NIGHTLINE

NIGHTLINE

History in the Making

and

the Making of Television

TED KOPPEL AND KYLE GIBSON

TIMES ⒯ BOOKS

RANDOM HOUSE

All rights reserved under International Pan-American Copyright
Conventions. Published in the United States by Times Books,
a division of Random House, Inc., New York, and simultaneously
in Canada by Random House of Canada Limited, Toronto.

Library of Congress Cataloging-in-Publication Data
Koppel, Ted
Nightline : history in the making and the making of television /
Ted Koppel and Kyle Gibson.
p.   cm.
Includes index.
ISBN 0-8129-2478-9
1. Nightline (Television program)   I. Gibson, Kyle.   II. Title.
PN1992.77.N54K66   1996
791.45'72—dc20   95-53838

Printed in the United States of America on acid-free paper
2 4 6 8 9 7 5 3
First Edition

BOOK DESIGN BY ROBERT BULL

For Grace Anne
—TK

For my parents, for my siblings, and for Mit
—KG

Acknowledgments

Bill Abrams was the one who realized that after fifteen years and four thousand broadcasts, *Nightline* had a history worth writing about. If we've mangled what he had in mind, he's been kind enough not to let on.

Our researcher, Eric Wagner, put in long, late hours in libraries and screening rooms, without sagging. So too did Amy Sills. We thank them both.

We especially appreciate the advice, support, and generosity of Tom Bettag. Thanks also to the current *Nightline* staff, including Phil Maravilla, Lara Bontempo, Kathy Kennedy, John Bibb, Lely Constantinople, Buck Parr, Debbi Estevez, Annemarie Powell, Dana Miller, Ted Gerstein, and Lynn Davis. And thank you to ABC's Sue Levkoff and Liz Hughes, who unearthed important old transcripts.

Travis Mier of Spirit Lake, Iowa, shared his computer expertise (badly needed), and Jan Bolluyt of Spirit Lake High School donated the summertime quiet of his classroom for some of the writing.

The un-fun task of coordinating our needs with assorted divisions of ABC News was assumed, with graciousness, by Malvina Csorba.

George Griffin performed every imaginable task, as usual, with wit and good humor.

We are grateful to Esther Newberg for bringing this project to the attention of Times Books, and for her encouragement.

Veronica Windholz, our copy editor, has a great eye. Her comments helped enormously. And we were lucky to have Benjamin

Dreyer as our production editor. Our readers will benefit from his contribution.

It was our great fortune to have Steve Wasserman, editorial director of Times Books, as our editor. Steve shaped this book. He guided our rather peculiar effort with patience and helped us to refine it with his remarkable talent. Steve has a gift for precision. Beth Thomas, his assistant, gave up many of her nights to retype much of the manuscript.

From the moment Peter Osnos, publisher of Times Books, took on this project, he has been there with energy and enthusiasm.

Finally, among the more than 125 men and women who were interviewed for this book, many have worked for *Nightline*. There are hundreds more, most of them the best in the business, who have worked for the broadcast since its debut. To cite every person who has contributed in the field, in the offices, in the editing rooms and tape rooms, in graphics and in the control rooms, would have resulted in a four-hundred-page thank-you note, which, in a manner of speaking, is precisely what this book is. We are sincerely indebted to all of those we could not name. So is *Nightline*.

Contents

Introduction

WHEN I WAS A child in England during the 1940s, the story of Sinbad the Sailor still had the power to amaze. At one point in his adventures, Sinbad discovered a crystal ball, similar in style to those once used by fortune-telling gypsies. He could look into this globe and see what people were doing hundreds, even thousands, of miles away; see and hear them. Now, that was miraculous! It's difficult now, looking back, to generate the feeling of awe that such a contraption once evoked; but it did.

In 1957, four years after my parents and I immigrated to the United States, I was a seventeen-year-old sophomore at Syracuse University. That was the year the Soviet Union petrified the Eisenhower administration by launching *Sputnik I,* the world's first orbiting satellite. The U.S. military was particularly concerned about the Soviets "dominating the high ground," a concept that has preoccupied the military mind since some of our earliest ancestors discovered that it was easier to hurl a rock downhill at an enemy than uphill. There is no record that anyone publicly anticipated the role that satellites would soon play in the field of communications.

I have no recollection of marking the launch of *Sputnik* as having any particular relevance to my life, either. A scant ten years later, though, when I was working as a correspondent for ABC News in Vietnam, occasional reports of mine would be shipped to Tokyo, where ABC had the capability to "satellite" them back to the United States. That significantly cut the time it took to get a battlefield report on the air; but we still had to physically transport the film to Saigon, drive it out to Tan Son Nhut airport, and put it aboard a flight to Tokyo. In early 1967 that remained the only point in Asia which had an "uplink" to a satellite. Once the film landed in Tokyo it would be sent by courier to a lab for developing, and finally it would be edited, placed onto projectors, and only then would the material be transmitted by satellite back to the United States. It was a process that saved the flying time from Tokyo to Los Angeles; and since these were days when ABC News had only an early-evening newscast on which such a report might be used, that could mean saving a full day. Even so, the lag between the shooting of a story in Vietnam and getting it on the air would still be one to two days.

Before another ten years had passed, film cameras had been largely replaced, at ABC News, by videotape cameras. It would no longer be necessary to "process" what the camera had captured. Videotape could simply be transferred from a camera to another machine capable of playing the tape. The lag time was getting shorter.

When, a couple of years later, American hostages were taken at the U.S. embassy in Tehran, we had reached the point of inviting guests into television studios around the world and putting them on the air "live." That was the technological environment into which *Nightline* was born some sixteen years ago. It was a time when *Nightline* itself was still nothing more than a nagging intuition in the fertile imagination of ABC News president Roone Arledge. The age of satellite technology was just about to flower, and the world of communication would never be the same.

Indeed, the world itself was quite different. The Soviet Union was more than a country; we referred to it and the countries under its hegemony as an empire. U.S. foreign policy was largely determined by the perception of the Soviet Union and its influence around the world. Mikhail Gorbachev was virtually unknown outside the Soviet Union. Bill Clinton was virtually unknown outside the state of Arkansas. South Africa, still in the firm grip of apartheid, was an international pariah. Nelson Mandela remained a prisoner whose face had not been publicly seen for years. Yasser Arafat was widely regarded as a terrorist. Neither the United States nor Israel would even speak (or at least officially acknowledge having spoken to) a member of the Palestine Liberation Organization.

The world had never heard of AIDS. No instance of the disease had yet been recorded. Iran-contra had not yet happened. Oliver North was an anonymous marine officer. Jim and Tammy Faye Bakker were happily married and the PTL Club was beginning to flourish.

It is already becoming difficult to remember, but there was a time when you could not simply point a television camera at an event in one part of the world and see it, instantaneously, around the world. There was a time when video images were carried aboard planes, rather than traveling at the speed of light. There was a time when satellites were so few, and the technology so expensive, that only governments and the three major television networks could afford to use them.

Early on in *Nightline*'s existence, someone in ABC's promotion division created an inspired line about the program: "Bringing people together who are worlds apart." It was true in a fashion that is all too rare in advertising. Literally and figuratively, *Nightline* has brought people together who are worlds apart. That was never possible in the age before satellites.

We have had generations in which to become acclimated to the miracle of sound, converted to electronic impulses, traveling at the speed of light over radio and telephone lines; but visual images, hurtling toward satellites from one part of the globe and then being bounced back toward another point on earth thousands of miles away in less than a second, remain a relatively new phenomenon. We are still in the process of adjusting. We *believe* ourselves comfortable and familiar with the phenomenon, but in truth, we are not. Our military leaders are still struggling to come to terms with a technology that enables news organizations to transmit live battlefield reports. Our national leaders have trouble adjusting to the reality of American television networks providing live coverage of U.S. bombs and missiles making impact on enemy targets. Our political and diplomatic leaders remain acutely uncomfortable with the instant demands and consequences of volatile images transmitted live from otherwise remote locations.

From both the journalist's point of view and that of the policymaker, there is a world of difference between dealing with a time lag of a day or two between an event and its appearance on television, and a live broadcast. Simply put, there is significantly less time for think-ing. The decision-making process is foreshortened.

The television anchor who is obliged to narrate, analyze, and put into context a live satellite transmission is entirely dependent upon instinct and experience. Such "editing" as is possible at all must be done instantaneously. That is difficult enough for the journalist with a reservoir of twenty or thirty years' experience. It is next to impossible for some of the younger men and women who sit at the local anchor desks around the country.

The point being that satellites have created more than simply the capacity to transmit and receive material instantly; they frequently create an imperative to do so. We can, therefore we must. To do any less would be to grant a competitive advantage to other stations, other networks.

The reach and stature of CNN have risen in direct proportion to that network's ability and willingness to cover any important event, anywhere in the world, "live." Which, in itself, has created an even more important and dangerous phenomenon: the need for policy-makers to react and respond according to the timetable of satellite technology.

The image of a U.S. Ranger's body being dragged through the streets of Mogadishu, Somalia, for example, created its own political imperative. Even if the White House had wanted to carefully consider the importance of the event and the appropriate response, the time available was hostage to the barrage of instant reaction from the media, the public, and politicians around the country. It is a phenomenon that simply requires greater discipline than most recent occupants of the White House have been able to demonstrate: to refrain from reacting publicly to an event when everyone else is.

Some years ago, my colleagues and I produced a documentary titled *Revolution in a Box*. The reference, of course, was to television; but more specifically, it was to the democratization of television and the increasing availability of its technology. Hi8 cameras are not only capable of producing broadcast-quality videotape, they are small enough and cheap enough to be accessible to almost any-one—certainly, almost any group. They and their compatible edit-ing equipment and videotape recorders have given millions of people the capacity to engage in video journalism. The point is that a technology that was once available only to the very few has become ubiquitous.

Miracles of communication that were still the stuff of fairy tales a mere fifty years ago are now accessible to groups, if not individuals, all around the world. That technology helped bring down the Soviet empire and the structure of apartheid in South Africa. That technology empowered the Palestinian intifada in Israel and Lech Walesa's Solidarity movement in Poland. That technology terrified the gerontocracy in China when they realized how widespread its impact could be. It gave what little voice there was to the victims of slaughter in Rwanda and multiplied the available images that came out of Bosnia.

It is a reflection of how quickly the technology has evolved when one considers that *Nightline*'s life span encompasses much, if not most, of that extraordinary development. When, in early 1980, we brought guests together, simultaneously, from Moscow, Tehran, and Washington, to engage in conversation and debate, that was a breathtaking technological achievement. Now it is within the capacity, and frequently even the repertoire, of every large, independent television station around the United States.

Our continuing challenge, these last sixteen years, has been to keep pace with television's expanding capacities while keeping track of the seminal events of our time. What is surprising and sometimes amusing is how obsessive we have frequently been about the trivial. What is less amusing is how dismissive we occasionally are about events that prove to be monumentally important. The S&L crisis would be an apt example of the latter; the PTL scandal would be a fair example of the former. But you can judge for yourselves.

Kyle Gibson and I have talked at great length about the various phases in *Nightline*'s existence, about the fundamental realities that cause some people to hesitate about coming on the program and the motives that impel others to do so. She has conducted more than 125 interviews with primary sources—former and current staffers and an astonishing number of former guests, whose stories about the negotiations that often precede such appearances tell much about the role that a television news program like *Nightline* has played throughout the 1980s and well into the nineties. Frequently, people will appear as a "last resort." Lani Guinier was actually in the process of being dumped by the White House as its nominee to the Justice Department when she finally agreed to come on the program. Gary Hart used the program in a vain attempt to jump-start his moribund presidential campaign. Ferdinand Marcos seemed to believe that a *Nightline* appearance might rekindle support from the Reagan administration. Michael Dukakis was running out of time, money, and support in his presidential campaign late in October 1988 when he sat down for a ninety-minute interview. Pik Botha, the former foreign minister of South Africa, felt that his country might be able to promote itself out of its international pariah standing when he agreed to let *Nightline* visit in 1985. Kyle has spoken to many of these guests and others who occasionally shed remarkable light on why people appear on the program at all.

There is always a motive, though. That, Kyle and I agreed, would be the thread that ties many of these otherwise unrelated stories together. We have consulted often, but this book is principally the fruit of her labor. She is particularly well suited to the task in that she worked on the program as one of our very best producers for eight years, but has gone on to work as a correspondent for ABC News and as a freelance writer. Kyle has been close enough to the program, in other words, to bring familiarity and affection to the project but is not so close anymore as to have lost all perspective and objectivity. Suffice it to say that I have contributed to this book, influenced it; but in the final analysis, Kyle wrote it.

Most of what you are about to read is written in the third person. Every broadcast, after all, is a collaborative effort. It would have been simpler to present the story of *Nightline* strictly from my perspective. It is, however, the diversity of perspectives that contributes to every broadcast, and it is a multitude of memories, not just mine, that best documents the history of the show.

At the very least, *Nightline* has been a reflection of what we *thought* was important at the moment that we covered a story. That says something about us, but since we operate within a commercial arena and are therefore also concerned about attracting an audience, it also says a great deal about what interested American viewers during any given week. Already, after only sixteen years, that has the capacity to surprise. It's strange to recall that the national attention was once focused as raptly on herpes as it would later be on AIDS; that a war between

Britain and Argentina could be the object of such interest; that giving, or refusing, assistance to a band of guerrilla fighters in Nicaragua once seemed so important that it led to decisions which nearly toppled the Reagan administration.

Perhaps it is merely an illusion, but it seems to me that the shifting focus of our attention and interest has barely kept pace with our accelerated capacity to transmit information. We get it faster. We absorb it faster. We discard it faster. We have become purveyors of an intellectual fast food: McThought.

More than four thousand programs produced and consumed. Some of them were pretty good, a great many of them were forgettable; but a handful may even be worth a book.

See what you think.

NIGHTLINE

ONE
Held Hostage

IT WAS BAD ENOUGH to have the Sunday shift. Worse still, there wasn't any news.

On the second floor of a battered brick building on Connecticut Avenue, what passed, in the late 1970s, for the Washington bureau of ABC News wasn't much more than a cluster of rusting metal desks scattered over a threadbare carpet. But Frank Radice, the twenty-nine-year-old man in charge that day, was too busy scanning wire copy to care. A hyperkinetic sort who derived sustenance from chaos, Radice leaned back in his chair and wondered what story he could drum up for the evening news. There was the ongoing energy crisis, but the best part of that story had happened back in the summer with the long gas lines. There was also Senator Edward M. Kennedy's challenge to Jimmy Carter for the Democratic nomination, but Kennedy, Radice knew, wasn't in Washington that weekend, and besides, Kennedy wasn't slated to formally announce his candidacy for another few days.

The best story that day was probably the exiled shah of Iran. The shah was in New York to be treated for cancer. His powerful American friends, including Henry Kissinger and David Rockefeller, had lobbied the Carter administration to permit the shah into the United States on humanitarian grounds. Carter had reluctantly agreed, despite his fear of retaliation by the radical Shiites who had overthrown the

Iranian monarch. After all, the shah had been sentenced to death in absentia, and Iran was seeking his extradition. That morning the wires had carried a brief item about several Iranians taking over the Statue of Liberty, but it appeared they were about to turn themselves in; tracking that story was the responsibility of ABC News New York headquarters. With President Carter at Camp David for the weekend, Washington, this Sunday, was quiet. So Radice slumped lower in his well-worn chair, sipped coffee, and flipped through the newspapers, looking for inspiration.

Then the dinging began. It was the bells of the bureau's wire machines. Radice sat up. In the days before computerized wire reports, the dings heralded an adrenaline rush. Somewhere, someone had news.

The bulletins were datelined Tehran. The American embassy had been overrun; between sixty and sixty-five Americans were taken hostage; their captors were identified by the Iranian government as "students."

Radice dialed ABC's diplomatic correspondent at his home in suburban Maryland. The correspondent was Ted Koppel. For the previous sixteen years, Koppel had covered the American civil rights movement, Latin American coups, Asian politics and economics, the Vietnam War, and Henry Kissinger's shuttle diplomacy in the Middle East. Radice asked Koppel what he made of the bulletins out of Tehran.

Koppel's response: "This story's gonna die."

Summer 1977

ROONE ARLEDGE WANTED AIR. There was no way he could begin to build a first-class news operation without more airtime. ABC wanted him to do for the news division what he'd done for sports, but it wasn't that simple. All of the imaginative sports programming for which Arledge was legend—shows like *Wide World of Sports* and *Monday Night Football*—would still be ideas instead of institutions if the network hadn't provided the airtime. It would be hard enough to lure viewers to a news division that, in thirty years, had never been considered competitive; it would be harder still, given that the only daily program in the division was the evening news. Arledge was already considering a revamped evening news with a "whip-around" format; the show would feature several anchors located around the world. But he couldn't build an empire on thirty minutes a night. It wasn't even a half-hour, really; minus commercial time, the evening news ran under twenty-two minutes.

One idea was to expand the evening broadcast to an hour. The notion was hardly original. All three networks had been lobbying their affiliates for years to give them an hour at dinnertime. One hour was their holy grail. But local stations hated the idea. The extra half-hour was simply too profitable; the early-evening slot returned a fortune when a station ran a game show like *Concentration* or an *Odd Couple* rerun. CBS couldn't even get Walter Cronkite a full hour. Arledge had concluded that if CBS couldn't get the extra time at dinner, neither could he. The affiliates had said as much. They were always telling Arledge the same thing: "You haven't proven you can do a *half*-hour show that's competitive yet; why would we give you an hour?"

So Arledge set his eyes on late-night. "Why can't we do what we do at the dinner hour with the eleven o'clock news?" he wondered. "At dinnertime, we have half an hour of local, or an hour of local, followed by half an hour of network. Why can't we have local news at eleven o'clock followed by a network news program?" But Arledge quickly discovered that "nobody thought it would work."

Johnny Carson owned late-night. He *was* late-night. NBC had ruled the time slot with *The Tonight Show* since the 1950s, first with Steve Allen and then Jack Paar. But for the past decade and a half, 11:30 Eastern, 10:30 Central was Carson Time. Watching Carson was a kind of ritual that united late-night America—and, in a sense, defined it.

Arledge suspected, however, there was an audience Carson wasn't reaching. There were probably millions, he guessed, whose appetite for news was whetted by the late local broadcasts—viewers who would welcome an extra half-hour on some interesting story of the day. But how to convince the skeptics at the affiliates? ABC already provided its local stations with a package of old dramas and sitcoms like *Police Woman, Baretta,* and *The Love Boat.* The package wasn't exactly Carson, but it was cheap, and palatable. It was the sort of light fare that most station executives—most network executives, for that matter—believed people wanted at the end of a busy day. In the words of one of Arledge's deputies, the network sought "pure, passive relaxation and entertainment for late night. People don't want news; that was the rule."

Arledge decided to hammer down conventional wisdom, one special television show at a time. "I wanted to prove that you could get an audience in that time period," he would remember, "so we started doing these 'instant specials.' " First he tried out a couple of shows in July 1977 about a blackout in New York City. But he quickly concluded he didn't want to wait for crises to steal the slot. "I wanted us on at eleven-thirty constantly. The show could be about anything that had happened that day. *Anything.*"

The siege began with Elvis. On the night of Elvis Presley's death, August 16, 1977, ABC News took over at 11:30 Eastern Time, with *Elvis Love Me Tender: A Memorial Salute to Elvis Presley.* When Groucho Marx died a few weeks later, ABC News grabbed the coveted time slot with *Remembering Groucho.* Just days after that, Jimmy Carter signed the Panama Canal treaties, and ABC News pounced again.

Elvis, Groucho, and the Canal were just the beginning. Over the next two years there would be more than forty late-night specials: *Skylab Falls Back to Earth, Andrew Young Resigns, President Carter in the Middle East, The U.S. Recognizes China, Bing Crosby: A Memorial, John Wayne: Homage to the Duke.* Some subjects seemed more worthy of a special report than others. A Russian ballerina who was being detained at John F. Kennedy Airport because her husband had defected might not, strictly speaking, have merited the same kind of attention as the death, say, of Pope Paul, but both events served Arledge's assault on late-night.

Though it was difficult to predict whether one-time audiences would return, Arledge's "instant specials" seemed to attract viewers. So did the mid-1978 launch of *20/20,* the network's first prime-time newsmagazine. At that point "expansion was the key," according to one of the division vice-presidents, Richard Wald. Wald, an erudite former president of NBC News and a college classmate of Arledge's, pushed in particular for as many of the 11:30 specials as the network would allow. The specials, he pointed out, not only demonstrated the commitment of ABC News to breaking events, but also helped divert attention away from the evening news, which was experiencing predictable glitches during its transformation into a multiple-anchor format.

Wald, however, wasn't the one who had to seek permission from network higher-ups every time the news division wanted to put an "instant special" into the late-night slot. Arledge left that task to the other vice-president of the division (and another longtime friend), David Burke. So Burke would trot over to the office of the president of ABC Television, Fred Pierce, and make the case again . . . and again.

Burke knew how to persuade. He was blunt and outspoken. A former administrative assistant to Senator Edward Kennedy and chief of staff to New York governor Hugh Carey, Burke had about him an air of propriety, a kind of righteousness. When he felt strongly about an issue, he'd flush with passion. His biggest problem was that it was getting harder for him to drum up even a pretense of enthusiasm about subjects that ranged from Skylab to a Russian ballerina. All the trips to Pierce were beginning to make Burke feel a little like the song-and-dance man of ABC News. Every time he got the go-ahead for another special, Burke would return to Arledge's office and launch into song: "Give 'em that old razzle-dazzle!"

In October 1979, Arledge and Burke persuaded the network into ceding a whole week of late-night for a visit to America by Pope John Paul II. "For people who cared about the pope, we were the only link they had once he left New York, unless you were watching the local news someplace," said Arledge. The ratings were high. But the pope couldn't tour America forever, and the network was not about to permanently turn over the slot because of one good week. Arledge knew he needed a real crisis—one with "legs" to it—a story so compelling, so potentially profitable, and just long enough, that watching late-night news would become an American habit.

ON NOVEMBER 4, 1979, Ted Koppel, for one, didn't think "students" taking over the embassy in Tehran would be a crisis at all.

When Frank Radice first called with the bulletins out of Tehran, Koppel reminded Radice that the previous February, a Marxist faction of Iranian militants had attempted to seize the very same embassy and that the American ambassador and the deputy prime minister of Iran's provisional government had worked together to quell the takeover attempt within a matter of hours. Koppel was certain this new attempt would be resolved by the time he made it from his home in Maryland to the office. Besides, it was a lovely, cool fall Sunday. Koppel's mood soured at the thought of losing a day off with his family.

Still, Koppel was a professional, and Americans taken hostage in an embassy merited something for the evening news. He relented and drove to the State Department. "I went in and did just a typical short, stand-in-front-of-the-limp-flag piece for the evening news. But I did not think the takeover was going to last. The Iranian government, after all, was still maintaining that this was happening in spite of their best intentions. They were implying that 'these students who are doing this are just a bunch of wild, crazy, uncontrollable kids. But don't worry, we don't want anybody to get hurt. We'll take care of it.' "

No one in ABC's news division disagreed with Koppel's assessment. Roone Arledge didn't even begin to think about a late-night special until Monday had passed into Tuesday, and Tuesday into Wednesday, with the Americans still held captive. By then it had become clear that top officials in the Ayatollah Ruhollah Khomeini's regime—rather than the "students"—were masterminding the takeover. On Thursday, when the militants paraded a blindfolded hostage in front of television cameras, Arledge wanted a special. He sent David Burke on yet another mission for clearance from Fred Pierce. A special on the crisis was a no-brainer, really, Pierce reasoned. Besides, it would only be for one night.

Jeff Gralnick, the executive producer of *World News Tonight,* was told he would be producing the broadcast. That afternoon, Gralnick met with his staff to mull over possible titles for the show. Gralnick was struck by how the crisis had paralyzed the nation. "Look at what's happening in Washington," he pointed out. "Look what's happening to us in the media. Look what's happening to the psyche of the American people. We really are being held hostage by this thing." The title was obvious.

That night, November 8, 1979, after the late local news, at 11:30 P.M. Eastern Time, Frank Reynolds, serving as anchor, hosted what nearly everyone at ABC figured would be the first and last late-night report on the crisis: *America Held Hostage.*

REYNOLDS: Look at this. One American, blindfolded, handcuffed, today in the courtyard of the American embassy in Tehran.

The half-hour broadcast offered reports from several correspondents on every possible angle of the story: Bob Dyke in Tehran, Sam Donaldson at the White House, Brit Hume on Capitol Hill, Ted Koppel at State, Anne Garrels on the reaction of the American public. The Garrels piece in particular revealed intense national interest in the hostages:

GARRELS: At New York's Kennedy Airport, transport workers announced today that they won't service Iranian aircraft until the American hostages are freed.

TWU OFFICIAL: We only hope that what we're doing here today will start—and we're sure of this—will start a chain of protest throughout the United States by American labor unions.

GARRELS: Longshoremen in New Jersey agree. They've refused to unload cargo from Iranian ships, but some want even more action.

FIRST UNIDENTIFIED MAN: I'd like to see us go right in there and get our hostages. If it means a quarter more a gallon for gasoline, I'm willing to pay it, and I think all the rest of the people are.

SECOND UNIDENTIFIED MAN: When I watch TV, the news, and I see what they do to that flag, it gets me in the heart.

That was the voice of Arledge's audience: an angry public, getting angrier with each passing day that the hostages weren't released. Still, there were no plans for another special. No one thought the crisis would last.

The day after *America Held Hostage* aired, Arledge had to fly to Lake Placid to look over the preparations for the 1980 Winter Olympics, the coverage of which still fell to him as president of both the sports and news divisions at ABC. Afterward, Arledge held a press conference to talk about the network's Olympics preparations. But Arledge would remember that "half the questions were about the hostages. And I noticed that every time I'd go up and down in an elevator, or a taxi, or whatever, people were always talking about the hostages."

When Arledge returned to New York, the takeover was a week

old. An anti-American fever inflamed Tehran. Thousands of Iranians had marched to the American embassy chanting, "Death to the Americans." Women swathed in chadors would confront American camera crews, shake their fists, and scream anti-American epithets. Khomeini had denounced President Carter as "an enemy of the people." Back in the United States, meanwhile, ordinary Americans began staging rallies demanding the deportation of Iranians living in America.

Arledge, fired up by his conversations with taxi drivers and elevator operators and mesmerized by the volatile images out of Iran, was mystified to discover that a second special wasn't even in the planning stages. When he asked why, he was told there wasn't anything new to say. You announce the hostages are still held hostage, went the argument, but what do you do for the next twenty-nine minutes? "That argument," recalled Arledge, "pissed me off. I said, 'You don't understand. People care; they cannot get enough about this.' " Every night without a show on the hostages, Arledge would grouse to Burke, was a night wasted. This was their chance. They should seize late-night for the Iran crisis, and make it interesting. The Iranians were making a mockery of America; the American public wanted anything on it.

Eleven days into the crisis, Burke won Pierce's go-ahead for a second installment of *America Held Hostage*. When the broadcast went to air, Gralnick had tacked *Day 11* onto the title. At midnight, a few minutes after the broadcast, Burke's home phone rang. He picked it up; it was Arledge wanting to know what he thought. Burke said it was time to claim the slot. "Roone, you've got to tell them you want the slot till the crisis is over."

The next day Burke and Arledge went to see Pierce. There was an audience for the Iran crisis, they said. You only had to walk down a street and talk to people to see that.

"News wants the slot," said Arledge, "as long as the crisis continues."

"Define," Pierce said, " 'as long as the crisis continues.' "

"Three, four weeks tops," Arledge estimated.

"All right, you're sure it's only three or four weeks?"

"Yes. Three or four weeks. These things don't last."

"ONLY A FEW WEEKS." That was the mantra. The reporters, producers, and editors whose hours were extended day after day were reassured that the crisis couldn't possibly go on for more than a month.

Frank Reynolds—who was anchoring both the evening news and the specials—believed it . . . Even the *White House* believed it. The administration clung to "a hope and a possibility that negotiation was going to bring a resolution just around the corner," according to Hodding Carter, who served as the State Department spokesman. The White House actually *liked* the ABC hostage specials—at least in the beginning. For one thing, the newscasts nicely served the administration's domestic political agenda. The focus on a foreign crisis took the spotlight off Ted Kennedy's campaign for President; at the same time, it gave Jimmy Carter the chance to look presidential. More important, the late-night specials were seen by the administration as a forum through which it could reaffirm, each night, that it wasn't forgetting the hostages. Military action, after all, at least in those first weeks, was not a possibility. In lieu of action, the White House had only one option: talk. *America Held Hostage* was a useful platform. Hodding Carter would remember the thinking within the President's inner circle: "Here is the government responding to all of this, here is the government talking, here is the government engaged. And the fact that it did not always make it look like we knew what we were doing was irrelevant, since there was nothing we could do." Early on, Hodding Carter went so far as to call and thank Reynolds for the specials. The more that the administration encouraged and participated in a kind of national dialogue about the crisis, it hoped, the less it would be required to try something riskier.

AT LEAST ONE CORRESPONDENT, however, was getting mighty tired of the pap from the State Department. Ted Koppel wondered why he had to file on every last word out of Hodding Carter's mouth for the Iran specials and why ABC was even airing specials on the nights when there was nothing new to say.

It took Koppel weeks to see what Arledge was really up to.

Journalism was only part of it.

This was the seizing of 11:30.

America Held Hostage was holding a *time slot* hostage, and Roone Arledge was not going to let go.

A BROADCAST THAT OPENED every night on a big title graphic showing a picture of a blindfolded hostage and *Day 45* above it . . .

then *Day 55* . . . then *Day 65*—was not what the White House had
had in mind. It seemed to some officials that the numbers were getting bigger, taking up more of the screen. They were not. Thanks-
giving passed, Christmas passed, 1979 was history, and still the hostages
were hostages. Now no one was making predictions anymore, not
even President Carter's own advisers. Whatever benefits they had
derived from the Iran crisis were long gone. Whatever benefits they
had derived from the early ABC specials were long gone, too. If anything, the specials were beginning to make the administration look
impotent. Now the White House *wanted* Arledge to let go—if not of
his coveted time slot, then at least of the topic of the hostages. Arledge
wouldn't do it.

Hodding Carter would later rue the early days of the takeover,
when the administration had decided to put so much attention on it.
His side, he realized, had cut a Faustian deal. By mid-winter, "we
were caught in an embrace with the media. We'd been dancing the
same dance to the same music." And once the administration wanted
the dance to stop, "we did not know how to stop it." The only way
to have stopped the dance, Carter later concluded, would have been
for the administration to have ceased commenting on the hostages.
Completely. In fact he did try, for a time, to reduce the State Department briefings on the crisis from three a day, to two, then to one.

Arledge had refused to take the hint. No news today? Then we'll
go *deeper*.

ON SLOW NEWS DAYS, the show would explore and explain the
issues behind the crisis. One broadcast defined the difference between
Sunni Islam and Shiite Islam. Another examined what the term *mullah*
meant. The results, by all accounts, were often fascinating. Watching
ABC late-night was like attending a seminar on Iran, Islamic fundamentalism, the hostages, the hostages' families, the shah's ailments, the
shah's travels in exile, the impact of the crisis on American foreign policy, and the effect on Jimmy Carter's presidency. Robert Siegenthaler,
an ABC veteran who was executive producer of *America Held Hostage,*
would later laugh: "Perhaps I should have been a schoolteacher. It just
seemed to me that the American people didn't know the nuances of
these subjects and would benefit from having them explained. We
even did shows about geography." Arledge felt they were the sort of

broadcasts that belonged on the air late at night, when the audience was winding down and had time to peruse a subject.

Covering the crisis was turning into a journalistic marathon. In two and a half months, *America Held Hostage* had begun to drain the life out of its ad hoc staff, made up of producers, reporters, editors, and technicians normally assigned to other broadcasts. "I'd gotten people I thought were good," said Siegenthaler, "and had just borrowed them, never specifying how long I was borrowing them for." The joke was that Siegenthaler's staff was being held hostage. "We never got any permanent staff; all we got was better catering as the ratings went up," said Siegenthaler.

Frank Reynolds had dropped out of the marathon in mid-December. His duties as Washington anchor of *World News Tonight,* he said, were enough. Without fanfare, the anchor seat had been handed to a man who hadn't had a regular anchor job since the Saturday evening news a few years back. But since late November, he had filled in for Reynolds several times, and Siegenthaler liked him, and the brass thought he was smart. Besides, no one was thinking too much about the long-term. For now, they concluded, ABC's diplomatic correspondent, Ted Koppel, would do fine.

Koppel loved the job. "I looked forward to it, enormously. Even when you have a beat like the State Department, you never get a chance to strut your stuff. Whether this program was fifteen minutes or a half-hour, it was mine."

The story suited Koppel's intellect. He'd been reporting on the relationship of foreign events to the United States for years. But it was television's new technology—which continued to advance in quantum leaps that very winter—that redefined what Koppel could do, and how far he could reach, from the anchor chair. Satellites were proliferating so rapidly and ground stations were becoming so ubiquitous that for the first time, an anchor could talk with someone located almost anywhere on the planet. The more the show harnessed the technology, and the more it concentrated on live interviews, the more its producers would cede editorial control to Koppel as the anchor.

Siegenthaler had his own reasons for welcoming the technology. "Day-old news" was anathema. ABC had recently started phasing out the use of film, which had always caused a delay in relaying pictures because it had to be processed in a lab. The advent of videotape introduced the instant replay. Video shot in Tehran after ABC's evening news was off the air could now be turned around and fed via satellite for the late-night special. And if there wasn't much new tape, Siegenthaler knew that a few live interviews would freshen the broadcast.

Set designers had built a large screen near the anchor desk. When Koppel interviewed someone, he would be turned toward the screen, and what viewers saw on it was the face of the guest. In fact, what Koppel was looking at was a monitor positioned just out of camera range, next to the screen. The screen, which was a bright green color, was blank. The control room would "key out" the green and replace it with the face of the person being interviewed. It was the only way to preserve a sharp picture of the guest. The technique of using a "chroma-key screen" wasn't new. "*MacNeil/Lehrer* had being doing it," said Koppel. "Ed Murrow did it in the fifties on his show *Person to Person*. But it occurred to us that if we could carry the interview from across town, we could do it transoceanically, too. And if we could do it with one person, we could do it with more than one person."

Soon Koppel began holding three- and-four-way conversations via satellite—live. It was as if he were hosting an intercontinental salon. "This was what had never been done on television before," said Koppel. "We would take people in remote locations and say, 'Here, talk to each other, disagree with one another, fight with one another, argue with one another.' "

Arledge noticed. *America Held Hostage* began to redefine the art of the television interview, its uses and purposes and its future. It was convening opposing forces in the American living room. Arledge likened the technology to taking two electric chords and touching them to one another and letting the sparks fly.

BY EARLY JANUARY 1980 Arledge felt the courtship of viewers was over; this was a full-fledged relationship. He was convinced that even when the hostages were released, the audience would be there, out of habit, looking for more information on an interesting story of the day. Enough of the affiliates had ceded the slot to news; why give it back to old reruns? So Arledge ventured once more to the office of Fred Pierce and claimed the slot like a squatter declaring rights to an abandoned building. Pierce understood that Arledge was arguing something along the lines of "possession is nine tenths of the law." But Pierce also thought Arledge was right. "You can have it," Pierce told him. "But only twenty minutes, Monday through Thursday."

Arledge grabbed the offer. He didn't tell Pierce that he had his eyes on a half-hour, five nights a week. But that was his plan. He also didn't tell Pierce who the anchor would be. But that was because he didn't yet know.

THE UNSEEN ARMY of workers behind *America Held Hostage* needed relief. Siegenthaler was scheduled to oversee ABC's coverage of the upcoming presidential primaries, and most of his troops on *America Held Hostage* were wanted back on the shows from which they'd been borrowed.

Arledge wouldn't staff the new show himself; that's what an executive producer was for. He awarded the post to Bill Lord, a wiry, brittle, and brilliant ABC veteran who had once served as senior producer of the evening news out of Washington. Recently, Lord had been running the news segments on *Good Morning America*. He understood that Arledge was anointing him to oversee the most important ABC News project of the year, and he wasn't sure he wanted it.

Lord walked into the office of Av Westin, who'd been appointed to revamp the newsmagazine *20/20* and to oversee the development of late-night projects. Westin was a legend, a pioneer from CBS, where during the 1950s and 1960s he had orchestrated some of the first international "live shots" ever seen on television. "What I'm about to tell you could be the end of my career here," Lord told Westin, "but I've got to talk to somebody. They want me to do this program, and I don't think I know how to do it."

Lord had never seemed to lack confidence before. Westin suspected that confidence wasn't really the problem now. "I had a feeling," Westin later recalled, "that Lord didn't think it was going to last." Lord was being asked to leave a solid, certain newscast for something that, once the hostage crisis was over, had no clear future. But after an hour with Westin, who knew how to pump up the troops better than anyone and who salivated at the idea of adventure and experimentation, Lord was soothed and agreed to try it.

· · ·

FOR TED KOPPEL, January passed with no word from above about his future. He suspected Arledge's list of potential anchors had his own name at the bottom. "I kept hearing rumors," Koppel remembered, "that they were talking to Dan Rather, talking to Tom Brokaw, talking to Roger Mudd. And so I sort of had the sense that the only way I was going to get it was if everybody else said, 'No, thanks.' "

David Burke, whom Arledge had appointed to court stars, later admitted that ABC was doing a lot more than talking. Burke and Arledge knew that even one famous name defecting to ABC News meant the network would be taken seriously. "We were trying to build a news organization," Burke said. "It was very crass, but we were just trying to do what we had to do to bring credibility to the division." Burke went after Dan Rather of CBS, "shamelessly," he would later boast, and after Rather refused, Burke pursued Tom Brokaw and Roger Mudd, both of NBC. The offers generally involved millions of dollars and the one prize each of these men had yet to attain: the throne, the anchor seat of the evening news. It was a win–win strategy. CBS and NBC would have to put their own thrones into play. Walter Cronkite, the Most Trusted Man in America, would probably have to step aside for CBS to keep Rather—and dethroning Cronkite was as good for ABC as winning Rather. Brokaw and Mudd would probably stay at NBC only if NBC would topple the popular and respected John Chancellor and David Brinkley. Burke summed up the game in a tidy maxim: "If you can't beat the opposition, you at least discombobulate them terribly."

The strategy, however, had an unfortunate side effect: it left Koppel feeling "discombobulated," too. He knew that Burke was whispering "late-night" in the ears of bigger stars. Burke would later admit as much: "We were doing anything we could to get Rather." If the CBS star had wanted late-night in addition to the evening news, it was his. But Rather was skeptical that the show would outlast the hostage crisis. So even while Arledge and Burke played anchor chess with CBS and NBC, they knew that the endgame didn't include a solution for late-night.

Bill Lord began meeting with Arledge, Burke, and Wald about Koppel. He "wasn't the natural choice," Lord recalled. "A guy like Frank Reynolds was the natural choice, but an impossible one," because he was needed to co-anchor the evening news. There could be no doubt that Koppel had the credentials. More than a decade and a half with the network, eight years at the State Department, Latin American bureau chief, Hong Kong bureau chief, three and a half years covering Vietnam, Laos, and Cambodia. The problem wasn't Koppel's résumé but the fact that his résumé didn't seem to have aged him. At thirty-nine, he could pass for twenty-nine on camera. "Roone had an image of an anchorperson," said Burke, "and Ted wasn't it."

Koppel knew that. It was Arledge who, upon taking over the division, had almost immediately maneuvered Koppel out of the anchor seat on the Saturday evening news and, eventually, back to the State Department. Koppel figured that the only reason he'd been picked to take over *America Held Hostage* was that no one was thinking at the time about a permanent anchor, or even a permanent show. Koppel had been intended as something of a benchwarmer.

But what he'd done was make the most of it.

By January 1980, *America Held Hostage* was stretching live technology to its limits. It had evolved into a unique broadcast requiring different skills than most anchors were called upon to exercise. It needed someone who was comfortable juggling three and four guests at a time. The consensus at ABC, a view shared by even the once-skeptical Arledge, was that Koppel looked more than comfortable. He looked like he was having fun.

One show in particular, featuring Secretary of Defense Harold Brown in Washington, as well as guests in London and Tehran, caught Arledge's attention. Koppel coolly threaded all the points of view into a cohesive discussion. "This was a virtuoso performance," Arledge recalled. "Ted had a great ability to remember a point someone had made earlier and bring it back into the conversation."

Then came President Carter's State of the Union speech and, after it, another remarkable special hosted by Koppel. The guests were an obscure but articulate Soviet commentator named Vladimir Pozner, ABC's Moscow correspondent Charles Bierbauer, Senator Joseph Biden, and Senator Richard Lugar. Koppel conducted the four-way conversation like a maestro.

The next day Arledge was reviewing a tape of the broadcast when Av Westin walked into his office. "Roone was nodding at Koppel's performance," Westin remembered, "and he was saying, 'That's the way to do it.' "

"Not many people had that skill," Arledge acknowledged. "Not many had even tried it—where you have a conversation going around the world, and you keep up with it, and interrupt, and bring it back to the point. By then, it became obvious that Koppel was the best person for the new show." What Arledge can't recall anymore was why he waited to tell Koppel.

Olympics fever, maybe. In February, *America Held Hostage* was preempted for two weeks by the Winter Olympics. Arledge was in Lake Placid, back at his first love: coordinating the coverage. The joke inside ABC was that the most interesting venue of the games was the central control room, where Arledge presided. Every camera relayed its pictures to Arledge, who wove the feeds into a single coherent drama, jumping from one event to another. Arledge, like Koppel, thrived on "live."

One day, as Arledge commanded the Lake Placid control room, Ted Koppel appeared. With no hostage special to anchor, Koppel had a few days to kill. Lake Placid, he thought, wouldn't be such a bad place to kill a couple of those days . . . and, well, perhaps if he was a candidate for the new show, perhaps if he just happened to catch Roone's eye . . . perhaps he'd get an idea of his chances. So, less than eight weeks before the new show was scheduled to debut, Koppel poked his head into the main control room of the Olympics, caught Arledge's eye, and waved hello.

Arledge waved back. Arledge said nothing. Not a word about the new show, not a word about Koppel's performance over the past months. Koppel went back outside convinced there wasn't a chance in hell he was getting the new show. He went home to Maryland.

Two days later, Koppel got a call from Dick Wald.

"We would like you to anchor the new broadcast," Wald said. "Do you want to do it?"

Did he want to do it? It was Koppel's fortieth birthday.

A MONTH LATER, two weeks before its premiere, the show had an anchor but no format and no name. Arledge decided to settle on a name first. The network couldn't promote a show without a name. He summoned Lord, Wald, Burke, Westin, Lord's deputy Stu

Schwartz, and Koppel to his office. He said they weren't walking out until they had a title.

Wald would remember how cramped they were in Arledge's small, odd-shaped office. "It was a kind of funny, stuffy little office with a desk too big for it and a huge fish tank and couches and chairs. There was a group of us, and we were sitting on every available surface. And we were looking at the fish."

Arledge wanted new ideas.

Silence.

At first the only consensus was that the title should combine two words: *Night Brief*, perhaps, or *News Night* or *Night Time*. Wald had already lobbied for the word *night* to appear in the title. Now he pushed for a word like *journal*, or *tribune*, or *diary*, or *chronicle*. Arledge rejected those words as too rooted in print.

Lord liked the sound of *News Night*. He was a minority of one.

Someone else suggested *Night Wire*, but found no echo of enthusiasm.

"Roone kept saying no," recalled Wald. "He just kept saying no to everything."

"I was looking for a name that said *The Tom Snyder Show*," said Arledge. "I loved the look and the feel, the late-night feel, of the old *Tom Snyder Show*. He'd have those guests on and they were sitting there talking to each other, and cigarettes and all. It had a late-night, gritty feel to it. And I wanted something of that same look. And I wanted the name to recognize that it was at night. I wanted it to sound like something that had continuity. Something that wasn't too definitive, though. I didn't want *The Story of the Day*, or something like that."

"It was like trying to write a joke," remembered Koppel. "It seems so easy when you hear a joke, and it sounds so natural. But the ability to write a joke out of thin air is very tough, and the ability to come up with the title of a program that you hope is going to last for a few years is not that easy."

The problem was that they were trying to christen an amorphous half-hour of airtime. "We weren't sure exactly what the program would wind up being," said Wald. "So we wanted a title that would fit various possibilities."

More staring at the fish.

Somehow staring at the fish made Dick Wald think of horses. He began to focus on the purpose of the program regardless of format. One certain goal was to sum up something in the news of the day, or to give a preview of something important scheduled for the next day. "And in racing there is a thing called the morning line," Wald recalled. "And it tells you what horses will be running and which are the favorites. This was going to be at night. And it was going to be the night line. And rather than call it *Night Line,* I thought one word would do it. So, I proposed *Nightline.*" And . . .

"Nobody liked it," Wald laughed. "Everybody thought it was a stupid title."

Lord didn't like it because "it didn't say anything. It was not an English word." Arledge didn't like it, according to Lord, because "it sounded like phone line or clothesline or something like that." Arledge later remembered thinking it didn't sound distinguished enough, that it was "too lightweight."

All Koppel knew was that *he* had to anchor the thing, that *he* was the one who would have to say, "This is *Nightline,*" every night, and he hated the sound of it. *"Nightline!"* Koppel sneered. "What a crappy name!"

Wald replied, "All right, you come up with something better."

More fish-staring. Finally, Arledge said, "Well, maybe *Nightline* isn't that bad. If we call it *ABC News Nightline,* it sort of has a better feel to it."

Wald then argued that "the program would define the title. If the program was as good as we thought it would be, it would make *Nightline* a generic name, not a specific name." Burke added that whatever people thought of the show, that would be what they thought of the title.

Now only one problem remained: What exactly was *Nightline?*

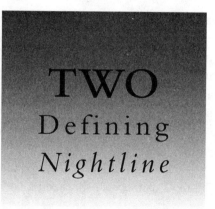

TWO
Defining
Nightline

ATOP THE U.S. CHANCERY building in Tehran, in a small, grimy room whose windows had been painted black since its conversion from an office into a prison cell, Richard Morefield was lying on a mattress when he heard footsteps. The door unlocked. An Iranian guard stomped in. The guard looked furious. "Your wife appeared on American television," he growled at Morefield. "She talked about your conditions here. The chargé of our country appeared with her. He said the CIA is stopping your mail, and your wife agreed with him. She said this was true about the CIA."

Morefield tried to conceal his excitement. The guard had revealed far more than he'd intended to. Until this moment, Morefield had had no idea whether the United States even maintained diplomatic ties with Iran. After nearly five months as a hostage, he knew that if ties were cut, the chances for his freedom, and that of his fellow hostages, would be slim. And until now he'd had no idea whether the average American still worried over the hostage situation in Tehran. There had been no way of knowing, since he'd been forbidden to listen to the radio or to read a newspaper. He'd even been denied his mail. But now the guard had unwittingly given Morefield some answers.

Even fifteen years later, Morefield's eyes would brighten at the memory. "First, this told me the U.S. government was still trying to work it out diplomatically; that we hadn't broken off relations, that we still had dialogue.

"Second, if my wife was appearing on national television, that meant that the hostages were still in the public eye. The American people had not put us on the back pages.

"Third, our condition was an issue.

"Fourth, the problem about the mail was getting attention, and that was a very sensitive issue."

As for the guard's taunt about Morefield's wife agreeing with the Iranian chargé, "I knew damn well she hadn't said the CIA was in on this."

Morefield immediately started spreading the word to the other Americans. He tapped a code through the walls and whispered to the hostages he passed in the exercise yard. Some television show had really irked the Iranians. Morefield wanted his fellow captives to understand there was good news in it.

Richard Morefield could not have imagined, then, that his wife and the chargé had confronted one another electronically, with the entire continental United States between them; the technology of debate-by-satellite had really only been harnessed in the months since the hostage-taking. And it would be almost another year before Morefield would learn of a show called *Nightline,* or that the debate that so infuriated his captors had happened to occur on *Nightline*'s debut, March 24, 1980. All he knew was that a few days after the visit from the angry guard—Morefield wasn't sure what date, precisely—someone opened his cell door and handed him his mail.

THE MORNING OF THE DEBUT, the show had a name and an anchor. That was about it.

There was still no consensus on focus, or on guests. Most important, there was no consensus on a general format. "I was filled with immense trepidation," Lord remembered. "Ted and I respected each other, we knew that we were going to have a good time together, but we had very powerful managers on top of us, and each had a different view of what the show would be." One idea was to use the show as a late-night wrap-up of the day's news; another was to mix up the format with regular segments on sports and weather.

Koppel was mystified, however, by all the anguished indecision.

"I mean, to me it seemed kind of obvious. We would continue what we had been doing. I mean, you know, you dance with the gal that brought you." The "gal," of course, was *America Held Hostage*. The story on which it had built a loyal audience was still a story. The hostages were still hostages. "I thought it should be the same program, with a new name. That's all. The only thing different was that we were not going to go away, even after the crisis was over."

By then, *America Held Hostage* had been refined into a smooth and dependable format: a four-to-five-minute taped "background piece" pertaining to the crisis, followed by live discussion with two or three guests. The format suited the story and the story still drew an audience, Koppel had argued. Why fix what wasn't broken? "We had an advantage that almost no other program in the history of television has had, and that is, we had been on the air night after night after night after night, and we had done very well, thank you very much. People respected the program. They watched the program in huge numbers, so why screw around with it? It just didn't make any sense. There was no reason to tell people, 'Yeah, you may have liked what we've been doing for the past four months, but now we're going to do something different.' "

Lord wasn't so sure. He thought *Nightline* would eventually *have* to evolve into something different once the hostages were free, and that its debut should signal changes to come. Whatever sort of program *Nightline* would become one day, Lord felt, it should start becoming now.

On the other hand, March 24 dawned with some interesting and unexpected developments involving Iran. The exiled and ailing shah of Iran had arrived that very morning in Cairo, having fled Panama only a day before Iran was to present the Panamanians with a request for his extradition. Iranian officials had ordered a retaliatory protest march on the American embassy, scheduled, as it happened, to coincide with the unveiling of the new show.

The story was too good to ignore. Lord decided to go with it. He'd have a live report from correspondent Bill Blakemore at the parade in Tehran, followed by two live interview segments. For the first segment, Lord wanted Koppel to interview a relative of one of the hostages. For the second segment, he wanted a representative of the Ayatollah Khomeini's regime. The program would close with a look toward Tuesday's New York presidential primary and a taped package about Senator Edward Kennedy's chances of winning.

Within hours, *Nightline*'s bookers, whose job it was to find guests, had lined up the wife of a hostage, Dorothea Morefield. Her husband, Richard, had been consul-general at the U.S. embassy in Tehran before his captivity. Mrs. Morefield would appear from a studio in San Diego, her hometown. For Koppel's second interview, Iran's chargé d'affaires in Washington, Ali Agah, agreed to appear. But he had one condition: even though the Iranian embassy was just a few blocks from the Washington studios, *Nightline* would have to bring a camera and a microwave truck to the embassy. The embassy was encircled with protesters, and Ali Agah feared trouble if he went outside. Lord told Susan Mercandetti, the head of the booking staff who'd been talking to Ali Agah during the day, to go ahead and take a camera crew and truck to the embassy and set up Ali Agah in a room there.

But as evening fell, what had concerned Lord for days—that *Nightline* would be nothing more than *America Held Hostage* with a new name—gnawed at him. Some of the three-way and four-way satellite interviews, the "intercontinental salons" that Koppel had pioneered on the *Held Hostage* shows, were more original than anything planned for *Nightline*'s debut. Lord got to thinking about the guests. They were supposed to talk to Koppel separately. But what if Koppel asked them to talk to one another? As of that moment, almost five months into the hostage crisis, no television news program had managed to bring together a relative of a hostage and an official representative of Iran. *Nightline*, Lord decided, should try to make the connection electronically. It would be confrontation-by-satellite.

Lord called Mrs. Morefield to ask if she'd be interested in an opportunity to speak directly to the chargé on the air. "I was frightened of the idea," she later recalled. What if she confronted the chargé and the Iranians retaliated by harming her husband? "I couldn't be sure that somebody wouldn't get mad and beat him or something. So the idea of actually going on television and confronting somebody, you know, I really agonized over it."

Less than an hour before air, Mrs. Morefield told Lord that she would do it. "It did seem to me," she said later, "that it was a good thing that this man had to confront the family as opposed to talking to officials."

Ali Agah, however, still had no idea of the impending face-off. Lord didn't want him to know until the show was on the air. And he saw no reason to notify Mercandetti, who was already inside the embassy. Why bother?

AT 11:30 EASTERN TIME, Roone Arledge sat next to Bill Lord in the New York control room as a gesture of support on opening night. By 11:30:30 Arledge was annoyed. He thought the opening animation looked silly. It featured a moon rising over a silhouette of a city. Arledge hated the moon. He made a note to himself that the moon would have to go.

Lord didn't pay much attention to the moon. He was keeping one eye on a monitor of Ali Agah's face, wondering if the chargé would bolt when Koppel announced the confrontation with Mrs. Morefield. Lord leaned over a console, curved his back, and yanked his shoulders up; his new staff would learn to recognize Lord's hunched frame as a sign that a program might be in trouble. Koppel introduced the show. His first few words, which he'd written himself, were low-key. It seemed, at first, that perhaps *Nightline* would not offer anything extraordinary at all. It certainly didn't sound like an introduction for a debut . . . which was exactly how Koppel wanted it.

> Good evening. This is a new broadcast in the sense that it is permanent and will continue after the Iran crisis is over. There will also be nights when Iran is not the major story, when we'll bring you briefly up-to-date on Iran but will focus on some other story. That's not the case tonight.

Koppel did have one small enticement. Mrs. Morefield knew it was coming. Ali Agah did not.

> For the first time on television we'll provide for the wife of an American hostage to speak live with an Iranian official.

Lord saw Ali Agha's eyebrows go up. A phone rang on the control room console and Lord picked it up. He'd expected it.

"Bill! Do not do this!" It was Mercandetti. Lord could not see her on the video feed from the Iranian embassy, but he knew that she was crouched somewhere between the camera and Ali Agha's now scowling face. She must have been listening to the introduction through an earpiece. "Ted cannot, absolutely cannot, let her talk to Ali Agah!"

"Yes he can," Lord answered coolly.

"No he can't." Mercandetti complained more loudly that Koppel had just sandbagged her guest. "Ali Agah wasn't told about this! Why didn't you tell me you were doing this?"

Lord suspected that Mercandetti was raising her pitch for effect: a good tirade might fool the chargé into believing that it was working, and that he wouldn't be asked to address Mrs. Morefield after all. But Lord could also tell that the tirade wasn't just for show. Mercandetti lowered her voice to a hiss and warned, "He's gonna walk."

Lord didn't reply. He could see on the monitor that the chargé was staying put, his attention diverted, either by Mercandetti or by the beginning of Bill Blakemore's live report from Tehran, where it was already morning and where tens of thousands of citizens were gathering for the protest march on the U.S. embassy.

BLAKEMORE: It seems clear from some new anti-American films that appeared on television here last night and this march here today that we're in for some renewed anti-American dramatics at least.

In a studio in San Diego, Dotty Morefield listened to the report from Tehran and steeled herself. How would these Iranians react, she wondered, to having one of their diplomats challenged by the wife of a hostage? A few minutes went by as she privately said one final prayer that what she'd agreed to do wouldn't bring more harm to her husband, or to the other hostages.

KOPPEL: It occurred to us here that you two might have a lot to say to each other, particularly Mrs. Morefield. Is there anything you would like to ask Mr. Ali Agah?

Mrs. Morefield looked straight into the camera. She wore large glasses, which made her appear at once unaffected, substantive, and somewhat innocent, almost bewildered by the crisis.

MOREFIELD: Well, certainly my first question is how can the government of Iran, in view of the fact that your president admits what has been done is a breach of international law the UN has condemned your country for, how can you continue to hold these innocent people?

For an instant, the chargé's eyes flashed wide, as if he'd believed that Koppel wouldn't really go through with this; then he glowered. At that moment Mercandetti understood what Lord was after. "Just the look on Ali Agah's face . . . it was unbelievable."

AGAH: It is mostly how could you remain silent in the past twenty-seven years when your government was involved in torturing, killing, and doing all kinds of corrupt actions against our people.

That response intimidated Mrs. Morefield. "I was scared. No matter what you would say, they would talk about forty years ago. I was up against a professional who had the line of patter that they had been mouthing for years down cold."

The chargé pressed on. He seized on the show's new name as a propaganda tool.

AGAH: I should thank at least for the title of this show that has been changed from *Iran Crisis: America Held Hostage* into *Nightline.* Even these small changes, you know, can have effect on the subconscious of people, especially like yourself, who are, you know, concerned certainly more than anyone else.

KOPPEL: Mr. Ali Agah. Permit me to interrupt for a moment, just to give Mrs. Morefield another chance to get a question in.

MOREFIELD: Why are we not being allowed to hear from the hostages? Why are we not corresponding with them? Why are there so few phone calls coming out? Why isn't there mail coming out of that embassy in Tehran?

AGAH: Well, perhaps one reason is because your CIA is sophisticated . . .

KOPPEL: Do you buy that, Mrs. Morefield?

MOREFIELD: No, I don't. I don't see how a letter from my husband to me or a phone call from my husband to me could be a threat to your security in any way.

Arledge turned to Lord and said, "Keep it going. Keep it going." Lord had the taped story about the New York primary scheduled for the final segment. Arledge was encouraging him to stick with the live debate.

"You see, on that very first night," Lord recalled years later, "*Nightline* was defining itself right on the air."

AGAH: Well, remember some of the letters were kept here, and they were told here in the media that they were kept in your Department of State. How do you know that they are not holding the letters from your husband?

MOREFIELD: I see that would serve them no purpose. Why, if you think the State Department, don't you let a third party in—a Swiss or someone—why are there not photographs being taken and sent out of all the hostages? Why do we only see a few?

AGAH: You see, I do not know about that.

"You know," Koppel would say after the broadcast, "it really *wasn't* terribly fair to put the chargé up against Dorothea Morefield. It was a little bit shameless. There really wasn't any way that Ali Agah could do anything about the mail. He was sitting here in Washington. He wasn't controlling the flow of mail in Tehran." In fact, when the broadcast was over, Koppel rated it as nothing special.

Lord, on the other hand, bounced out of the control room. He thought the Morefield–Ali Agah confrontation was "television magic. It wasn't something finely crafted ahead of time, in an editing room. It was something magic that happened on the air, live. We had created an atmosphere, an experience, that did not exist prior to bringing the two people together."

The debut was a television version of a Rorschach test. Everyone seemed to see something different in it, even the people within ABC.

Richard Wald and a number of network executives who'd watched from an office above the control room agreed with Lord. Wald, in particular, thought the first *Nightline* "thrilling."

Arledge thought it was fine, a decent beginning.

And Koppel rated it "flat." Good thing, he thought, that television critics would sample the show for a while before weighing in on it. There was time, he assured himself, to tinker.

Thirty-six hours later, on Wednesday morning, Koppel woke up, opened his *Washington Post,* read the first two paragraphs of the television column, and winced.

On the Air
by Tom Shales

No less a world figure—and no more—than the Iranian chargé d'affaires, Ali Agah, took note of the fact that Day 142 of the Iranian crisis saw an end to the ABC News broadcast hysterically titled "America Held Hostage," and a beginning for a new, Monday-through-Thursday late report called "ABC News Nightline."

The program, supposedly a breakthrough, is the first regularly scheduled and permanent (in the transitory TV sense of the word) late-night newscast, but to judge from its premiere, it is not likely to see America Held Spellbound.

Tom Shales was one of the most respected and influential television critics in the country. Koppel felt sick.

As for the program, it represents at best a great leap sideways and at worst a pratfall backwards for network news. The premiere did not provide viewers with anything worth knowing, and the broadcast looks to be merely another unpleasant side effect of the Iranian mess, since it would never exist if the nightly hostage reports hadn't earned boffo ratings for ABC.

The first program was weighed down with a

contrived confrontation between this Agah fellow
and Dorothea Morefield, wife of an American
hostage. When anchor Ted Koppel announced that
"for the first time" on live TV such a clash would
occur, he sounded like the host of one of those old
bleeding-heart and humiliation TV shows of the
50's—"Strike it Rich" and "This Is Your Life," and
that sort of thing.

The gambit was cheaply theatrical, mawkish and
self-promotional. It was preceded by soap operatic
tape of the Morefield family in San Diego . . .

Of course, it wasn't really news at all. It was new
news, neo-news, non-news, pseudo-news, a sugary
news substitute. Newsohol. In fact the program was
produced like an entertainment show, starting with a
dizzy, busy, outer-space motif at the outset . . .

In television it is commonly felt now that more
news is automatically good news and that even a news
cocktail is preferable to more stale beer from the
entertainment producers of Hollywood. There is
merit to this argument, but it almost evaporates in the
face of something like "ABC News Nightline." It is
difficult to see what is accomplished in the name of reality when the news is dressed up in a clown suit and
paraded in the center ring.

. . . Past performances by the likes of Geraldo
Rivera and shows like "20/20" suggest ABC News is
unembarrassable, but shows like "Nightline" must be
producing a few red faces around the shop, at least
among the old-timers who still remember what news
used to be.

Koppel would remember that review for years. "Shales shredded
us to bits. It was devastating. I make it a practice not to complain when
critics go after you, because if I'm prepared to accept their praise, I'd
better accept their criticism. But I felt terrible for all of us. So I called
Tom and I said, 'Look, I think that was dreadfully unfair. Here's a program that's going to be on the air night after night after night, and you

get us on our first night out, and okay, so maybe we weren't great, but why couldn't you wait for two or three weeks?' "

Shales told Koppel that he'd wanted to hold off but that his editor had pushed for a review of the first show. For the sake of fairness, Shales promised to come back and review *Nightline* again in six months or so.

BILL LORD HAD no doubt that Shales would come around. After weeks of grappling for a concept of what *Nightline* should be, Lord was convinced that he'd found the formula with the Morefield–Ali Agah debate. "We would bring people together who were worlds apart, using the most advanced technology available. With the right guests and a fine focus piece up front, and with Ted's intellect as the inquisitor, I knew it could be extraordinary."

Lord envisioned applying the live technology and Koppel's interviewing skills to a wide range of subjects: to stories about science, and to natural events like storms and earthquakes. He saw no reason why *Nightline* couldn't tackle those subjects, and he saw no reason to wait for the release of the hostages to try. It was a given that every broadcast would include an update on the hostages until they were free. But the freedom of running a broadcast called *Nightline* instead of one called *America Held Hostage* was the freedom to deviate from the Iran story when there was nothing new on it. Lord wanted to stretch the editorial reach of *Nightline* immediately.

Koppel did not. "I had a mind-set at the time," Koppel explained, "that we were the Iran hostage program. I did not feel confident enough about the program yet; I was really nervous that if we strayed away from the hostage story, we were going to lose all the people. I thought what the audience was tuning in for, night after night, was to hear about the hostage crisis. And I was not ready to let go of that life preserver."

So Lord gradually tugged Koppel away from the "life preserver" with topics that suited Koppel's intellect and experience: politics and the presidential primaries, the economy, U.S.-Soviet relations, and the Middle East. Then Lord tugged a little more forcefully. Three weeks after *Nightline*'s debut, he called Koppel at his home one morning. Not much news was coming out of Iran, Lord observed, but there was this—Lord paused—this volcano in Washington State, and . . .

Lord detected nothing but absolute silence on the other end of the phone. He could almost hear Koppel thinking, *A volcano?*

Lord went on. The volcano, he said, Mount St. Helens, had begun to rumble and smoke and spit ash. *Nightline* could show it live. Now he paused for a response.

Silence. Then, in a low, you-should-know-better tone: "Bill." Lord thought Koppel's jaw sounded clenched. "Bill, *that* is not *Nightline.*"

Lord offered a snappy retort. "Well, Ted, *I* think it is *Nightline.*" They could have tossed that one back and forth all day.

For Lord the whole point was the live shot. Producer David Bohrman had flown out to Washington and had rigged up a series of microwave hops and satellite links that would allow *Nightline* to broadcast a live picture of the rumbling volcano, which would be visible because it was so far west that the sun would just be setting behind it at airtime.

Koppel, for his part, understood that Lord was enthralled with natural cataclysms and exotic live pictures, but what did a rumbling mountain have to do with a show like *Nightline?* Besides, the volcano hadn't even *erupted* yet. Koppel relented, although Lord would tell a colleague that in the minutes before air, "Ted was not at all happy" about the topic. Until, that is, the shot came up of a scientist standing in haze caused, in part, by smoke from St. Helen's. It was so hazy that the mountain wasn't even visible, but the scientist, a man named Dr. Stephen Harris, conveyed the feeling that he stood near a monster that was about to awaken after 120 years.

HARRIS: St. Helens is one of the most violently explosive volcanoes on the Pacific Rim . . . the fact that the earthquakes are continuing as the mountain is being continuously shaken indicates that there is hot magma—that is, liquid rock—moving underground, which is generating the earthquakes. And as long as these continue, the possibility of a major eruption is there.

Koppel was captivated. "Bill was absolutely right about that one," he said afterward. Within weeks, the volcano erupted so violently that it heaved clouds of ash up to twelve miles high. Koppel offered no resistance to another broadcast on it. That night Lord went to the control room earlier than usual, waiting for the live satellite picture of the volcano. When the picture came up, a shot of the mountain with its upper third missing—blown away by the eruption—Lord whooped (like his hunched shoulders, his whoops were also a signal, his staff would learn, but this one positive). The volcano, he believed, symbolized *Nightline*'s first "watershed": it redefined the show's editorial reach, and—just as important—its technological reach.

Lord began to envision *Nightline* as more than a public-affairs show; now and then, it could turn the viewer into an armchair traveler. The same advancements in satellite technology that permitted Koppel's pioneering multilateral, multinational interviews also allowed, from Lord's perspective, the exploration of events and locations in parts of the world that viewers might previously have only read about. By exercising newly developed technological muscle, *Nightline* could transport the viewer into remote and exotic pockets of the world, live.

Koppel, on the other hand, worried about "the technological tail wagging the editorial dog." Yes, he had originally hated the idea of a show about a volcano, and yes, in retrospect, he'd been wrong about that one. But Mount St. Helens was actually an active scientific phenomenon. What Koppel feared was that television news in general, if not *Nightline,* stood in danger of choosing live locations first and coming up with stories to justify them second. (Fifteen years later, he'd note the proliferation of local, cable, and network reporters standing in remote locations by their individual satellite dishes, too busy "reporting live" to actually have time to travel around an area and learn something, and he'd conclude that his fears, for television news in general, were justified.)

Occasional dust-ups between the executive producer and anchor over live shots were therefore inevitable, like the one over "sunrise in the Sudan." Lord's enthusiasm for that one would seem especially quaint with a few years' hindsight, but Koppel, at the time, saw nothing quaint about it. He groused that once he'd informed the audience that it had the privilege of witnessing the first live shot in history of sunrise over the Sudan, what would he talk about for the next twenty-nine minutes? But the two men had come to a tacit understanding by then about what to do when they disagreed over a subject for the broadcast. Whoever felt most passionately, for or against the story,

won. Sometimes it was Lord, sometimes it was Koppel. In the case of
sunrise over the Sudan, it was Lord. He tied the live shot to a program
about political developments in the region, where the rise of Islamic
fundamentalism was said to have played a role in the recent murder of
Egyptian president Anwar Sadat.

Lord also felt more passionately for, than Koppel did against, pursuing the Mount Everest of live television, which, it so happened, *was*
Mount Everest. At the time, television did not even exist in the Hindu
kingdom of Nepal. But Bohrman had heard about a group of Canadian
mountain climbers who were about to ascend Everest with small
hand-held cameras. Their plan was to hand the videotapes off to sher-
pas, who would carry the material back down the mountain to base
camp, where it could be picked up and driven to Katmandu and then
fed from Katmandu by satellite. "Envision this," Bohrman told Lord.
"A live shot from Mount Everest. A live shot not *of* Mount Everest,
but from the *top* of Everest."

Bohrman proposed setting up a series of microwave dishes between Katmandu and the base of Everest. If the climbers made it to
the summit with a video camera, they could send a live shot from the
highest point in the world back through the Himalayas by microwave
to Katmandu, where a satellite would feed the shot on to New York.
Lord paused perhaps a second or two before saying yes to the effort.

Bohrman and another producer, along with a crew of ABC cameramen and technicians, flew into Nepal with over twenty cases of
gear and equipment. At the airport, Nepalese officials performed an as-
siduous examination of each and every item in each and every case. It
occurred to Bohrman, as the authorities carefully wrote down his explanations of what each item was called and what it did, that he could
simply make up names and functions for the items, since the officials
had no idea *what* they were looking at. Eventually, the gear was approved and moved to a hotel in Katmandu. There Bohrman met with
experts who knew the terrain, and together they plotted a series of
microwave "hops" through the mountains between Katmandu and
Everest. In the end it took five microwave dishes to establish a television signal between the city and the mountain. Then a yak ran into
one of the microwave dishes. That remains, as far as anyone has been
able to ascertain, the only time a yak and a microwave dish have ever
collided.

Bohrman got it all fixed, and weeks before the climbers had even reached the summit, a camera stationed next to one of the microwave dishes was transmitting a live picture of Everest back to Katmandu. It was not a view from the summit, but any live shot of the mountain was a first, and Lord wanted it on the air. He'd do another broadcast, he told Bohrman, when the climbers reached the top. Lord decided that the first Everest broadcast would open on the live shot and then go to a taped story by correspondent Jack Smith, a veteran climber himself, who'd traveled with a camera crew to the climbers' base camp. The live guest would be a spokesman for the Canadians stationed at the Katmandu hotel. All Lord really wanted was to plant the television equivalent of a "*Nightline* Was Here First" flag on Everest. And as far as he was concerned, the flag was planted when Koppel opened the broadcast with these words:

KOPPEL: What you see behind me is the first live shot in history of Mount Everest.

While Lord whooped in the control room, Koppel tried to fend off a bad case of ennui. All he could think, as he looked at the monitors of the satellite feed was, *It's a* mountain, *for heaven's sake. It's just sitting there, like mountains do. It could be a* postcard.

But Lord loved it. It reminded him of a broadcast with Edward R. Murrow in the fifties, when Murrow showed a live shot of the Brooklyn Bridge, then switched to a live shot of the Golden Gate Bridge, all the while marveling at the wonders of technology that allowed the viewer to stride the continent in a heartbeat. Bohrman loved it because his intricate web of microwave and satellite signals, the yak mishap notwithstanding, worked. And Jack Smith loved it because he could claim that his stand-up from base camp set a new world record for the highest stand-up in the history of broadcast news: 17,500 feet above sea level.

A week later, two of the climbers were making the final push to the summit when they decided to lighten their load by getting rid of the camera. But David Bohrman was a producer possessed; he arranged for a STOL (Short Take-Off and Landing) plane to fly ABC's cameraman over the mountain as the two men reached the peak. The camera fed the picture from the plane, through the microwave hops and satellites, back to America. The only problem was that the video signal from the plane came up just seconds after *Nightline* went off the air. But Canadian television picked it up and broadcast the picture of the men on the summit to a proud Canadian nation. All the effort had paid off . . . if not for the audience to which the effort had been originally dedicated.

Bohrman looked back at the Everest adventures years later and reflected, "All of us at *Nightline* in those days, we felt like pioneers. There were no rules. We had to figure out, 'What kind of program are we?'"

The trick was to see what worked and to keep it, to see what didn't work and throw it out . . . to let the show gradually, as Lord put it, "define itself." Experimentation wasn't a risk but a necessity. From the producers, for example, he encouraged provocative, unconventional "focus" pieces, the introductory taped stories that set up the issues to be discussed in the live interviews. He wanted the stories to have a point of view, he told the producers. Any guest who might take issue with that point of view would have the opportunity to do so. What was important was that the piece serve as an intellectual springboard to the interviews.

"There was a feeling," said Tom Yellin, one of the original field producers, "that if you didn't know what you were supposed to do, then you could make it up. Which made it so exciting."

Lionel Chapman had worked with Koppel on *America Held Hostage.* But *Nightline,* he found, was a whole new environment. "I remember being pushed to do things differently. In my case the pushing came from Ted. We were encouraged to test ourselves and to try things."

Bob Jordan and Pam Kahn, two of the other original field producers, would find themselves in remote parts of the world with little, if any, instruction from Lord and Koppel. "But if you were thrust into a story somewhere in the world where things were unfamiliar and the logistics difficult," according to Jordan, "Ted would say, 'Just tell me what you see.' It was the best advice a producer in the field could get, and it's what all of us at *Nightline* operated on."

THE BOOKERS, for the first half-year or so, were having adventures of another kind. Sometimes Koppel would pass by Susan Mercandetti's office and overhear her on the phone: "K-O-P-P-E-L. Ted Koppel. He used to be at the State Department. *Nightline*. No, *Night-line*. It's a new show. Right. At eleven-thirty. No, that would be Johnny Carson. Our show is on ABC. No, *Night-line*."

Not many guests worth booking understood why they should put off sleep until some ungodly hour to appear on a program they'd never heard of. Those who were aware that ABC had *something* on opposite Carson thought it was still strictly a hostage-update show. They certainly saw no payoff in staying up until midnight to appear on it. Who'd be watching? In the early days there were only two bookers, Mercandetti and Nadine Muchin, and it was up to them to figure out how to get people to come on. Mercandetti would recall that "the toughest to convince were the Washington power figures. There was no nightlife in Washington, especially back in the early eighties. Official Washington tucked in early."

Several important politicians and diplomats tried to negotiate a pre-taped interview—something that could be done earlier in the evening. But Roone Arledge issued an edict that every guest, regardless of rank, celebrity, or power, must appear live or not at all. "Once you start taping people," Arledge had warned Lord, "nobody's going to want to stay up until eleven-thirty at night in Washington to come into the studio. And by pre-taping we'll lose all the spontaneity." Arledge had another concern. "If we get into pre-taping interviews, Ted will be interviewing one guest at a time, and that means we won't have the ability to let the guests debate one another." Arledge was betting that, over time, potential guests would appreciate that "live" meant their words would be unedited. He was also betting that Koppel's focused interrogations would burnish *Nightline*'s reputation as a serious, even prestigious, forum. Once a few important events unfolded on *Nightline*'s watch, Arledge felt certain that its reputation would grow.

MEANWHILE, WORKING IN near anonymity had its benefits. It united the staff. So did the whispers—inside and outside the network—that a show that owed its existence to the Ayatollah Khomeini wouldn't last long. The day Bob Jordan was hired from a Boston affiliate, he ran into some old friends who worked for other ABC broadcasts. "You're going to work for *Nightline*?" they scoffed. "It's not gonna survive. Six months tops. ABC's crazy if it thinks this show's gonna work." The sense that they were outsiders at ABC News, as well as the underdogs of late-night, forged a bond among *Nightline*'s bookers, producers, reporters, and researchers.

The only real divide was geographic. Half the staff worked out of New York, the rest, out of Washington. Arledge wanted the executive producer and the control room for the broadcast in New York, at ABC News headquarters, so that he could be involved with the development of the broadcast. He would have preferred having the anchor in New York, too, but Koppel had settled his family in Maryland many years earlier; he had no intention of uprooting them. So Lord had hired an even number of staff members for the two cities. He bridged the divide by institutionalizing a morning conference call (which would continue to launch the *Nightline* workday a decade and a half later). The call began with a producer summarizing what had happened in the world overnight, after which the staff would pitch story ideas until Lord and Koppel settled on a topic for that night's broadcast (subject to change in the event of breaking news).

There was an innocence about those early days. For several months, the New York staff, except for Lord, didn't even have office space. For conference calls with Washington, they'd cram into Lord's office, some sitting on the floor, some huddled together on a frayed couch, all packed together so tightly that formality was impossible.

The collegial environment and underdog mentality paid off. The staff responded as a team when signal events began breaking on *Nightline*'s watch, beginning with a startling post-midnight announcement out of the White House in late April 1980. Koppel had just signed off the broadcast when the White House released the news of a secret military mission to rescue the hostages. Dust storms in the Iranian desert and problems with helicopters had forced President Carter to order the mission aborted; but one of the helicopters had collided with a C-130 cargo plane, the White House said, killing eight men of the Delta Force. Koppel returned to the anchor chair for a five-and-a-half-hour special report, an all-night marathon of satellite feeds. There were live reports from ABC correspondents stationed overseas, who described worldwide reaction to the aborted mission, with live pictures from Tehran, where citizens were swarming the gates of the American embassy, denouncing Carter as Satan.

Operation Blue Light was the worst debacle of the Carter presidency and a defining event in the evolution of *Nightline* into a program that viewers would turn to for late-night breaking news. A fledgling cable network called CNN would launch a twenty-four-hour-a-day news service that same year, but *Nightline* had at its disposal the global resources of ABC, including state-of-the-art technology, vast numbers of foreign and domestic bureaus, seasoned correspondents, and talented producers. *Nightline* could respond to crises almost instantly, almost anywhere, and not just in Iran.

In fact, Koppel was not all that surprised one December night, while dining out before the broadcast, to be pulled from the table for an urgent phone call. He figured it was either something about the Americans still held captive in Tehran or something about Poland. That very night, in just over an hour, he was scheduled to interview the Soviet commentator Vladimir Pozner about the possibility of Soviet intervention in Poland. The caller was Lord. John Lennon, the former Beatle and an icon of rock and roll, had been shot outside his Manhattan apartment building. By the time Koppel and his colleagues had made it back to the studio, Lennon was dead. About thirty minutes were left before airtime to scrap the top half of the line-up on Poland and replace it with a live report from correspondent Lynn Sherr, who was at the hospital where Lennon lay dead, and for a reminiscence from *20/20*'s Geraldo Rivera, who had at least met Lennon. At 2:30 A.M. Eastern Time, Koppel anchored an entirely new edition on Lennon for the West Coast. By then ABC had set up a camera outside the Dakota, Lennon's Manhattan apartment building, the scene of a strange and impromptu vigil. Hundreds of men and women had converged around the dark Victorian building where Lennon had been shot. In the wee hours of that winter night, the mourners held candles and sang Beatles songs. The microphone caught an echo as their voices bounced between brick and concrete and drifted into Central Park.

Breaking stories would spike the ratings over the years, but had *Nightline*'s success depended on them, it would have faded away before the hostages were even released. In fact, the aborted attempt to rescue the hostages, in April, and John Lennon's murder, in December, were about it when it came to crises breaking on *Nightline*'s watch for the first year. Something more fundamental distinguished the hundreds of shows that aired between April and December: the live interviews.

The topicality of the interviews, the electricity attendant to their being live, and the sense that on any given night Koppel might be holding a conversation with someone halfway around the world began to command attention. Television critics commented on what they usually described as Koppel's "unflappable" demeanor. One reviewer even referred to a night when Koppel seemed to lose his cool with some Iranian protesters as an example of his, and *Nightline*'s, spontaneity. Koppel conceded to the reviewer that he had had trouble disguising his anger with the protesters' defense of the hostage-taking. But even then, his ire manifested itself more in the way he phrased his questions than in his tone of voice or demeanor. "Calm" simply came naturally to him. So did live broadcasting, as naturally as breathing. Once he told a colleague that if someone were to measure his pulse at noon and again during a broadcast, he doubted if there would be any difference at all. The medium suited Koppel. And his demeanor suited the intimacy of the medium, especially late at night.

Reviewers also made note of the fact that Koppel actually seemed to be listening to his guests. He was. Susan Mercandetti would remember how she'd learned that. The day after *Nightline*'s debut, she walked up to Koppel and handed him a neatly typed list of questions that she thought he might want to ask a guest that evening.

Koppel looked Mercandetti in the eye and said, "Do not ever, *ever* give me questions." Mercandetti was mortified. She never did hand him another list, nor did she ever see him prepare one.

Koppel refused to work off prepared questions because he wanted to hear what the guests had to say and to build on the conversations naturally, the way people did in real life, around dinner tables or in seminars. Guests could say surprising things. Koppel knew he'd better be listening and not looking at notes. He would be freer, that way, to take the conversation on whatever tangent seemed right. The results were some electrifying debates that first year, on everything from the equal rights amendment to the *Voyager* space probe, from the baseball strike to the ethics of the death penalty, from riots in Miami to the reemergence of the Ku Klux Klan. The fact that everything was live, and that the show was electronically convening guests who often lacked the means or the inclination or the will to debate face-to-face, meant that neither the guests nor the audience nor Koppel could ever be certain where the conversations would end up.

In November 1980 *The Christian Science Monitor* wrote that "a quiet revolution in late-night network news has erupted while most of the nation slept . . . or watched Johnny Carson . . . *Nightline* is the thinking man's alternative to late network viewing." The *Monitor* cited as evidence a two-and-a-half-hour special edition that aired the night after Ronald Reagan's landslide election to the presidency. It was a technological marvel for its time, an electronic international whip-around anchored by Koppel, Frank Reynolds, and Barbara Walters. Reynolds chatted with the President-elect and Mrs. Reagan, who appeared from their home in California and still seemed to be adjusting to the news that they'd won; Walters talked to Soviet commentator Vladimir Pozner in Moscow, who speculated that Reagan's hard-line views would hurt U.S.-Soviet relations; ABC's Pierre Salinger reported from London on European reaction to the election; and from Washington, the columnist George Will appeared and accused religious conservative activists of hogging too much credit for the election.

Koppel anchored a multilateral debate featuring senators George McGovern, Birch Bayh, and Frank Church, and two conservative political activists, Paul Weyrich and the Reverend Jerry Falwell. The three senators had been tossed from office the previous evening by a new wave of conservative voters. They seemed to relish the chance to confront their conservative nemeses, if only by satellite.

BAYH: I say to Mr. Falwell, I am a Christian. I was reared by Christian grandparents, baptized in the Church of Christ. . . . I think that most of us are moral, whether we are on the right or the left. We want to do the right thing.

FALWELL: . . . I have nothing but love and appreciation for these gentlemen . . . And I have never spoken an ill word about any of them . . .

CHURCH: . . . Now these gentlemen talk, you know, within the bounds of sweet reason on this program. But when I see literature of that kind spreading around this state, I'm not

only disturbed, but I'm frightened that this tendency
could lead us into hatred, intolerance, and bigotry. . . .

WEYRICH: . . . I want to address what Senator Church was talking
about, because, as Holy Scripture says, "By their fruits ye
shall know them." And the fruits of a member of Congress is his voting record. . . . And I don't think if you
take a look at the voting records of the senators who are
here on this program, that really you can put them in the
category of people who support the traditional family,
people who support traditional moral views.

KOPPEL: Gentlemen, each of you seems to be astonishingly capable of quoting Scripture. And I just wonder how it is that
this impression is abroad and in the country now that
your groups are hate groups.

WEYRICH: Well, I don't know . . .

McGOVERN: . . . These . . . right-wing extremists . . . have been getting away with dirty tactics in American politics for too
long a time. . . . They've said they'll lie. They've said
they'll twist the facts. They've said they'll do anything to
defeat humane and progressive senators that don't fit their
mold of what an American ought to be. I personally regard them as a menace to the American political process.

Jeff Gralnick, the executive producer that night, thought the five-
way debate was a milestone. "Ted choreographed a conversation
among all those people. And this was in the days before Ted had monitors to see everyone—I had all the monitors in the control room, but
he couldn't see all the guests. So I'd have to say in his ear, while he
was listening to the conversation, 'It looks like McGovern wants in,'
and he'd go with it. And it was so good that the show went on for two
hours and forty minutes—the longest post-election special in history."

Tom Yellin stood in the control room at 1 A.M. as the debate raged
on and realized that "there was this real true exchange. It was like having these people in your living room. It really had the intimacy of a
personal encounter." This was the night, said Yellin, "when, after
seven months on the air, *Nightline,* I thought, had finally matured.
What made that show different was that for the first time you had real

people at the center of a news story offering not only their insights and analysis of a story itself—but they felt comfortable enough on this night to reveal themselves."

NOT LONG AFTER THAT broadcast, Bob Jordan started hearing from the same former colleagues who had teased him back in March about joining a show that had no future. Jordan's old associates now wanted to know about the rumors that *Nightline* was going to be expanded to thirty minutes, five nights a week. The rumors were true, Jordan informed them. Would it mean, they asked, that there might be openings on the staff?

AT THE TURN of the year, Tom Shales honored his promise to Koppel to revisit the program. In the January 8, 1981, issue of *The Washington Post,* under the headline "THE LATE BLOOMER; A NICHE IN LATE-NIGHT; TED KOPPEL OF 'NIGHTLINE': FROM HOSTAGES TO HOT," Shales wrote:

> The man most responsible for the success of "ABC News Nightline" is the Ayatollah Khomeni.
> The man second most responsible is Ted Koppel.
> If not for the hostage crisis and ABC's commitment to broadcast nightly reports on it, "Nightline" would perhaps never have become a permanent network fixture, as it did last March. This week it expanded from 20 to 30 minutes, and in April goes from four nights a week to five.
> This man Koppel—short, pugnacious, cocky, droll, 40—has helped pull off a double garbanzo: first that a news show would give Johnny Carson a run for the late-night ratings (occasionally beating him, never getting creamed by him) and second that ABC News of all Newses would come up with a broadcast this smart, classy, and relatively shlockless.
> "Nightline" represents the most successful programming initiative in ABC News history. Executive producer William Lord can take bows, but Koppel gets a medal. He's moved to front and center of network news.

> He's a smoothie. He's a pro. He's a rocket. What
> makes "Nightline" click is Koppel's bull's-eye inter-
> viewing style, a verbal and rhetorical combination of
> Sugar Ray Leonard and Mikhail Baryshnikov—a suc-
> cession of jabs, rejoinders and judicious-to-delicious
> interruptions: Koppel a cappella.

In ten months the critics had come around, major players in politics, culture, and diplomacy were accepting invitations to appear, and
the affiliates considered the show enough of a ratings success to grant
its expansion from twenty minutes to a half-hour. And yet, still, the
specter of the hostage crisis loomed over every broadcast. Koppel's
sign-offs were all variations on a theme: "It is day 399 for the hostages
in Iran." "Today marked the four hundredth day of captivity for the
Americans being held in Iran." "This is day 401 of the Iran hostage
crisis." *Nightline* was sticking by its commitment to provide updates
on the crisis every night, no matter what the main topic of the broadcast. In fact, since the failed rescue mission, almost half of all the
Nightline broadcasts had been devoted entirely to Iran or the hostages.
Without a resolution, *Nightline* was still, the joke went, "the show
brought to you by the Ayatollah Khomeini."

By then several of the wives of the hostages had been interviewed
by Koppel so often that their faces were better known than those of
their spouses. Louisa Kennedy, whose husband had been the third-
ranking diplomat in Tehran before his captivity and who, along with
Dorothea Morefield, appeared on *Nightline* frequently, couldn't walk
through a grocery store without attracting attention. Programs like
Nightline, Mrs. Kennedy realized, had ushered in the era of the "global
village." Viewers, she said, "knew us by our first names."

Some columnists and politicians argued that by keeping the spotlight on the hostages, the wives had made it more valuable to Iran
to prolong the crisis. The wives, obviously, did not agree. Louisa
Kennedy would say later that had *Nightline* and the rest of the American media simply ignored the hostages, "I'm afraid the Iranians would
have simply kept them locked up and thrown away the key." When
her husband was released, he would learn of the intensive coverage
and of his wife's appearances and would concur that they'd helped
more than hurt the hostages. Television, said Moorhead Kennedy,
"did far more to rally the American people against the Iranians and to

strengthen the hand of Mr. Carter in not making concessions than would have been the case" without the coverage. In fact, Kennedy remembered that his captors had complained to him that the American media was engaged in "disinformation" against the Iranians. "What should the media have said that it didn't?" he would challenge his guards. They had never offered much of a reply.

JANUARY 21, 1981, day 444 of the hostage crisis, it ended. Minutes after Ronald Reagan took the oath of office, Iranian officials put the Americans on a plane for home. Richard Morefield stepped off the plane during a stop in Algiers and waved to the television cameras. Morefield did not know that his wife was watching that scene, live, from their home in San Diego, nor would he have dreamed it possible. He'd been gone so long and kept so isolated that Morefield had no idea about the recent advancements in television that allowed it to bring people together who were "worlds apart." And he had no idea about a show called *Nightline*.

One week later, he was on it. With his wife at his side, Morefield watched as Koppel ran a clip from the premiere show, when Mrs. Morefield confronted Ali Agah about the mail. Morefield then recounted to Koppel the story of how he'd learned from the angry guard about the confrontation between his wife and the chargé and how he'd tapped the information out to the other hostages, to let them know that "they weren't forgotten." And Morefield beamed when he remembered the thrill, a few days after the guard's visit, when someone opened his cell door and handed him letters from his family, the first mail to reach him during all those months in captivity.

After the program, Koppel pulled the Morefields and the *Nightline* staff into a studio and brought out champagne. At long last the hostages were free. Finally, *Nightline* was completely free to define itself.

SOMEWHERE ABOUT THIS TIME, Lord, Koppel, senior producer Stu Schwartz, and writer Steve Steinberg, all of whom had worked for ABC back in the days when people called it the "Almost Broadcasting Company," adoped a new motto. They might be discussing some story idea or reviewing a broadcast at midnight or even scrambling to change the show, and one of them would pause and smile and say to another, "*These* are the good old days."

· · ·

ROONE ARLEDGE WOULD PINPOINT the show's coming of age to an event that occurred a few months later. The broadcast had invited Secretary of State Alexander Haig to appear from Ottawa at the end of an economic summit. Haig, who was in Ottawa with President Reagan, sent back a message that he was planning to ride home with the President to Washington on *Air Force One,* at precisely the hour when *Nightline* was on the air. If *Nightline* wanted him, said Haig, it would have to pre-tape the interview.

At the time Arledge still insisted that all of Koppel's interviews be live and had warned Lord not to set a precedent by giving in to anyone. "Live" was part of what defined the show and gave it an edge. Lord thought that perhaps an interview with the secretary of state was worth a pre-tape. He called Arledge and asked permission to break the rule against pre-taping just once.

Arledge said no.

In the end Haig agreed to miss his ride on *Air Force One.* He remained behind in Canada to appear on *Nightline.*

Even fifteen years later, Arledge savored that memory. "That was a defining moment. The fact that Haig stayed up in Canada to appear live kind of reinforced in our minds how important the program had become."

THREE

Belushi, the Blues, and Art Petacque

FRANK RADICE HATED to be the guy to burst the bubble. It hadn't been a week, even, since the champagne celebration with the Morefields and the joy of it still lingered around the office. The release of the hostages had given Koppel and his producers a whole new freedom to experiment. The affiliates had given them an expanded time slot in which to do it.

So it was going to be a tad embarrassing for Radice to have to tell Koppel that he couldn't get his first assignment for the newly expanded *Nightline* off the ground. He shuffled into Koppel's office and asked, "Do you have a minute?"

"Sure," Koppel answered. "What's up?"

Radice flopped down in a chair. This could be awkward. How do you tell the anchor that the network correspondents rate working on a *Nightline* story about as exciting as a stakeout in the rain? "I can't find a correspondent," Radice announced.

Koppel wasn't surprised. "You mean you can't find a *willing* correspondent," he replied. It was no secret to Koppel that few of ABC's on-camera reporters wanted to work for the show. Even though a typical *Nightline* focus piece ran five or six minutes, which was much longer than standard evening-news stories, most reporters believed that the advantage of more airtime was outweighed by the disadvantage of a smaller audience, compared to the numbers who tuned in to *World News Tonight*. And though it was true that after ten months on the air *Nightline* was beginning to receive favorable reviews, the accolades were for Koppel's skills as an interviewer, not for the taped pieces. *Nightline* had two correspondents of its own, James Walker and John Martin—and, for a time, Charles Gibson as well—who participated in the overall editorial process of choosing stories and who enjoyed the best of exotic travel and interesting assignments. But those correspondents were often on the road and overbooked, which meant that it was up to the ABC News assignment desk to drum up some reluctant reporter to file for the show.

On this particular Friday, Radice had informed the desk that he needed a reporter for a story on organized crime in Chicago. They'd have to travel that night; the story was scheduled for Monday's broadcast. About an hour later the desk editor had called him back and said there simply wasn't anyone available. Radice was nonplussed. No one? Not a single paid on-camera employee of ABC News was free to go to Chicago? Nope, was the answer.

Radice had then phoned Bill Lord in New York to tell him about the problem. Lord's response: "You're a clever boy. You'll think of something." Click. That had been it.

So now it was Koppel's turn to listen to Radice's plight, and to watch his producer sink lower and lower in a chair. But Koppel had an idea: "Go find the best crime reporter in Chicago, someone who's covered the Mafia for years. Doesn't matter whether they work in television, radio, or on a newspaper. Sit down and interview him on camera. Have him give you all the details, all his memories of covering the Mob. Then cut his answers into a narrative."

Radice flew to Chicago with a camera crew and tracked down a reporter with the *Chicago Sun-Times* named Art Petacque. Petacque was a classic: a gruff-voiced, heavy-set, street-smart newsman who'd covered the Mob for years. He took Radice through the structure of the Cosa Nostra, through its history, through the best anecdotes. Radice had more than enough for a ten-minute narrative.

Because Petacque's stories weren't scripted, and because his voice wasn't trained for broadcasting, the narration had a raw, natural feel to it.

PETACQUE: The outfit in Chicago, the crime syndicate as we call it, plays this kind of a role in the daily life of people like you and myself. . . . In Chicago, I could tell you that they've been in legitimate businesses that ranged from the crib to the grave. And I say that literally. Now, Fred Evans, who is the Meyer Lanksy type in Chicago, owned a diaper company. Now, that's the crib bit.

After the interview, Radice spent an afternoon roaming around Chicago, shooting locations referred to by Petacque. He had a *Nightline* assistant dig up old stills and file footage of Al Capone and the other Mafia figures Petacque had mentioned. Then he edited the interview into a cohesive narrative, and covered it with the appropriate pictures.

The format wasn't new. Documentary films often structured narratives out of interviews, and the network news shows had toyed around for years with stories built strictly out of "natural sound." But the Mafia story was the first attempt at the technique on *Nightline*. It worked so well that within weeks, several producers were cobbling stories without correspondents. And over time they learned to weave narratives not with one voice but with a series of voices from the field. Children of divorce talked about pain, children of alcoholics about fear, children of Israel and of Palestine about their dreams for peace. Lord dubbed the format "the Petacque."

What was different about "Petacques" on *Nightline* was the way the broadcast married the format to breaking news. When a man with a rifle walked into a McDonald's in San Ysidro, California, opened fire, killed and wounded adults and children, and laid siege to the restaurant, a local ABC affiliate positioned a camera crew across the street and broadcast live reports. Producer Bob LeDonne arranged a feed of those reports to New York, where he edited them together chronologically to re-create the unfolding tragedy. Within two hours of its conclusion, after police stormed the restaurant and killed the gunman, LeDonne had the piece ready for broadcast. The natural sounds and the voices, all recorded in "real time," held the viewer in close to the confusion, commotion, and fear.

After San Ysidro, whenever there was late-breaking news of national interest, if a local affiliate could feed video to New York in time for the broadcast, the assignment would go to LeDonne. So one summer night when the calls came in that a passenger jet had just crashed outside Dallas and *Nightline* was scheduled to go on the air in an hour and a half, it was LeDonne who ran to an editing room and waited for the pictures to come in. When they did, he was stunned. The camera roamed inside a mass of torn and smoking metal. Only one rescue worker popped in and out of the frame. LeDonne realized that the cameraman who'd captured this must have been one of the first people to reach the crash site. What was most startling was the sound: there wasn't any. There was a ghastly silence—the sound of death.

LeDonne culled seven minutes of the scene. Using strictly natural sound, he edited the material into an eerie tour through the wreckage: Rain and mist mix with smoke to drop a foggy gray shroud on every image, creating an impression, especially with the silence, of an awful dream. The quiet eventually gives way to the faint wailing of sirens until, finally, the shouts of emergency workers pierce the air. A man with a bullhorn yells, "Leave the bodies where they are."

The package drew an unusual review from Tom Shales, who rarely wrote about *Nightline*'s focus pieces: "What a viewer got from these seven minutes was a more immediate and authentic impression of what the crash was like, and what its effects were on those involved, than a reporter standing in front of the carnage with a microphone could possibly have provided. Indeed, it reaffirmed the fact, often overlooked in TV news, that the camera is still the most essential correspondent. . . . There were no wasted motions and no excess words."

OTHER EXPERIMENTS SPUTTERED. There was the story about cocaine, for example, in which producers videotaped a performance by modern dancers whose movement was supposed to be an interpretation of how cocaine affected the brain. The best that can be said about the effort was that it didn't work.

Cartoons pretty well flopped, too. There were a number of attempts during the early years to close the show on editorial cartoons. The idea was to marry the cartoons to actual video. That concept didn't work, either.

KOPPEL COULD ACCEPT the failures. They were a sign of health, a symptom of vitality and innovation. It was important to keep searching for new ways to tell stories. It was equally important, Koppel knew, to be searching for new stories to tell. The development of the broadcast demanded a wider range of topics than what might be considered inside the "safe zone" of international affairs and public policy. But the day came when Lord wanted to venture so far out of the zone that Koppel was fairly certain his executive producer had lost his mind. And by dinnertime that day, Koppel's colleagues would see him stalk out of his office, slam the door behind him with a force so hard the wall shook, and disappear out of the Washington bureau and into the March night.

It was the worst editorial conflict between anchor and executive producer in the two years that *Nightline* had been on the air. And what had triggered it, of all things, was the death of John Belushi.

The day had begun quietly, with guests booked and a taped piece ready to go for a program on rising unemployment. But in the early afternoon David Bohrman walked into Bill Lord's office holding some wire copy. "Bill, you need to look at this," Bohrman advised. According to the wires, John Belushi, the comedian and actor, had been found dead in a bungalow of a Los Angeles hotel. The cause of his death had not yet been determined. He was only thirty-three years old.

Bohrman, who was himself only twenty-six, reminded Lord that to the baby-boom generation, Belushi was an icon, one of the wildest of the original cast members of *Saturday Night Live,* and, more recently, an oddly charismatic movie star. The pudgy-faced, nonverbal, sweet, and vulgar fraternity brother in *Animal House* was a rebel for the eighties: a rebel against yuppiedom, against cleaning up one's act, against acting like a grown-up.

Lord was thinking about the audience. This was a Friday. Ever since the show had expanded from four nights a week to five, he'd wanted Fridays used for slightly offbeat, less serious subjects. Lord's philosophy was that "Friday is when people sort of unwind, go out and have dinner, perhaps, and they don't want to come back and see some heavy foreign-policy thing. It's important to find topics that are a little looser, that will help us gain an audience based on the interest that they might have on a Friday night . . . something a little more comfortable and relaxed."

Furthermore, on Fridays, what followed *Nightline* was ABC's answer to *Saturday Night Live,* a comedy show targeting young viewers. It made sense for *Nightline* to complement the midnight show with stories that might appeal to a slightly younger audience. Lord had turned to none other than Elvis—or the ghost of Elvis—to set the tone; the very first Friday *Nightline* had aired, it had featured an exclusive video tour of Elvis Presley's home, Graceland.

It so happened that on this particular Friday, Lord had agreed to a subject as serious as unemployment because the country was in a recession, and that very morning, the Labor Department had issued a grim unemployment rate for February: 8.8 percent of Americans were officially without work. The rate wasn't much higher than January's, but it suggested that the recession wouldn't be over soon. The statistics justified a broadcast, and besides, Koppel felt strongly that it was the right one to do. The executive producer had therefore acceded to it.

Still, Lord kept revisiting the decision. He just didn't think that viewers looking for a respite from the workweek would be wild about tuning in to a show on unemployment. So the news out of Los Angeles caught his attention.

Lord called Bob Greene, a nationally syndicated columnist who lived in Chicago and often reported on cultural stories for *Nightline*. "If we were to put together a program on John Belushi," Lord asked Greene, "how do we justify it?"

"Well, he really was the John Lennon of television comedy," Greene replied.

Lord called Koppel. "Ted, you've seen the wires about John Belushi. I think we've got to change the show."

"What?"

"Yeah, you know, the bumblebee guy, the *Saturday Night Live* guy."

Koppel dropped his voice to the icy-cold tone, low and ominous, that he used to convey both disgust and stubbornness. "Bill . . . I gotta tell ya . . . I feel very, very uncomfortable with this idea."

That was as pleasant as the conversation got. Koppel felt strongly about the economics show; unemployment was a story people cared about. It was timely. It was, from Koppel's viewpoint, the sort of subject that *Nightline* was all about.

Lord thought Koppel's attitude on this was "stuffy." Koppel hadn't balked at the Elvis show, had he?

But tonight both Koppel and Lord were digging in for a fight. Lord told Koppel that he was going to have the bookers start lining up live guests on Belushi, and that only if they came up empty would he use the unemployment show as a backup. Koppel protested one more time, hung up the phone and, after slamming his door, disappeared.

While staff members quietly made bets with one another over who would back down, Lord or Koppel, correspondent James Walker worked with several producers to pull together a taped profile of Belushi's career. The bookers began the search for guests. What they found was that not only were Belushi's closest friends too distraught to consider an interview, but that anyone who had so much as nodded to Belushi in a hallway was too distraught to do an interview.

What happened next is still unclear. What Lord remembers is that someone told him that the bookers had come up dry in the search for one of Belushi's friends, but that they had been able to lock in the legendary comedian Milton Berle. Berle, Lord was told, had appeared as a guest host with Belushi on *Saturday Night Live*. What the bookers and their assistants still insist, to this day, is that *no one* booked Milton Berle and that he miraculously appeared, out of thin air, at the ABC studios in Los Angeles and told the news desk that he was there to come on *Nightline*.

No matter how Berle came to be booked, Lord felt he had what he needed to go ahead with the Belushi show. The bookers had also lined up a critic from *TV Guide,* and Bob Greene was writing a commentary on Belushi's roots in Chicago. Now the question was, where was Ted? It was 10 P.M. and Koppel still hadn't returned to his office.

Lord's phone rang. It was Koppel, calling from a restaurant in downtown Washington. "What have you got?" Koppel asked tersely.

"Well," Lord tried to sound upbeat, "we've got Milton Berle, and—"

"*Milton Berle?* What the hell does Milton Berle know about John Belushi?"

"Well, he was on *Saturday Night Live* once, and he's apparently got some good stories . . . it'll be fine . . . really, it'll be great."

Koppel paused for a moment before responding. "All right, I'm on my way back in."

Lord wondered, for the first time that night, for the first time in two years, in fact, if it were possible that Koppel had considered *not* coming back.

In fact, Koppel had sulked for the better part of two hours in a restaurant booth with his young son, munching on a hamburger and hoping that somehow Lord would come to his senses, that maybe the bookers' phone lines would go dead. But to ditch his responsibility as the program's anchor was not an option as far as Koppel was concerned. Still, he walked back to the studio in a foul mood.

Five minutes before air, Koppel was still peeved. *John Belushi? Milton Berle?* He took his anchor seat and was about to hook on his microphone when he was told that he had an important call from the Los Angeles studios. Koppel picked up the phone next to his desk.

"Hello?"

"Ted?"

"Yes."

"Milton Berle. What the *fuck* am I doing on your show?"

OVER A DECADE LATER, Koppel remembered the call from Milton Berle better than he remembered what followed, perhaps because what followed wasn't memorable. Berle had called to point out that other than having chatted with Belushi in a dressing room at NBC, he hardly knew the man, so how much in heaven's name could he say?

"Well, you're it, Milton," Koppel had responded. "You're all we've got." On the air, Berle smoothly and enthusiastically compared Belushi's talent as a physical comedian with some of the old legends', and Bob Greene offered a perspective from Belushi's hometown, but the conversation begged for someone who knew Belushi personally. And yet Lord would look back on that broadcast years later and still insist that although the show might not have gone well, it was the right one to do. And Koppel would always insist that it wasn't.

IF KOPPEL DIDN'T THINK that *Nightline*—at least in its formative years—had any business shortchanging hard news for the death of an entertainment figure, he felt just as strongly, a year later, that the ABC entertainment division had no business producing a drama that hyped the threat of a real nuclear holocaust. In the fall of 1983, he sat in his office screening an advance copy of what the entertainment division hoped would be a blockbuster. It was a film, scheduled to air during the November ratings sweeps, called *The Day After*. The made-for-television movie told the story of a midwestern town hit by Soviet nuclear missiles.

The Day After coincided with a nadir in U.S.-Soviet relations. In September 1983 the Soviets had shot down a Korean airliner and accused it of spying, and in October the Reagan administration had reaffirmed its commitment to a stronger nuclear defense system. For

Americans who might be feeling a wee bit nervous about the Cold War, *The Day After* was just the thing to make them positively terrified.

Koppel watched it and cringed. "The premise was bogus. It was meant to instill in viewers the fear that the Soviets were ready to launch nuclear missiles at the slightest provocation and that the White House was capable of engaging in a nuclear attack without a prolonged debate. And I knew that was simply not the case." Koppel knew because he had witnessed "war games" at the Pentagon. The games presented officials with plausible high-pressure scenarios. Sometimes the threat of war or a nuclear crisis loomed; sometimes the crisis revolved around terrorism or a hostage-taking. The officials were required to deliberate and make decisions as if the crisis were real. What had impressed Koppel about those games was how quickly the officials at the table seemed to forget that their crisis was fictional. "They'd throw themselves into it. You could feel the pressure. What it took for officials even to consider the possibility of a nuclear strike— even a make-believe one—involved long, drawn-out, tortured deliberations." Although he hadn't witnessed anyone from the Reagan administration play the game, he knew that administration members often did. "And I thought that if *Nightline* could shed light on those deliberations, on what it would really take before American officials would come to a decision for or against the use of nuclear weapons, it would serve Americans far better than a melodrama about blinding light and mushroom clouds."

Nightline, Koppel decided, would produce a drama of its own about the Cold War. It would stage its own "war game." And it would broadcast the game in the week just following the heavily hyped premiere of *The Day After. Nightline* viewers would witness the sort of deliberations that would, in real life, precede the decision to use nuclear force or the decision to avoid it.

Jay LaMonica, an investigative reporter who had worked with Koppel for years on stories involving national security, lined up military and intelligence experts to help design the game, while *Nightline* senior producer Bill Moore constructed a set to resemble a "war room" on the top floor of ABC's Washington bureau. The room looked mundane, but the technology it concealed was complex and state-of-the-art. Moore had bright lights recessed behind slits in the ceiling and cameras hidden behind fake television screens, so that the players would not be distracted. The proceedings would be recorded on tape machines located on a different floor. And they would be carried to another room, where the "control group"—the military and intelligence experts responsible for the scenario—would periodically escalate the crisis by giving the players new developments to deal with. The control group would be coordinated by Leslie Gelb, the former director of political and military planning at the State Department.

Former U.S. senator and secretary of state Edmund Muskie accepted *Nightline*'s invitation to play the President. His cabinet was comprised of officials from the Nixon, Ford, and Carter administrations. There were former secretaries of defense—James Schlesinger and Clark Clifford. There were former members of the National Security Council—William Hyland, Richard Pipes, Richard Holbrooke, and Winston Lord. There was Antonia Chayes, the former undersecretary of the Air Force, and General Edward Meyer, a former chief of staff of the U.S. Army. And there was Hodding Carter, the former spokesman of the State Department. These were people who had not only participated in war games inside the White House situation room; as officials they had grappled with real international crises. Over two days—a total of sixteen hours—they immersed themselves in a hypothetical confrontation between U.S. and Soviet forces in the Persian Gulf.

CHAYES: I am not willing to go all the way, and I think we've got
            to face that, too. I don't think the American people are,
            would support that. . . .

CARTER: If there were an all-out Soviet assault on our forces, calling into question their survival, it would be a declaration
            which would be so explicit on their part that we indeed
            have to answer yes, we will go all the way.

The faces around the table looked pinched. As the hours passed, the closer the Soviets moved toward U.S. forces and strategic oil fields, the more Muskie's cabinet fell into some classic—and surprisingly hostile—deliberations about the policy of "first use."

CLIFFORD: I cannot picture an American President ever being the
            first to use either a tactical or a strategic nuclear weapon.
            That would be, I think, an absolute policy as I see it.

SCHLESINGER: Mr. President . . . the policy of no first use is detrimental to our position in Europe, and I beg of you to postpone any decision with regard to the suggestion of the secretary of state.

MUSKIE: We are not reviewing nuclear policy at this point. I have no intention of reviewing nuclear policy at this point.

Muskie said afterward that he'd felt he "was really dealing with all these problems. Even, you know, the loneliness of a presidential decision on the nuclear option." He spared himself the nuclear option by sending a message to the Soviet president proposing a mutual superpower pullout from the area. The control group had the Soviet leader "agree," conditionally, at which point the control group declared the game over. Just three days later, Muskie had a heart attack. He recovered, but the timing of the coronary underscored the almost inhuman pressures of a nuclear age presidency.

The Crisis Game was broadcast as a series. Producers had pared the tapes of the game down from sixteen hours to four, which were spread across four nights of programming, one hour every night. It was not only riveting television; Richard Pipes, who was one of the players and who had, in real life, served as an adviser on the Soviet Union to President Reagan, guessed that tapes of the series would make their way to the highest levels of the Soviet government. "I think it's good for them to see it," he said at the time. "I think they will see the prudence, the intelligence, and knowledge that goes into making these decisions."

DRAMATIZING THE BRINK of Armageddon was one thing. But *Nightline* takes you to . . . D Day? It sounded like a bad imitation of the old CBS series *You Are There*. Still, the idea was Rick Kaplan's, and Koppel didn't want to dampen Kaplan's spirits. Kaplan had only been running the show a few days.

Bill Lord had been producing *Nightline* for four years when Roone Arledge asked him to take over the helm of the evening news. *Nightline* went to Kaplan, a veteran of both the *CBS Evening News,* with Walter Cronkite, and ABC's *World News Tonight*. At thirty-seven, Kaplan had carved out a reputation as a forceful, imaginative broadcast journalist; he threw himself into projects as if they were military battles.

Kaplan arrived at *Nightline* looking for a big project, fast; he

wanted his own imprint on the show. He set his eyes on D Day because its fortieth anniversary was only weeks away. And he locked
onto the idea of time travel precisely because *Nightline* had never tried
it. Kaplan loved "firsts."

KOPPEL: (*introduction*) We ask you to help us by stretching your
            imagination over this next hour so that we can bring you
            D Day now as we would have brought it to you then. . . .

            The long-awaited invasion of Hitler's Europe is
            under way. Allied troops have stormed ashore in Nor-
            mandy and are now consolidating their beachheads.

            We begin with our correspondent at the War De-
            partment, John McWethy. Jack, do we have any sense of
            surety yet that the Allies have been able to take the beaches
            at Normandy? Have they moved inland as far as they're
            expected to move? Are they going to be able to hold it?

MCWETHY: They have not moved as far as planners had hoped they
            would be by tonight, Ted. Nonetheless, they are on the
            beaches, and with the exception of Omaha, they pushed
            about five miles in the other major beaches, the British
            and the Americans. On Omaha they are still having very
            tough going. They have encountered some stiff German
            resistance and the casualties have been quite heavy.

Some of the reporters on that broadcast would later express a
twinge of discomfort about the concept. Wasn't this the equivalent of
acting? But Koppel, whose first reaction to the idea of the program
was that it was "dumb," concluded afterward that the experiment had
been "refreshing."

Kaplan was so pleased with it that he decided to apply time travel
to the anniversary of VJ Day—with a twist. He sent Jean McCormick,
Nightline's chief of research, to the bowels of the National Archives in
Washington to dredge up every document she could find about how
the Allies would have attacked the Japanese mainland had the atomic
bomb not come first. McCormick spent months piecing together the
contingencies. The battle plan for the invasion that never happened
became the blueprint for a *Nightline* adventure to an event that never

was. State Department correspondent Barrie Dunsmore served as the "war correspondent," and White House correspondent Sam Donaldson "reported" from the Truman White House:

DUNSMORE: The final assault on the Japanese home islands has begun. The War Department announced a short time ago that Allied forces under the command of General Douglas MacArthur are now ashore on Kyushu, the southern-most of Japan's four main islands. Enemy forces are said to be putting up a ferocious defense . . .

DONALDSON: This afternoon Mr. Truman called in reporters to talk informally about the invasion, which is the first major decision on the war he's had to make. Looking grim, the President said he'd hoped to avoid an invasion, but in the end could not. He did not elaborate on that, but he bristled at one reporter's suggestion that continued aerial bombing alone could soon bring Japan to her knees.

To follow this broadcast required a kind of intellectual triple somersault in the suspension of disbelief. Viewers had to imagine that they were back in 1945, that *Nightline* and all of its technology existed then, that Hiroshima and Nagasaki had never been bombed, and that the end of the war now depended on the invasion of Japan. Staff members would debate the merits of that one for years.

But Kaplan's early efforts did help the staff to understand that experiments were his drug. The new executive producer didn't whoop in the control room when a show was good like the old one did, and he didn't lift his shoulders and curve his back when a show was bad, but he did have a style that was, well, distinctive . . .

"Listen, everybody, *tonight's show stinks*! Everyone out here, *now!*" Kaplan's command was impossible to ignore. He'd been running the show for almost a year and everyone had learned by then that his bellow at the dinner hour meant what the old bells of the wire machines used to mean: it was going to be a long night. Those producers and reporters who weren't on the road that evening along with researchers and production associates, scurried out of their offices to an area near the wire machines.

"I hate what we've got planned for tonight," Kaplan announced. "I've looked at the guest line-up . . . and, it's no one's fault, but this show is going to be boring as hell. I've talked to Ted. He agrees. We're starting over. And . . . I have absolutely no idea what we should do."

It was dinnertime. Whatever story they would choose, the staff would have less than four hours to pull together a focus piece, to find the right guests, and to arrange the logistics—limousines and satellite transmissions—required to get the right guests on the air.

Kaplan was holding a hat. "Everyone write down a story idea on a piece of paper, fold it up, and put it in the hat. The first idea I like, we're doing tonight."

The group quickly dispersed, and reconvened a few minutes later, each staff member dropping a piece of paper into Kaplan's hat.

No one who was there remembers what was on the first few slips that Kaplan opened and read aloud, but everyone remembers that his face brightened at the fourth. "A debate over *Huckleberry Finn*. There's a school in Chicago that's presenting a theatrical version of *Huck Finn* and some people are trying to shut it down as a racist play. That's it!"

The idea had come from Jean McCormick, the researcher, who had read a small item about the debate that morning in *The New York Times*. For an instant, McCormick puffed up with pride, and then she realized that she'd be the one doing the last-minute research for the broadcast and her shoulders slumped.

Kaplan scanned the room. When he spotted correspondent Jeff Greenfield, he stopped. "Greenfield! Have you ever read *Huck Finn*?"

"Well, yeah. Sure."

"Great. You're doing the piece."

Kaplan assigned several producers to work with Greenfield on the taped setup story, which required, naturally, video of the play. ABC's Chicago bureau would have to send a cameraman to the play to shoot it, and to feed it in time to weave it into the piece. The bookers started dialing numbers in Chicago to find guests. Somehow it all got done.

Two days later, a major newspaper carried a review of the broadcast, praising *Nightline*'s producers for having "predicted" this important debate over the *Huck Finn* play and for having "prepared" a show in advance that would be ready to air the night the play opened.

The author of the laudatory article was never informed that the *Huck Finn* program had been pulled out of a hat, literally. But the morning of that review, Kaplan sent Jean McCormick a single red rose, as a thank you and as a symbol that good ideas would *always* be the lifeblood of the broadcast.

EVERY NEWSCAST HAS its own behind-the-scenes character. *Nightline*'s was, in a word, irreverent. The punishing hours may have had something to do with it. The pressure certainly did. The more that *Nightline* garnered respect from critics, viewers, guests, and other news organizations, the more its staff felt a responsibility to uphold the standard, or to raise it: Tuesday was good; Wednesday should be better. And there was always the possibility, every night, that news would break and Kaplan would charge out of the office and change the show. It was only natural, then, for the people crammed into their pressure cooker to look for some safety valves.

The tension release could come in small ways, like Nerf basketball in producer Herb O'Connor's office, or the uncontrolled fits of giggling in the control room during the pre-production of a story about dirty lyrics in rock music . . . or moonwalking on the anchor desk (which only happened once. The moondancer wore sunglasses and a glove. He looked a lot like the anchor, but he may have been the anchor's evil twin. The anchor would later claim amnesia).

Koppel does own up to a story about him and Pierre Salinger in Vienna, where they had traveled to conduct a joint interview with Austrian president Kurt Waldheim about Waldheim's Nazi past. Just before leaving their hotel for Waldheim's palace, Salinger asked Koppel to come to his room. When Koppel walked in, Salinger said, "I have something to show you," and dropped his pants. Salinger proudly displayed a pair of boxer shorts with hearts and arrows on them. "These were a gift from my wife to wear to the interview," he told Koppel, "since it's Valentine's Day."

"Well, Pierre, my friend," Koppel replied. "Now I have something to show *you*." Koppel undid his belt and dropped his pants. He, too, wore boxers with hearts and arrows. "These were Grace Anne's gift to me for Valentine's Day."

"So there we stood for a moment," Koppel would remember, "Pierre and I, in our goofy boxers, laughing at one another. And then we put our pants back on and off we went to the palace."

Thus the tension attendant to a nightly broadcast manifested itself in laughter . . . sometimes. On other occasions it manifested itself in a collective deranged attitude. One night a major story broke not long before airtime, which led to a mad scene in the editing suites, where a team began slamming together a piece by Jeff Greenfield. The staff had divided the script into sections. Each section had a producer and editor, with one producer responsible for "marrying" all of the sections just before airtime.

On this night, the floor where editing was done was chaos; tapes seemed to be flying through the air. All of the editing rooms surrounded one large room, at the center of which stood senior producer Bob Jordan. Jordan's Zen-like calm during crises was something of a trademark, so his colleagues, who whirled around him screaming out things like "Someone has the tape I need, now give it up!" thought nothing of Jordan standing very still, an island of serenity in a sea of bedlam. No one realized that one reason Jordan was standing so especially still was that he thought he had the flu and might faint.

Nightline's director, Marv Schlenker, arrived from the control room to find out just how badly things were going. Schlenker took refuge next to Jordan in the middle of the whirlwind when Jordan mentioned that he thought he had the flu. "I've felt really crummy for a couple of a days now," Jordan said. "And now I'm feeling dizzy." Schlenker looked at Jordan's face. It was white as parchment. "Lie down." Schlenker instructed. "Lie down right here. Lie down *now*."

Someone popped a head out of an editing room, saw Jordan lying on the floor, and shouted, "I think Bobby's fainted!" The editing rooms emptied out and everyone converged around Jordan. They told him not to move while someone phoned 911 and someone put a jacket under Jordan's head and someone else elevated his feet with a box.

The producers-cum-paramedics were suddenly interrupted by the voice of Susan Mercandetti, who by now had become a producer herself. Mercandetti was the only one who had not left her editing room because she was the one in charge of the completed Greenfield piece. "If he's conscious," she yelled, "keep editing!" Mercandetti would later amend this version of events. She would claim that she shouted, "If he's *alive*, keep editing!"

Jordan, now lying smack in the middle of all of the editing rooms, would later remember his colleagues leaping over his body, passing tapes back and forth above his face. Sometimes someone would pause before stepping over him to ask him if he was feeling any better and to remind him not to move.

At about this point, Mercandetti realized that she'd never received an important shipment of tapes from the video library and that without it, the story couldn't be completed. She flew over Jordan several times, hurling insults at the video-library couriers, who, of course, weren't there. Mercandetti did stop once before jumping over Jordan to say, "Are you all right? Well, *we're* not, and we're not going to make air. There's a whole damn cache of tapes missing."

What neither she nor anyone else knew was that the tapes were located right below her in the box that was propping up Jordan's feet.

Jordan heard someone say that a paramedic had arrived. Then he heard someone else say, "That's not a paramedic, that's our pizza delivery man." Greenfield took the pizza and began handing slices into the editing rooms. He was about to step over Jordan again, but seemed to think better of it. Greenfield paused, leaned over, looked at Jordan, and said, "Pizza?"

The pizza delivery man, taking all this in, did not leave right away. He stood there and watched. To no one in particular he said, "This looks like a Fellini film."

Mercandetti figured out a way to finish the piece—barely, without the tapes—and by the time the show was off the air, the paramedics had come and led Jordan out the door. Fifteen minutes after that, nearly all of the producers who had used Jordan's body as a hurdle poured into the emergency room where he was being checked out. Everything was fine, they were told. (Jordan would learn a few days later that the problem had been something with his inner ear.)

It was left to a couple of production assistants to clean up all the detritus in the editing suites that night. One of them was about to move the box that had been used for Jordan's feet when she decided to see what was inside . . .

The "missing" tapes, having served at least some purpose, if not for the Greenfield piece, went back to the library.

THE IMPORTANT THING about the loose atmosphere was that it bred creativity. Koppel and producer Steve Steinberg were exchanging bits of trivia about one of their mutual passions, the blues, when Steinberg remembered a sweet piece of irony. "Guess where the world's largest archive of the blues is?" "Where?" "The University of Mississippi." Koppel raised an eyebrow. That really was a piece of irony. Inside the school that as recently as 1963 had refused to allow

James Meredith, a young black student, to register stood the world's largest repository of indigenous African-American music. "Want to do a story on it?" Koppel asked.

Within a week or so, Steinberg and correspondent Jed Duvall were on their way to Oxford, Mississippi. They unearthed some remarkable music: Big Mama Thornton singing "You Ain't Nothin' but a Hounddog," and "That's All Right," by Arthur "Big Boy" Crudup. Both songs had been recorded almost a decade before Elvis Presley would record them again. Duvall laced the old recordings around a narrative about the lost pioneers of the blues, but the words were secondary to the music, its scratches and hisses a testament to its originality.

For an evening, *Nightline* was a blues club. The show pioneered the use of the live segment for something other than conversation. Why waste time talking when the guests are B. B. King and Wynton Marsalis? Koppel faded into the background and gave them the show. Their impromptu duet, a coast-to-coast electronic jam session, conveyed an aura of intimacy and magic.

"Blues Night" launched a new genre for *Nightline*. Harry Connick, Jr., would come on and demonstrate how to play jazz piano. Gregory Hines and Sammy Davis, Jr., would demonstrate the art of tap dancing. The day would come, years later, when the show actually featured poetry reading.

A program born of an international crisis had evolved by the mid-eighties into a program that could focus on just about anything for a night: a Soviet sub spying on Sweden, penguins in New Zealand, the opera. There was even a show about Liberace, memorable for the return of a very special guest: Milton Berle.

The occasional spicy topic or "fun" show was good for *Nightline*. What wasn't so obvious was how to better cover the weightier issues that were *Nightline*'s meat. Then came the decision to completely uproot the broadcast and to move it nearly eight thousand miles away, for an entire week of programs devoted to a single issue that most Americans didn't exactly understand and weren't even talking about. The decision was inspired by a combination of restlessness and naïveté, and by a smidgen of tension between the anchor and the executive producer. It would prove to be one of the most important decisions in the show's history.

FOUR
South Africa

KOPPEL WAS ACTING strangely and it was getting on everyone's nerves. Various members of the *Nightline* staff would peek around corners to spy on him. They'd pull one another aside to gossip about it. *"He's smoking,"* they'd whisper. He hadn't smoked in years. But now, as he wandered the studios of the South Africa Broadcasting Company (SABC), a white haze, like the specter of all that could go wrong, hovered over him.

The anchor wasn't exactly exuding confidence. Neither was his executive producer. Rick Kaplan would stare at the snake of smoke coiling above Koppel and wonder if they'd made the greatest miscalculation of their careers. "I thought we had a chance to make a bit of history here," Kaplan reminisced later, "but I also knew that if we screwed it up, we'd be laughingstocks. We'd be international *jerks*. And then I got to thinking about Ted and I said to myself, 'He's gonna be the jerk on camera. He's got to carry it off. We've built him a stadium and now he's got to hit a home run.' "

Kaplan focused on Koppel because he couldn't bear to face what really worried him: the fate of the next five broadcasts was almost entirely out of their hands. They'd brought *Nightline* to a volatile, violent country. Anyone and anything could disrupt a broadcast, including the reactionary siege mentality of the South African government. Many of the programs scheduled for the week, because of their focus

on apartheid and on the opponents of apartheid, were illegal according to the restrictions imposed on South Africa's own television networks. Yet the plan, as it stood, and as agreed to by the government
of South Africa, called for each broadcast to air inside South Africa
about twelve hours after it aired in America, the delay ostensibly due
to the time difference. Kaplan wondered whether the government
would stick to that commitment. Also, South Africa's own reporters
were prohibited from quoting some of the very people whom Koppel
planned to interview, like the wife of imprisoned black political leader
Nelson Mandela. Would the government really allow *Nightline* to go
ahead with those interviews? As for the guests, there were scores of
ways and reasons for every one of them to back out. Some already had.
Not one booking was certain. Nothing was certain.

Well, *one* thing was certain: *Nightline*'s week in South Africa was
going to cost almost $600,000—about four times over budget. At that
price, Kaplan and Koppel couldn't even guarantee an audience.

They couldn't even guarantee a show worth watching.

Their biggest gamble would be the first broadcast. For the first
time in history, on March 18, 1985, a black leader would publicly debate an official of the white South African regime.

An hour before the show was to air, Koppel dragged on his
umpteenth cigarette, typed out an introduction to the program, and
wondered what would happen if one of the two invited guests decided
not to address the other. Or would it be worse if the debate actually
took place? The government, after all, controlled all the broadcast facilities. No one could be sure of the outcome. In particular, no one
could predict the consequences for the black priest who was about to
challenge the apartheid system.

Desmond Tutu walked into a small study of his church. He
watched the cameramen and technicians organize their equipment.
The television lights already seared the air. The room was stifling.
Tutu maintained the serene demeanor befitting his position as Anglican bishop of Johannesburg. And yet, he remembered later, "I was
churning inside. I was very concerned that I could end up with a lot
of egg on my face. And it would not just be me: I would have let down
very many people who did not, at that time, have too many spokes-
persons. And that was a fairly big burden to carry. And so the calm and
the serenity that one appeared to project were not entirely real."

Tutu was also confounded by something. He could not fathom why "the South African government was willing to take the chance that they just might not pull it off, that they just might play second or third fiddle in the encounter."

The answer was that F. P. "Pik" Botha, the other guest, had no intention of playing second fiddle. Poised and self-assured, the South African foreign minister strode into the television studio in Cape Town. He had been an actor in his youth. He enjoyed the limelight. Botha also had an agenda: "So often the events in this country were portrayed abroad really in a way which did not reflect the truth. The truth might have been bad, but it was never as bad as the picture portrayed of South Africa." *Nightline* would be his platform to say so. Botha felt confident.

Not Koppel. He would later admit that he "was a nervous wreck" an hour before airtime. He had gone around with Kaplan to calm the staff and "tell everyone how great the program was going to be and how excited we were. Then Rick and I were standing in a stairwell outside the control room, just the two of us." They wished one another luck. Then Kaplan asked Koppel, "Are you as scared as I am?"

"You better believe it. I'm ready to barf right now."

"So am I," said Kaplan.

THEY'D BEEN WORKING together by then for nine months, and the fact was that those first nine months had been rocky. "We tolerated each other," Koppel would later say of their early rapport, "but there was no warmth between us." D Day notwithstanding, Kaplan's earliest attempts at shaking up the show had struck Koppel as not terribly sophisticated; if anything, Kaplan's first offbeat experiments worried Koppel because they suggested that Kaplan was casting about for a vision, that he had no real battle plan to move the show's coverage of substantive issues in new directions. *Nightline* was in its fifth year, after all, and Koppel thought that it was no different than most shows in their fifth year—a little predictable, slightly stale. Even the offbeat topics were still being presented in exactly the same format that *Nightline* would present a show about the budget. ("Blues Night" was still years away.) Besides, it wasn't going to work if the show had to go "soft" to be creative. The most important challenge, Koppel thought, was to come up with new ways of covering the serious issues, the kinds of stories on which *Nightline* had made its name. Every time it tackled something important in foreign policy or politics, there was a sort of sameness to it all.

In fact, Koppel had seethed privately for months about the show having missed a big opportunity. In the very early stages of the Ethiopian famine, he had wanted to go to Ethiopia himself, to move the broadcast there for a few days and spotlight the tragedy from inside. But the whole idea came up just as Kaplan was coming on board as executive producer, and the British Broadcasting Company got into Ethiopia first and essentially "owned" the story from then on.

Kaplan was well aware, over the course of those first few months, that the anchor wasn't sure Kaplan was up to the job of *Nightline*'s executive producer. That was discomfiting, but so was the fact that he actually agreed with Koppel that the show wasn't taking enough risks on the serious stories. Then one day, while he'd been thinking about how to redefine *Nightline* and how to redefine his relationship with Koppel, a memo from producer Lionel Chapman crossed his desk. It was one in a series from Chapman about South Africa.

FOR ALMOST FOUR DECADES, whites had held blacks in a suffocating stranglehold known as apartheid. Blacks comprised 73 percent of the population, yet they were denied the right to vote. They could not own property. They were consigned to live in desolate "homelands." They could not travel freely, nor could they so much as commute to work without government-issued identity cards. No other country's government had so completely incorporated racial segregation into its laws, its culture, its economy, its way of life.

Yet South Africa in the mid-1980s in no way resembled the tranquil, neatly segregated society envisioned by the Dutch descendants who had designed the apartheid system. Black resistance flourished. The father figure of the anti-apartheid movement hadn't been seen publicly since 1962, the year he was carted away to prison. It didn't matter; Nelson Mandela's invisibility made him a legend. His party of resistance, the African National Congress, had been outlawed for decades. It thrived anyway. Sharpeville and Soweto had come to signify not so much townships as indelible and hallowed sites: the scenes of brutal crackdowns. Although the first tricameral parliament of 1984 included some minorities, it still excluded blacks; their absence only exacerbated tension. Moreover, the ugly stain on South Africa's image was spreading overseas. In Washington, a series of sit-ins outside the South African embassy beginning in late 1984 coincided with talk in Congress of economic sanctions. Already, a number of American universities were divesting their endowments of companies doing business in South Africa.

Chapman's memo noted the escalating bloodshed and the protests and the fact that although *Nightline* had occasionally focused on apartheid, it had never sent one of its own producers to South Africa. Chapman, an African-American, wanted to go.

Kaplan read the memo and remembered Koppel's campaign to move the show to Ethiopia. Why not South Africa? He called Koppel. "Let's go to South Africa. We'll take everyone. We'll devote an entire week of broadcasts to apartheid."

Koppel thought the idea "breathtaking." He thought it was the right thing to do. He also thought no one would watch. Racial violence in South Africa had been going on for so long that Americans seemed inured to it. The embassy sit-ins and academic debates about divestment never garnered headlines. American viewers might have heard of apartheid, but few—in particular, few white Americans—had any idea of what life was like for South African blacks. But Koppel agreed with Kaplan that the story was important, that *Nightline* had a rare opportunity to help shape a moral and political agenda.

When Kaplan put the idea to ABC News president Roone Arledge, Arledge agreed that not many viewers would have the patience to tune in—five nights in a row—to a country and a political system so removed from their own lives. But he too concluded that it was the right thing to do.

David Burke, Arledge's deputy and a close friend of both Kaplan's and Koppel's, was in the meeting when Kaplan made his pitch. Burke thought *Nightline* needed shaking up. Walking out of Arledge's office, Burke urged Kaplan, "Go to South Africa as soon as you can."

TEN DAYS LATER, Betsy West, a *Nightline* senior producer, sat on her bed in a Cape Town hotel room and dialed into a conference call with Koppel in Washington and Kaplan in New York. Across the room from West, listening in on a separate extension, was Tara Sonenshine, one of the show's bookers. West, who was responsible

for most of *Nightline*'s foreign stories, and Sonenshine, whose forte
was finding compelling guests, had been dispatched to meet with
South African officials about the proposed programs. West gave
Koppel and Kaplan the good news: the government had agreed that
Nightline could visit. The only thing it refused to do, she said, was to
permit a debate between one of its officials and a black anti-apartheid
opponent. Sonenshine began to give the details of what the government had called "alternative ideas" to a debate, when Koppel cut
her off.

"Come home." His voice dropped. "Cancel whatever meetings
you have left, and just come home."

West and Sonenshine were speechless. They exchanged lifted-
eyebrow, what's-*this*-about glances. "Tell the South African government," Koppel continued, "there will be no apartheid on our
broadcast. Your visit there is over."

Koppel wasn't making sense. His tone was stilted, dismissive, and
completely unfamiliar. If this mission was a debacle—and the two
staffers hadn't thought so until now—it wasn't *their* fault. Was Koppel
really surprised, they wondered, that the South African government
had a few reservations?

They didn't get a chance to ask. Koppel hadn't finished talking
when Kaplan launched in. "If you two can't get done what we've sent
you to do, the hell with the project! We're not cutting any deals with
the South Africans."

West and Sonenshine had apparently forgotten something Koppel
warned them about before the trip. "Our assumption," said Koppel
later, "was that the phone was tapped. I thought Betsy and Tara would
remember that I had said to them the phones would likely be tapped."
His ultimatum was for Pretoria's eavesdroppers. Underneath Koppel's
icy edict was a demand intended for the government of South Africa:
one of its officials *must* agree to debate a black opponent of apartheid
or *Nightline* would cancel its entire week of shows.

Sonenshine thought everything was off. She had seen the fallen
faces of officials every time she had mentioned "interaction" between
a government representative and a black opponent. "They were incredulous. It was as if we had suggested that they all go to Mars. The
notion of interaction was impossible." It was Foreign Minister Botha
who had suggested "alternative approaches," such as separate inter-

views. All that West and Sonenshine were trying to do on the phone now was to convey Botha's suggestions to Koppel and Kaplan. Instead, the women were getting their heads handed to them for even mentioning a compromise.

They hung up and stared at each other. West finally blurted out, "Why are Ted and Rick acting like such jerks?" Neither of them remembered Koppel's warning about the phones.

The next morning, before they'd had a chance to inform the South Africans they were going home, Sonenshine's phone rang. It was a government press aide. "Something can be worked out," he said. West and Sonenshine never learned whether the call with Koppel and Kaplan had been overheard. All they knew was that, suddenly, the government was agreeing to the debate and that Pik Botha himself wanted to appear.

Botha would later explain that he had personally lobbied his colleagues in the government to realize the unique opportunity presented by *Nightline*. As foreign minister, Botha knew better than most officials that apartheid was pummeling South Africa's image abroad. His own people told him so. "It was my staff, my ambassadors, my representatives. They were exposed all these years to the chagrin, to the attacks. They were the ones—*my* department was the department that was painfully aware of our image, and trying to make recommendations as to how to improve it." Since the interviews with Koppel would be unedited, Botha figured *Nightline* would at least give the government a fair chance to present its case. "The ugly will come out," Botha advised his colleagues, "but the good will also come out."

Botha had a second motive, he would later claim. He had heard that the South Africa Broadcasting Company, whose facilities *Nightline* would be using, wanted to run the series inside South Africa. Botha thought it a splendid idea, for he privately believed that it was time to dismantle apartheid. He wanted the broadcasts to affect the whites of his homeland, he would insist many years later. Botha was reminded of the prayer "that God may grant us the gift to see ourselves as others see us." It was time for white South Africans "to see themselves as others see them. And, from my point of view, South Africans were entitled to know, rightly or wrongly, how the world saw us." *Nightline* would be their mirror.

Sonenshine suspected that what ultimately attracted the government was the cost of American advertising. One official had asked her about the price of a commercial minute on *Nightline*. He seemed interested in tallying the total number of commercial minutes in a week's worth of programming. His conclusion, apparently, was that ABC was offering the government millions of dollars worth of publicity.

As for Botha's opponent, the motive was clear. Bishop Desmond Tutu was the obvious choice to represent the black resistance to apartheid. The government could hardly brand the Anglican bishop of Johannesburg and Nobel Peace Prize winner a sinister force. Tutu understood why he was acceptable to the government. What concerned him was the political leadership of the black resistance movement, namely the outlawed but thriving African National Congress. Tutu asked that *Nightline* get the ANC to approve his appearance in the debate.

No big deal, thought Sonenshine. She had to work with the ANC anyway, since virtually all of the anti-apartheid activists worth booking for the week were affiliated with the organization. And why *wouldn't* the ANC welcome an American broadcast that wanted to examine apartheid? "We had gone in assuming the ANC would be totally thrilled about this."

The assumption was naive. "We got caught in what was then still a lot of division in the ANC between the far left and the middle. We went through elaborate negotiations to try to get the ANC on board this thing." First, the ANC demanded that Tutu and Botha not sit in the same location. That was fine. *Nightline* convened its guests by satellite all the time. Tutu would appear from his church in Johannesburg; Botha would sit in a studio in Cape Town. Second, the ANC wanted every detail laid out: who would speak first, how much time would be allotted to the interviews, the subject matter to be discussed. Sonenshine found the process excruciating. "It felt like years that Betsy and I were over there, running back and forth between the government side and the ANC." Finally, the ANC gave its blessings to the debate.

Koppel and Kaplan were exultant. Six weeks later, they flew toward Johannesburg. A team of producers and reporters was already in place, finding guests and preparing taped background stories. The twenty hours it took to fly there only underscored how remote South Africa was from the United States. Koppel still doubted that many Americans would watch—unless, of course, something unforeseen and unpleasant happened. In recent weeks race-related violence had

seemed to escalate. Koppel was prepared to gamble the show's reputation on the project. But he was not willing to let his program be manipulated by Pretoria, which, after all, controlled the broadcasting
facilities *Nightline* would have to use. He worried over the show's possible political impact. Might it make a bad situation worse? Well, there
was nothing to do about it now. All Koppel knew to do was something he hadn't done in years. He pulled out a pack of cigarettes, and
on the long flight to South Africa, he wrapped himself in a blanket of
smoke.

ON MONDAY MORNING, March 18, less than twenty-four hours
before the first show would air in the United States, Pik Botha summoned Koppel to lunch in Cape Town. Koppel faced the week as if
he were standing on the edge of a cliff; the last thing he wanted or
needed was to have to get on a plane and fly to Cape Town for lunch
with the foreign minister. "But it was made very clear to me that if I
expected this thing to come off, the foreign minister was expecting me
for lunch."

So Koppel and Sonenshine flew to Cape Town. They walked
into a spartan room in the Foreign Ministry, where lunch had been
set up. Botha was there with a number of aides. He sat at the head
of the table, with Koppel on his left. "We began to chat," Koppel
remembered, "and lunch was served, and Tara and I began to eat.
No one else did." Suddenly Koppel realized why the South African
side of the table wasn't eating. "Let's say grace!" Botha announced.
Koppel and Sonenshine, embarrassed, put down their silverware and
Botha said grace.

"All right," said Botha, turning to Koppel. "Now, tell me, what is
this program we're supposed to be doing tonight?"

Koppel tried not to show his alarm. *Supposed to be doing?* he
thought to himself. He wondered what Botha was up to. Koppel
looked Botha carefully in the eye and said, "Mr. Foreign Minister, as
you know, we're very grateful and delighted that you're going to be
participating in what promises to be an historic broadcast and that you
and Bishop Tutu will be appearing together for the first time tonight."

"What?" Botha's stentorian tone had served him well as an actor.
"I don't know anything about this! No one has told me anything
about this!"

Koppel knew this was no time to be coy. He decided to use an old tactic he had learned from Henry Kissinger. "Mr. Foreign Minister, I can only assume that if you really had not heard about this before, you would fire everyone on the other side of the table here."

Botha smiled and went on to another subject. There was no longer any talk about whether he was going to do the program.

That evening Kaplan and Koppel stood in the stairwell outside the control room, commiserated about their nerves and nausea, and proceeded to their positions. It was now fifteen minutes until air. Tutu took his seat in the church study, under the steaming lights. A fly buzzed around his head. He seemed not to notice. All his thoughts were on the debate. "One could quite easily have come a cropper," he explained later. "There were very considerable butterflies fluttering in the pit of my tum-tum when this great occasion arrived."

Botha sat down in the chair of the Cape Town studio. He reminded himself of some advice ABC's Barbara Walters had once given him: don't use notes, and speak from the heart.

Koppel took his place at the anchor desk in the Johannesburg studio and clipped a microphone to his tie. In the control room, Kaplan stared at the monitors and jiggled a leg. Next to him sat Roone Arledge, who had flown in to show his solidarity with the project.

In the director's chair was Roger Goodman, a master at coordinating the look and production of ABC News special projects. Goodman had directed everything from the Olympics to political conventions, but the sort of obstacles he'd encountered at South African Broadcasting Company were unique. The facilities and equipment were most definitely *not* state-of-the-art. Goodman looked around the control room and hoped the technology would work, at least through the first show. Tomorrow, he could worry about the rest of the programs.

Ten minutes before air, the satellites came up. One monitor in the control room carried the feed from Cape Town: Pik Botha. A second monitor displayed the feed from a church in Johannesburg: Desmond Tutu.

Kaplan watched their faces and reminded himself that "these men had never really spoken before. They were two of the most powerful people in all of South Africa, and they'd never had a conversation."

Koppel had to test the audio before air. "Good evening, Bishop," he intoned.

TUTU: Good evening.

KOPPEL: Good evening, Mr. Foreign Minister.

BOTHA: Good evening.

KOPPEL: Mr. Minister, would you say hello to Bishop Tutu?

Silence.

Oh no, thought Koppel. *Botha's not going to talk to the bishop. This thing is going down the drain.*

The silence, he would say later, "seemed eternal. Oh, it seemed like forever."

Kaplan thought it was a technical problem. His stomach dropped to his toes. Oh my God, he told himself. They can't hear each other. This isn't working!

It turned out that Botha wouldn't pause forever but for four or five seconds. Finally, he complied. "Good evening, Bishop."

"Good evening, Mr. Minister," said Tutu. "How are you?"

Kaplan heaved an enormous sigh. Koppel smiled slightly. At least they're in place, he told himself. At least they're going to talk to each other.

NEAR THE CONTROL ROOM, Lionel Chapman had gathered with other *Nightline* producers and SABC staff members to watch the show. "You could feel the tension, the excitement and, frankly, the amazement."

KOPPEL: For the next five nights we'll show you many different sides of this rich, fascinating, and terribly controversial country. And you will hear and see South Africans, black and white, in and out of government—people who have never talked to each other publicly before, doing just that.

"I felt tense for Ted," recalled Chapman. "Tense for us. People would look at each other and there would be nervous laughter."

Chapman's anxiety was based on personal experience. He had been traveling around South Africa for several weeks with correspondent Jeff

Greenfield, preparing the taped background pieces that would lead the broadcasts. And what Chapman had found in his travels was even weirder than what he'd imagined. There was the night with the prosperous Afrikaner farmer, for example. "He was a very generous person," Chapman recalled later, "and he invited us to a huge barbecue at his place and ended up inviting us to spend the night there." As the day wound down, Greenfield and Chapman were admiring a spectacular sunset when their host launched into a litany of complaints about the blacks in his country. He contrasted them to black Americans. "Your black people are not like our black people," the farmer said. "American black people are different." It dawned on Greenfield and Chapman that the Afrikaner had no idea that Chapman was, despite his light skin, black.

Greenfield interrupted the Afrikaner's tirade. "Excuse me, but do you know that Lionel is black?" The farmer appeared slightly embarrassed, but after a minute or two, he pointed to Chapman's achievements as support for his argument. "Well, you are exactly what I mean," he told Chapman. He noted that Chapman was educated and "ingrained into the dominant culture in America." Chapman said nothing.

On another day, in a suburb of Cape Town, Chapman, Greenfield, and the crew asked their driver to stop at a roadside restaurant for lunch. When they got inside, Chapman realized that the driver—a black South African—hadn't made it through the door. His skin was darker than Chapman's. When Chapman realized the man wouldn't be allowed in the restaurant, he pushed everyone back in the car. He wanted to scream. "It was the only time in my life, actually, where I've ever encountered a situation where I was denied or I saw somebody denied service because of the color of his skin."

In Soweto, Greenfield tried to interview Percy Qoboza, a black journalist. Greenfield heard commotion and looked out a window. He saw a group of black schoolchildren in uniforms running down the street. "Somebody came in and said, 'These kids have just killed two suspected informers and they're heading this way. They think you're with the SABC'—South Africa Broadcasting, which was, of course, government-run." Qoboza ran into the street and told the students who he was and that the men inside were not South African government officials but American journalists. The students backed off.

Now Chapman watched a monitor and hoped Koppel would have an easier time of it.

KOPPEL: There is about Bishop Tutu so much bubbling enthusiasm, such a buoyant optimism, that it's easy to forget that this man is walking a political tightrope from which he could tumble at any moment. Bishop Tutu, for example, is widely thought to support the policy of disinvestment—that is, encouraging mostly American businesses to pull out of South Africa as a moral gesture against apartheid. But were he openly to support disinvestment, Bishop Tutu would face up to five years in prison.

Tutu listened, and feared "that I would let our side down badly. I knew that the case I was going to have to make was unassailable, but that didn't necessarily mean one would have been able to handle such an opportunity with aplomb, and with the expertise that it required."

KOPPEL: The foreign minister of South Africa is almost universally known in this country as Pik Botha. The Pik is an abbreviation of the Afrikaans word for penguin. But as his adversaries have discovered, this is no man to be taken lightly. He is one of the most popular politicians in South Africa. A former ambassador to the United Nations, he has always been an eloquent spokesman for his government, charming, a brilliant debater and, some say, an excellent actor when necessary. Pik Botha is also said to have an explosive temper.

Botha knew better than to unleash that temper at the top of the show. He depicted the government as accommodating and flexible.

BOTHA: We are for a change in a controlled fashion, believing the people of various communities ought to absorb the change. We also believe that our black communities ought to change, and that many of the traditions of the black communities ought to change. So it's not only whites that ought to change. We've got to do this on a quid pro quo basis.

KOPPEL: Let me see, Bishop Tutu, whether I can get agreement here or disagreement. There is indeed a great deal of talk of change. Does that talk—has it been translated into reality, into action?

TUTU: I'm very glad that we are agreed about one thing, that the policy of apartheid is so ghastly and vicious that it ought to change. I think that we ought to commend Mr. Botha, the state president, for his courage.

In a room not far from Koppel, Jeff Greenfield sat with a group of South African journalists who had been invited to watch the program as it was fed to America, since the show wouldn't air inside South Africa for another day. Greenfield studied their reactions. "I believe that may have been the first time that anybody there, whatever their political sentiments, had actually seen a black person and a white person debating like this. I wasn't sitting with government stooges; these were real journalists. And they were looking at this as though they were watching broadcasting from another planet."

One of those journalists was Arrie Rossouw, a syndicated political correspondent for the newspaper *Beeld*. Rossouw was thrilled that the debate was happening. He wanted his countrymen to hear it. He had always opposed the government's refusal to engage in a dialogue with the ANC. This debate, he was certain, would open a door to real dialogue, eventually, and he was sure that once the door was open, it would never be shut. But Rossouw also felt a mixture of embarrassment and envy that this enormously important step was being initiated by Americans. "I felt cheated," he would recall later. "Why couldn't a South African newspaper or a South African broadcast present this sort of thing? And yet, it was so important that at least the process of communication had begun." Rossouw was especially pleased that Tutu was so articulate. "Everyone inside South Africa knew that no matter what the government said and no matter what Tutu had to pretend in order to do this, he was the de facto spokesman for the ANC. So if he could seem so human, the message was clear. The ANC wasn't the 'devil' that the government had made it out to be."

By then Tutu had gone so far as to explicitly introduce the name of Nelson Mandela, an outlaw, as the "authentic" representative of the black community. Negotiation must proceed, he said, but only with leaders like Mandela—now in his twenty-fifth year in prison—at the table. Botha was ready for that.

BOTHA: Mr. Mandela is now jailing himself, because all that was required from him was a statement or some indication that he would abandon violence to achieve political ends and objectives, and then he could be set free.

The two men fell into a dispute over the constitutional right to protest. Suddenly Tutu seemed frustrated by the legal jargon. He reached for something deeply personal. Out came a searing oration about identity:

TUTU: I'm a bishop in the Church of God! I'm a bishop of one of the most important dioceses in South Africa. I'm fifty-three years of age. You would, I suppose, say that I'm reasonably responsible. In my own country I do not vote. According to this government I am not a South African. My travel document says of my nationality that it is indeterminable at present. So that blacks have been turned into aliens in the land of the oppressed.

Just last year, one hundred sixty thousand blacks were arrested because they tried to sell their labor, and therefore, because they did not have the right pass, they were not allowed to sell their labor. Men are made to leave their homes, to live in single-sex hostels for eleven months of the year. This Christian country destroys black family life deliberately. This Christian country has destroyed stable black communities, uprooted three and a half million blacks. And we are saying we seek to change the system. It's no use talking about selective morality. We, the victims of this vicious system, are saying, for goodness' sake, when are you going to listen to the victims and stop listening to the perpetrators of something as evil as Nazism and Communism?

The South African journalists watching at SABC fell utterly still. "Nothing could compare to that statement by Tutu," Arrie Rossouw remembered. "The power of it was that it was true. And the emotions of it rang so true. There was no way for Botha to really answer it." The statement would later crop up in nearly every South African news report on the debate. And it would be repeated, again and again, by critics of apartheid in America. The one-minute appeal for dignity "was hardly the most devastating thing that anyone had said about apartheid," Koppel thought later, "but for some reason it had an impact."

All Tutu knew was that he was trying to express the feeling of being treated as nonentities. "For so long we had been treated as anonymous, as being there without being there." Tutu also felt that his plea was, "in a sense, unanswerable."

Botha had to try to counter. He attempted to ascribe independence to the desolate homelands, or "national states" as he called them, to which blacks were involuntarily consigned.

BOTHA: As far as the citizenship issue is concerned, I admit we have run into difficulties, and it's one of the highest priorities of the special cabinet committee, of which I'm a member, to look into this issue . . . To compare us with Nazis is an insult to the more than one hundred thousand South Africans of Jewish origin who came to this country and to our forefathers who fought with the Allied powers against Nazi Germany. . . . Where in the rest of Africa do black people enjoy the standards they enjoy here? In Africa five million children will die this year, thirty-three million are faced with starvation. . . . We all have reasons for what we're doing. I don't say that they are always good reasons from a moral point of view, but we have admitted this.

Koppel asked Tutu to clarify the goals of the resistance movement.

TUTU: You bring about political change either by the exercise of a vote. But blacks don't have a vote, so that is out of the question. The other way of bringing about change is through violence, and most of us eschew violence; we avoid violence. The third possibility is the one that I have been calling for, the assistance of the international community to bring pressure on the South African government to urge it to go to the conference table before it is too late.

Tutu offered a passionate closing.

TUTU: They can't say to us, "Don't use violence," and then, when we try to use nonviolent means, that too they take umbrage at. And we ask, what else is left for us to use? What option have we got? And I myself believe that it is possible for apartheid to be dismantled and for this country to become what God intends it to be, a glorious country, a country where all of us, black and white, will be able to stride with heads held high into the glorious future that God holds for us.

Botha had a warning:

BOTHA: If only the outside world could stay out of it a little bit, because there is where the trouble starts. I mean, the outside world shouldn't come and prescribe to us, either black or white. We should come to the solutions ourselves.

KOPPEL: If the outside world, Foreign Minister, if the outside world weren't—and forgive me for using a rather crude term—holding your feet to the fire, do you think even the changes that have been made over the last five years would have been made?

BOTHA: Yes, perhaps faster. It would have been made faster because there are black leadership negotiating with us and talking with us and persuading us. It's a give-and-take process. But if the impression is created also, as far as black leadership is concerned, that outsiders are making our decisions for us, then that kind of pressure tends to slow down the process of reform. I'm sure you can understand this.

As Rossouw and the other journalists filed out after the show's end, Jeff Greenfield looked at their shell-shocked expressions and had no doubt that twenty-four hours hence, when the show aired inside the country, viewers would be transfixed. "I'm fairly skeptical about the transcendent power of media," Greenfield would say later, "but in this case, you could tell these people had seen something they'd never seen before."

Rossouw felt elated. "I knew that a seed had been planted. It was that simple. Whether the government wanted to admit it or not, a dialogue had taken place between one of its own and a man whom everyone knew represented the ANC. And the important thing was that Tutu was so human, so *reasonable*. No one could watch Tutu without thinking, What he says is reasonable. I was certain that South Africans would watch this and wonder, 'Now, what's so awful about at least talking with these people?' "

Tutu was ecstatic. He sensed that the show had "helped to give an enhanced legitimacy, because there we were, engaging this particular person who was a high government official and who had not, up to that point, thought that they wanted to engage with any of those who were not within their own system. And that it was happening on a major, major program—for us it was an incredible feather in our cap."

Meanwhile Koppel wondered if he had bombed. He took off his microphone and looked around. By now the long-established routine at *Nightline* was that producers and staff would amble into the studio after the credits and chat with Koppel about the show. But now, after the biggest gamble in Koppel's five years at *Nightline,* no one walked in but Roone Arledge. Koppel took the absence of his colleagues as a tacit message. "I thought there'd at least be a little bit of high five," said Koppel, "and there wasn't any of that. I sort of had a feeling that everyone was kind of disappointed in the program. And I felt really low." What Koppel didn't know was that Kaplan was trying to protect him from an onslaught of staffers—not just *Nightline* people, but the SABC crowd and the journalists.

Koppel slunk back to his hotel room, dejected. "I had a sense that the show hadn't gone that well, that it was okay, but it wasn't anything—it certainly wasn't anything historic."

The next morning Koppel picked up a South African newspaper outside his hotel room. The headline: "PIK, TUTU IN LIVELY TV DEBATE."

That same morning, a clock radio awoke Betsy West in her Johannesburg hotel room. The top of the news, she later remembered, was the Tutu versus Botha debate. "I'd never been in a situation where we were making so much news that we had become the story. The attention this began to get in South Africa was extraordinary."

The show wouldn't air inside the country until that evening, yet "it was all anyone could talk about," remembered one South African reporter. "South Africans had never seen the other side on television—or anywhere else." That night, just after the show was broadcast, a woman who worked at South African Broadcasting returned home to find her husband sitting in a chair, looking dazed and devastated. "What's wrong?" she asked.

"I just saw the Pik Botha–Desmond Tutu interview. This has really changed my life." The man was an Afrikaner. He was also a member of the Broedderbund, a secret organization devoted to white supremacy. "I can never look at apartheid the same way again," he told his wife. The broadcast, he said, had "shattered" him.

THERE WERE STILL four shows to do, and "crises—crises nonstop," in the words of Tara Sonenshine. "Some guest was always pulling out, and someone else was always threatening to. Guest number two didn't want to appear with guest number four, and number four was pulling out unless we dropped guest number three." Koppel and Kaplan didn't have much time, therefore, to glory in the South African headlines. Nor did they have time to worry about why Roone Arledge had suddenly left town.

They'd soon learn, though. While Arledge had been in Johannesburg, supporting this gamble with ABC's reputation and money, ABC had been sold to a media company called Capital Cities. Arledge had to fly to New York to meet his new bosses. "Here would be the moment," Kaplan reflected later, "when the folks from Cap Cities are getting their first look at the president of ABC News, and he's endorsing this million-dollar series of shows in South Africa—all of which could have blown up."

In fact, things *were* blowing up. The South African government hated what led each American broadcast: the taped and edited background pieces over which the government had no control. After the initial two broadcasts aired in the United States, an emissary was sent to meet with Koppel and lodge a formal complaint. The government was considering "pulling the plug" on the remaining programs. Sonenshine remembered "a lot of talk about whether we were all going to be on planes the next day."

Having once aired its grievances to Koppel, however, and having aired them immediately afterward to the press ("NAT COMPLAINT OVER 'BIAS' IN U.S. TV SHOW" was one headline), Pretoria decided not to shut down the remaining programs. Instead, South African officials continued to do what they had done with the first broadcast, censoring the versions that ran inside the country, deleting the taped pieces. On the fourth show, the government deleted a taped interview between Koppel and a woman who was forbidden by law from speaking to him: Winnie Mandela.

Mrs. Mandela had recently been released from internal exile. She was still under house arrest, however, which meant she could not leave her home between six at night and six in the morning. And she was still "banned"—on the list of those ordered by the authorities not to speak to the press. The press also was forbidden from quoting anything she said to anyone. "At the time, she was a heroic figure," Koppel recalled. "She was trying to keep a movement alive while her husband was in prison. You must consider all the psychological pressure that they brought to bear on her, the number of times that she and her children would be rousted out of their home, the number of times that she'd have to leave and find another community, until finally they moved her into the Orange Free State, where she was surrounded by nothing but enemies. This was and is a woman who had endured an enormous amount. I must confess, I was very much moved when I met her."

On March 21, 1985, the twenty-fifth anniversary of the Sharpeville massacre, Winnie Mandela broke the law and met Ted Koppel on a street in Johannesburg. She was dressed in a flowing purple robe. Her hair was braided in intricate cornrows. Koppel felt that "she had a majesty about her. She had presence." He recalled that "she and I walked through the streets toward a park bench, where we were to hold the interview. And as we were walking along, she took my hand. And I thought, What the hell, I don't give a damn. If they want to make something of the fact that I'm walking down the street holding hands with Winnie Mandela, so be it. So we walked down the street hand in hand to the park bench."

When they arrived at the bench, Koppel was handed a note from one of his producers. There had been a funeral march in Uitenhage, near Port Elizabeth, that day. Police had opened fire on the mourn-ers—scores were reported injured, and some had died. "I still re-member that moment," said Koppel, "when I learned that a lot of people had been injured and a few people had been killed. And, look-ing back on it, I've always prided myself on maintaining a certain dis-tance from anyone that I interview, whether I dislike them or like them, admire them or have contempt for them. On that particular day, I did not."

Koppel asked Winnie Mandela about the violence in Uitenhage.

MANDELA: This of course brings particular emotions to me. This is what our leaders went to prison for, those twenty-three years ago. This confirms what we've been saying all along: There has been no change in this government, there have been no changes whatsoever. . . . This coun-try has enough wealth to look after all its inhabitants. Late as it is in the day, in the African National Congress we still believe that we are prepared to accommodate each and every one in this country. We cannot wish away even the racists who have violently governed us these past thirty years.

Mrs. Mandela echoed Bishop Tutu's statement that negotiations were desirable but impossible if the black leaders who should be doing the negotiating—in particular, her husband—remained imprisoned.

MANDELA: There is no way the South African racist government can negotiate any type of freedom with men behind bars. Only free men can negotiate.

KOPPEL: You've used a great many eloquent words, but what you're saying is really one word: impasse.

MANDELA: Precisely. I'm afraid so. I'm afraid so. Unless the govern-ment releases the leaders unconditionally, unless it dis-mantles apartheid, there is no way they can negotiate with anyone else.

Arrie Rossouw, the correspondent with *Beeld,* watched the in-terview with Mrs. Mandela at SABC as he had watched the other programs. Because she was a "banned" person, he could not quote her directly. In fact, the press restrictions meant that Rossouw had never had the opportunity to interview Mrs. Mandela, or even to observe her, before this broadcast. "Remember, this was before she got into trouble later," Rossouw would later recall. "She was not as controversial then. And I was struck by her poise. It was the first time I'd ever really seen her as a politician."

The next day, the Washington correspondent of a South African newspaper suggested that the government's attempts to censor Mrs. Mandela had only enhanced her stature: "The fact that she has been silenced in her homeland for many years gave additional force to her eloquence and unbowed testimony." The omission of the Mandela interview hardly helped the government. By now, the show's South African viewers had heard from a black union leader, a black journalist, and from white opponents of apartheid, too. Among the guests scheduled for the final broadcast was Oliver Tambo, a top leader of the ANC.

The big question was whether viewers also would hear from P. W. Botha, president of South Africa. Botha, *Nightline* had learned, was seriously considering reneging on his earlier commitment to appear in the final broadcast. Botha's misgivings were an open secret. *The Johannesburg Star* reported on March 21, "The Government [says it is] deeply unhappy with the bias against the South African authorities, which has been a feature of the series so far. A senior Government source said: 'They are showing the worst possible aspects of the country and then throwing them in the face of Cabinet Ministers and expecting instant, simple answers. The President is viewing the whole thing with concern and is reconsidering whether he will take part or not.' "

"*Nightline* had quickly become a part of the internal political debate," said Jannie Botes, an anchor and producer with SABC. "You had government officials, through the press, arguing about whether they should be on the show or shouldn't be on the show. And those who did appear that week were then criticized for what they did say or didn't say."

President Botha's quandary about whether or not to appear was complicated by the Uitenhage massacre. The tragedy dominated Friday's front pages, as did the response of George Shultz, the American secretary of state. He had reacted to the massacre by publicly branding the system of government in South Africa as "evil and unacceptable." Shultz's condemnation alarmed Pretoria. Despite his complaints about *Nightline*'s "bias," Botha decided to go ahead with his interview with Koppel, intending to use it to defend himself.

That morning Roone Arledge arrived in Cape Town after an all-night flight back from New York—his third intercontinental flight in five days. He joined Koppel at President Botha's "summer house." There, in an elegant room whose furniture was etched with gilt, two camera crews were set to go. Botha entered, and greeted them coldly. His face was red. He was clearly agitated. He carried sheaves of papers, "a whole list of things," Arledge recalled, "that he was going to refute Ted with—things that he thought we had done that were terrible." The atmosphere reminded Arledge of the Soviet Union. "It was all very frigid and uptight."

Koppel began the interview by asking for Botha's response to Shultz. Botha was dismissive.

BOTHA: I don't think your secretary of state is capable of judging South African conditions, because he's never been here. And I cannot recollect that he went out of his way to get to grips with our problems. Secondly, I find it rather awkward for other governments to interfere in the internal affairs of another country. I thought that was one of the principles on which the United Nations came about—namely, that no country has the right to interfere in the affairs of another country.

Botha then turned to the subject of "errors" in *Nightline*'s taped background pieces:

BOTHA: You created the idea that our medical services are bad and that blacks have no proper medical services. Now, the facts are in that in South Africa there is one medical doctor for every 1,500, including blacks. In all of Africa, there is one medical doctor for every 10,000. . . .

KOPPEL: That's on average, sir.

BOTHA: On average.

KOPPEL: You remember what Mark Twain said about averages.
             He said . . .

BOTHA: Oh, yes, I read Mark Twain.

KOPPEL: "If I have one foot in a bucket of hot water and one foot
             in a bucket of ice, on average I'm comfortable."

Botha launched into a litany of statistics to defend the resettlement
of blacks onto what he called "viable" land.

KOPPEL: Some of your black opponents in this country say to you,
             If the land is so good, we'll make you a deal. We'll let the
             whites in South Africa take all the land, and we'll then
             take the land the whites have.

BOTHA: Yes. I wonder what our farmers in the vast areas of the
             Cape province would say about that, where the rainfall
             is a quarter of the rainfall in the areas where these black
             people live.

KOPPEL: You think they'd willingly make—

BOTHA: I don't think that they will be able to live on this arid
             land where our people are farming with sheep.

Koppel asked Botha about the violence at Uitenhage. Botha's excuse was a Cold War classic.

BOTHA: You have a fight between the superpowers of the world,
             the United States and Soviet Russia. And they are both
             trying to influence Africa and also South Africa. And
             under the leadership of Soviet Russia there came about
             the Communist party with its headquarters in London,
             operating from there. Under their control they have the
             African National Congress and their people. And these
             people get their instructions from the Communist
             party. . . . They want to make this country ungovern-
             able, and we're not going to allow it.

KOPPEL: Are you suggesting that those demonstrations yesterday were Communist-inspired?

BOTHA: Yes. I say that part of it is influenced by people who do not have the real interests of those people at heart.

Botha hurled blame at the East and the West. What wasn't the fault of the Communists was the fault of America's messy democracy.

KOPPEL: Why would the U.S. secretary of state describe the South African system in such unprecedentedly harsh terms for this administration?

BOTHA: I'll tell you why. I have the impression—and I think my impression is right—that you Americans are fighting your elections in America on South African grounds. . . .

KOPPEL: Mr. President, normally you'd be quite right about that. This is one of those rare periods where there is a lull in the electioneering that takes place in the United States. We just had elections a few months—

BOTHA: No, you always have elections. You have elections right through. You have too many elections. That is my complaint against your country. You can't lead the Western world with all the elections you have. You're weakening yourself.

KOPPEL: What are you suggesting for us?

BOTHA: Well, I'm not interrupting in your affairs. I might state my abhorrence of some of your policies. But I object to you interfering in mine; why should I interfere in yours?

KOPPEL: It is not exactly interference, Mr. President, for the secretary of state of a sovereign nation to express his opinion—

BOTHA: Oh, yes. And if they come to us in a decent way and ask us the reason why we act in a certain way, we shall give them . . . But South Africa is a tough country. We nearly brought the British empire to its knees. And I would advise some superpowers not to try to destroy us.

Finally, Koppel asked Botha to address the issue of pass laws and influx-control laws. Would they be eliminated soon?

BOTHA: In the first place I'm also carrying an identity card. And I think all South Africans should carry one.

KOPPEL: But you don't have to?

BOTHA: I have to. I'm forced to carry it. All South Africans are.

KOPPEL: But you are limited to—

BOTHA: I have one now on me.

With a flourish, Botha pulled out his identity card and held it up to the camera.

The gesture fooled no one. "Most people were ashamed to their *teeth* when Botha did that," said Jannie Botes, the SABC anchor. "People thought, This man is making a fool of us. Yes, whites carried identity cards. But we never had to show them to police in order to travel from one part of town to the other. What P.W. said was simply not true."

An editorial in the *Cape Times* called Botha's appearance a "missed opportunity": "As far as the South African reform lobby and American public opinion are concerned, President Botha's appearance was a public relations disaster. . . . To an American audience which is probably half convinced that what happened in Uitenhage was a deliberate massacre, President Botha's showing was a boost for the disinvestment lobby. To anyone at home or abroad with even a moderate understanding of South African affairs, his evasive response to a question on influx control and the pass laws—producing his own identity document—was manifestly misleading . . . As South Africa lurches ever deeper into crisis, it is evident that the Botha administration has lost the reform initiative. Black areas are becoming ungovernable. Communication between blacks and white authority has broken down. . . . The unrest goes on, no matter how many demonstrators are baton-charged or shot dead . . . blacks are determined that they will no longer suffer the system of apartheid."

"What *Nightline* had produced in a week was nothing short of a revelation to white South Africans," recalled Botes. "Everybody talked about it. At least every intelligent friend I had was talking about it. The government failed miserably to present its case, in the eyes of intellectual South Africans. The show was ruthless, in a way, in terms of what it exposed. It opened the eyes of a lot of people. And it made fools out of the [ruling] National party, because it broke all the old stereotypes that they'd been trying to sell for so long, and that they could sell and control because they controlled the SABC. For the first time, South Africans saw the ANC as real people. And then strange things started to happen. Most important, the ANC got 'de-demonized.' It wasn't the group of devils that the government had painted them to be. Some of these people really made sense. There was also the realization that, eventually, we have to deal with these people. We can't wish them away. By coming and showing us these people, *Nightline,* in a sense, broke the control of the government." Botes added: "But there was a sense of shame that this was being exposed worldwide."

The South African newspapers generally extolled the series. One editorial called it a "shock to the white public, shielded daily by the SABC from the true reality of South Africa and the discomforting views of the representatives of a large proportion of the population."

Koppel, for his part, felt uncomfortable with the attempts to measure the series' political impact. "The media," he told a South African journalist, "is rarely, if ever, a primary player. I think that it is not that *Nightline* has moved anyone in South Africa one step further than they were prepared to be moved. It is that the government was prepared to take a rather risky gamble in letting us in because it felt that it had more to gain than to lose."

But Arrie Rossouw disagreed. "The series had a major impact, especially where it mattered, in the political circles. Everyone could see that these people in the ANC were reasonable people, and that it only made sense to talk to them as a way of breaking what was becoming a terrible impasse. People started saying, 'It is possible, after all, that the government is wrong.' The younger politicians were especially affected by the broadcasts, for they realized that everything about the ANC being made up of devils wasn't true. They pushed particularly hard for communication. And what you had, not long after those broadcasts, were different officials and members of parliament beginning to 'talk about having talks' with the ANC."

The most tangible impact of the *Nightline* series was on the South

African press—the journalists, like Rossouw, who felt "embarrassed" that it had been Americans who'd exposed the system. One editorial after another made the same complaint: "Why was it necessary for a United States television, ABC, to conduct the debate? SATV is quite sophisticated enough to put on programmes like this of its own. It does not have to take them second-hand from a visiting team of Americans—though second-hand is better than not at all when we are at last allowed to see confrontations between the Minister of Foreign Affairs and a less-than-docile black South African."

"At SABC, we were jealous and angry that it took *Nightline* to come do this," said Jannie Botes. "In a way, the government had allowed *Nightline* to make us look like fools. We had always wanted to do such a program, but we were never allowed to." Another SABC producer remembered that "we all said things to each other like, 'Look, for the first time you can see and hear both sides. Isn't it sad that we can't have that debate ourselves?' " "So the people running SABC had to save face," said Botes. "*Nightline* had shown us so clearly a different example of broadcast journalism, that SABC had to try to move in that direction."

Not many months later, a group of producers from SABC traveled to New York and Washington, where they observed *Nightline* in production. The result: a new South African broadcast featuring live interviews called *Network*. Koppel took the imitation to heart. "It is, after all," he would later say, smiling, "the sincerest form of flattery."

One of the co-anchors of the new program was Jannie Botes. Although he would encounter far more government resistance than *Nightline* had encountered in trying to give airtime to anti-apartheid leaders (ANC members were still banned from the airwaves), Botes got more than a few who opposed apartheid on his broadcast.

In America, where Koppel, Kaplan, and Arledge had predicted that few people would watch the series, the show's week in South Africa attracted a million more viewers than normal. Representative John Conyers of New York, a co-founder of the Congressional Black Caucus, said that *Nightline* had "alerted the country and the rest of the world to the situation in South Africa. By upping the issue's visibility, Koppel's shows put enormous pressure on the Reagan administration to do what it did not want to do."

What the Reagan administration "did not want to do" was to impose sanctions. But by early April 1985, twenty different bills were pending in Congress, each designed to pressure South Africa to end apartheid. Seven major American banks announced they would ban further loans to South Africa, and almost half of all U.S. companies with business in South Africa had become signatories to the Sullivan Principles, a code requiring equal treatment for black workers. Meanwhile, anti-apartheid protest spread to college campuses across the country. By summer, more than two dozen American cities were pulling their investments out of South Africa and foreign banks had begun to call in their short-term loans. Finally, in 1986, President Reagan, under pressure from Congress, announced economic sanctions.

By then the "talks to have talks" had led to a number of private, informal contacts between South African political leaders and representatives of the ANC. The minister of justice even paid a call on Nelson Mandela. A number of prominent South African academics were paying regular calls on the ANC headquarters in Lusaka. The Broedderbund, the secret organization of Afrikaners, voted to press for political reform. And the chairman of the Broedderbund began his own series of talks with leaders of the ANC, including a meeting with the ANC foreign minister, Oliver Tambo, on Long Island.

P. W. Botha, however, remained violently opposed to the contacts. On the very day that some intermediaries who'd met with the ANC were supposed to meet with Botha, in May 1986, Botha ordered air raids on ANC bases in neighboring countries and declared a new state of emergency. The flowering of the South African press was one of the casualties of Botha's new restrictions. *Network* wasn't canceled, but Jannie Botes, after several months of hectoring his bosses for permission to interview more opponents of apartheid, was yanked off the show. He was told that he needed, it was decided, some "political experience" and was therefore going to be posted as a reporter covering parliament. But Botes understood what was really happening. He would, in fact, shrug it off as an example of what was happening to journalists all the time: "I was not the first or the last to be pulled off the air for political reasons." A few months later, he took advantage of an invitation from the U.S. Information Agency to spend time observing journalism in America. "The time had come," he explained later, "when it was no longer possible to work towards presenting all points of view within the SABC. It was time to leave it, and begin a new career."

The U.S. sanctions, along with those imposed by other nations, slowly strangled South Africa's economy. Just as important, the attempts by P. W. Botha to shut down all the dialogue with the ANC were futile. The communication had already happened. It was impossible to turn the members of the ANC back into demons.

On February 12, 1990, after several more years of bloody upheaval, Nelson Mandela walked free.

By the time, five years after that, when Nelson Mandela was elected president of South Africa, Bishop Tutu was Archbishop Tutu. Yet he was still the same exuberant, passionate man whose optimism in the face of oppression had so impressed his own countrymen, white and black, in 1985. Not long after Mandela's election, a jubilant Tutu reflected on *Nightline*'s first visit to South Africa. His voice chimed high and low, joyous and musical, even as he remembered the tension he'd felt leading up to the debate with Pik Botha. He chuckled at the memory of the "butterflies" in his stomach. But Tutu thought it was right that he'd been nervous. "Those programs were an important milestone in our struggle against a vicious system."

By then, of course, Pik Botha had relinquished the post of foreign minister for the less exalted title of minister of mineral affairs in Mandela's coalition government. Yet he insisted he had no regrets. He remembered that in the weeks following his debate with Bishop Tutu, one friend after another had castigated him for it. How, they would ask, could he have done it? Why had he participated in such a thing? "What bothers you about it?" he would challenge his critics. "What did you hear that has you so agitated? Is it the truth?" He would remember, a decade later, feeling pleased that *Nightline* had discomfited his fellow Afrikaners. And he would also remember what he had told himself back then: "It is *time*."

FIVE
The Wall

HANAN ASHRAWI AND her husband, Emile, set out long before dawn. The trip to Jerusalem from their home in Ramallah shouldn't have taken more than thirty minutes, but there was a checkpoint to pass. The Ashrawis feared that Israeli soldiers would detain them. Emile slowed down as they neared the roadblock. Hanan held her breath.

Suddenly, the soldiers raised their hands and gave Emile an official military salute. Emile, with his big beard, was a dead ringer for Amram Mitzna, the commander of Israeli forces in the occupied West Bank. The Ashrawis had often heard comments about the striking resemblance, but the Palestinian couple had never thought they would welcome the comparison.

They arrived at the Jerusalem Theater just behind four busloads of Palestinians. One group of Palestinians had traveled in the dark early morning from Gaza; the other had come from the West Bank. Only a special dispensation from the top levels of the Israeli government allowed the Palestinians to be here. The *Nightline* producers who had escorted them in from the territories cleared the buses and exchanged glances with one another that said, So far, so good.

The activity inside the theater, however, suggested that trouble was expected. In a control room above the auditorium, a security guard issued gas masks to *Nightline*'s production personnel. Ted Koppel reviewed contingency plans with Rick Kaplan. If violence erupted, Koppel was to grab two guests and race for a tiny backup studio nearby; correspondent James Walker was already seated in front of a camera, to sub-anchor until Koppel could get there. Meanwhile, one floor below Kaplan and Koppel, the Palestinians who had come in on the buses lined up with Israeli citizens to pass through metal detectors.

In just over an hour, on the stage of this theater, with television cameras broadcasting live to America, Israeli and Palestinian leaders were scheduled to debate—face-to-face—for the first time in history. In the audience would be Palestinians from the territories side-by-side with Jewish citizens of Israel: ancient enemies who had never congregated publicly, except to fight.

ABC News president Roone Arledge looked in on the auditorium and wondered whether he should have canceled the whole experiment. A few days earlier, Israeli defense minister Yitzhak Rabin had hosted Arledge, Koppel, and Kaplan at a breakfast, during which he had predicted that the *Nightline* town meeting would be incendiary. Rabin warned that extremists would likely throw a stink bomb or, worse, some kind of grenade into the auditorium.

"Rabin thought we were crazy," Arledge recalled later. "These were his words: 'You guys are nuts.' He was angry we were doing the program. He told us that there would certainly be violence. He said that there would be somebody who would pull out a PLO flag, and someone would jump him, and people would be attacking each other, and that we might be responsible for deaths." After the meeting with Rabin, Arledge had returned to his hotel room to consider the defense minister's warning. "The worst-case scenario," said Arledge, "was that not only could there be violence, and there could be people killed, maybe, but on top of that we would be the cause of it all. If something bad happened, it would not only be a terrible event, but it would be indefensible that we went ahead, particularly if people found out that Rabin had told us we were crazy.

"So I'd called Rick and the other people we had there, and I'd asked them to double and triple the security. We had to be a hundred percent certain that everything was secure. And even then I was nervous about it, about the idea—I hate to put it in this context—the idea that we'd be naive and foolish enough, and so arrogant—this distin-

guished program—to think that we could bring all these people together in one auditorium."

But at this moment Arledge noticed that Palestinians and Israelis
were obediently passing through the metal detectors and quietly
taking their seats in the theater. Nonviolence was a possibility, too.
So far, so good.

One reason the adversaries in the audience may have assembled so
quietly was that something on the stage had them mesmerized. It was
obvious that the two large tables on either side of the stage were for
the panels. But what was that *thing* in between them?

Hanan Ashrawi walked out from the wings to inspect the setup.
She examined the strange obstacle. She knew what it was and why it
was there. She had demanded it. And yet, looking at it now, Ashrawi
couldn't help but think to herself, How ugly it is!

IT HAD TAKEN three years for Kaplan and Koppel to come up with
"the next South Africa." Not many stories warranted the kind of commitment *Nightline* had given apartheid in 1985. The challenge was to
find another conflict with international relevance, with complexities
suitable for a week-long examination, with political adversaries who
were ready and willing to debate. The conflict must also be situated
somewhere suitable, from which they would broadcast live. "It's not
easy to find subjects like that," said Koppel later, "because not only
does it have to be of national interest in the United States and of some
interest to an American television audience, but you also have to be
convinced that you're going to be able to find enough people who
speak English well enough that they can convey their point of view
with some eloquence.

"We had thought about going to Northern Ireland. And I suppose, theoretically, we could have done something with the Iranians
and the Iraqis, but that would have been such a huge problem in terms
of language and such a huge problem in terms of getting permission to
travel around the country and shoot."

In December 1987, Palestinians living in the Israeli-occupied
territories of Gaza and the West Bank launched an uprising. For the
most part, the "intifada" entailed demonstrations and stone-throwing
at Israeli soldiers. But when the soldiers began using tear gas, and
sometimes real bullets, to quell the protests, violence fueled violence.

By early 1988, the intifada was attracting international attention. In America, the evening news led night after night with fresh pictures of the upheaval. At the very least, the Palestinians had executed a brilliant visual maneuver. The video of children throwing stones at men with Uzi machine guns suggested a replay of the biblical tale of David and Goliath. Only this time, Israel was Goliath.

What intrigued Koppel was that the violent images didn't explain the conflict, and that most Americans had no idea of the Palestinians' heritage, their identity, their struggle. "Americans had a very one-dimensional vision of Palestinians. Palestinians were a bunch of bomb-throwing terrorists. They sort of looked like Yasser Arafat, and they were killers and hijackers and terrible people. I think that we always do ourselves an injustice when we stereotype any entire group of people that way. It doesn't matter who it is."

Koppel and Kaplan realized they had found "South Africa II." It was Israel. The equivalent of Bishop Tutu versus Foreign Minister Botha would be the Palestinians versus the Israelis. *Nightline* would assemble them for a town meeting in Jerusalem. This time the opposing sides would convene without satellites, without electronic wizardry. This time, the enemies would actually meet, face-to-face, on one stage.

It would be important to get the right representatives for the two sides; Koppel and Kaplan were committed, once they'd settled on the concept, to having genuine political leaders on the stage. Philosophers and intellectuals wouldn't do. The debate had to have political credibility; otherwise, why go through all the risks and the dangers involved?

The biggest danger, in fact, was this: the show might kill the guests . . . literally. Any Palestinian who would agree to debate an Israeli official would have to be possessed of a death wish. The Palestinian leadership had declared a boycott on contact with Israeli officials; to permit contact, it was believed, would be to legitimize the Israeli leadership. In fact, in early 1988, just as Kaplan and Koppel were hatching their plan for *Nightline* in the Holy Land, a well-known Palestinian author and professor named Sari Nusseibeh was accused of meeting secretly with an Israeli official. Nusseibeh was badly beaten up.

The Israelis would have their own problems with a town meeting. Because the Palestine Liberation Organization had a history of terrorism and continued to call for the destruction of the state of Israel, it was illegal for an Israeli official to speak to any Palestinian who didn't first disavow allegiance to the PLO. And yet the Israelis knew that the only credible Palestinian leaders were by definition allied with the PLO. At that point, the PLO embodied Palestinian dreams of independence. No Palestinian would, or could, repudiate the PLO.

The issue of the PLO was a political tinderbox in America, too. In the late 1970s, Andrew Young, who was serving as Jimmy Carter's ambassador to the United Nations, had been forced to resign for having had an unauthorized conversation with a PLO delegate to the UN General Assembly. Then, after the Israeli invasion of Lebanon in 1982, and the unraveling of an Israeli-Lebanese peace accord in 1983, the Reagan administration pulled back altogether from peacemaking in the Middle East. Only as the Reagan presidency closed in on its final year did Secretary of State George Shultz launch one final attempt to bring Israel and the Palestinians back to the table. The effort involved some bizarre rituals. American emissaries couldn't be seen speaking directly to officials from the PLO, so they met instead with Palestinians who were not official members of the PLO but de facto members. Then the de facto members would travel to Tunis for meetings with the official members and report back to the American officials. As one U.S. official described the curious process, "Diplomacy in the Middle East was filled with fig leaves and fan dances because the domestic politics of negotiation had become so loaded."

By late January 1988, the fig leaves and fan dances of the negotiators had yielded exactly nothing. So when Kaplan and Koppel began to test their town meeting idea with sources in the Middle East, the first word they heard back was *impossible*. Stringers, reporters, and producers in the region, experts who knew the landscape and the labyrinthine politics of the place, academics, and politicians all informed Kaplan that his plan was lunacy. Yes, the town meeting was a fascinating idea. But an impossible idea.

The word *impossible* had the effect that it usually did on Kaplan and Koppel. They pressed on. They decided to send a *Nightline* emissary to the Middle East, someone exuberant, intelligent, and just naïve enough not to realize the obstacles. They picked Gil Pimentel, a Harvard-educated twenty-nine-year-old *Nightline* booker. He habitually wore big glasses that conveyed a kind of nervous, wide-eyed innocence. Over the previous four years on the show, Pimentel had booked everyone from Boris Yeltsin to Ginger Rogers; yet he was, in his own words, "this dufus who didn't know shit about Middle East politics." Pimentel's orders were to go to the occupied territories, to find the most credible Palestinian leaders, and to convince them to break their own rules and debate Israeli officials for a live American television program.

Koppel was the one who actually pulled Pimentel into his Washington office and gave him the assignment. Pimentel should begin, Koppel told him, by finding Yasser Arafat, the chairman of the PLO. Arafat's blessing was critical to the project. Besides, Arafat had been interviewed by Koppel several times over the years and was familiar with the format. As Koppel later remembered it, "We knew that the Palestinians insisted that the PLO was the only legitimate representative of the Palestinian people. So, we had to talk to Yasser Arafat. I wasn't sure that Arafat could help set it up, but I was sure that Arafat could have stopped it dead in its tracks. I felt it was a necessary stop. We had to pay our institutional respects. We had to go and say, 'You're the boss.' "

Pimentel would remember that he offered up a cheerful "Okay. Sure." But he wasn't *that* naive. "My inner response was to leap up and go racing out of the room, just sort of jump out of a window and go running down the block yelling and screaming, and never show up again."

ON A SNOWY, frigid January day, less than twenty-four hours after receiving his marching orders from Koppel, Pimentel was on a plane bound for Baghdad. When he landed the next morning, a PLO functionary met him and escorted him to a hotel. For the next three days, Pimentel waited for word about his requested meeting with Arafat. On the fourth morning another PLO functionary drove him to a new house located in the suburbs. In walked Yasser Arafat, who, despite his perfectly pressed and tailored military uniform, struck Pimentel as somehow looking "like a psychiatry professor at the University of Chicago. His beard was very closely cropped and immaculately groomed."

Arafat asked how Koppel was. Pimentel said fine, and handed over a letter from Koppel that explained the town meeting. "Mr. Arafat," said Pimentel, "we are hoping for the first time to present the Palestinian point of view, without editing, and to present it on equal footing with the Israelis'. It's never been done on American television. And we want Palestinians themselves to explain their point of view, and to explain it to the American public."

Arafat smiled and said, "I think it's a great idea. I will help you in any way I can to see that through. That's all we've ever wanted: the opportunity to speak for ourselves. Whatever you need, you will have."

"Well, what I need you to do, sir, is to send out the message through whatever means you have to the territories that the people who participate in this program are participating with your blessing and that they should not be attacked in any way."

Arafat promised that the message would go through.

HANAN ASHRAWI DOESN'T remember ever receiving such a message from the PLO. What she does remember is opening her door one day, in the West Bank town of Ramallah, to discover an earnest young man wearing large spectacles who had never been to her part of the world before and didn't seem to understand its byzantine ways, and whose mission was, in her words, "crazy."

Pimentel had been told that this magisterial, chain-smoking professor from Bir Zeit University was closely tied to the PLO. He also knew that Ashrawi was familiar with the leaders of all the Palestinian factions. (The information had come from ABC's John Cooley, who was one of the network's producers in the Middle East, and from Betsy West, *Nightline*'s senior producer based in London. Both West and Cooley had met with Ashrawi several times.) Pimentel laid out the concept of the town meeting. Would Ashrawi help him find four Palestinian political leaders willing to debate officials from the Israeli government?

There was something so unrealistic about Pimentel's plea that it touched Ashrawi. "The thing that worked most in favor of this was Gil's innocence. He was so naive! I was amazed that ABC would send somebody so green. But it worked in his favor, because all my maternal instincts came out. Really, I felt that this poor guy didn't know what he got himself into. Now, had they sent somebody who was sophisticated and cynical, I probably would have dismissed him. But this guy was just so innocent that I have to say I knew he needed protection." Ashrawi also knew that there might be benefits from such a broadcast. "We felt the time was coming to go public, to present our case, to face the Israelis." She believed the boycott against public contact with Israeli officials had hurt the Palestinian cause. The Israelis had been able to control the debate, to define the Palestinians as terrorists. "It was time to present our people as human beings. I felt we had to take the Israelis on. We were ready for them. And we had a much better case to present than they did."

Ashrawi decided she would help this naive young man find his panel.

Meanwhile, Pimentel's counterpart, the booker assigned to lock in the panel of Israeli officials, began to realize that she and Pimentel were wading into a booker's quagmire. At first, Heather Vincent had been rather pleased with her progress. She had met with Ehud Olmert, leader of the right-wing Likud party and a member of the Israeli parliament, the Knesset. Olmert proclaimed himself a longtime fan of Koppel. He would be happy, he said, to participate in the town meeting. Years later, he explained his reasons: "I felt that this was an excellent opportunity. We were at that time accused of being intransigent and inflexible and so I felt this was a good opportunity. We were likely to come out more moderate and more reasonable. So I felt that, at least in terms of propaganda, it could do a good job for us."

There were, however, a few problems. Nineteen eighty-eight was an election year in Israel, and it was against the law to negotiate with representatives of the PLO. It would be difficult to convince an aspiring politician to break the law. Though *Nightline* was assured by the government that it would take no legal action against Israelis who participated, there was still enormous political risk. Olmert was already hearing from the far right in his own party that any kind of dialogue would result in retribution at the polls. Olmert told Vincent he would have to have a list of the names on the Palestinian panel before he could convince anyone to join him in the debate. He had to be able to show his colleagues that none of the opposing panelists was tied to the PLO. Vincent was not much more savvy about the Middle East than Pimentel, but she knew one thing: the panels were now mired in a catch-22.

PIMENTEL HADN'T EVEN GOTTEN to the point of worrying about what to tell the Israelis. He couldn't even organize a panel that was *allied* with the PLO. He wanted a representative from each of the major Palestinian factions. But despite Arafat's blessing, and despite the assistance of Hanan Ashrawi, the divisions within the Palestinian camp were deep enough to disintegrate every group Pimentel tried to put together. "There were just so many personal rivalries and disagreements. Person number four wouldn't like person number two and person number four would drop out. And then a new person number four would come in and person number two would drop out. And then a new person number two would come in and then person number three would drop out."

The only panelist Pimentel was certain of was Haidar Abdul Shafi. The seventy-year-old physician from Gaza was the grand old man of Palestinian independence and a founding father of the PLO. He was old enough, and secure enough, not to fear the ramifications of sharing a stage with the Israelis. He shared Ashrawi's conviction that it was time to challenge the Israeli government in a public forum. Most important, Abdul Shafi's name had been vetted with the Israelis. Ehud Olmert pronounced the Palestinian doctor acceptable. Olmert later explained that Adbul Shafi was "not a pussy cat, but he was not associated with terror." Olmert sent word that as long as the Palestinian doctor presented his views as his own and did not portray himself as a spokesman for the PLO, the Israelis were willing to have him on the stage.

Now that the Israelis were willing to accept a founding father of the PLO into the debate, Pimentel realized there was hope. Most of the Israeli government, it seemed, wanted the town meeting badly enough that some of its officials were willing to go to extraordinary lengths to make it happen. After all, recalled Pimentel, they "knew exactly who Abdul Shafi was and they chose to ignore it." In fact, the Israelis came up with an ingenious fig leaf for the PLO problem: since Abdul Shafi lived in Gaza, they reasoned, and since, at that time, it was illegal for people in the territories to be members of the PLO, then logic would dictate that no PLO member could be living in Gaza. Therefore, since the good doctor did live in Gaza, he could not really be a member of the PLO. Pimentel was beginning to enjoy, if not entirely understand, the logic of the Middle East.

Still, Adbul Shafi wanted veto power over other contenders for the panel. He insisted that Pimentel clear the list with him. More than one candidate fell by the wayside because, as Pimentel recalled, "Abdul Shafi would say, 'I'm sorry, I just can't be seen with that person.' "

The problem, as Ashrawi saw it, was that what *Nightline* wanted to do was "break a taboo. It was trying to break with customs and with historical, traditional behaviors." Tradition had it, for example, that even at the UN, if Israel spoke, the Arabs walked out.

So, as Ashrawi and Pimentel made their rounds through the occupied territories and pled the case for the debate, two factions of the Palestinian movement refused to cooperate. One of the factions, the Popular Front for the Liberation of Palestine, warned Ashrawi that it would publicly denounce the town meeting and would tell Palestinians not to participate.

A WEEK BEFORE the town meeting, Kaplan arrived to discover that not only was Pimentel's panel nonexistent save one, Vincent's panel was in trouble, too, and her problems with the Israelis were bound up in Pimentel's quandary. Several potential panelists from the Knesset refused to commit until they knew who was appearing on the Palestinian side. Some Israelis who initially expressed interest balked when they saw that Abdul Shafi was on the show. One right-winger in the Likud who had agreed to go on pulled out, telling Vincent it was "too risky." Kaplan felt that time was running out and that both sides were paralyzed by fear: "The Israelis were afraid of being totally ostracized, and the Palestinians were afraid of retribution by their own people, and it was a nightmare."

Vincent assured Kaplan that Ehud Olmert was a certainty, or, as Vincent described him, "my brave one." But even Olmert said that unless they could book a couple of others on the Israeli side, he'd have to back out. He couldn't look as if he were sticking his neck out all by himself, he told Vincent. The other sure booking was Dedi Zucker, a Knesset member and a founder of the Peace Now movement in Israel.

As the week wore on, Vincent got a commitment from another Likud Knesset member. His name was Dr. Eliahu Ben-Elissar. His credentials—former chief of staff to Prime Minister Menachem Begin and the first Israeli ambassador to Egypt—were so impressive that he couldn't be easily tarnished by agreeing to participate. Vincent also found Knesset member Haim Ramon. He belonged to the Labor party, which favored dialogue with the Palestinians. His appearance, therefore, carried less political risk than the appearance of the Likud members. Even then, Vincent knew that should Pimentel come up with a panel of Palestinians deemed "unacceptable" to her panel, the Israelis would walk.

PIMENTEL WAS GETTING DESPERATE. A week before the broadcast, he had only one Palestinian locked in. Ashrawi felt that time had run out. She made one last attempt to persuade a member of the intifada leadership to join the debate, but when he turned her down, she called Pimentel. "Gil, I'm so sorry, but it's not going to work. I just don't think it's going to happen. It's just too risky."

Pimentel began to scream. "Look, all we've heard for years and years is you people saying you get a raw deal, that the American media only listens to the Israelis. Now you're being offered unlimited network time to express in your own way exactly what you think, and you're not taking it! You're being offered this opportunity on a silver platter, and because all of you are afraid of what other people will think, you're going to miss out on it. Don't complain to me about our biased coverage! If it doesn't happen, it's all your fault!" Then Pimentel hung up on the soft-spoken professor.

Ashrawi was shocked. "I thought he'd lost his bearings. Maybe he thought I was working for ABC or something." Within minutes, she called Pimentel back. He remembered her voice "trembling with rage. She was clearly about to cry." "Never in my entire life," Ashrawi sputtered, "has anyone ever talked to me that way. How dare you speak to me that way when all I'm trying to do is help you. And this is the way you treat me! Nobody has ever treated me this way."

"I'm really sorry, Hanan," Pimentel replied, "but you have to understand how much pressure I'm under. I'm in a terrible situation. I'm young, I'm inexperienced. Everybody is saying, 'How could they possibly have sent him to do this?' ABC has staked its prestige on this show. I could be fired if this doesn't work. I'm standing on the brink and I'm terrified."

By the end of Pimentel's apology, Ashrawi took him back under her protective, maternal wing. "All right, then. We'll continue to work on this and see what we can do."

Until now Ashrawi had insisted that her role should remain strictly behind the scenes. But Pimentel's breakdown softened her resolve. He urged her to join the panel. If she agreed, he pointed out, they needed to find only two more. Ashrawi agreed.

Within a day or two, over a dinner at the Jericho home of Saeb Erakat, an important Palestinian journalist and professor, Pimentel persuaded Erakat to join the panel. All that was needed now was one more. Pimentel decided that if they couldn't find someone suitable, he could live with three. Still, he was terrified that something—or someone—would cause the Palestinians to cancel at the last minute. So Pimentel set about trying to book "backup" panels. He tracked down people who were more teachers and philosophers than activists, but if worse came to worst, at least he'd have a full set of Palestinians at the table.

But what Pimentel began to discover was that one by one, his "backups" were backing out. Someone seemed to be tracking down and intimidating every person Pimentel contacted. A day and a half before the scheduled broadcast, it was clear that if his "credible threesome" fell through, there would be no emergency panel, no Palestinian panel at all, no town meeting. That night, just thirty-six hours before the show, Pimentel was at Ashrawi's house when a call came from Gaza. Mamdou al-Akhar, a doctor and a key figure in the Palestinian independence movement, agreed to participate. Ashrawi had been lobbying him for days. Ashrawi hung up the phone and turned to Pimentel. "Congratulations," she said, smiling. "You've got yourself a panel. Now, what about the booths?"

"Booths?" Pimentel asked. "What booths?"

"The booths that will separate us from the Israelis."

"Who said anything about booths?"

"Well, Saeb said he was going to talk to you about booths."

"Saeb talked to me about having a booth that separated you from the Israelis, and I told him, 'No way, that's not going to work. This is a stage.' "

"Well then," Ashrawi sighed, "I don't think we can do it."

Pimentel felt dead.

From across the room, Ashrawi's husband, Emile, suddenly erupted: "How could you all be so worried about this? How could you let this opportunity like you have never had before . . . how could you possibly let it slip by because of what some people could say? Don't let it go by."

"We need a separation," Ashrawi explained. "We cannot be seen talking to them directly."

Emile suggested, "What about a symbolic separation? How about if you took a roll of barbed wire and you spread it down the stage in the middle of the two participants? And, you know, it serves as a visual metaphor and people will understand what's going on. And you only talk to Ted."

Oh, right, thought Pimentel. He imagined the press release: *Koppel's going to leap a barbed-wire fence over and over again while simultaneously mediating the first confrontation in history between Palestinians and Israelis, for over three hours, in front of millions of Americans.* Pimentel suddenly envisioned Koppel catching his pants—or something worse— on the wire.

"No, Emile. Barbed wire won't work."

Emile wouldn't give up. What about a wall? "You know, a little symbolic wall just running down the length of the stage."

Ashrawi liked the idea. And Pimentel was thinking that at least a wall couldn't actually hurt Koppel in any way. By the time he returned to his hotel room in Jerusalem, however, Pimentel realized he was in deep trouble: how do you debate face-to-face through a *wall*? He put in a call to Rick Kaplan, who was staying across town at the King David Hotel. He knew Kaplan was out to dinner with Israeli officials, so he left a message that said, in essence, "The Palestinians want a wall. Call Gil."

When Kaplan got the message, the town meeting was set to begin in less than thirty-six hours. Nearly a million dollars had already been spent to move *Nightline* to Jerusalem for a week. He'd flown in scores of producers, researchers, reporters, editors, and technicians. Most important, he had brought Koppel to Israel. No, the culmination of *Nightline* in the Holy Land was not going to be Ted Koppel running into, leaping over, peeking over, or otherwise negotiating a wall.

Over at the American Colony Hotel, Pimentel could not fall asleep. He was tossing and turning when the phone rang. Pimentel picked it up. The caller didn't identify himself, which would have been a silly thing to do since it was clear after a word or two that it could only be Kaplan: "No . . . fucking . . . wall! Do you hear me! No fucking barbed wire, no fucking wall, no fucking anything! This is gonna be a benign . . . fucking . . . stage. Do you understand me? *A benign fucking stage!*"

Boom! Dial tone. Pimentel never did fall asleep after that. The next morning, as the hours ticked closer to showtime, he paced the

Jerusalem Theater, wondering whether he could get a job at CNN. Kaplan walked in. Pimentel started trembling. He felt his eyes welling up. "Rick, I don't know what I'm going to do." Pimentel's voice was breaking. "In the past twenty-four hours, I've put together four panels of Palestinians. And each one of them has collapsed. And now I've got a panel together and if this panel collapses, I don't know what I'm going to do."

Kaplan put an arm around Pimentel and dropped his voice. "What's it gonna take?"

"A wall!"

"What kind of a wall?"

"A . . . little . . . *bitty* . . . wall." Pimentel began to sob.

NOW, AS THE AUDIENCE slowly filled the auditorium, Hanan Ashrawi stood on the stage and stared at the barricade and thought to herself, *What an ugly wall.* It stood no more than three and a half feet tall, finished in what appeared to be rec-room mahogany. Ashrawi wasn't thinking about the fact that *Nightline*'s set designers, under the supervision of director Roger Goodman, had been given less than twenty-four hours' notice to come up with something high enough to resemble a wall and low enough for the two sides to see one another. All Ashrawi could see was that the wall didn't look at all indigenous. Nothing about it seemed Palestinian, or Israeli, or even Middle Eastern. What it looked like was something that might support an artificial shrub in the lobby of a Des Moines Holiday Inn. But Ashrawi had to smile to herself. At least her poor naïve Gil had come through with a wall.

Pimentel had no time to take pride in the prop. He had another crisis. Mamdou al-Akhar had the flu. At least that's what his wife had said when she phoned Pimentel just forty-five minutes before the show was to air to explain that the doctor would not be able to appear on the broadcast. Pimentel had feared this possibility ever since the previous afternoon, when al-Akhar had visited the theater. "He had a look of terror in his eyes," Pimentel recalled. "He was wide-eyed. This was pure stage fright."

Flu or stage fright, the Palestinians were now reduced to three. Pimentel had a backup in mind, a prominent lawyer who was scheduled to be in the audience. But when Saeb Erakat and Haidar Abdul Shafi arrived, they met with Ashrawi privately and returned with a veto. For political reasons, they did not approve of this particular Palestinian for the panel. They would go on as three.

As dawn broke over the theater, the panelists took their seats onstage. Koppel walked on and noticed that the Palestinians were dressed in Western-style clothing. None of them wore any kind of traditional Arab or Palestinian garb. He thought to himself that if nothing else was achieved, perhaps some stereotypes would be shattered in the next few hours.

But would nonviolence hold that long? By now Koppel knew the route to the backup studio if trouble erupted, and he'd seen the gas masks in the control room. He looked out across the audience, at this gathering of mortal enemies, and decided to make an appeal for peace. "The broadcast is about to begin. Please have enough respect for one another to resort only to ideological battles." He paused, smiled, and offered one last instruction. "Have a good time." At that, the first nonpartisan laughter of the evening echoed across the auditorium.

At precisely 11:30 P.M. Eastern Standard Time, 6:30 A.M. in Jerusalem, Koppel introduced the broadcast with a reminder to viewers in America:

KOPPEL: What you are about to see is live. . . . (*camera pans audience in Jerusalem Theater, then pans Koppel and panelists onstage*) It has been suggested to me that if we truly understood what we are trying here today, we would never have done it. There's probably some truth to that. If anyone has come here today determined to disrupt, to prevent rather than encourage dialogue, that won't be difficult. If all of you are determined to satisfy only your constituencies at home, to say only those things that your neighbors will applaud, we'll have to live with that. Many, but not all, in our American television audience will appreciate how much courage it took for some of you to come here.

Koppel launched the show with a taped piece by correspondent James Walker and producer Deborah Leff. The story focused on violence in the town of Nablus, and on a Palestinian family whom

Walker and his camera crew happened to be visiting when Israeli troops began shooting and firing tear gas just outside the family's home. Almost a dozen such pieces prepared over the previous weeks by *Nightline* producers and reporters were ready to air. Some of the stories were told from the Palestinian perspective, some told from the Israeli point of view. They were to be threaded into the program to provoke discussion.

But for all the drama of those carefully packaged stories, nothing, it would turn out, proved more provocative or memorable than the prop in the middle of the stage. As he was about to introduce the panelists, Koppel paused to explain what it was that divided them.

KOPPEL: You may have noticed this little fence that I'm sitting on here. It has been suggested to me—and it is perhaps symbolic of the delicacy with which the negotiations proceeded just to bring this panel together and to bring this audience together—but it has been suggested to me that we need a symbolic divider between our Israeli guests on the one hand, our Palestinian guests on the other. I must tell you that it has been so difficult to arrange this broadcast that this was one small price that we were prepared to pay. So here it is. I will try and spend as much time on one side as on the other.

Then Koppel executed a graceful scissor-step over the wall, a step that gave tacit emphasis to the inscrutable politics of the Middle East. Nervous laughter resonated through the auditorium. It would be the last bipartisan response from the audience.

Ehud Olmert stared at the wall and thought to himself that he and his Israeli colleagues were looking at the ultimate propaganda tool. "The Palestinians couldn't have provided us a better opportunity," he explained later. The Israelis would use the obstacle as proof that "these [Palestinians] don't want to talk, they want fences."

Ben-Elissar had the same idea. He was the first to mock the barricade.

BEN-ELISSAR: First of all, why don't you remove this fence? We don't need this fence! Who needs this fence?

KOPPEL: The Palestinians need this fence.

BEN-ELISSAR: They need it. I know that maybe they need it. We
               don't need it. I don't need it. The Israelis don't need this
               fence. If there is one thing that is sure, that is definitive,
               it is that in this country Arabs and Jews will have to live
               together. Precisely as they will have to live forever—
               together in the Middle East. There is no other choice. So
               we don't need this fence.

Ashrawi thought Ben-Elissar's comment was "his unmasking. Of
course [the Israelis] didn't need the fence—they were running our
lives." But onstage, Ashrawi and her colleagues ignored the gibes
about the fence. They were determined not to appear defensive or intimidated. The goal of the Palestinians, after all, was not to change the
attitude of the Israeli leadership but to affect the attitude of American
viewers. The Palestinians wanted to be seen as dignified and confident.
Most important, as far as Ashrawi was concerned, was the effort to
portray the Palestinian people not as terrorists but as "human beings."

ASHRAWI: There is a contradiction in the term "benign occupa-
               tion." Occupation is unnatural. It is abnormal. We are
               here at great personal risk. Each and every single one of
               us has had to suffer lots of harassments, different types of
               interrogation, imprisonment, lack of ability to travel or
               move around, and . . . after a lot of soul-searching and
               agonizing we decided to come here, not to have dia-
               logue with the Israelis, because the correct address as I
               said is the PLO, but rather to express our opinions
               clearly, because for years we have relied on the justice of
               our cause in order to make our points clear, but it is ob-
               vious that the Americans and the rest of the public opin-
               ion has to know that justice is not sufficient to give us
               our rights. So we are here to address you directly, to tell
               you that we need our own basic rights, to be recognized.
               We need to be recognized as people. We don't have to
               humanize ourselves. We are human beings. And this has
               been neglected and ignored for centuries. Thank you.

Ashrawi's eloquence was underscored by her low, mellifluous voice, her sophisticated, slightly British accent, and her Western dress. She even held a long cigarette holder, like an old-time American movie star. She was doing an elegant job of shattering stereotypes.

Unless, that is, one happened to belong to the panel opposing her. Ehud Olmert thought Ashrawi was "the most eloquent, no doubt. I was immediately impressed with her full English, which was perfect. The best that any Palestinian ever spoke on TV that I have heard." But Olmert felt like smirking at Ashrawi's cigarette holder. He considered it a ridiculous and diminishing accessory. "I thought she was naïve about how silly—how pampered—she looked," he said later. "She was supposed to be speaking for the common man." Olmert saved his attacks, however, for contradictions not in Ashrawi's image but in her message. He recalled the story of Nusseibeh's beating earlier that spring.

OLMERT: First of all, I would like to say that no harassment allegedly perpetrated by the Israeli government can match the harassment which is perpetrated against them by their own people. All this talk about the attitude of the Israeli government, with all due respect, is ridiculous. Sari Nusseibeh, who was interviewed here, once met with me. Two days later he was almost killed by Palestinians because he dared speak with an Israeli.

Olmert was leading up to his own well-aimed barb at the wall.

OLMERT: They demanded the fence. I'll tell you why, Mr. Koppel. Because they might be endangered by their own extremists within the Palestinians. The Palestinians kill more Palestinians than ever were killed by Israelis.

What Olmert never pointed out—because it would have weakened his argument—was that the wall gave as much political protection to Olmert's side as it did to the Palestinians. The Israeli panelists would be just as free, later on, to exploit the wall for domestic political purposes, as a shield against right-wing extremists opposed to dialogue. But Olmert was here to portray the Israelis as ready to negotiate.

OLMERT: We are prepared to start negotiations without any pre-
            conditions . . . I'm ready to sit with Palestinians with-
            out Jordan. But I'm afraid that they will not be ready
            to do it—

A member of the audience shouted, "That's a lie!"

Heckling would continue to erupt, now and then, from both sides
of the audience. Israelis pelted Ashrawi with derisive hoots when
Koppel asked her about the violence of the intifada.

ASHRAWI: Violence I'd say on the part of the Israelis. Symbolic vi-
            olence on the part of the Palestinians. You cannot equate
            stone-throwing, which is essentially a symbolic act, with
            the military machine—

            (*hooting from audience*)

            —with the might of rubber bullets, which people say
            don't hurt, with tear gas that we've all experienced that
            can cause miscarriages as well as deaths, with live ammu-
            nition—do you call that parity in a situation like that?

KOPPEL: It's not parity, but if someone is confronting me with a
            slingshot as I said a moment ago, I may lose some of the
            sense of the symbolism there.

Koppel knew full well that symbolism and substance were en-
twined. *He* was the one, after all, who had to scissor-step a wall every
time he wanted to move from one panel to the other. And what he
began to notice, each time he stood near the Palestinian table, was that
none of its representatives would look at the Israelis. Ashrawi, Erakat,
and Abdul Shafi seemed to be trying to ignore the Israelis. It was the
viewing audience that the Palestinians hoped to reach.

Eventually, though, Saeb Erakat's rage broke his determination to
avoid eye contact. The Israelis had been accusing the Palestinians—
and the PLO—of intransigence. Suddenly Erakat's eyes flashed. He
paused and glared directly at his opponents.

ERAKAT: Am I a human being or not? Give me my rights! I want
            my daughter to live in peace! And stop this cycle of

violence! Your army's no longer the IDF, the Israeli Defense Army, it's an army of woman and child chasers. They enter the refugee camps, kill and destroy. . . . You know, I'm Semite. We're cousins! Very strange cousins, but we're cousins. We're the sons of Abraham. So no one call me anti-Semite. I'm Semite whether you like it or not. I'm Semite!

Erakat couldn't contain himself now. Nor could the audience.

ERAKAT: Occupation is the highest form of terrorism. And Hitler—

              (*boos and shouts of protest from the Israeli section of the audience; Erakat turned and glowered at them*)

ERAKAT: —excuse me, I hate Hitler more than any of you.

A journalist seated in the audience heard an Israel woman mutter, "I hate you."

Eventually, Ashrawi too became enraged. What triggered her furor was a taunt by Ben-Elissar:

BEN-ELISSAR: What you are doing is sending out children and women to the streets to cope with Israeli soldiers. You are afraid to go out into the streets to do it yourself. You are doing it with your children. And you know very well, you know very well that we Israelis and that we Jews have a very special feeling, and a very special attitude that is not known in maybe your circles, for children and for women. And this is why you are hiding with this kind of innocence, bashfulness, you're hiding behind kids and women.

Years later, Ashrawi still flushed at the memory of Ben-Elissar's put-down. "That hit where it hurt most, really. I was a mother who was so hurt and pained by what my children had to go through, and how we had to live under occupation and the kind of fear and insecurity and danger that my kids were going through. And Ben-Elissar had the audacity and lack of feeling and inhumanity to strip me of my humanity and to accuse all Palestinians of not having feelings for their children, and to say that only Israelis have those feelings for their children. That is terrible. The nerve. The racism. Many Israelis have developed a sort of racist mentality and a blindness to our humanity. I felt that racism had to stop right there and then . . . I couldn't help it."

ASHRAWI: I think I have heard enough tonight. People analyzing our motives. People putting words into our mouths. People twisting what we say. And people refusing to hear what we say. And to culminate, we have heard, frankly, outright racist statements, which have been underlying the whole talk this morning, or this evening in the States.

Ashrawi had one more message. It was illegal for her to claim allegiance to the PLO, but the broadcast offered a unique platform, a platform wasted, in her opinion, without declaring:

ASHRAWI: We see the crux of the matter is the total Israeli refusal to address the PLO as our representative. This is going to solve the problem. Address the PLO. Have the international negotiations. We want peace. If you want peace, take that step.

By now it was nearly three o'clock in the eastern United States and mid-morning in Jerusalem. Nothing had been resolved. Nothing was supposed to be resolved.

"I think this was probably the first time," Koppel said later, "that a large American audience saw, on network television, Palestinians and Israelis speaking in a sense past one another, but at least as equals, as equal human beings, with equal standing on the stage and equal standing in the audience. And I think after that, it may have been a little more difficult for people just to dismiss Palestinians as a caricature. And if we accomplished that much, that's a hell of a lot."

Koppel closed the broadcast, the members of the audience filtered out, and the panelists left the stage. All that was left were the two tables and, between them, a bit of scenery that spoke to all the history, the animosities, the bloodshed, the refusal of the Israelis to recognize the Palestinian leadership, the refusal of the Palestinian leadership to recognize Israel's right to exist.

Three and a half years later, following the Gulf War and the expulsion of Saddam Hussein from Kuwait and the demise of the Soviet Union, Middle East peace talks opened in Madrid. The Palestinian delegation included Erakat, Ashrawi, and Dr. Abdul Shafi. One of those involved in setting up the Madrid talks thought *Nightline*'s town meeting may have played a role, albeit a small one, in spurring dialogue. Richard Haass, a Middle East adviser to the National Security Council under President Bush, credited the show with moving the peace process along "at the margins. The fact that these people could appear together in public—the wall notwithstanding—was something of a psychological breakthrough."

Ashrawi agreed. "The show broke barriers. It made acceptable the idea of an encounter between Palestinians and Israelis. After that, we made a qualitative shift in our approach and in the level of communication with the Israelis, which prepared the ground for negotiations." The show, she said, "also brought greater awareness to the world of who the Palestinians are and the complexities of the conflict. I got calls from the States, and had lots of letters. And the show had tremendous impact in the Arab world. I got calls from people who'd seen the broadcast in Lebanon. There was a sympathy for the Palestinians and there was a sense of pride that these Palestinians stood up to the Israelis."

The Israeli panelists didn't see it that way. Ehud Olmert thought the Palestinians had lost the debate as soon as it emerged that they were the ones who had demanded the wall. He felt that the Israelis demonstrated openness. "You know, when you meet privately, there is always some mystique or some mystery or the possibility of some secret deal—who knows what has been discussed? But when you discuss it all on TV, then you prove you are not hiding anything." Olmert also heard from viewers in America, viewers who thought *his* side had carried the debate. "Soon afterwards, there was this sense that this was more than just a TV show, that this was a political event, an international event, that TV had become more than just a technical instrument."

The wall itself may have been an instrument. Richard Haass, for one, suspected it had an impact. "The silliness of the wall, in a funny sort of way, may have played into things, because it showed some of the absurdity of the situation in the Middle East. People who live next door to one another, who lived among one another, and who could talk privately—suddenly the politics of the two sides made it necessary to go through this elaborate charade, the construction of this symbolic wall. I think for anyone who had a working intelligence, it was intellectually embarrassing, even humiliating. The fact that politics necessitated doing this for political protection. For thinking people on both sides of the Israeli–Palestinian divide, the wall can't but have helped to have made people somewhat uncomfortable, with themselves and their own predicament. So the fact that the town meeting provided something of a breaking of a taboo, and the fact that the wall made people more uncomfortable with reality, I think it helped at the margins. And that's not bad. A lot of history happens at the margins."

All Gil Pimentel knew was that without that ugly bit of scenery dividing the stage, the town meeting would never have happened. When the Madrid talks were about to begin, Pimentel wrote a piece about the wall for *The New Republic*. He included advice for the American delegate to the talks, Secretary of State James Baker. "In the months ahead," wrote Pimentel, "the secretary of state may also discover he has to build a wall to break down a few barriers. If so, he should call me. I can get him a used one, cheap."

SIX

Shows We Wish You Had Never Seen

LE DUC THO'S ANSWER was endless. He rambled on and on as if to a captive audience when, in fact, his only captives were Ted Koppel and Henry Kissinger, and Kissinger was signaling that he wanted to escape. As for the other estimated six million listeners who had the power to tune out, Koppel figured that many already had. From an air-conditioned room of the old Caravelle Hotel in Vietnam, Le Duc Tho prattled on. Kissinger, in ABC's New York studio, rocked in his chair and whispered off-camera that he wanted to bail out. On the roof of the Caravelle, the sun was beginning to melt Koppel into a small pool of sweat. If the sun didn't, he knew the lights set up to offset the high-noon sunshine would. Boom! A light exploded. There was only one thing remaining that could go wrong . . . New York? Hello? Are we on the air? The satellite had gone down.

There had been more than a few bad shows over the years, but nothing like this. Walk up to Koppel anytime, anywhere, and ask him which of four thousand shows was the worst, and he'll blurt out the answer without inhaling or blinking, as if it's always right there on his tongue, something bitter that he needs to spit out: "Vietnam, 1985."

IT HAD SEEMED LIKE such a fine idea. Ten years to the day after the troops of North Vietnam marched into Saigon, Koppel would be there—live—from what was no longer Saigon but Ho Chi Minh City. After weeks of negotiations, Koppel would be interviewing one of the most famous diplomats of the late 1960s and early 1970s: North Vietnam's representative to the Paris peace talks—Henry Kissinger's nemesis—Le Duc Tho.

The negotiations to book Le Duc Tho were an omen. Rick Kaplan knew that later. "I spent seven hours with Le Duc Tho's assistant convincing him to have Le Duc Tho do the program. He wanted to know the questions. We don't give anybody questions. Le Duc Tho's assistant stands up at one point and takes something we said wrong, and he says, 'Your B-52's did not intimidate me. You won't either.' "

Le Duc Tho finally consented. Kissinger eventually agreed to appear from New York. Le Duc Tho and Henry Kissinger, co-winners of the 1971 Nobel Peace Prize, together again for the first time.

Kaplan made arrangements for parity. Since Kissinger couldn't be face-to-face with Koppel, neither would his counterpart in Vietnam. Le Duc Tho would be placed in the Caravelle Hotel, near Koppel, where an aide seated at Le Duc Tho's side would hear Koppel's questions through an earpiece and translate them for Le Duc Tho. Then Le Duc Tho's answers would be fed into a nearby booth, where they would be rendered into English by a second interpreter. Thus, neither Kissinger nor Le Duc Tho would have an advantage. That was the point.

Meanwhile, Koppel needed a set that said "Vietnam." The decision was made for him to be seated outside, with Ho Chi Minh City behind him. A set was built for Koppel on the roof of the Caravelle. The only problem was that since the broadcast would air live, at 11:30 P.M. East Coast time, it would be 11:30 A.M. in Vietnam. Koppel would be broadcasting from atop a high-rise building in Southeast Asia with the sun directly overhead. But how bad could it be, the thinking went, for just one show?

Bad.

On April 29, 1985, Koppel sat under a blazing sun on the roof of the Caravelle Hotel and opened the broadcast:

KOPPEL: It is their big moment. Ten years to the day since the
            armies of North Vietnam and the National Liberation
            Front—the Vietcong—marched into Saigon and took
            final control of the whole country. It is that moment
            which is being celebrated here today with this parade in
            what is now known as Ho Chi Minh City.

Not a minute into the broadcast, Koppel thought he was being
burned alive. It wasn't just the sun. The set included several enormous
electric suns—lights so huge and strong they're called brutes—which
were required to combat the problem of shadows. The brutes kicked
the ambient temperature up to somewhere around the melting point
of lead.

Koppel began a Q and A with correspondent Richard Threlkeld,
who was covering the victory celebrations. By now any viewer could
see that Koppel was hot. His sweat glistened in the light of the fierce
brutes.

Koppel introduced his first guest:

KOPPEL: Mr. Le Duc Tho, you have spent a lifetime as a revolu-
            tionary, a lifetime fighting in one war after another. Is it
            all over now? Have you achieved what you set out to do?

                          (silence)

Koppel's question had to be translated. The viewers at home
couldn't hear the translation into Vietnamese; all they could see was
Le Duc Tho sitting there, apparently looking off-camera at someone.

KOPPEL: Mr. Le Duc Tho?

LE DUC THO: (answers in Vietnamese)

                          (pause)

INTERPRETER: I can say that we are quite satisfied with what we have
               achieved, yes.

The pace was glacial. Thirty seconds into the interview, one
would have thought it was time to say good night. Maybe one just
wished it. Although no one could—or was even meant to—hear the

aide who was feeding the questions in Vietnamese to Le Duc Tho, the interpreter who was translating the answers into English was, unfortunately, a woman with a soft voice—a voice that might have been perfectly audible had it not been for the sound of the wind, which whipped across the roof and hissed into Koppel's open microphone.

Koppel turned to Kissinger, who already looked annoyed.

KOPPEL: Dr. Kissinger, I guess the question I have to ask you at this point, as one sits here in Saigon there is a sense of inevitability. Did it always seem this inevitable?

KISSINGER: No, it didn't seem that inevitable to me—nor to any of our associates.

KOPPEL: Why was it that it took so long from the time that negotiations began—I realize they began first between you and Xuan Thuy and then only later on between you and Le Duc Tho. Why did it take so long for the negotiations to come to a conclusion?

KISSINGER: It took so long because Le Duc Tho and his associates wanted victory and we wanted a stalemate. We simply wanted to have South Vietnam under a non-Communist government and we had an enormous domestic opposition which was very skillfully exploited. But I frankly do not want to refight the Vietnam War on this program, as I've made clear repeatedly.

Kissinger wasn't just annoyed now, he was starting to give threatening, heavy-lidded looks sideways, to someone on the edge of the set, a *Nightline* booker no doubt. Kissinger clearly thought he had been duped about the subject matter, and he was indicating he wanted to leave.

KISSINGER: Well, I think there is something demeaning about having three networks covering a victory parade over the United States in the city of the country where the victory was achieved . . .

But is a tirade a tirade if the host hasn't heard it?

KOPPEL: Dr. Kissinger, you'll have to forgive me because the audio
                 from the United States right now is very garbled and I'm
                 not sure if I heard the entire answer to my question.

Kissinger tried again, turning now to a substantive analysis of
U.S.-Asian relations.

KOPPEL: Dr. Kissinger, as I said a moment ago, I'm afraid the
                 audio quality from New York right now is very bad, so
                 we will be rejoining you later in this program.

Oh, this was just fine. Koppel not only couldn't hear one half of
his all-star guest lineup, by now he was "sweating like a pig. It was
hotter than hell, humid as hell, and then those brutes made it even
hotter."
He went back to Le Duc Tho.

KOPPEL: Mr. Le Duc Tho, how do you evaluate relations be-
                 tween the United States and your government? Non-
                 existent?

LE DUC THO: The relation of the U.S. with Vietnam right now is not
                 yet a normal relation.

Uh-oh.

KOPPEL: I'm sorry. At this point I'm having tremendous difficulty
                 with our audio here, even within Vietnam.

Now he couldn't hear Le Duc Tho! The man was less than fifty
feet away, and Koppel couldn't hear him. He couldn't hear Kissinger.
He couldn't hear *anybody*. He was frying in the sun and he couldn't
hear anybody.
The show wasn't even half over, so Koppel didn't have much
choice but to try again. He asked Le Duc Tho something about relations with the United States. There was another lull while the first
interpreter finished giving the question to Le Duc Tho in Vietnamese,
and another lull while Le Duc Tho responded, until finally Koppel
heard the soft voice of the woman interpreting the answer back into

English. And then the answer went on, and on, and on. The answer went on "for about nine hours," as Koppel later recalled it.

Suddenly Le Duc Tho turned cantankerous; like Kissinger, he too now intimated he'd been duped about the topic of the broadcast.

LE DUC THO: I think you should—we could touch upon the things that we debated, we discussed yesterday.

Koppel tried a question about Chinese expansionism; Le Duc Tho ignored it.

LE DUC THO: You once asked me about negotiations in Paris.

(*booming sound, followed by sound of glass breaking*)

The lights. The brutes. They were tipping over in the wind now and exploding.

Le Duc Tho, meanwhile, tucked away in a booth, rambled on, oblivious of the turmoil.

LE DUC THO: Now I wish that you would ask me the question about those negotiations and then we can move on to the other areas that you are interested in.

KOPPEL: All right, well, would you be good enough just to respond to that question and then we'll go to a break and when we come back we will talk about the Paris negotiations.

Behind Koppel now, competing with the wind, the traffic, and the parade, was the distinctive sound of glass being swept.

LE DUC THO: Let us return to the Paris peace talks first, so let us do that.

KOPPEL: Mr. Le Duc Tho, you are giving great evidence of the stubbornness that you showed throughout some of these negotiations.

Koppel had over half an hour left. This was, after all, supposed to be a historic broadcast. But it was Le Duc Tho's show now. Once he

turned to the Paris peace talks, he seemed not to inhale. Koppel realized he had a new problem, a big problem, bigger than exploding brutes. He tried to interrupt Le Duc Tho, but Le Duc Tho couldn't
hear him. Only Le Duc Tho's interpreter could hear Koppel, since he
was the one translating Koppel's questions into Vietnamese. But the
interpreter refused to convey Koppel's interruptions to Le Duc Tho.

The Vietnamese had insisted on an interpreter from their foreign
ministry, and no one had really thought too much about it—until
now. "The guy sitting next to Le Duc Tho," said Koppel later, "was
also working for Le Duc Tho. And the interpreter was no fool. He did
not work for me. He worked for Le Duc Tho. And damned if he was
going to interrupt the boss for this guy who's just visiting. So he refused to interrupt. I had no way of cutting in."

Next, Koppel got word through his earpiece that even though he
still couldn't hear Kissinger, Kissinger could hear Le Duc Tho and was
slamming his hands down on the arms of his chair. He was demanding to know how long Le Duc Tho would be allowed to filibuster.
Koppel was on the air. "I had no way to get them to tell Kissinger to
calm down because I had no control over the thing."

KOPPEL: All right, you will have to forgive me, Mr. Le Duc Tho.
               I'm sorry to interrupt at this point (*Le Duc Tho continues*),
               but I'm afraid we cannot spend the entire—

               (*Le Duc Tho continues; English interpreter also continues;
               they're still on the Paris peace talks*)

KOPPEL: Forgive me, I wish the interpreter would interrupt Mr.
               Le Duc Tho. (*voice of Le Duc Tho continues underneath
               Koppel*) Please. (*camera cuts to Le Duc Tho still talking*) I'm
               afraid we're not going to be able to spend this entire time
               talking about the Paris peace negotiations . . . We're
               going to take a break.

               (*Le Duc Tho's Vietnamese is still audible during fade to
               commercial*)

Kaplan was running the show from a makeshift control panel situated at the other end of the same large room where Le Duc Tho and

his interpreter sat. During the commercial, Kaplan shouted over to the interpreter, "Will you please make Le Duc Tho shut up?"

"*You* make him shut up," the interpreter hissed back.

By now producers in the New York control room who could see Kissinger on a monitor were placing bets as to whether or not he would leave.

It got worse. After a commercial, Le Duc Tho finally agreed to move off the Paris talks and on to the current issues of MIAs and Vietnam's relations with its neighbors. It hardly mattered by then. He complained about sanctions, and about Chinese expansionists in Kampuchea, and whatever else he wanted to talk about.

LE DUC THO: (*voice of interpreter*) We are demanding equal treatment. . . . Every year there are hundreds of Americans coming into Vietnam . . . even our famous pianist, Dang Thai Son, who'd already signed a contract . . . and there should be facilitating conditions about the U.S. . . .

KOPPEL: Let me just—

After what seemed an eternity on the issue of relations with Kampuchea, Le Duc Tho paused just long enough to give Koppel the chance to say the interview was over. Le Duc Tho started up again. He had a word for "the American people."

LE DUC THO: On the occasion of the celebration of ten years of liberation of the south, we wish to profess gratitude to the American people for their support and contribution to our present victory. We hope that all the American wives and mothers will never again allow their husbands and sons to go to die in another Vietnam War anywhere in this world. We hope that the friendship relations between our two peoples will grow ever more, and we hope that the normalization of relations between our two countries will come soon so as to pave the way for the growth of relations of friendship and cooperation between our two peoples. May the American people live in peace and happiness. Thank you.

Then this:

> I'm Charles Gibson in Washington, and what you are
> seeing is the uncertainty of live television in many of its
> facets. And because of technical problems we have lost
> our satellite contact with Ted Koppel in Vietnam for a
> moment and we're trying to reestablish contact. But
> with us now is former secretary of state Henry Kissinger.

That's what viewers got. What Koppel got was: "Ted? This is
Rick. Our satellite is down. The States can't see us."

Charles Gibson, who had been asked to stand by in Washington
for precisely this contingency but who, as he watched the program,
had begun to pray that none of it would fall to him, was fated nevertheless to bear the brunt of Kissinger's wrath:

KISSINGER: I think what we saw is a defeat which we inflicted upon
ourselves. And it is quite significant that Le Duc Tho
thanked his American supporters at the end of his remarks . . . And I must say that the difficult portion in
this program between the American point of view and
the Vietnam point of view and the absolutely one-sided
account of the correspondents is one of the explanations
of how we got to where we are. And I don't see any
point in engaging in a long debate in the two minutes
that are left.

GIBSON: Well, we have more than two minutes, and I don't want
to engage in a debate at all. . . .

KISSINGER: But I won't repeat—I hate to do this on the air. I said before I went on the air that I saw no point on the tenth
anniversary of the withdrawal from Saigon for an American to debate the Vietnam War, and I'm not going
to do it.

GIBSON: I don't want to re-debate the war, but when you watch
Le Duc Tho, that is the first exposure, I would expect—

KISSINGER: Well, that's *your* problem—

GIBSON: —that many Americans have had to him.

KISSINGER: I was told you were going to discuss the future. This has
              not happened. But I think we should drop it at this point.

Now Gibson was holding up a hand, as if to say, Enough! This isn't
even my show! I don't even want to *be* here!

GIBSON: Well, let's move to it. I just couldn't let his style go with-
               out comment and the way he, in effect, decided what his
               agenda would be in talking to Ted and simply plowed
               ahead with that, come what may.

KISSINGER: Well, that's what we did experience.

For Koppel the final indignity was the news that the satellite was
working again and that he could rejoin the discussion. After a couple
of tense exchanges with Kissinger about negotiating with revolution-
aries and about negotiating on behalf of a democracy, Koppel ended
the pain and said good night from Ho Chi Minh City.

When the show moved to its next stop in Thailand, Kaplan was
informed that it would please his hosts if a Buddhist monk blessed the
set. Kaplan was more than happy to oblige. After Vietnam, the monk
couldn't hurt.

ANYTIME INTERPRETERS WERE INVOLVED, the chances of
a *Nightline* broadcast going awry escalated dramatically. One night
there was an especially nervous interpreter in New York who, when
the moment came to translate into English, froze. Years later, no one
remembered anymore who the guest was, only that he spoke Italian.
The interpreter was in a soundproof booth separated by a window
from the control room, where Kaplan was seated.

After Koppel's first question to the guest, when it came time for
the translator in the booth to put the answer into English, there was
silence. Koppel wondered if he was the only one not hearing the
interpreter. He wasn't.

Kaplan couldn't go into the booth where the interpreter sat, because the mike was open. What everyone in the control room remembered was that Kaplan walked up to the window of the booth,

leaned his six-foot-seven-inch frame against it, pressed his hands to the glass, and pleaded, "Translate! Please! *Translate!*" They also remembered the interpreter's frightened expression when he looked up and saw this large man splayed against the glass, yelling something that was impossible to understand from inside a soundproof booth.

WHAT MAKES A bad show? "There are, after all, a number of things that can happen in the course of half an hour to make the show bad," said Koppel. "I can be off. Guests can be off. The piece can be off. The subject can be off. And sometimes, when you're really lucky, all four are."

"Herpes Night" was one of those shows. The subject was children with herpes. Koppel and his guests had waded deeper and deeper into a swamp of misunderstanding.

KOPPEL: But the more serious herpes, herpes simplex two—

DOCTOR: I'm sorry. Herpes simplex two is not the more serious, sir. There is no difference between herpes simplex one or herpes simplex two when it affects any part of the body. They both can cause the same type of either no disease, mild disease, or severe disease. In a baby, for instance, either type one or type two herpes causes the same disease.

KOPPEL: All right, Doctor, it is, I am sure, my fault, but I am more confused now than I was when we began this program.

A parent chimed in that her child had neither strain "one" nor "two," but a totally different strain.

Koppel kept trying, but "no matter what I asked, the person giving the answers just made it more complicated, more opaque, more dense, more difficult to understand than it had been before." He eventually turned to another parent, who wanted children with herpes barred from her children's school:

KOPPEL: You have heard what the doctor has had to say. I must confess, I'm still a little bit confused. But perhaps with everything you have heard before, you understand that apparently there is little or no danger to your children. Is that what you understand?

PARENT: Yes and no. It kind of comes back to me as more confusion, just like it got to you—

KOPPEL: Why have you kept your children out?

PARENT: Because I don't feel it's right that they should be, oh, how to say, put up against this. It's not fair to them and it's not fair to the child that has the virus himself.

KOPPEL: All right. But, I mean, I assume that your school district, or at least this particular school, has gone to the trouble of bringing a doctor in to answer parents' concerns. Have they done that?

PARENT: Yes, they did.

KOPPEL: And what did the doctor tell you?

PARENT: He scared us to death. He told us—

KOPPEL: Why?

PARENT: He told us that we all have had it. He did make that very clear. He said that he's sitting there in front of people that probably are just secreting with it now. And that was scary.

KOPPEL: Even though you've made it through life fairly well. I mean, in a sense, obviously doctors mean that to be reassuring. If so many of us have had it, and if by the time we reach middle age we have overcome it, then clearly it is not that horrible disease that we're thinking of. And, indeed, you just heard Dr. Nahmias say that we're not talking here about genital herpes.

PARENT: Right. Yeah.

KOPPEL: But you're still scared.

PARENT: Yes.

Koppel was feeling scared too. He was scared he had just taken a common virus and turned it into something inscrutable and terrifying to parents everywhere. So he tried one last time to demystify a story about a baby with herpes, and he got confused all over again.

KOPPEL: Should we go back to calling them cold sores again? Would that be one answer?

DOCTOR: No. Because apparently that baby did not have cold sores. It had herpes as a baby, which is different from a cold sore.

"It just got worse and worse," Koppel recalled. With only forty seconds left to try to calm the audience, Koppel described herpes as "a relatively mild disease," and the doctor tried to reinforce that fact to a frightened parent.

DOCTOR: Sir, it is all over the medical literature. And I'm sorry you have not been able to see it, but it's there.

PARENT: That's part of the problem, is education.

KOPPEL: I guess it is, and I apologize if we have done an inadequate or certainly an incomplete job. I thank all of you for joining us this evening. Try not to worry. I suppose that's the best we can do at this point.

"*Try not to worry*"? "*That's the best we can do?*"
Koppel and Kaplan commiserated after the show. How could they leave the audience more confused than when they began? They agreed they would have to do something. "Where is it written," one of them said to the other—years later, neither remembered who said it—"that we can't do the show again and try it with a couple of guests who can actually give decent answers?"

"First, do no harm," says the Hippocratic oath. The following *Nightline* began thus:

KOPPEL: We have rarely, if ever, done this before. But our program last Friday evening on the subject of children and herpes apparently succeeded in raising more questions than it answered and alarming more people than it reassured. Those of you who didn't see the broadcast, don't worry. You're probably better off. Those of you who did, give us another chance. We're about to try it again.

With the help, in particular, of Dr. Tim Johnson, ABC's medical correspondent, the second show, at the least, did no harm. Some people thought it even made sense.

A BAD SHOW IS one thing. A bad year isn't quite so funny. Nineteen eighty-three was the Year of Bad *Nightlines*. Actually, the experiment to stretch the broadcast to an hour only lasted seven months, but it felt like a year, and it yielded results that were, for the most part, "truly awful," according to Bill Lord. He should know. He was executive producer at the time.

The push to extend *Nightline* past midnight occurred when the network's most recent attempt at developing a program to follow *Nightline* failed. Roone Arledge concurred with network executives that *Nightline*'s loyal viewers might not want to commit to a whole new program at midnight but that they might stay up for more of *Nightline*. The show was by now an established hit. Extending it to an hour each night made sense. "We went to an hour because we thought it would be successful," said Arledge. "The show was doing very well and it was still fresh and new and people liked it and the other things weren't working. So it seemed a logical thing, first of all, because the program was good. Second, we could hold viewers over the midnight hour with it."

Koppel knew that such a change meant altering the format. *Nightline* would have to give up its one-theme-a-night approach. "There are only some nights when you can really use an hour for a subject. But if you've got a dozen of those a year, you're doing pretty well. Most nights you can't really do an hour on anything. It's not fascinating—especially at that time of night. And so we just figured, all right, well, instead of doing just one subject a night, we'll do three subjects a night."

Three subjects a night, five nights a week, equals fifteen subjects a week. It was only a matter of days before the broadcast was stretching for interesting topics—topics like "Organic Gardening," "Baldness," "The World Series of Poker, "Cats."

"If you're doing, let's say, twenty-five minutes on the big news of the day, we had the feeling that you needed to put something softer in, a little more featurish, just to give some pacing to the hour," Koppel explained. "And I think that's where we really lost it."

The subjects were so diverse that to watch a whole hour was to submit to intellectual whiplash.

KOPPEL: We'll try to find out how serious the danger from dioxin really is. Also tonight, romance novels. Half a billion dollars' worth are sold every year. And we'll look back at some of the highlights of the flight of the space shuttle *Challenger*.

One broadcast included segments on skin cancer and tanning, the deaths of journalists in Honduras, and post-traumatic-stress syndrome in Vietnam veterans. Another hour began with a story on minorities and achievement, followed by ten minutes on the British elections, after which Koppel interviewed a heroic air traffic controller, and then the winner of the National Spelling Bee. Suddenly *Nightline* resembled a morning program, only not as organized, and certainly not as happy.

Nightline viewers, then and now, tend to be a clever bunch, often cleverer than the folks who bring them *Nightline*. A jumble of topics suggested to viewers that there wasn't any single pressing story worth losing sleep for. The audience began to tumble off, or perhaps drowse off.

What worried Arledge was that Koppel's live interviews, which had become the centerpiece of the half-hour *Nightline*, were being applied to the silliest subjects: "I was afraid that the whole concept would become a caricature." After about seven months, Arledge laid the one-hour experiment to rest and *Nightline* returned to its original half-hour format.

WHICH IS NOT to say the show never tanked again. One broadcast went from dull to stupefyingly dull because of Koppel's insistence on repeating at regular intervals what a loser of a show it was, right on the air. He did everything but yawn on camera. His guests rightfully found him a bit rude.

The original theme for the program—at least as the guests understood it—wasn't all that bad. The idea was to examine the "style" of the Bush presidency—to review how, over the course of his first year in office, President Bush's personality had manifested itself in his leadership. The subject was certainly an appealing alternative to the historically soporific ritual known as the State of the Union address to Congress, which would air just a couple of hours before *Nightline*. For ten years, now, *Nightline* had tried to follow up the State of the Union message with some examination of it. None had ever worked. Koppel laid the blame on the predictability of the ritual. "Usually, the State of the Union address is an exercise in caution. The President tries as best he can to say things that aren't going to piss too many people off at the same time. So the addresses don't very often lend themselves to interesting follow-up shows." Brit Hume, ABC's White House correspondent, shared the sentiment but would word it a little differently: "The last memorable State of the Union address was given by Gerald Ford when he said, 'The State of the Union is not good.' Other than that one night, it's always been a dreadfully dull event." So when Hume was invited to come on *Nightline* to *not* talk about the evening's message to Congress but about Bush's first year, he said fine.

Nightline correspondent Jeff Greenfield was actually rather excited about the show. He had cajoled two of the newer stars in journalism to appear live with him and Hume from a Washington studio: Alessandra Stanley, a senior political correspondent for *Time* magazine, and Maureen Dowd, the White House correspondent for *The New York Times*. Stanley and Dowd were of the new generation of reporters who wrote about not just what a politician said but how he said it. Dowd in particular was considered something of a pioneer in "personalizing" the presidency. She had an eye for Bush's odd, revealing gestures. Greenfield knew that Dowd could toss out lines like Dorothy Parker, which might explain, in retrospect, why he got a little carried away with his vision of some new electronic version of the Round Table. Somehow—he wasn't thinking so much of Hume, now—it would be Greenfield sitting between "these two really bright, bright women," exchanging witticisms and clever political banter.

Dowd was apprehensive. She worried that Koppel might throw a curve into the conversation by moving it toward his favorite topics and not hers, like nuclear-weapons issues or something. But Stanley, her good friend, told her it would be "fun." The theme, Stanley pointed out, was their cup of tea. Dowd had written a lot about Bush's "preppy" imprint on the White House. "Come on," Stanley said. "We'll have a good time."

So that evening, after confirming once more with a *Nightline* booker that Koppel was not, absolutely not, interested in anything from the State of the Union, Dowd sat in the *Times* newsroom preparing some notes for the broadcast. She thought of a few snappy phrases that depicted the "Bush style," she culled a few good anecdotes about Bush's relationship with the press, and at some point, she realized she was having fun preparing for the show and decided that it just might be an enjoyable night. The voice of the President addressing Congress droned on a television in the background. Dowd heard him say something about troop cuts in Europe, which was sort of a surprise, but she paid scant attention to the details. She could do that tomorrow. She had to prepare for *Nightline,* after all. No sense in not being prepared. But to be on the safe side, Dowd called one of the *Nightline* bookers once more, just to make certain that Koppel didn't want to talk about what Bush had told Congress. "Don't worry," the booker answered, "Ted has no interest in discussing the military budget. This show is not going to be about the State of the Union."

When Greenfield walked into the studio that night, there were Dowd and Stanley, both of whom, he thought, looked smashing, even glamorous, and he felt pumped up all over again. "I thought, This is gonna be great. It will sort of be like . . . Tony Orlando and Dawn."

It was not Tony Orlando and Dawn.

Koppel seemed to have forgotten the theme. He led his guests almost immediately into the conversational equivalent of a desert. His first questions were so dry they were parched. "How solid is Bush's approval rating?" "To what extent is Bush committed to being the education President?" "Is there an inner toughness to Bush?"

Hume tried to muster up some decent responses. Stanley tried. Dowd tried. Greenfield tried. But all four looked a little stunned, as if they wanted to shout, "Come *on,* Ted!" to the lifeless queries. Within minutes the show seemed to have no "there" there. In fact, it seemed to have no Koppel there. For a "chat" segment, things seemed to be getting awfully quiet.

Hume finally tossed out some meat just to get Koppel's juices flowing: Bush, Hume noted, had surprised everyone with his announcement of troop cuts in Europe. Koppel took it . . . and tossed it to Dowd.

KOPPEL: Maureen, how important is that going to be, both in terms of what it signals about the U.S. presence in Europe and in terms of—

Uh-oh, thought Dowd. *Is he going where I think he's going? This can't be happening . . .*

—we keep hearing about the peace dividend—

The military? The budget? What happened to the "Bush style"?

—if you bring back 65,000 or 75,000 troops from central Europe, what does that translate to in terms of big bucks?

Dowd felt she was in the middle of an "exam nightmare, where you go into class to take a test and you can't answer the questions. But with a nightmare, you wake up. And I couldn't wake up. I felt like about five years passed before I opened my mouth and babbled something about Gorbachev and Bush." In fact, Dowd managed a deft bit of speculation, suggesting that Bush had used the announcement of the troop cuts to steal attention away from Gorbachev. But when Koppel asked her if that wouldn't be "silly" of Bush to do, Dowd sagged and Hume stepped in to rescue her, like a big brother, by interrupting that it "wouldn't be silly if you were in the administration."

Koppel now latched the conversation onto the State of the Union, the one subject the program had been arranged to avoid. He ticked off issues from Bush's speech and asked Stanley to comment on them, which she did, but her eyes were as wide as a deer's. Dowd looked devastated, and a fog of silence descended on the conversation.

Greenfield, like the nervous host of a bad party, struggled to fill in the lulls:

GREENFIELD: Could I just mention one quick thing? What happened to the war on drugs?

Had this been a cocktail party, Greenfield might have been the guy shouting, "I know, let's play Charades!"

Hume, playing the role of a gracious guest, picked up on the issue of drugs and offered a pertinent response. So now Hume and Greenfield gamely lobbed the issue back and forth for a minute, still trying to make a go of having a decent time, when the host interrupted:

KOPPEL: I'm sitting here watching and listening to you folks for a moment, and I have the sense, as I suspect some of our viewers do, that all of us are kind of winding down on the subject. We have barely filled, you know, fifteen minutes, talking about George Bush, and talking about George Bush's speech, and we've sort of run out of things to say. What does that tell you?

Greenfield's reaction: "I was ready to kill him." They still had half a show left to do, and Koppel was pronouncing it dead—live. What were the four supposed to do now? Get up and leave? Nothing like having the host of the party announce that it's a dud right in the middle of it. Dowd noticed how quiet everything seemed. She thought it all would work as an episode of *Tales from the Crypt*.

Hume for some reason tried one last time to revive things with a piquant analysis of Bush versus the Democrats. Then Greenfield and Stanley made a valiant effort to draw something interesting out of the very fact that Bush really was kind of boring to the public. Dowd decided to just clam up and pray for midnight to come quickly. But now the host was on to another theme. His new theme was that the show was a disaster.

KOPPEL: We're going to take another break. We'll catch fire when we come back in a moment.

Koppel didn't want viewers to think that *he* thought the show was any good. He would later offer the lame explanation that "every once in a while I sort of have this feeling that if I don't say something about how boring it is, there are going to be a thousand letters saying it, but if I admit it, then the viewers will say, All right, well, at least you recognize it was a boring show and you won't do it again."

So after a commercial, Koppel made sure that viewers would

understand. He indicated that not only did he recognize that the show was a flop, he had worried all day that it would flop.

KOPPEL: Brit, I confess to you, and through you to our audience, that we sort of agonized on whether we should even do a show on the State of the Union tonight. . . . What, if anything, do you think is going to be remembered—I shudder to say a year from now—a week from now about this State of the Union address?

Hume did the smart thing: he conceded that State of the Union messages—and by implication shows about them—were historically dull. The only problem was that Hume didn't use up enough time. So, with a minute left, Koppel turned back to Dowd. All Dowd wanted now was to get off the air and go home and hide. But Koppel wanted her to elaborate on exactly how boring Bush's speech really was. *Is there no respite from this horror?* Dowd wondered. Somehow she managed to dredge up the observation that Bush used the word *freedom* a lot in his speech, and that his devotion to his family, and his emotions, seemed more genuine than those of his predecessor, Ronald Reagan.

But Koppel couldn't help himself:

KOPPEL: All right. All right, well, listen. I thank all of you, Alessandra, Maureen, and Brit and Jeff. We must do this again one day. . . . *Not too soon.*

Stanley's jaw dropped. Hume and Greenfield rolled their eyes. Dowd wasn't even sure she had heard Koppel correctly. Did he say, "Not too soon"? "It was a dreadfully rude thing to say," Koppel would admit later, smiling sheepishly, like an ornery adolescent. "It was very rude of me to say it to them . . . but you know, it really *was* a boring show."

Dowd and Stanley shuffled like zombies out of the studio. Greenfield sulked over his ruined dreams of witty banter, while Hume sought to console the two women, who seemed to be in shock. He thought it best to point out that at the very least, well, they looked good. "Maureen really did look wonderful that night," Hume would remember. "And it was all I could think to say . . . I just kept telling her, 'You know, Maureen, you've never looked lovelier.' "

After a few hours commiserating with Stanley in the bar of the Mayflower Hotel, Dowd, still in search of solace, drove to her sister's house, for which she had a key. Dowd crept into the bedroom where her sister was sleeping and shook her awake. "Was it really that bad?" Dowd asked softly.

"Yes. But your makeup looked good."

It wasn't long before both Stanley and Dowd received notes of apology from Koppel—"sweet" notes, according to the recipients. And it wasn't all that long before their friends tired of teasing the two reporters about that awful night. It did, however, take about a year before Dowd could watch *Nightline* again without wincing. And when a magazine ran a tribute to her erstwhile tormentor, Dowd couldn't resist the opportunity to torment him in return. She mailed the article to Koppel after underlining a reference to the anchor as a "gentle interrogator"; she had jotted next to it, as she recalled later, "something along the lines of, 'As *if*!' "

Still, Dowd would insist that her personal trauma on *Nightline* never affected her general "admiration" for the broadcast. Would she agree, then, to give another go to an interview? When Koppel called with one such invitation, she replied, "Mr. Koppel, you've taught me that television is not my medium." Koppel laughed and replied, "Bullshit!"

But as of this writing, Dowd has never appeared on *Nightline,* or on any other television program, again.

SOME OF THE TRULY bad shows weren't boring at all. They were mesmerizing, like watching a house burn down or watching someone fall slow-motion into a cake—live.

"The thing about *Nightline*," said Rick Kaplan, "a great *Nightline*, is that you're always on the edge. Because you never know what some guest is going to say next, or even what Ted's going to say next. And there is always that potential for an audio line to fail or for a camera to fail or for a satellite to explode—anything." Nothing, in fact, can muck up a broadcast more thoroughly than a technological glitch.

There was a period in the mid-1980s, for example, when you could just about guarantee a disaster on the Fourth of July. During Kaplan's reign as executive producer, bad shows on the Fourth became a sort of holiday ritual, almost a point of pride. "In a way," recalled Kaplan, "if a Fourth of July show had worked out, we would have been horribly disappointed, because it was kind of a tradition: we expected to walk into the valley of death and not necessarily come out. And that was okay."

Once, Koppel was to interview the author George Plimpton about his obsession with fireworks. Everyone at the show imagined how wonderful it was going to look because Plimpton would be standing in front of a fireworks display. But no one paused to consider the audio. So Koppel went to Plimpton, and behind Plimpton, viewers could see sparkles and rockets and glittering "spiders" exploding and cascading in the air. They could also hear lots and lots of noise.

KOPPEL: George, what is it that causes all of us, not just Americans, to love this notion of setting the sky on fire? What is it in our soul that makes us delight at that?

PLIMPTON: Well, Ted, I think it's a matter of—I'm sorry?

KOPPEL: No, I didn't—I've said all I was going to say. There was the question. You go with the answer now.

PLIMPTON: I'm having a very hard time hearing you. Forgive me. The traffic is roaring; my ears are somewhat gone from the fireworks. I think you asked me what this great love of fireworks is about. Is that right?

KOPPEL: That's close enough, George. Go with it.

PLIMPTON: Well, I think that it's a great art form. It's the eighth art. It is an art that really is a painting in the sky, if you will, and there's nothing really quite as magnificent in the fields of art. I'm sorry, I hear nothing but music and things breaking up here, so it's hopeless.

KOPPEL: Well, I'll tell you what, let's see if you can hear me now. Can you?

PLIMPTON: I can hear twenty-five voices speaking.

KOPPEL: All right. Well, I tell you what. See if you can focus on one.

Koppel would automatically cringe, even years afterward, at the memory: "He couldn't hear what I was saying and no one could hear what he was saying, because the damn fireworks were going off."

Not to worry! The second half of the broadcast would save it: a live concert in Texas, featuring Willie Nelson and Kris Kristofferson, both of whom were standing by to be interviewed. Their barbecue/concert had been under way since early afternoon . . . which meant that Nelson and Kristofferson stood on a stage enveloped by a horde of rowdy, hooting Texans, tens of thousands of whom had been drinking beer for close to eight hours straight. The rock band behind them wasn't feeling any pain either, and it had no intention of stopping its set while *Nightline* was on the air. Clearly, the *Nightline* staff had taken a collective mental holiday. Again, no one had asked the obvious question, which was, "If a concert is under way and the audience is likely to be—er—happy, and Kristofferson and Nelson are standing on the stage, near the band, a rock band that will be performing no doubt *not* softly, how are the two guys going to hear Ted?" Answer: "They're not."

KOPPEL: Joining us live now from South Park Meadows in Austin, where the celebration is being held, is Kris Kristofferson, one of the country music artists taking part in the festivities, and the man after whom this picnic is named, Mr. Willie Nelson. Willie, can you hear me?

KRISTOFFERSON: (*turning to Nelson*) He said good evening.

NELSON: Good evening.

KOPPEL: Good evening, that's very good. Kris, I tell you what, if you can interpret for me.

NELSON: We're having a good time over here. I can't hear a lot that's going on over there, but I hope everybody can understand. We're having a big time down here in Austin, Texas, for our Fourth of July picnic, and thanks for dropping in on us. Right, Kris?

KRISTOFFERSON: Well, we had a lot of great music.

KOPPEL: I'll tell you what, Kris. Why don't you send him back onstage, because he can't hear a thing anyway and we want to hear him sing in just a minute. Let's you and I talk for just a second. What is it, do you think, that brings thirty, forty thousand people in there to sit cheek by jowl for twelve hours in the sun? What kind of a celebration is that? (*pause*) I don't know what you guys are hearing, but it's not me, right?

KRISTOFFERSON: I think it's music, doing a lot of people here a lot of good, though. A lot of different people getting together. (*pause*) I feel stupid, Willie. Bail me out, man.

KOPPEL: I'll tell you what. Kris, can you hear me at all?

NELSON: Huh? I don't know. I don't know what happened.

KOPPEL: What we're trying here, I think, is beyond the power of television to handle. There's so much noise going on back there, you guys can't hear me at all, can you? (*silence*) Kris, if you can hear me in any way, why don't you tell Willie to get back onstage because I know he's going to sing in just a moment. I hope he's going to—

KRISTOFFERSON: The band is doing great out there.

NELSON: Great job out there.

KRISTOFFERSON: Yeah. There's a hell of a show going on out here.

KOPPEL: I'll tell you what. Why don't we take a look at it? I think we need to do that. Why don't we ask Willie to get back onstage, folks?

KRISTOFFERSON: Hey, that was great, Willie.

KOPPEL: There are some things, I think it goes without saying, that even live television cannot handle. This is one of them.

Settings explode. Technology explodes. On occasion guests explode, or implode. Most guests, though, are polite. Some are anxious. Once there was a young boy on a show about children and the fear of nuclear war. He had tried to calm himself down before the broadcast by doing breathing exercises, but by the time Koppel got to him, the boy was hyperventilating. He said "whew" a lot. On another show, "there was this kid from military school," Koppel remembered. "He was absolutely great in the warm-up. And then when the camera light went on, he just froze."

When the show is live and a guest tanks out, Koppel's usual safety net is another guest. But not on the legendary "Vegetable Night." The broadcast was about the censorship of books in schools. It featured a man from Texas named Mel Gabler, who, with his wife, had set up a clearinghouse that reviewed textbooks and books that might be in school libraries for offensive material. The other guest was a woman from the American Library Association's Office of Intellectual Freedom.

The conversation was taking a lively turn, as it usually does when *Nightline* focuses on censorship. Suddenly, the man from Texas held up a book, the sort of book he wanted banned. He then offered up a passage from the book, just to make clear exactly what it was he objected to. In other words, the man shared something he considered offensive and wanted banned with a couple of million viewers: "And this is a book," he said, "that we find in many public schools for the teaching of sex education, and so forth. For instance, it encourages women to masturbate using a peeled cucumber!" It remains one of the racier remarks ever made on *Nightline,* and it was made by a man advocating censorship.

How to respond? Sometimes that's what other guests are for. Koppel turned to the woman from the American Library Association in Chicago. Only one problem. "Ted?" It was Bill Lord in the control room. "Ted, we just lost the satellite to Chicago."

Koppel went to a commercial.

Afterward, Lord walked out of the control room and sighed. "I suppose I'll be hearing from the National Vegetable Growers' Association about this." He didn't.

But Koppel got a letter: "It was from a group of women from Smith College, thanking me for the information."

THEN THERE WAS the cosmonaut.

On the twenty-fifth anniversary of the launching of *Sputnik,* Koppel's guest was a veteran of the Soviet space program. Koppel remembered the man possessing "this adorable face. He looked like George Gobel. Crew cut. Cherubic. Ruddy cheeks. The sweetest childlike smile. And absolutely none of his answers bore any relationship to my questions."

KOPPEL: What to you is the most exciting thing about what has happened in space in the last twenty-five years?

(cosmonaut's eyebrows shoot straight up, as if yanked by a puppeteer; they drop back down, and his face opens into a broad, sweet smile)

COSMONAUT: Uh, today is twenty-five years I took part in the launch in the first official satellite, *Sputnik.*

KOPPEL: Where do you think we will be twenty-five years from now?

(cosmonaut's eyebrows shoot up again; he looks like someone pinched him)

COSMONAUT: Uh . . . I was twenty-six and very young engineer.

It dawned on Koppel that his guest understood no English.

Koppel desperately needed to giggle. The image of the cosmonaut's eyebrows inspired one of his own to twitch up and down until he forced it into an inverse arch. The Soviets had assured *Nightline* no interpreter would be necessary. They had said the cosmonaut spoke English, which was only true if you counted five or six pre-rehearsed sentences.

Koppel tried to ask another question while simultaneously trying to bite the inside of his cheek, which made it appear as though moments ago he'd received a shot of Novocain.

KOPPEL: Do you—

(cosmonaut's eyebrows shoot up again)

Koppel dropped his head to compose himself. His shoulders shook. The cosmonaut, who couldn't see Koppel, had no idea that his host was anything other than rapt. He pressed on.

COSMONAUT: As a young boy in Russia . . .

Koppel lifted his face to try to give the director a chance to cut to a shot of him listening, but the director, a wise man, stayed off it. Koppel was still trying to affect fascination, or at least interest, but now both eyebrows were cocked in odd shapes. One eyebrow suggested "I'm somber," the other suggested "I'm going to lose it."

In the control room, Bill Lord pointed out Koppel's monitor to other producers. Lord did not sound upset when he advised the room, "Watch Ted."

Now Koppel's mouth had this weird curl to it, which he tried to hide by tipping his head down and grinning oddly at his desk. He froze like that for an instant, pulled down the corners of his mouth, paused, and started to ask something when the cosmonaut cut him off and launched into another attempt at "It all began."

Koppel lost it and flopped over his desk like a rag doll. He didn't make a sound, but his whole upper torso heaved. The cosmonaut stumbled on. Lord couldn't say anything to Koppel, because Lord, too, was giggling uncontrollably. Koppel finally composed himself long enough to go to a commercial, at which point he yanked off his microphone, threw back his head, and howled.

Viewers never saw any of it. This was one of the rare interviews back in the early 1980s that wasn't live. Given the time difference between New York and Moscow, the interview was pre-taped. Which was why, Koppel later recalled, he allowed himself to let go. "If it had been live, I wouldn't have thrown it in."

Lord found something else to put in the broadcast, but the tape of the cosmonaut still exists. Copies of it get passed around on a slow day.

SEVEN
Koppel on
The Interview

T HE LIVE INTERVIEW on television is a different animal than any other kind of interview. A taped interview, conducted for later broadcast, can be edited so that if you've done something embarrassing, the producers and editors can keep that embarrassment from becoming public. But when you do something live, if you're great, you're great; if you stink, you stink.

There is a dynamic at work here. In a live format, you are doing more than conducting an interview. You're also thinking about how much time you have. Unlike a taped interview, a live interview requires you to ask the right questions within a finite period of time. Which means that instead of taping the interview and editing it later, you are quite literally editing the interview in your head. You have to keep several factors in your head. You're constantly thinking such things as, Let's see, we haven't gotten to the main parts of this yet, or, This is boring, we've got to cut this now, or, This man or woman is going on too long; they're not responding to the question.

June 9, 1988
Guest: Vice-President George Bush

BUSH: I mean, Ted, if you'll let me get on to some of the positive things about this administration.

145

KOPPEL: Well, I'll tell you what. You said we've got forty minutes. We don't have quite that long. I've still got a few questions on this issue, if you don't mind.

It's so much easier not to antagonize the guests when you're not live, because you can let them answer every question at length, which gives them the illusion that they're able to say anything they want to say. They don't know that you'll cut their words down later in the editing room. Same thing with a newspaper: you're going to cut them, but you'll cut them when you write the story. When you're doing a live interview on television, the cutting has to be done in front of everybody. If someone is going on too long, you can't say, "Cut," because it would sound rude or disrespectful. I'll say something like, "Sorry, we don't have all night," or, "We have a very short period of time left, and it seems to me we haven't addressed the most important issues." Over the years, I've used a hundred variations of that line, but they all amount to the same thing: cut, cut, cut.

April 25, 1986
Guest: Lyndon LaRouche, political activist

KOPPEL: Mr. LaRouche, I don't want to cut you off, but we've got an awful lot of territory to cover . . .

March 23, 1987
Guest: Robert Schuller, televangelist

KOPPEL: Dr. Schuller, forgive me, that is one of the longest and most eloquent evasions of a question I've ever had, but let me see if I can bring you back to the question.

There is a chemistry, a relationship that takes place among the viewer, the interviewer, and the interviewee. Almost inevitably, a viewer begins by identifying with the interviewer. The interviewer, after all, is your surrogate. If you're watching a television program, no matter who is being interviewed, the interviewer is the one who, if he or she is doing the job properly, is asking the questions that you wish would be asked. You want him to get to the point, and you want him to provoke the answers that you want to hear from the guests. So the interviewer starts off with the allegiance of the audience, but he can lose them. For example, if he jumps in too fast, if he seems to be pressing too hard, too early, if he seems rude, then he loses the allegiance or identification of the audience. So you'll find that for the first question or two, I usually let people ramble.

May 28, 1992
Guest: Daryl Gates, Los Angeles police chief

KOPPEL: Chief Gates is our guest tonight, and he joins me live here in our Los Angeles bureau. Chief Gates, let's see if we can begin on a note of agreement. Do you agree that there's a dysfunctional family, official family, here in Los Angeles?

GATES: Well, I think there are—through the past year there has been some unhappiness on the part of some of us. I think you've shown some of that. I've been unhappy with the mayor, he hasn't been happy with me, but that isn't just this past year, it's been for a long period of time. I don't think that's hampered anything, in spite of how much I disagree with the mayor. I think we have put together over the years a disaster plan in this city that's unparalleled anywhere in the United States. The mayor's been part of that, I've been part of that. We have a plan. I brought the plan, if you'd like to read it.

KOPPEL: Well, I mean, go ahead and show it, and tell me what's in it. (*Gates shows thick sheaf of paper*) That's obviously a very large plan.

GATES: Well, yes it is.

If I've allowed the guest to go on a little, if I've given him or her time to deliver perhaps a longer, maybe even slightly boring answer, then there comes the moment when I imagine the folks back home are saying, "Ted, come on, get in there!"

KOPPEL: And let me just ask you, before you, you know, flaunt all these pages in front of me here, Chief, is that the plan for the day the verdict came down on the Rodney King trial, the beating of Rodney King? Is *that* what the plan is?

GATES: See, one of the problems with people like you, Ted, is
          you don't know enough about what we do in dealing
          with unusual occurrences and disasters.

June 9, 1988
Guest: Vice-President George Bush

BUSH: Let's talk, you don't want to talk about the good stuff?
          You sound like—and I understand it—but you sound
          like Mike Dukakis and Jesse Jackson, pessimistic and
          everything.

KOPPEL: No. I'll tell you what, that's why I tried to say at the be-
          ginning of this program, and you recognize—

BUSH: You did, that's right.

KOPPEL: And you recognize this.

BUSH: I take that back, you—

KOPPEL: You're going to take the positive issues in your campaign
          speeches and your advertising. It's up to me to raise some
          of the negative ones.

March 28, 1983
Guest: Bo Gritz, former Green Beret

KOPPEL: You have spoken, Colonel Gritz—

GRITZ: Ted, let me respond, if you don't mind, because—

KOPPEL: No, I do mind, Colonel, because we're going to do this
          on my basis, if you don't mind.

November 9, 1989
Guest: Vitali Kobesh, Soviet commentator

KOBESH: Ted, tell me, would you like Germany to be united but
          friendly?

KOPPEL: I'll tell you what. When I come on your program I'll answer your questions; now you're on my program. You
answer mine, all right?

*I almost never have prepared questions in front of me. I don't believe in
preparing a list of questions ahead of time. I usually have an idea when I walk
into the studio about where I want to begin, but that's about it. The reason is,
I want to be engaged in a genuine conversation with my guests. And in a conversation, you listen to the other person; then your next question is provoked
by what the person has just said. So even when the executive producer is signaling in my earpiece that it's time for a commercial or when another guest is
waiting anxiously to join in, my job is to listen to the one guest who's speaking. A word, a nuance, or a casually uttered phrase might contain the most important information of the evening.*

March 24, 1987
Guest: The Reverend Jimmy Swaggart, television evangelist

SWAGGART: I felt that entire [PTL] debacle was a cancer that needed
to be excised from the body of Christ. It's a very painful
experience, but it was something that needed to be
done. . . .

KOPPEL: I'm assuming that what you're accusing Jim Bakker of is
sexual misconduct. Am I wrong on that?

SWAGGART: Are we're talking about the Jessica Hahn story?

KOPPEL: No, we're talking about what you said to me about five
minutes ago on this program.

SWAGGART: I did not tell you or anybody else what that conduct was.

KOPPEL: You said it was of the same kind—you said you didn't
know anything about the Jessica Hahn story but that
there were other incidents like that. Now, maybe I in-
ferred something you didn't—

SWAGGART: There were others—

KOPPEL: —but then you go ahead and straighten me out on it
right now.

SWAGGART: There were other similar incidents, but I will not state—
            say what they were. Because it was just rumored.

KOPPEL: Fine. Well, now, *wait* just a second. When you say it was
            just *rumored,* I want to get back to this one more time,
            and I apologize, because we've got Cal Thomas sitting
            by here, but he'll be joining us in just a moment.

Swaggart's use of the word rumored *had surprised me. Swaggart had
slipped up, revealing that he had spread unconfirmed gossip about a rival.
Sometimes all it takes to change the course of a conversation is a single, spon-
taneously chosen word.*

KOPPEL: When you say it was just "rumored," in other words you
            don't know these things to be fact?

SWAGGART: No, I do not know them to be fact.

KOPPEL: Well, then why in heaven's name did you pass it on to
            anyone?

SWAGGART: I didn't say that I passed it on to anyone except those
            gentlemen [the executive council of the Assemblies of
            God], because I felt there was some truth in it, but if
            there is not anything that you can prove, well, you don't
            accuse somebody of it, unless you can prove it.

KOPPEL: Well—

SWAGGART: —did not enter into any kind of investigation.

KOPPEL: I've got to tell you, Mr. Swaggart, before I would refer
            to you as a cancer that has to be excised from the body
            of Christ, based on that kind of thing, I would want to
            have more than rumor and innuendo to go on, and I as-
            sume you had more.

SWAGGART: Well, I felt I did have more, and I felt what I knew was
            factual, and I felt it was the truth, but I couldn't prove it.

KOPPEL: And you still can't.

SWAGGART: I don't really want to prove it at this particular time. It's
            not necessary to do so.

KOPPEL: Well, I, forgive me for bearing in on this, but it seems to me that there's an awful lot of mudslinging going on around here, and I'm simply asking you not to prove it at this point, not to go into specifics, but simply to tell me whether you think you have proof.

SWAGGART: I'm sorry, I didn't hear the last part of the question.

KOPPEL: Whether you think you have proof. I mean, that's different from saying you've heard rumors that you believe are true. Do you have proof? Do you know them to be fact?

SWAGGART: I told you that I did not have the proof, but as far as I am concerned, they are true. But I could not prove them and made no attempt to prove them.

When a guest is reluctant to divulge information, the interview can become the rhetorical equivalent of a treasure hunt, as demonstrated by the inscrutable guru known as Bhagwan Shree Rajneesh. In the early 1980s, Rajneesh, a native of India, was the spiritual leader of a free-love commune in Oregon whose members had seized political control of a nearby town. While Rajneesh luxuriated on a $60 million ranch, replete with a fleet of ninety Rolls-Royces, he avoided deportation by consistently denying that the cult was religious. One evening in 1983, Rajneesh appeared on Nightline *and told my colleague Charles Gibson, who was sitting in the anchor chair, that the commune members were not his "followers," only "friends." But not long after that appearance, the guru attempted to flee federal charges of fraud by chartering a private plane for Bermuda. He was arrested during a refueling stop in North Carolina. The next night he talked to me by satellite from jail.*

October 28, 1985
Guest: Bhagwan Shree Rajneesh

RAJNEESH: I have not left America.

KOPPEL: Well, you were trying to.

RAJNEESH: No.

KOPPEL: Well, Bermuda is not part of the United States, the last time I looked.

RAJNEESH: No. I was going to be somewhere in the United States.
            I don't know where my friends were taking me. . . .

KOPPEL: Bhagwan, I don't mean to be offensive, but I must tell
            you it stretches credulity that a man would get on an air-
            craft and not know where he's going.

RAJNEESH: I depend on my people for almost everything.

KOPPEL: What do you mean, your "people?" Your followers?

RAJNEESH: Yes.

KOPPEL: Yes. Your followers.

RAJNEESH: Yes.

KOPPEL: Now, I come back once again to a conversation you had
            with my friend Charlie Gibson less than a month ago.
            You swore up and down you had no followers.

RAJNEESH: You are calling them followers.

KOPPEL: I asked you. I asked you twice. That's why I repeated it.

RAJNEESH: You asked me, and I said yes, because those people think
            them followers. I think myself they are my friends.

KOPPEL: Well, it's more convenient to have them as your friends
            when in fact you're trying to deny that what you have is
            any kind of religion. But again, we're getting into legal
            complications now, because that's one of the hooks by
            which the state was coming after you, wasn't it?

RAJNEESH: That is no problem. As far as I am concerned they are my
            friends. And there is no religion.

Euphemisms—words like Bhagwan's friends *instead of* followers*—are
the tools of obfuscation. It is essential to bring them to light and to weed them out
of the conversation. In the end, the goals of every interview are the same: clear expression of thought and comprehensible arguments. If those fundamentals are
missing, it is the job of the interviewer to help the guest hone his or her response,
even if it means asking the same question again and again . . . and again.*

March 25, 1988
Guest: John Strauch, attorney for R. J. Reynolds Tobacco Co.

KOPPEL: If indeed it can be proved that thirty years ago or more you already knew what the dangers [of smoking] were, but did not warn the public, then you would have a liability, wouldn't you?

STRAUCH: Well, now that you bring up thirty years ago, let me point out that in 1954, in an interview in *U.S. News and World Report,* E. Kiler Hammond, who was the director of statistical research for the American Cancer Society, was bluntly asked, Does smoking really cause cancer? His answer to that was, That's what we're trying to find out.

KOPPEL: Yeah, look, Mr. Strauch, forgive me. We're not going to get anywhere if you're going to quote, you know, what the surgeon general or folks like him said thirty years ago—then you're also going to be stuck with what the surgeon general today says, and the surgeon general today is totally unambiguous on the subject. What I'm asking you is, if the defense of nonliability is that you had adequately informed the public of that danger thirty years ago, then you might be liable?

STRAUCH: Well, you know, that is a position that has been taken here, but that overlooks the fact that, as I started to say, if you have American Cancer Society people at that time doubting causation, certainly the industry ought not to be condemned for taking that point of view, and you've had twenty-some years of warning labels with people free to either smoke or not smoke as they choose.

KOPPEL: I must congratulate you, you evade answers about as elegantly as anyone I've ever had on the program, but this—

STRAUCH: Well, Ted—

KOPPEL: The question that I'm asking is not who else knew it but whether you folks knew it, whether the tobacco

industry knew it. I don't care what anyone else was saying in 1954.

STRAUCH: Well, all right, that's different. I think that's a different
question you've been putting, and the answer to that—

KOPPEL: No, it's precisely the question I've been putting. . . . Mr.
Strauch, call me a silly romantic fool, but I'm going to
try one more time. If you folks are not the ones that are
putting that message on the side of the cigarette packs, if
that's us, the public, which insisted that they do it, on
what basis then are you folks not liable if it can be proved
in court—and I recognize it hasn't been yet—if it can be
proved in court that the tobacco industry knew twenty-
seven years ago that it was dangerous?

STRAUCH: Oh, of course, I don't think that's going to be the case.

*Over the years, most of my interviews have been conducted electronically.
Some guests are halfway around the world; others are in the same Washington
building that I'm in, but in a different studio. The guests are asked to look
straight into a camera to address me, while my voice is fed to them through an
earpiece.*

*The uninitiated often complain that the format is unnatural. But on
evenings when there is more than one guest, the arrangement is pragmatic: it
gives me the ability to control the conversation and to keep it flowing. When,
as is often the case, there are several guests located at disparate points around
the world, no one has an advantage in getting my attention or in dominating
the debate. The director, meanwhile, will impose the faces of all of the participants on the screen, as if they are gathered in an electronic salon.*

*The effect, back in the early 1980s, was original, and so striking that it es-
tablished* Nightline *as a unique international forum. Over time, the format of
keeping me separated from my guests had become a hallmark of* Nightline, *so
it was not something that the show's producers were anxious to change. In fact,
up until 1987, face-to-face interviews were forbidden. ABC News president
Roone Arledge was worried that once we permitted them,* Nightline *would
look like every other program, and that if one guest got the privilege, every guest
would want it.*

But in the summer of 1987, Richard Harris, a Nightline *producer, began negotiating with former senator Gary Hart about the possibility of an interview. Senator Hart had ended his campaign for the presidency earlier that spring because of the controversy surrounding his relationship with Donna Rice. Now there were signs that Hart might reenter the race. He had yet to talk about the Rice affair. Hart told Harris that he would appear on* Nightline *if I would guarantee not to raise the subjects of Donna Rice and his marriage. At that point, I called Hart and said: "Look, Senator, there is no way that I can do an interview with you for half an hour without raising those issues. It's why you had to step down from being a candidate. And if you're thinking of coming back as a candidate, you can't do it without addressing the subject."*

Hart conceded that point. "But," he said, "if I'm going to be addressing that issue, I'm not going to do it sitting off in some other studio with an earpiece in my ear. You've got to acknowledge that that's a personal enough subject that I want to be able to look you in the eye when I do it."

And I said, "Fair enough. I think that's a legitimate point. But it's up to the president of the news division. I'll have to argue the point with him."

So I called Arledge and said, "Hart has agreed to the interview, and has agreed to answer a couple of questions pertaining to the relationship with Donna Rice, but he won't do it unless he can sit in the studio with me. And I think he's right. I think he has a fair point." And Roone said, "Go ahead."

September 8, 1987
Guest: Gary Hart

KOPPEL: I'm sure there are a great many of you watching tonight who are interested in hearing the thoughtful and substantive views that the senator is eager to share on the subject of defense and education, welfare and taxes, but I have no illusions, and I suspect Senator Hart harbors none either, that there are two questions in particular that most of you want to hear asked and answered. Both of them will be asked.

Senator Hart and I do share at least one common interest. We would appreciate the company of as many of you as possible beyond the first two or three minutes of this broadcast, so hang in there. The questions will be asked, but not just yet. . . .

(*to Hart*) First, let me ask, long before the name

Donna Rice was known in this country, the issue of womanizing was raised against you. It had been raised in 1984. It was something that, I am told, members of your staff raised with you and said, "You've got to reassure us that that's not going to happen again in 1988." Does that not make it a legitimate issue?

HART: . . . It is no secret, Mr. Koppel, in the twenty-nine-year history of our marriage, almost three decades, that we had two public separations. We have been open and honest about our relationship, or tried to be, and I think, perhaps more than almost any public figures in our society, have had to answer and have answered embarrassing questions about our relationship with each other and the nature of our marriage. Certainly there have been rumors. It is not unique to me. Rumors about public officials and Presidents have gone back, I think, to the beginning of the republic, certainly starting with Jefferson, maybe even Washington—certainly some of the best Presidents of the twentieth century have had rumors circulating about them. I think what was different in my case was that rumors became news last spring—that is to say, the facts that there were rumors were printed as news, and one or two news organizations, based upon tips or information they got, decided to set up surveillance, and I think come very near if not invade my own personal privacy to prove those rumors were true. Now, having said all that, I apologize for this long answer, but it is an important question.

KOPPEL: It was a long question.

HART: I made a serious mistake. I should not have been in the company of any woman not my wife who was not also a friend of mine or my wife. On the other hand, I, throughout my life, and including my public life, have treated women and men equally. And I've always had the opinion if I went out in public with those people that

that was my best defense against those rumors. I should
not have been with Miss Rice. That was a serious mistake.

*My assumption is always that the audience is listening closely. When I
ask a question, it's something I think the viewers want asked. I'm their representative.*

KOPPEL: Senator, I suspect, and we're going to take a break, because I'm going to come back to the issue, but I suspect
that there is a certain amount, and forgive me for putting
it so indelicately, but a certain amount of snorting and
thigh-slapping going on around the country right now
when you couch all of this in the context of, in effect,
equal rights, that you treat women as you treat men. . . .
Senator, we're not now talking about having men and
women for friends, we're talking about something that
certainly has about it every possible impression of im-
propriety. . . .

HART: I'm not a perfect man, Mr. Koppel. I'm a human. I commit sins. The Bible I read says we all commit sins, and
mine happen to be pretty visible.

KOPPEL: I told you some days ago when we spoke, and I told our
audience this evening, that I would ask you both questions. I will ask you the first now, just before we take a
break, because I think I know what your answer is going
to be. Did you have an affair with Miss Rice?

HART: Mr. Koppel, I was asked a question last spring which I
refused to answer, and your clip showed that. The articles to which you've referred have commented not only
on Miss Rice, but, I must say, an outrageous number of
people with whom I have been linked, a large number
of whom I have never met, let alone been involved
with. It has also been suggested that I don't tell the truth,
because I would not reveal all about my personal life.
And I've tried to figure out the best way to answer these
questions, not only for my sake, but for other elected

officials' sakes in the future, other candidates for national office, and so it seems to me I have no choice but to answer the question that was asked me last spring, and I will do that. If the question is, in the twenty-nine years of my marriage, including two public separations, have I been absolutely and totally faithful to my wife, I regret to say the answer is no. But I also am never going to answer any specific questions about any individual. I have no privacy. My wife has privacy and other innocent people have privacy, and I don't care what questions are asked tonight or any time in the future, I'm not going to answer them on any specific instance. Now, I've been made, I've been forced to make a declaration here that I think is unprecedented in American political history, and I regret it. That question should never have been asked, and I shouldn't have to answer it, but I will say to you this—I would say this to the national press corps—never ask another candidate that question. It isn't anyone else's business but that individual and his spouse or her spouse, and I think questions like that have the very real danger of seriously undermining the credibility, and the competence and quality, of our national leadership. We shouldn't ask those questions.

It later occurred to me that had Hart been afforded the rules of the interview used in Japan, then he would have been given a piece of paper before we started, with all of the questions written down. He could have looked at the piece of paper and have known those would be the only questions that would be asked. I think it's a particularly useless way of doing an interview, because it's not really an interview at all. The guest can just mail in the answers.

But even if the guest doesn't know all of the questions ahead of time, if only the interviewer has decided on what he or she will ask, then it's not an interview. The interviewer will not react at all to the odd or truly newsworthy statements the guest might be making.

KOPPEL: I would maintain, Senator Hart, that in most instances, the press tries very hard to be prudent about this kind of thing, to be evenhanded about this kind of thing, and I would—

HART: I wouldn't call hiding in bushes and attempting to put lis-
             tening devices on people's walls prudent and restrained.

KOPPEL: Now, who tried to put listening devices on your walls?

HART: I understand that's what one news organization tried to
             do to me.

KOPPEL: Did you ever find those listening devices, or is it just a
             rumor that you heard?

HART: I have reason to believe that the attempt was made, but
             the point is, new ground rules were drawn up here.

*Sometimes what's most critical to listen for isn't what the guest has said
but what he* hasn't *said. This was the case when I asked Hart the second of
the two questions that I'd touted at the top of the program:*

KOPPEL: Are you back in the race for President?

HART: Mr. Koppel, I'm not a candidate for President, and I'm
             not making any plans to become one, and I also want to
             say that I don't float trial balloons, it's not my style, and
             if I've got anything to say about running for office, I'll be
             the one to say it. . . . I care about this country. . . . The
             idea was never just to be President. It was to change the
             future and the direction of this nation. Now I've got to
             figure out a way to try to do that. . . . I am going to try
             and have an impact.

*Again, my assumption is that if an answer seems imprecise to me, it
probably seems imprecise to the audience. If I'm wondering about nuance, so
are they.*

KOPPEL: Now, I think you gave me a rather definitive answer, but
             I know there are going to be people out there sitting
             there saying, "That wasn't assurance. He left a crack
             open in the door." Do you do that deliberately?

HART: No. Well, I suppose I did, but not for, not for political,
             tactical games.

When, in fact, Hart did reenter the race three months later, my role was slightly different. This interview was not so much to hear him out but to hold him accountable for his statements to me and to the audience in September. My role had shifted even more into that of surrogate for millions of angry viewers.

December 15, 1987
Guest: Gary Hart

KOPPEL: Senator Hart, I suspect you've been too busy today to be able to listen to a lot of radio talk shows. I heard a number driving to and from work, and I must tell you, at least here in this town—and this is Washington, D.C. and you're not running here right now—but [there is] outrage at what is perceived as your arrogance in putting yourself forward as you have now as a leader who stands above and beyond what these other six Democratic candidates have to offer, particularly in the area of moral leadership. Now if you were confronting one of those outraged persons, and you're confronting some of them tonight, what do you tell them?

HART: Well, first of all, I haven't sought to put myself above the other candidates, perhaps apart from them a little on the issues, but under no circumstances would I want anyone to think that I was attempting to suggest that I was above anyone else. . . . We're going to do our best, and we'll reach out, but whatever candidacy I have, as I said today, is based upon the power of ideas. And I can't see how that power can threaten anyone.

KOPPEL: Senator, forgive me. There's a certain hypocrisy inherent in what you're saying here. If, on the one hand, you don't believe that you have any chance knocking these guys off, then there's not much point in getting into it. And if, on the other hand, you do believe you can knock them off, then you've got to be able to understand that they're a little bit resentful at this late date, of Gary Hart suddenly rising from the grave and coming back again.

Anyone who is running for office is fair game as far as I'm concerned. I'm not addressing him as a private individual. I'm not talking to him in his capacity as a human being. I'm addressing the candidate, the one who is asking the public to elect him.

October 8, 1987
Guest: Pat Robertson, presidential candidate

ROBERTSON: The unit where I served was on the border of North Korea. We were about 2.7 miles off the so-called front.

KOPPEL: Seoul is only a few miles from the border of North Korea, Mr. Robertson. . . . I want to ask you straight out, I mean, you know and I know what combat is, and I'm not asking you were you within range of artillery shells, were you in combat? Were you out in the trenches?

ROBERTSON: Ted, I'm sorry, but the brave people who support a combat division—there are twenty thousand men in a division; there are about two thousand men per regiment, so at best there are six in the infantry regiments and maybe two thousand artillery, so that leaves twelve thousand support troops.

KOPPEL: I'm not quarreling with you what the breakdown of a Marine division is, I'm simply asking you if you were one of those in the trenches.

ROBERTSON: Well, that is your definition. I'm telling you—

KOPPEL: It's not my definition. I'm just asking you a question. I wasn't defining anything.

ROBERTSON: I was at the division headquarters. The headquarters was the command center that controlled those regiments that were in the trenches.

Those who actually attain public office are undoubtedly fair game. Elected or appointed, they must be accountable, and that gives me all kinds of rights to press hard.

May 28, 1992
Guest: Daryl Gates, Los Angeles police chief

GATES: . . . the lieutenant had withdrawn the forces where that intersection is, and he should have redeployed them . . .

KOPPEL: Would it be unfair at this point to say, Should the commander of all commanders, the chief of police, have been off at a fund-raiser during precisely that period?

GATES: You know, Ted, that's another thing. It's very irritating.

KOPPEL: Sure, it's irritating.

GATES: I have not—I have never said at any time—I've said on national television over and over again, the answer is no. I should not have been there. But it wouldn't have made any difference, because it was—

KOPPEL: But if you're blaming the lieutenant—

GATES: —wait a minute, Ted, but no, I'm not blaming the lieutenant.

KOPPEL: If that lieutenant had gone off to a fund-raiser, if any of your officers had gone off to a fund-raiser, you probably would have had them cashiered.

GATES: And I have said I bear a responsibility.

KOPPEL: What responsibility? You're leaving in a few weeks. What responsibility are you bearing?

GATES: You think I have not beared [sic] any responsibility this whole year and this particular thing? I haven't seen your name on the front page of every newspaper. I haven't seen your name on television as being the one who incited the riot. I haven't seen your name in any way connected with this, but I have, and I've accepted the responsibility that I may have—

KOPPEL: You make precisely my point, Chief.

GATES: And let me just—let me just finish, though.

KOPPEL: You make precisely my point there.

GATES: If I had been in my office twiddling my thumbs for twenty minutes, instead of that fund-raiser, no one would have paid any attention.

KOPPEL: Two hours, Chief. Not twenty minutes.

GATES: But it just happened to be—no, no, no, no, twenty minutes.

KOPPEL: You weren't back until eight-thirty.

GATES: That—I was at that location for twenty minutes.

KOPPEL: It took you a while to get there; it took you a while to get back. Two hours. You were gone from six-thirty to eight-thirty.

GATES: Well, you haven't any idea where I was. You haven't any idea. You never asked where I was.

KOPPEL: You were in Brentwood.

GATES: I know that. But you don't know what I was doing after I left there. You have no idea. You've never asked that question, and I don't deign to answer your question now.

November 20, 1987
Guest: Evan Mecham, governor of Arizona

KOPPEL: [You said,]"Anybody who'd break the law shouldn't have a job in government. It's up to me to uphold the law. A homosexual act is against the law." Now, that sure sounds to me as though you're suggesting that homosexuals shouldn't be in government.

MECHAM: Mr. Koppel, we've had a thirty-minute program. You spent the first part of it telling all about the things. Would you allow me just to respond in a positive way to some—

KOPPEL: No, no, Governor, I tell you what. You can make all the
             positive announcements that you want to in the state of
             Arizona. I told you from the very beginning, and I've
             tried to be as candid with you as I can, you're not here
             to talk about your accomplishments in office. You're
             here because you've become a national figure of consid-
             erable interest, not because you opened a trade office in
             Taiwan, not because you've been tough on drugs. Try
             and answer the question. . . . Now, let's just for a mo-
             ment, let's play by my rules for a moment, let's go back
             to the question that I asked you initially and which, it
             seems to me, you evaded the first two or three times that
             I asked you. Were you not calling for the elimination of
             homosexuals from government office because in your
             view they break the law?

MECHAM: We have spent so much time on homosexuals.

KOPPEL: You have spent so much time evading, if you'd just an-
             swer the question a little more directly, Governor, then
             we could have gotten through this in about a minute
             or two.

*By then I wasn't really talking to Mecham anymore; at that point I was
talking directly to the audience. And I was saying to the audience, in effect,
"You haven't missed any of this, have you? Because if you've been out in the
kitchen for a moment, let me just explain to you that this guy has not answered
a single question I've asked, and you ought to know that."*

MECHAM: I have looked at no homosexuals in state government.
             But I've looked at vetoing the tax increase, I've looked
             at hiring . . .

KOPPEL: If you are not going to answer my question at least be
             forthright enough to say, "Ted, I'm not going to answer
             your question."

*According to my definition of a "bad guest," Kurt Waldheim was a clas-
sic: extremely polite, well mannered, and consistently disingenuous. In 1988 the
Austrian president was under siege. Documents had emerged indicating that in*

the Second World War, Waldheim's military unit knew of and probably participated in the deporting of Jews to concentration camps. A commission of historians appointed by Waldheim to exonerate his reputation had done the opposite. Although the commission couldn't prove that Waldheim himself had committed atrocities, it found that he had to have known about them and that his cooperation with the Nazis helped make it easier for war crimes to happen. There was also evidence that the Soviets had known of Waldheim's past for decades, and that they had used that information to manipulate Waldheim, even when he was the secretary-general of the United Nations.

Waldheim's defense was to act like the quintessential headwaiter. The technique worked especially well because Pierre Salinger and I were on Waldheim's turf, inside his palace in Vienna. We interviewed him on the very night he had announced that he would refuse to resign in the wake of the commission's report. And, like a good headwaiter, he stayed aloof, unflappable, detached; no matter how rude we might become, he was determined to remain professionally cool and polite. The message conveyed by his demeanor was that he'd dealt with even ruder people than we, and that nothing would interfere with his sangfroid.

February 15, 1988
Guest: Kurt Waldheim

WALDHEIM: There is no evidence.

KOPPEL: They [the commission] think otherwise.

WALDHEIM: Members, yes, they made a mistake in regard to my political past, there is the same inconsistency with the conclusions of the report and the facts which are contained in the report . . .

KOPPEL: Yeah, I mean, with all due respect, Dr. Waldheim, we're referring here to what all the commissioners have signed as their finding, and they find that in each instance every one of the claims that you made is not substantiated by the documentation.

WALDHEIM: Well, I can only reject this, because it is quite clear that the facts contained in the report do not correspond with the conclusions, and I will maintain this, my opinion, because I'm convinced that this is the case.

He was not going to get angry, because that would have been a victory for the "rude" guests—in this case, Pierre and me. He wasn't about to give us that satisfaction.

WALDHEIM: Here in Austria people who elected me, they knew exactly what I did and what I was during the war; they elected me because this was the normal fate of a young Austrian of, let's say, twenty, twenty-two years of age. To make him responsible for the wrongdoings of Hitler and of the Nazi army, which I contend of course, this is not fair.

KOPPEL: And I don't think, with all due respect, Dr. Waldheim, that that is the charge, the principal charge that's being leveled against you.

WALDHEIM: And what is the principal charge?

KOPPEL: The principal charge that's being leveled against you is that you've been less than honest in the way you have dealt with these matters, most particularly over the last two years, but also over the last forty years, that you have concealed, that you have misled, that you have diverted, that in some cases you have flat-out lied, and what this report appears to do is confirm that.

WALDHEIM: Well, that is your opinion, not mine.

I could have said, "Waldheim, you are a bloodthirsty butcher who was responsible for the deaths of innocents," and he would have simply responded by saying, "Mr. Koppel, I'm so sorry that you feel that way. You clearly don't understand the facts."

David Duke's demeanor was similar: on guard, slightly cool, and very much suggesting that I just didn't understand. I interviewed Duke when he was running for governor of Louisiana, but the issue was his past. He'd been a Grand Wizard of the Ku Klux Klan and a neo-Nazi. He was therefore a perfect example of the guests who resort to code language, which they know how to use very well. It provides them with the excuse that, Hey, I never said anything about the Jews, I never said anything about the blacks, I never said anything about Catholics.

November 15, 1991
Guest: David Duke

KOPPEL: You have become—and I say this with a certain grudg-
ing respect—you have become extraordinarily adept at
saying some of the same things that you used to say in a
very harsh and offensive manner back in the days of what
you describe as your youthful indiscretion. You say them
now with a lot more gloss, with a lot more polish, but
you know what people mean by code messages, and the
code messages you're putting out are essentially the same
as things that you were saying in a far more blunt fashion
a few years ago. No?

DUKE: No, I don't think you're right at all. I think the liberals
make that code. I think reverse discrimination is the real
racism today, but it's not called racism, it's called affirmative action.

KOPPEL: Talk to me about what differences, if any, you see
between blacks and whites. Are there fundamental differences beyond the obvious skin pigmentation?

DUKE: Well, I think—well, I think there are differences among
all people, as we all have different talents in certain areas,
and I don't—I couldn't begin to be able to identify what
those talents are. But certain races have certain proclivi-
ties in certain areas of music or athletics or different pur-
suits. But I think the best way to determine who's the
best qualified is through testing, is through job record
and performance, and I object to these programs of racial
discrimination. I don't like it when someone takes a test
for a job and scores in the nineties, if he's white, and has
that score dropped by twenty points, or if a person who's
a minority takes a test and has the score raised twenty
points. I think you should have—

KOPPEL: You keep—

DUKE: —what you score on the test—

KOPPEL: You keep saying that as though somehow there were a
              federal affirmative action program which does that, and
              they don't . . . Let me get you back to where we were a
              minute ago. You were starting to say that there were cer-
              tain natural proclivities among certain races. Are you say-
              ing that one race or another is better inclined as a racial
              matter, or just that there seems to be a larger number
              within one race or another?

DUKE: Well, there's—there's probably—there are probably
              group differences, sir, there's no question about that. But
              I couldn't begin to identify what those group differences
              are—but I think we got to have a system in this country
              that pushes for equality of rights and opportunity for
              everyone.

   *With people like that, it is almost impossible to do an effective job of ex-
posing them in the brief time that a live interview allows. At most, when the
program runs the usual half-hour, the total interview time is about eleven minutes. Now, there are a lot of interesting things you can do in eleven minutes. But
when you're up against a skilled politician or a diplomat, and someone who has
gone through this experience before, they're on guard; I don't care how good an
interviewer you are, there's a limit to what you can achieve in eleven minutes.*
   *Something else about David Duke's responses reminded me of Waldheim:
both blamed the media for their troubles, the mainstream media in particular.*

KOPPEL: How did a political race in Louisiana end up becoming a
              national campaign, Mr. Duke?

DUKE: I think the reason why we're having racial tensions in
              this race is because of the liberal media. . . . What about
              Jesse Jackson and "Hymietown" in New York City? I
              don't see the media take him to task so much.

KOPPEL: Oh, I recall Jesse Jackson being taken very much to task.
              Indeed, it probably cost him many, many tens of thou-
              sands of votes.

   *There is a whole category of guests who come on because they're in some
kind of trouble—legal, political, ethical—who assume the posture that says,*

You media guys have this fixation about issue x or rumor y, and you just don't understand. You don't really want to do a fair interview; you just want to use the opportunity to make me look bad. By going after "mainstream media," of course, they're going after me. I'm the villain—sometimes implicitly, sometimes explicitly.

January 28, 1994
Guest: Oliver North

NORTH: The American people watched for six long days while I was testifying at a hearing I didn't want to go to, and we certainly didn't want to make public. You know, what astounds me is that the American people—because it was run gavel to gavel—right there looking at the tube, without the—no offense intended—without the—

KOPPEL: Oh, go ahead.

NORTH: —intermediaries of the media interpreting it for them, the American people had a chance to decide exactly what was going on, and they concluded—

KOPPEL: And they liked what they saw—

NORTH: —they concluded that it was the arrogance on the part of the professional politicians and that inner circle of elites in Washington that never should have done that to a lieutenant colonel in the United States Marine Corps.

Oliver North is especially fond of beginning an interview with someone from the mainstream media by essentially talking over the head of the interviewer to the viewers. He begins with a tacit announcement that says, "Hey, you folks out there know what's going on here, don't you? The mainstream media doesn't like me. The mainstream media can't get over Iran-contra, they're obsessed with it. So nothing I do is going to be fairly treated, anyway."

NORTH: Ted, I'm going to give you a provocative notion, that someday, somebody will get it right, even you.

In general, when guests go after the media, my tendency is not to try to fight that point too long. Sometimes that disappoints people. They want to

*know why I don't defend media coverage more. It's more productive, in my
view, to regain control of the conversation by returning the focus back toward
the guest.*

February 14, 1992
Guest: David Miscaviage, Church of Scientology official

MISCAVIAGE: I'll tell you, the person getting harassed is myself and
the church. . . . Here's the common mistake the media
makes. I can give you a hundred thousand Scientologists
who will say unbelievably positive things about their
church to every one you add on there, and I not only am
upset about those people not being interviewed, they are
too. . . . Not just myself, any Scientologist will open up
a paper, will watch this program, they're probably laughing right now, saying, "This isn't Scientology." That's
what makes media. Media is controversy. I understand
that, and if you really looked at the big picture of what's
happening in Scientology, it isn't really controversial,
certainly to a Scientologist.

KOPPEL: I hope you understand that there's a little bit of a para-
dox in your saying that "we're not going to get a chance
to listen to what Scientology is all about." We have with
us, since you were courteous enough to join us—

MISCAVIAGE: Oh, absolutely. I'm just trying—I'm just trying to correct this, that's all.

KOPPEL: I understand, and we're going to be spending the rest of
this hour, in which I'll have a chance to talk to you and
you can clear up some of the misconceptions we have.
Okay?

MISCAVIAGE: Okay.

*On-camera, I rarely change my demeanor in deference to the stature of
the guest. Were my respect for the rank, fame, or accomplishments of a guest to
impede my line of questioning, the discussion would suffer. And there are few
exceptions to that—a sitting President is one, the Pope is another; also, the*

president or prime minister of another country. Except for those, I approach al-most every guest as if, until midnight, we are on equal footing.

October 31, 1994
Guest: Edward M. Kennedy, senator running for a sixth term

KOPPEL: You're not a spring chicken anymore and, forgive me, you're overweight. Why put yourself through this?

February 16, 1994
Guest: Philip Heymann, former deputy attorney general

KOPPEL: You may be a good lawyer, you may be a good law professor, you may be a good analyst of what solves crime, but you're a lousy politician, you know that.

HEYMANN: Well, I'm not positive of that. We'll see what happens, Ted.

January 12, 1983
Guest: Frank Rizzo,
former mayor of Philadelphia,
running for mayor again

RIZZO: The ADA is an organization that never supported me and some other people like me who had the same philosophy.

KOPPEL: No, I mean, that's understating, isn't it? I mean, they hate your guts.

RIZZO: Beg your pardon?

KOPPEL: I say they hate your guts.

RIZZO: Well, let me say this—

KOPPEL: And you're not too crazy about them, either, are you?

One guest who simply refuses to regard any interviewer as a conversational equal is Ross Perot. Perot "tolerates" another person on the set—e.g., me— while he gives a speech. He really does not believe in interviews. Perot does not deign to acknowledge that he's being interviewed. You, the interviewer, are the price that has to be paid for getting half an hour of free television time. Like Oliver North, Perot talks past the interviewer, directly to the audience. If you try to intrude by asking a difficult question or one that's not what he cares to talk about at that time, he treats you like an unruly schoolboy.

February 17, 1993
Guest: Ross Perot

KOPPEL: What are you suggesting that he's going to have to do with regard to Congress? I mean President Clinton.

PEROT: No, Congress and the President, see. The people in this country—and that's why all of the people want to stay organized and build the organization. If we're big enough in every congressional district, the congressmen and the senators will listen, right?

Some of the toughest interviews over the years have been with those I call "the scoundrels." They are scoundrels precisely because they've been able to maintain a devoted following even as they betray and possibly exploit these same constituents. Seventy percent of the American public may have no illusions about the scoundrel you are interviewing. They know that the guest may even be a crook. But 30 percent think he's just absolutely wonderful. Maybe it's only 20 percent. That's still tens of millions of Americans. You cannot treat those millions with a lack of respect.

Jim and Tammy Faye Bakker epitomized this problem for me. At the time of my interview with them, in May 1987, the Bakkers had lost control of PTL, their televangelism empire, and the Heritage USA religious theme park in South Carolina to the Reverend Jerry Falwell. Falwell and a number of others were accusing Jim Bakker of raping a church secretary, Jessica Hahn, and of other sexual misconduct. Jim and Tammy Faye were also accused of misappropriating PTL's funds for personal use. There were reports that even the doghouse on the Bakker property had air-conditioning and heating.

At that point, neither of the Bakkers had been indicted. Jim Bakker had admitted to a one-time liaison with Hahn, but he was also accusing Falwell and others of trying to steal Heritage USA and PTL. Over the years, the Bakkers had drawn donations from millions of Americans. And a good number of donors, in that spring of 1987, still believed in Jim and Tammy Faye. Hundreds of thousands, if not millions, still genuinely believed that Jim and Tammy Faye were a man and a woman of God who were doing their best to help heal the sick and those with psychic injuries, and that they were doing their best to put people in touch with the Lord.

Because of their devoted following, and because Bakker had been neither convicted nor even indicted, I was nervous. What concerned me was, What if I've misjudged these people? What if they really are people of God? What if they really are good human beings, and they're just sort of folksy, and maybe they've gotten a little carried away with their own success? I don't want to be the instrument of hurting anyone who has genuinely tried to ease people's lives. I was really worried about going after them too hard.

May 27, 1987
Guests: Jim and Tammy Faye Bakker

KOPPEL: Why are you willing to talk now?

JIM BAKKER: Well, we have been quiet for these many, many weeks, and it's been devastating to us, what we've been going through, and if I could just give you one Scripture that's kind of set the stage for what God has given to us, and this was the scripture that the Lord gave me, in Psalms 38, verse 12: "Meanwhile, my enemies are trying to kill me. They plot my ruin and spend all their waking hours planning treachery. But I am deaf to all of their threats. I am silent before them, as a man who cannot speak. I have nothing to say, for I am waiting for you, O Lord." The Bible says that they who wait upon the Lord will renew their strength. And Tammy and I have gone through a devastating time. Tammy started first with pneumonia, and then we went through with Betty Ford's program, and then this thing came and just crushed us so deeply, and we didn't want to get in the fight. It was like a circus. We couldn't believe it. We wanted to protect our children. We wanted to really just cling to each other and see God. But it won't stop, and we're getting, really, thousands of letters. And people said, "We want to hear from you, Jim and Tammy. We want to know what went on. We want to know where you are and how you feel." And we chose to come out today, and we actually chose your program. We even had—I guess we had invitations to just about every program to come on, but I felt that you're not only tough, but I felt that you would be fair and give us a chance to share with people all over the country.

KOPPEL: All right. Well, I hope I live up to both your expectations. Let's start with the tough. You may consider this to be a tough question, Mrs. Bakker. Is it going to be possible to get through an interview with both of you without you wrapping yourselves in the Bible? I don't mean to demean your faith in the Lord. I don't mean to demean whatever faith you have in the Bible, but sometimes one gets the sense, in listening to the two of you, that whenever you get into trouble, you wrap yourselves in that holiness which protects you, because folks don't like to poke through that too much.

JIM BAKKER: Well, that's—

KOPPEL: Let me—let me see if Mrs. Bakker can respond to that.

JIM BAKKER: Oh, okay. Good.

TAMMY FAYE BAKKER: Well, the Bible is protection. It's a very real protection. It's a comfort. That's, I think, the biggest reason we wrap ourselves in the Bible. It's so comforting. Jesus said, "When you go away, I'll send a comforter to you," and he has, and that's been our comfort during this.

KOPPEL: Yeah, but you know what I'm saying.

TAMMY FAYE BAKKER: Sure.

I knew I had to deal gently with people who kept wanting to invoke the Bible. I have contempt, however, for people who use the Bible as their de-

fense against legitimate charges, and the two of them were trying to do that all the time.

BAKKER: You know the Bible says, "Ye without sin can cast the first stone," or "Ye that has spirit shall restore your brother in the spirit of meekness," and I—it's just such unscriptural activity for all of us to be debating back and forth publicly—

KOPPEL: All right, but you're starting to do what I was suggesting to you early on I wasn't going to let you do tonight, and that is, you're wrapping yourself in the Bible again—

BAKKER: But that's all I have.

KOPPEL: That's fine, I understand it may be the only protection you have, but it's not the only answer you've got. There have been some very direct charges made here.

I sometimes had to get a little bit angry, sometimes had to use a little humor. My message was: You believe in the Bible. Fine. Now let's talk about you.

KOPPEL: When Jerry Falwell stands up as he did today, and he levels charges against you—homosexuality from 1956 to the present, effectively engaging in something approaching rape with Jessica Hahn involving a second man, a third man who attempted to become involved but couldn't, then you, later on, in a kind of locker room braggadocio supposedly said, "Did you get her, too?" You could sue the pants off the man, if you wanted to, if he's lying.

JIM BAKKER: How else could they keep Jim and Tammy from being restored to their ministry unless they keep putting these charges on top of us?

KOPPEL: What I'm saying is, you could wreck him. There aren't enough millions of dollars in the coffers of Jerry Falwell's ministry to pay for the libel action you could bring against him if he's wrong, and none of those things happened.

TAMMY FAYE BAKKER: He is wrong, but we aren't going to wreck him.

JIM BAKKER: Scripturally, forgive me, but you're not to return evil
for evil.

*The issue, of course, wasn't whether some people are saints and some are
sinners. We are all varying shades of gray. The issue was how much or little
emphasis they put on spiritual salvation compared with how much emphasis
they put on where the viewer should send money.*

KOPPEL: How much money did you earn last year? How much
money were you paid in salary, in bonuses, in dividends,
in royalties? No idea? You're shrugging, Mr. Bakker.
You don't know?

JIM BAKKER: I don't have the exact figure.

KOPPEL: Not exactly, roughly. Within one hundred thousand to
two hundred thousand?

JIM BAKKER: I would say roughly my salary was $1.1 million and the
take-home pay out of that would be about five hundred
thousand to six hundred thousand, probably.

KOPPEL: All right, Mrs. Bakker?

TAMMY FAYE BAKKER: I honestly—honest, I do not know how much
I make. I've never thought about it.

JIM BAKKER: She don't.

TAMMY FAYE BAKKER: I really don't.

KOPPEL: Well, I mean, doesn't that—doesn't that strike you as—
if you were sitting out there right now watching this
program, as millions of people are, and you were—

TAMMY FAYE BAKKER: Yeah, it would strike me as funny.

KOPPEL: —and you were—you were a prayer partner who had
coughed up a difficult five, twenty, fifty dollars at some
point, would you feel comforted seeing Tammy Faye
Bakker sitting there saying, "I don't know how much
money I make"—it's your money, you know?

JIM BAKKER: Ted, that's our problem. That's our failure. Tammy and I were interested in building our ministry and working for the Lord . . . anybody knows that I worked day and night.

KOPPEL: No one—look, no one has ever accused you of being lazy, to my knowledge.

Obviously, the best way for Jim and Tammy Faye to defend themselves was to say that their accusers weren't coming after the Bakkers, they were coming after the PTL followers. They were coming after the Lord. Every scoundrel who has ever used the pulpit and the Bible as means of raising money for himself or herself uses that argument.

Some people say that patriotism is the last refuge of scoundrels. I don't think so. I think the Bible is the last refuge of scoundrels, and Jim and Tammy Faye were two of the more colorful scoundrels that have ever plied that trade.

KOPPEL (*to Tammy Faye*): [The board of directors] said you were kind of like a shopping machine. I mean, you would go out and—

TAMMY FAYE BAKKER: I do like to shop. I probably am well known for my shopping.

KOPPEL: Yeah, it's—

TAMMY FAYE BAKKER: But I am a bargain hunter! (*smiles*) . . . I enjoy shopping. It's kind of a hobby to help my nerves. Better than a psychiatrist! (*chuckles*) . . .

KOPPEL: The doghouse. You've got to tell me about the doghouse.

JIM BAKKER: Oh, my. Our poor dogs don't have a home right now. I found the canceled check for that, by the way. I paid for that, for the materials for that house, and one of the guards had a—supposedly, an old air conditioner put in, and so it would have heat for the dogs in the wintertime. I think that's probably the most famous doghouse in the world, but poor Max and the rest of them are without a house.

TAMMY FAYE BAKKER: We're sorry, Snuggles.

KOPPEL: It's kind of a symbol of wretched excess, right?

JIM BAKKER: You know what I think? I think the people who watch our program know we're a tad flamboyant . . .

A "tad flamboyant," perhaps, but the Bakkers were eminently watchable; their interview garnered the highest ratings of any Nightline *program in the seven years the show had been on the air. Years later, I would look back on my fear before the broadcast, the concern I had over the possibility that I was about to hurt two decent preachers, and I would conclude that all the fret was for naught. They really were scoundrels. Scoundrel is almost the wrong word, because it has a tinge of affection to it.*

JIM BAKKER: We'd go back to PTL and work for nothing if God wants that.

KOPPEL: Yeah, well, maybe you would, but you didn't. And the fact of the matter is, not only did you not work for nothing, you worked for a great deal.

Exactly five months later, I interviewed Bakker again, but this time without Tammy Faye. By then, Bakker was reportedly the target of a federal grand jury probe into criminal tax fraud and mail and wire fraud, and he'd been defrocked by the Assemblies of God; Jessica Hahn had told reporters that Bakker had indeed forced himself on her; and PTL had filed for bankruptcy.

But Jim and Tammy Faye Bakker were still at it. They had launched a 900 number—which issued a daily recording by them in exchange for a dollar and a half from the caller. They had hired a publicist, and they had announced that they hoped to go on tour. By then there was just no doubt in my mind that they were both outrageously nasty people. I was angry. It showed.

October 27, 1987
Guest: Jim Bakker

BAKKER: What we need to do is to begin to concentrate on what God called all of us ministers to do.

KOPPEL: I'm sure you haven't forgotten, Mr. Bakker, because it must be a very big part of your life, that you're not a minister: You're an ex-minister.

BAKKER: (*laughs*)

KOPPEL: You're laughing. Why?

BAKKER: Well, I just feel like the call of God comes from God, not from man. . . .

KOPPEL: If you were a man who was genuinely sorry, there are lots of ways you could demonstrate that, not the least of which would be to go out among the poor and show that you are first and foremost a man of God who wants to help people find God, who wants to be charitable. Instead, old Jim Bakker seems to be doing what Jim Bakker has always done, and that is hustling a buck.

BAKKER: Well, I'm sorry you feel that way.

KOPPEL: It's not a question of how I feel. I mean, you've got a 900 telephone number. Think people can pay a buck-fifty to listen to you and Tammy talk about chickens that she either did or didn't raise from the dead? I mean, that's not, that's really not bringing people closer to God, is it? . . .

BAKKER: Jessica Hahn is simply not telling the truth, and I don't think I need to belabor that. I really don't.

KOPPEL: Well, I mean, you say you want to set the record straight. I don't know how you're going to set the record straight without belaboring some of these things and substituting your truth for what you say is a lie.

BAKKER: Well, I think perhaps in our book we will deal with the subject, but I feel, as I said before, I think it's very ungentlemanly to discuss these things on public television, I feel like it's been discussed enough, and I feel very sorry for her. Very, very sorry.

KOPPEL: You've kind of lost me there, Mr. Bakker. It's ungentlemanly to discuss it on television, but if folks will wait for your book, then you're going to discuss it there?

BAKKER: No, because you can sit down and you can very carefully
            make the words . . .

KOPPEL: I hope that you and your wife can live in tranquility for
            the rest of your lives. But the question is, why does Jim
            Bakker have to inflict himself on the public? Why is it
            necessary for you to maintain—I mean, what kind of a
            role model do you think you are?

BAKKER: Well, I hope I haven't inflicted myself on the American
            people. And the only role model I hope I could be is a
            sinner saved by grace. And that there's hope for me and
            there's hope for everyone else.

KOPPEL: That's fine. But, I mean, why, why should you be
            preaching anything? Why should you be restored as a
            minister?

BAKKER: Are you asking that as a prejudgment, that you don't
            think I should be?

KOPPEL: I'm asking that with certainly a healthy dose of cynicism.

*The only guests who pique my exasperation more often than scoundrels are
diplomats. They're trained to obfuscate. I've said as much on the air.*

May 19, 1987
Guest: Nizar Hamdoon, Iraqi ambassador to the United States

KOPPEL: Are you telling me that if and when that request [for
            compensation to the dead] comes into the hands of your
            government, that your government is prepared to honor
            that request?

HAMDOON: I think Iraq will look into it based on international norms
            and goals and practices, and I am sure that my govern-
            ment will look into it in a very cooperative manner.

KOPPEL: Ambassador Hamdoon, I know that you have had an-
            other career before you became a diplomat, so perhaps
            you will take some pity on me. I'm not a diplomat. I

don't understand what those phrases mean. Does that mean yes or no?

As obfuscators, the Soviet diplomats were in a league of their own. They'd say whatever they were told to say, and no matter how absurd it might be, no matter how incredulous my reaction, they would hold their ground. Every Soviet spokesman knew better than to ever concede a point, especially within the necessarily circumscribed minutes of a live interview. Eugene Pozdnyakov was an extreme. He was a Soviet attaché in Canada who had agreed to discuss the nuclear reactor meltdown in Chernobyl a week after scientists in Europe first noticed a dramatic increase in radioactivity in the atmosphere. I wanted to know why the Kremlin had waited for several days before notifying neighboring countries of the accident when Chernobyl's fallout had placed those countries in danger.

April 30, 1986
Guest: Eugene Pozdnyakov

POZDNYAKOV: It happened on Saturday, and the governments of proper countries are usually on holidays on the weekends.

KOPPEL: Oh, come on! Come on—

POZDNYAKOV: On Monday, on Monday they received—

KOPPEL: Oh, no, no, no, no. Now, Mr. Pozdnyakov—

POZDNYAKOV: —they received information.

KOPPEL: I would be astonished—and I don't think you're going to tell me—that the Kremlin closes down Friday evenings and opens up again on Monday mornings. I can assure you that's not true.

POZDNYAKOV: I didn't say the Kremlin. I said the proper governments.

KOPPEL: I can assure you that the State Department doesn't close down, I'm sure Whitehall doesn't close down, the Élysée Palace doesn't close down. Every government in Europe has duty officers on who could have accepted a call like that. Now, now that's nonsense when you say it was over the weekend.

POZDNYAKOV: Well, but it was over the weekend.

KOPPEL: But this is nonsense . . .

The art of evasion didn't disappear with the Soviet Union; other diplomats have refined it. During a visit I made to Baghdad just after the invasion of Kuwait, I interviewed Tariq Aziz, the foreign minister, and asked about Westerners being detained by Iraq. Among them were some young American children, one of whom was ill.

August 15, 1990
Guest: Tariq Aziz

AZIZ: I hear this story for the first time, now we are on TV . . . I will immediately take care of that, and see what we can do.

KOPPEL: Can you do that? I mean, do you have the power to do that?

AZIZ: Of course. Of course. The government of Iraq can do that.

KOPPEL: All right. Let me just make sure, because you're a diplomat, and one has to be careful when listening to diplomats to hear precisely what is said. Are you telling me that those children will be released?

AZIZ: Well, it is not in the power of the foreign minister to decide on their release.

KOPPEL: That's what I was asking you a few moments ago.

AZIZ: Yeah, yeah. I am a member of the government, and I can ask my colleagues who are in charge of this matter to handle it, because I know the intentions of my government. You see, we don't have any hostile intentions against those people. We don't want them to be harmed by any reason.

KOPPEL: You said you—you've said you can ask them. Forgive
             me for pressing you. Will you ask them?

AZIZ: I will, of course.

KOPPEL: Thank you.

AZIZ: No. Of course. I said, no problem about it.

*Unfortunately, all I'd squeezed out of Aziz was a commitment to "ask"
about the children. By the time I returned to Washington, not forty-eight hours
later, not only had no one been freed, there were reports that all the hostages
had been moved to an undisclosed location. On* Nightline *that night, Ambassador al-Mashat claimed ignorance as to where the hostages had gone; then,
in almost the same breath, he promised they were safe.*

KOPPEL: Mr. Ambassador, let the record show . . . you're giving us
             assurance about the safety of people whose whereabouts
             you know nothing about, as you just conceded to us.

*Al-Mashat was hurling euphemisms into the conversation as if they could
curtail further inquiry. The invasion itself, he insisted, was an "annexation" of
a territory that had always rightfully belonged to Iraq. Kuwait had "invited" Iraqi
forces to move in. The United States, by sending troops to Saudi Arabia, was the
"aggressor." The Westerners inside Iraq weren't hostages, they were "guests."
Euphemisms are never to be ignored. They are rhetorical shields. The interviewer
who points them out lays bare the propaganda that hides behind them.*

KOPPEL: I'm not quite sure whether you regard these "guests"
             of yours, whom I still insist on describing as hostages,
             whether you regard them as a domestic matter or a
             foreign policy matter.

AL-MASHAT: No. I protest vehemently that you use the word
             hostages. Please don't.

KOPPEL: I'm still asking you for your definition of a hostage. If
             people are being kept against their will, and if there is a
             condition for their release, which condition cannot, at
             the moment, be met, I would argue with you that those

people are clearly hostages. Now, if you have another definition, I would be happy to hear it.

AL–MASHAT: Now, this is not the time to involve in polemics with you on this.

The art of the interview, after all, is about clarification. It is about distilling what a guest truly knows or believes or feels out of what may be murky responses.

KOPPEL: Yes, well, since you were accusing me of engaging in polemics a moment ago, let me just, for the sake of the record, point out that what precipitated this crisis was not Americans going to Saudi Arabia, but the Iraqi government invading Kuwait, which preceded this event.

AL–MASHAT: Yeah, well, who authorized you to go there and build an offensive force? That is a Security Council resolution. He will take care of that. It is an Arab problem. It should be solved by the Arabs.

KOPPEL: Perhaps it was invited, Mr. Ambassador, by the same people who *invited* you into Kuwait, because, thus far, we haven't been able to find any of those people.

AL–MASHAT: No, no, this is two different issues. We are talking about two different issues. We are talking about offensive force—

KOPPEL: The one led to the other, Mr. Ambassador.

AL–MASHAT: No, no. No, the offensive force. You have no business of having offensive force to come and threaten the existence and threaten Iraq.

KOPPEL: Why was it necessary, before that force even arrived on the scene—

AL–MASHAT: It is not you to—

KOPPEL: —for Iraqi divisions to be massed along the Saudi border with Kuwait?

AL-MASHAT: This is not your business. This is the business of the Security Council of the United Nations.

KOPPEL: Well, if we waited for the Security Council to act in that regard, Mr. Ambassador, I presume that, by this time, Iraqi forces would have occupied not only Kuwait, but also parts of Saudi Arabia, because the forces were there.

AL-MASHAT: If we use this logic, we will not have international order. That means every strong country can take law by its hand, and then move forces, and the stronger will be and eat the weaker!

KOPPEL: You have summarized precisely, Ambassador al-Mashat, what Iraq did to Kuwait. And that is exactly why American forces are in Saudi Arabia today.

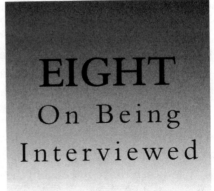

EIGHT
On Being
Interviewed

WHAT IN HEAVEN'S NAME was Ted Koppel trying to pull? Geraldine Ferraro was ready for him to be tough, but his demeanor was far more than tough, she thought; it was downright rude. Why was he being so arrogant? And pedantic. What gave him the right to talk this way to the Democratic nominee for Vice-President of the United States?

In the two months since becoming Walter Mondale's running mate, the first female vice-presidential candidate in history had spent almost as many hours studying policy papers as she had campaigning. Ferraro had devoted particular attention to international issues, especially arms control: these were issues that hadn't required her attention when she'd been a simple representative from Queens. But the invitation to appear on *Nightline,* almost exactly eight weeks before the November 1984 election, was, as far as Ferraro understood it, an invitation to discuss a wide range of issues with Ted Koppel.

Koppel didn't seem to see it that way. After a minute or so on the latest polling data, he plunged into the subject of arms-control negotiations with the Soviet Union. He asked Ferraro her position on "no first use" and on anti-satellite weapons. Ferraro offered fairly succinct answers, suggesting that there would be no agreement on "no first use" until the United States had parity in terms of conventional forces. But on the subject of anti-satellites, she said, negotiation was possible.

Then Koppel turned to the question of a mutual nuclear freeze. He suggested that when Ferraro had been asked about this subject in a debate, she had "ducked" it.

FERRARO: It wasn't that I was ducking it. Let me suggest to you, first of all, that we're not quite sure what the Soviet Union is suggesting when they're saying a nuclear freeze. What we're talking about is a mutual, verifiable nuclear freeze.

KOPPEL: Yeah, that's what I'm talking about, and what I'm asking is, how do you verify it?

FERRARO: By national technical means. And you know, Ted, as well as I, that those things are not—most of them are classified. The means by which we verify are classified, so you know that I cannot talk about them on television. But we would not enter into an agreement for any sort of freeze of any sort of weapons that would not be verifiable.

KOPPEL: Well, I'll tell you what. I just spent some time talking with some folks over at the State Department this afternoon. They don't have quite the same compunctions about not talking about those means as you do. We're talking essentially about satellites, we're talking about human means on the ground, although it's questionable how many we've got. . . .

FERRARO: As I've told you about satellite observances, I'm sure that you have information, perhaps classified information, as I do, about the type of things that you can see those satellites and verify as being built, as well as your ability to verify testing of various weapons. I'm kind of at a loss, Ted, because I don't want to violate the restrictions on classification. But you do know that we are capable of knowing precisely how many large weapons, submarines, and other things are being built.

KOPPEL: Well, submarines, you're quite right. I don't agree with
             you on the other point, and I'll pursue it a little further
             when we continue our conversation in just a moment.

Ferraro was getting angry now. Would Koppel ever ask about a
domestic issue? "I thought what he was much more concerned about
was not the concerns of the public at the time," she recalled years later.
"What [the public] wanted to know was, what was life going to be like
for them for the next four years." Even worse than the line of questioning, she thought, was Koppel's demeanor. "This was almost as if
I was running against *him*. I mean, this was his putting forward his
knowledge and being on the same level as mine. He went from being
a reporter to being almost an adversary."

What Ferraro didn't know until years later was that most of the
Nightline staff agreed with her. Producer Diane Mendez watched from
ABC headquarters in New York and shook her head. Koppel, she
thought, was being disrespectful. Rick Kaplan, the executive producer
at the time, thought so too. Kaplan told a colleague after the show that
"Ted was treating Ferraro badly, condescendingly."

FERRARO: *The Wall Street Journal* makes it look as if we're not build-
             ing any [nuclear warheads] at all. They're wrong.

KOPPEL: That's correct. No, what they're saying is that for every
             one that we're building, we have scrapped some others.
             So that in terms of accretion, we have not been adding
             to our stockpile of nuclear warheads.

FERRARO: We are building.

KOPPEL: We are adding?

FERRARO: We are building.

Ferraro later wrote of the moment in her memoirs: "I couldn't believe it. Now we were in a war of semantics. I'd never said 'adding.'
I'd said 'building.' "

KOPPEL: Well, I'm asking you, though, are we adding to the
             overall number? Because they point out that we've got
             21,000 and the Soviets have 29,000.

FERRARO: Ted, we have between us 50,000 nuclear warheads. Whether it's twenty-one or twenty-nine, you have to take a look at where those warheads, what missiles they are and what launchers, whether or not they're vulnerable or invulnerable. . . . You can hear *The Wall Street Journal* repeating what the administration says time and time and time again.

KOPPEL: Yeah, but we're talking—

FERRARO: No, no, let me finish.

KOPPEL: Yeah, but we're talking facts here, Ms. Ferraro.

FERRARO: No, but what you are saying and what *The Wall Street Journal* is saying and what the administration is saying is that we are not on an equal basis with each other, that we are an inferior force. And that is not a fact.

KOPPEL: No, I'm—

FERRARO: The Joint Chiefs of Staff—

KOPPEL: Forgive me, I'm not saying anything. I'm asking you, when you say between us—

FERRARO: Well, I'm saying no.

KOPPEL: When you say between us we're building five or six a day, I'm asking you, how many are the Soviets building and how many are we building?

FERRARO: You want me to say we're building three and they're building two, and one day they're building three and we're building two. I don't know, but between us—

KOPPEL: If that's the reality—

FERRARO: We have five or six a day.

KOPPEL: Of it, yes.

FERRARO: What one does is take a look at how many missiles are being built over a period of time and average them out to five or six a day. . . . But you know, the point is, I think this administration constantly says that we are

not—that we would freeze into inferiority. I think that's
the phrase that Mr. Bush and Mr. Reagan use constantly.
That is not a fact.

KOPPEL: Not overall, you're quite correct.

By now Kaplan thought Koppel was over the line. "He was not
being fair," Kaplan complained later. "He was holding her to a standard he didn't hold anybody else to and, frankly, nobody could be held
to. He was so . . . un-Ted-like."

As soon as Koppel went to a commercial, Kaplan talked into
Koppel's earpiece. "You know," warned Kaplan, "tomorrow, you're
going to hate this. You're going to be embarrassed by what you're
doing now."

Koppel responded, "You've just got to let me go."

Kaplan hadn't been running the show for more than a few
months. He had yet to establish much of a rapport with Koppel, and
tonight, he thought, both Koppel and Ferraro were paying the price.
Kaplan was angry that Koppel wouldn't listen to him. He turned to his
senior producer and said, "Fine. Ted will have to live with this."

Ferraro, meanwhile, began to realize that Koppel was never going
to turn to domestic issues. She would write of it in her memoirs:
"There I was, less than three weeks from Election Day, still undergoing a foreign-policy exam instead of examining the differences between the two tickets. How counterproductive. And how arrogant of
my interrogators."

KOPPEL: Is there a real difference between Camp David and the
               Reagan plan? Because I'm not sure there is.

FERRARO: Yes, there is.

KOPPEL: What is it?

FERRARO: Well, I think specifically the things that I've already
               referred to.

KOPPEL: Well, the only thing you referred to was that Jordan after
               five years would be asked to represent the Palestinians,
               which I gather is what the Israelis have wanted for a long
               time, too.

FERRARO: Well, quite frankly, I think that with the Camp David plan it leaves Jordan—it leaves Jerusalem to negotiation. It also leaves the West Bank and Gaza to negotiation.

KOPPEL: So does the Reagan plan.

FERRARO: No, it doesn't. In the Reagan plan, after five years the Gaza and the West Bank are non-negotiable. They transfer.

KOPPEL: It leaves Jerusalem for negotiation.

FERRARO: It does, that's the only thing it does leave to negotiation.

When the broadcast ended, Koppel barely had a chance to remove his microphone when a group of *Nightline* staffers came charging onto the set. Susan Mercandetti was among those who led the attack: "You were unfair," she told Koppel. "You were showing off, and you were rude. You wouldn't let her finish her sentences. And you never got off foreign policy." He should apologize to Ferraro, Mercandetti advised. Producer Deborah Leff, who had been in the control room, agreed. Leff told Koppel that she doubted he would have treated a male candidate so dismissively. Kaplan talked to Koppel by phone from the New York control room and echoed the criticism: Koppel had been too abrasive.

Koppel's staff was divided, however, as to whether or not he had been sexist. Some believed that, if anything, Koppel's problem was that he had treated Ferraro exactly the same way he would have treated a male candidate for Vice-President. Koppel told one colleague, "The point is that I felt foreign policy issues were fair game for the Democratic nominee for President of the United States. One could argue that I felt Ms. Ferraro was up to the challenge."

But did he think he was impolite? "Yes."

Ferraro received a note from Koppel a few days later, apologizing for his rudeness. Her supporters and advisers continued to seethe, however. A few weeks later, Ronald Reagan won his second term with ease over the Mondale-Ferraro ticket. No one in the Ferraro camp believed that the outcome of the election had been affected by Koppel's hostile interrogation, but the unpleasant memory of that interview lingered.

Just weeks after the election, Madeleine Albright, who had served as an adviser on foreign affairs to Mondale and Ferraro, called Ferraro to tell her about a speech given by Koppel at Georgetown University. Koppel had mentioned the interview with Ferraro in answer to a question. Albright, who was sitting in the front row, had interjected, "You did a number on her."

"Well," Koppel replied, "I've been accused of being professorial, prosecutorial, and pompous during that interview."

"All of the above," Albright said.

Ferraro included that anecdote in her book. But a decade after the interview, she remained bewildered as to why Koppel had treated her like a doctoral candidate. The reason, she ultimately concluded, was that he was "sexist. It was sexist, I think, in the way he addressed me, the questions, being argumentative." And if Geraldine Ferraro had been Gerald Ferraro? Koppel "might have been as argumentative with a man, because that's his style. But I think he would have been a bit more respectful to the office. And I think he would have had a wide range of topics. There was a double standard. If I had very little foreign policy experience, Reagan had less, and he was the man who was elected President of the United States. I'm sure that Ted would have never done that to Ronald Reagan in 1980. He would have never done it. What was Ronald Reagan's experience in the service? He had as much experience as I did."

At the time of the interview, Ferraro noted, she was a three-term member of Congress. "When men are elected to Congress, they're given the presumption of competence. Women have the burden of proof."

Still, Ferraro kept a sense of humor about her few months as the feminist icon of 1984. Four years later, she was in her den watching television with her husband. Dan Quayle came on and said, "No vice-presidential candidate has ever been subjected to the scrutiny that I have." Ferraro turned to her husband. "You know, he's young, but he's not that young. Doesn't he remember 1984?"

"UH-OH, I WAS WORRIED about this." The driver was really just addressing himself, but the two passengers in the back heard the muttering and peered over the front seat and out the window of the car. They saw a swarm of reporters and camera crews blocking the en-

trance of ABC's Washington bureau. The driver accelerated past the
building and turned the corner, then headed down an alley leading to
a back entrance. He pulled into the ABC garage, but as the gates came
clattering down behind the car, the swarm dashed up, and the cameras
and lights suddenly took aim through the mesh on the man and
woman getting out of the back of the limousine. The man felt sick to
his stomach. He grabbed his wife and dashed inside. He had always
loved appearing on *Nightline*. Tonight, he dreaded it.

A few months earlier, Richard Berendzen was one of the most
prominent, most successful university presidents in the country. In the
course of a decade he had dramatically raised the academic standards,
the public profile, and the endowment of American University. Educated at Harvard, he was a highly respected astronomer. Berendzen
had often appeared on television over the years to discuss the latest
discoveries involving the big bang theory, or to debate the merits of
creationism versus theoretical physics. He was well known in Washington for his energy, for his ardent courting of the media, for his intelligence, and for his disciplined devotion to the university over
which he presided.

But in late March 1990, Berendzen abruptly resigned his post, announcing that he was "exhausted." The truth, which emerged in the
press over the next few weeks, rocked Washington. Virginia police
had traced a series of obscene phone calls to the private phone in the
office of the president of the American University. Berendzen then issued another statement to announce that he was undergoing treatment
at the Sexual Disorders Clinic of Johns Hopkins University Hospital,
in Maryland. "I cannot begin to convey my embarrassment, or my torment," the statement said.

Berendzen remained hidden away for weeks of examination and
therapy at Johns Hopkins, but his wife, Gail, enjoyed no such privacy.
Reporters stalked her; camera crews and photographers surrounded
her home, day and night. One night, at about three in the morning,
she heard rattling out by the driveway and discovered strangers going
through the garbage cans.

Two months later, Berendzen was released from the hospital and
formally charged with two misdemeanors for making indecent calls.
Still, the scrutiny intensified. He and his wife were inside their home
and noticed reporters trying to peer through the slats in blinds. It got

to the point where the Berendzens put sheets over the windows. Years later, Berendzen would look back on that nightmare spring and describe the feeling of his life turning into a freak show: "I couldn't walk down the street, couldn't go get a haircut, couldn't go to the grocery store or a restaurant. And I thought, I can't go through life like this."

Berendzen decided to have the hospital make public all of its findings on him. "I thought rather than everybody speculate or dream up whatever they want to dream up, just give them the facts." The facts, according to the hospital, were that Berendzen had been severely sexually abused as a child and that his abuser had been a trusted adult. The phone calls were a symptom of a kind of post-traumatic-stress disorder, which had been triggered in 1988 by a visit to his childhood home upon the death of his father.

Berendzen knew he'd have to follow up by giving an interview somewhere. He had a number of requests from newspapers and magazines, but he worried that whatever he said for print would be filtered and edited. "So I decided [the interview] ought to be electronic." And live. "The highest tension, but, in a way, the most accurate representation, is live TV."

Berendzen phoned Koppel to talk about appearing on *Nightline*. Berendzen set only one condition: He would not identify the "adult woman" who had abused him as a child.

"Fine," Koppel replied. "I would not have asked you that question anyway."

The day of his *Nightline* interview, Berendzen appeared in court, his first foray into a public place in almost two months. With his wife by his side, he pushed through a wall of reporters and photographers, walked into the courtroom, and pleaded guilty to making obscene phone calls. By the time he arrived at ABC, he was emotionally drained, almost numb.

So now the Berendzens scampered out of the lights shining through the mesh of the ABC garage and linked up with Gil Pimentel, who escorted them to the greenroom. Berendzen had been in that room so many times, but on this night he felt strange. He wondered if he should back out. It was one thing to have the medical findings released, but "that's sort of at a distance. You're not personally there. But to now have to sit and talk, and to realize it's going nationwide—that was stirring the stomach. I really was afraid that the light would turn on and no words would come out, or I—I didn't know what would happen."

A *Nightline* producer handed Berendzen a thick stack of phone messages and said, "We've had quite a few calls here for you." Berendzen remembered feeling afraid to look. "But they were wonderful calls: 'We're with you'; 'We're praying for you'; and so on."

He took a seat in the studio with one of his doctors, Paul McHugh, who would be appearing with him. Berendzen was trembling almost uncontrollably. "Hang in there," said McHugh. The taped piece that led the show only heightened Berendzen's fear and dread. It included an interview with the Fairfax woman who had received his indecent phone calls. Berendzen had written the woman and her husband a letter of apology, but he knew the couple still planned to file a $15-million civil lawsuit against him. When Berendzen heard the woman's voice, he later recalled, "It hurt; it hurt very badly."

WOMAN: It took me about ten minutes into the conversation to figure out what I had, which was an obscene phone caller. So, within two hours we had a tap on our phone. . . . It's basically a form, in my opinion, of verbal rape. Over a two-week period of time, there were about thirty or forty calls, and that was what my goal was, to keep him calling me so that we could eventually find him, which we did.

The videotape included a scathing response from the woman regarding the Johns Hopkins report about Berendzen's childhood abuse.

WOMAN: I had tremendous childhood trauma of every shape and kind that you can think of. I am a very normal, healthy adult that does not make obscene phone calls . . . That is a cover-up, it's an excuse.

Koppel finally turned to Berendzen and asked him to reveal as much as he was willing about the details of his childhood abuse.

BERENDZEN: Ted, up until two months ago, I wouldn't have shared this with any human being on earth. Indeed, I had hoped that I would go to my grave not to have to share it with anyone. . . . It started about age eight and became much more intense around age eleven.

Berendzen would always cringe when he remembered these early minutes: "I felt like I was just pulling layers of skin off of me." Berendzen's pain was reflected in the face of his wife. Gil Pimentel, who was watching the interview from the greenroom with Gail Berendzen, thought that she looked as if she were trying to stifle actual physical pain. "She held herself with dignity. But you could see that it took all she had to maintain her composure. The only visible manifestation of her pain was that she would wince. Her face would just flash these winces, these moments of pain, as though somebody were taking a needle and jabbing her with it, but she wouldn't move in any other way."

Meanwhile, Koppel pressed Berendzen to explain the connection between what he'd said in his obscene phone calls to his own abuse.

BERENDZEN: The report, which I authorized the release of today, states quite clearly, the person on the other end of the phone turned out to be, essentially, a surrogate for my own victimizer . . .

KOPPEL: You hear what your—and I use the word advisedly, in this case—what your victim in this case has to say. Effectively, she said, it's all B.S. Now, can you understand why she feels as intolerant, and what response do you have?

BERENDZEN: Well, I certainly feel sympathy for her, because I gather she was a victim herself, and I certainly am sorry, deeply sorry, for intruding into the life of her and her husband, indeed, two days ago I sent them a written letter of apology, which is the soonest that my lawyers thought was advisable to do it, and they got it yesterday . . .

"I was almost on auto-pilot," Berendzen later said of these moments. "I was really very shaky. I didn't think I was going to make it through."

Koppel turned to Dr. McHugh for an explanation as to how the doctors at Johns Hopkins could be certain about something Berendzen claimed had happened over forty years earlier. McHugh cited the years of expertise represented by the clinic professionals, the thoroughness of their interrogations, and the tests.

KOPPEL: What kind of tests?

DR. McHUGH: Tests such as the amytal interview, which is the "truth serum" test. We had an expert lie detector work on Dr. Berendzen. We subjected him to a number of physiological tests themselves, all of which corroborate or discorroborate our opinion that this was a patient and not a person who was indulging in a kind of selfishness of conduct . . .

KOPPEL: If—let me use the term that society would use. Anyone who has engaged in perverse behavior, perverted behavior, isn't it inevitable that sooner or later you would find something in his or her past that would lead you to say, "Aha, that's the reason for it," and a reason becomes an excuse?

DR. McHUGH: No, that's not correct. When people are brought to us, we look at this behavior in the context of that life.

Koppel asked Berendzen what an eight-year-old child, or an eleven-year-old child, should do if he or she was being molested by a trusted adult.

BERENDZEN: I would hope that the youngster who runs into that problem would turn to help, perhaps turn to a family physician or seek professional psychiatric counseling. And certainly, if I didn't get it at age eleven, I should have when I was in my twenties or thirties. . . . And if there's any victim out there today who is in their thirties, forties, or fifties, I hope they will have the wisdom tomorrow to seek out the kind of counsel I didn't find.

KOPPEL: You say, turn to a psychiatrist, turn to a family doctor. Could you have done that when you were eleven?

BERENDZEN: I tell you what I did. I was puzzled. I was hurt. I was excited, I was traumatized, I cried. I couldn't turn to anyone. And so what I did was play games. I pretended it had never happened. And that worked for a year or two. And then I decided I would just forget it. And that worked for a few months. Then I decided that I would work terribly hard . . . And I learned, after a while, if you work sixty, eighty, ninety hours a week, one hundred, you don't remember. I do not consider the report from Johns Hopkins an excuse at all. No way whatsoever. I am making no excuse. Today I pleaded guilty to these two misdemeanor accounts of making the indecent phone calls. I must live with that shame for the rest of my days.

One reason Berendzen had agreed to appear was to reach, specifically, the more than ninety thousand alumni, faculty, staff, and students of American University.

BERENDZEN: The role of a university president is to be a role model. And so my pain is manifold: it was remembering the pain of years ago, it was the shame and pain of what I had caused to others recently, and then it was the letting down of students and faculty members. So my own anguish has been severe. And I hope the students would realize that, unfortunately, I'm vulnerable, and I failed, and I'm sorry.

After a commercial break, Koppel had a message for his guest.

KOPPEL: Dr. Berendzen, you might like to know that while we've been on the air, we just received a phone call from the president of the American University student government, who called to express his support and the support of the organization. I assume you can take good news where you find it these days.

BERENDZEN: Yes indeed.

When the program was over, Berendzen felt as if he had been examined by millions of voyeurs. He did not feel relieved. Not that night, anyway. He'd been far too exposed, the experience too raw for him to feel relief.

But early the next morning, the phone in the Berendzen home started ringing. Caller after caller wanted to share a secret with Berendzen. Almost all of the messages were variations on a theme: "It happened to me, too. And I haven't told anybody until now."

"I'd never gotten such calls before in my life—people that I didn't expect to hear from," he recalled. "Business executives and these tough macho guys were calling me up, and even though I was the one in the shaky state, they were the ones who were crying, and I was listening.

"Then I heard from eight people at American University," Berendzen said. "Eight different university people told me what had happened to them when they were kids. Four men and four women, on the staff and faculty. The four men who called, I had known for years. I can't even tell you now what I was hearing."

Then came the letters. Within a week, Berendzen had received more than a thousand. "Ninety-five percent to ninety-eight percent were wonderfully positive and supportive," he said. "People wrote things like, 'You touched my life.' Pastors wrote, and doctors wrote, and the AU family—students and faculty." One letter came from a woman in Phoenix. "It was handwritten, in ink. And about page four, it's all blurry; you can't read it. She'd gotten to the very end of the letter and then she wrote, 'I'm sorry about page four, but I'm crying as I'm writing. And the tears have blurred the ink.' "

Not long after the broadcast, Berendzen was walking by a famous Washington hotel, "and the doorman grabbed me on the sidewalk. I didn't know this man. Tears were running down his cheek. And then there was a cabdriver on M Street. He honked. I looked over, and he said in a thick accent—he may have been Ethiopian—'Saw you on TV.' Then he gave me the thumbs-up."

About that time, Berendzen invited members of the student government to his home to thank them for their support. "They didn't even speak at first. They just came and hugged me." Then one morning Berendzen received a phone call from a man whom he describes as nationally prominent—a man who had appeared on the cover of at least one major weekly newsmagazine. "Can we have lunch?" the caller asked. Berendzen accepted, and they met in a restaurant in downtown Washington.

Berendzen would remember that when the lunch began, "I didn't know what this was about. We sat there at first and had a nice conversation. Then we got to the end of the entree, just as the coffee and tea were coming. He said, 'I saw you on *Nightline,* very moving show.' And I said, 'Well, it was a very hard program to do.' "

Then, according to Berendzen, the man looked him in the eye. "He said, 'A similar thing happened when I was a boy, you know.' And I said, 'Have you ever discussed this with anybody?' 'Never.' 'Your wife?' 'No.' 'Why not?' 'I don't know how she'd respond.' 'Anybody at your work know?' 'No.' " Finally Berendzen asked the man, "Why are you telling me?" The man said he needed someone to talk to whom he could trust.

Years after the *Nightline* interview, Berendzen concluded that the pain of it was exceeded by the benefits. "Part of what I was trying to do was to address my fellow males. Without sounding too pompous about it, I was trying to say if a Harvard Ph.D., a university president, can find to his personal surprise that maybe he's more vulnerable—that he can be hit by a torpedo—more than he would have ever acknowledged, just maybe it could happen to you." Today, he believes that the degree of empathy he achieved—with everyone from the doorman to the cabdriver to the Washington "name" who asked him to lunch—was something far more profound than any professional connection he'd ever known.

The lawsuit by the Virginia woman was thrown out by the D.C. Superior Court in a summary judgment. When she announced that she would appeal, there was an out-of-court settlement.

Berendzen eventually returned to a post as a physics professor at American University. But even now, long after the crisis that brought his trauma into the open, he still has students who come into his office, shut the door, and ask to talk. Sometimes it's a roommate that the student has brought along to talk to Berendzen. "And then," he said, "I start hearing stories. Stories that you cannot imagine."

IT WAS JUNE 1993 and Lani Guinier was sitting in the greenroom in ABC's Washington bureau, about half an hour before airtime, when

Ted Koppel walked in. He told Guinier that he was glad she had come, "but I owe it to you to show you something before the program begins."

"I don't want to sandbag you on the air," Koppel said, "so instead, I'm running the risk that you will walk out on me. But if you think your nomination is still alive, take a look at these." He handed her what had just come off the presses: the first edition of the next day's *Washington Post:* "GUINIER NOMINATION NEAR WITHDRAWAL." Koppel also showed Guinier a fax from ABC's New York desk. It was the next day's headlines of *The New York Times:* "AIDES SAY CLINTON WILL DROP NOMINEE FOR POST ON RIGHTS."

"Look at all these quotes from 'senior White House officials,' from 'top White House officials,' " Koppel pointed out, "all of them 'conceding that the Guinier nomination is dead.' When you've been in this town as long as I have, you know that's it; it's over. Your nomination is finished."

"That's not what I'm hearing," Guinier replied.

"Well then, I don't think you are being well served by the administration." Koppel added that he was breaking one of his own rules by letting a guest know ahead of time what some of his line of questioning would be. "But I just didn't feel it was right to wait until we got into the studio before showing you these headlines. I thought you should know it is my intention to ask you about them when we're on the air. And I thought that you should know, judging by these, that tonight is probably going to be your only chance to defend your nomination before it gets pulled. Do you still want to come on?"

Guinier asked Koppel for a moment to scan the articles and to consult with the two administration aides who had accompanied her.

Until now, Guinier had not made one public statement in defense of her legal writings, even though criticism had mounted for weeks. Her articles, which had appeared over the previous several years in law review publications, addressed the political powerlessness of minorities. Guinier had written in one piece about "the tyranny of the majority" and the need for "proportional representation" in different levels of government. One article proposed increasing nonwhite nominees for federal judgships. Another talked about "result oriented" changes to boost the percentage of minorities in state legislatures.

The articles, in Guinier's mind, were an attempt to "communicate nuance and subtlety and complexity. I had written them with an expectation that was appropriate for the time that I was writing. I had been writing for tenure. I'd been writing for other scholars who were curious as to how my mind worked, and whether I was able to grapple with ideas in all of their complexity."

But once President Clinton had announced her as his nominee for assistant attorney general for civil rights, the readership of Guinier's articles reached far beyond the legal and academic communities. Clint Bolick, of the Institute for Justice in Washington, wrote on the op-ed page of *The Wall Street Journal* that Guinier was a proponent of quotas. The editorial page of the *Journal* echoed that view. Senate minority leader Bob Dole accused Guinier of advocating "vote-rigging schemes." And even several liberal Democrats in the Senate, including two members of the Judiciary Committee, Senator Patrick Leahy and its chairman, Senator Joseph Biden, expressed concern about Guinier's opinions. The American Jewish Congress also issued a statement that said Guinier's writings "raised substantial questions" about her approach to civil rights. Guinier's most fervent opponents dismissed her with a single epithet: "Quota Queen."

Guinier desperately wanted to respond to the accusations. "What happened to me is that all of these very complex and nuanced ideas were taken out of context, the nuance ignored, the subtlety destroyed. I was caricatured and distorted into a sound bite: 'Quota Queen.' "

Administration officials instructed Guinier to remain silent. The time to respond, she was told, would be in the Senate confirmation hearings. "I had been muzzled," Guinier later said. "It wasn't personal, it was policy, but I had been told that I could not speak throughout this process. I would wake up every day, dreading the morning when I would look at the newspapers or listen to the radio and hear what different people were saying about me and my views. It was as if they had discovered this human being who went by the name of Lani Guinier, who had these very bizarre views, and somehow it was as if I was on trial for her views. I didn't recognize the views as my own, and I was being tried for something this other person had allegedly said, and yet I wasn't even being given a chance to speak."

Finally, after weeks of allowing Guinier's adversaries to shape the public perception of the political agenda, administration officials arranged for her to meet the editorial boards of *The New York Times* and *The Washington Post*. Only later would she learn that on the very afternoon she sat in Manhattan with the editors of the *Times*, most of the key figures in the White House were concluding it was time to step away from her nomination.

Guinier was standing in LaGuardia airport that afternoon, waiting to board a shuttle for Washington, when a woman who identified herself as a *Nightline* staff member approached her and handed her a letter from Ted Koppel, inviting her to appear on his program that very evening. Guinier handed the request to an aide from the Justice Department, who said it would be passed on to the White House. "Would you want to do it if we get approval?" the aide asked. "Of course," Guinier replied. She went on to her meeting at *The Washington Post*, but soon Guinier was aware of a hot debate taking place—and getting hotter by the hour—between officials at Justice and at the White House over whether or not it was too late to have her defend her views on national television. "It was my sense," she later recalled, "that those who were lobbying to give me this platform basically felt that I was my best witness and so being on *Nightline* would be the best opportunity to provide the beginning of a rebuttal." As the afternoon faded to night, Guinier hung around in a conference room of the Justice Department, nibbling on pizza, waiting for an answer. It wasn't until almost 10 P.M., less than two hours before *Nightline*'s airtime, that an official told Guinier that she had authorization to do the show.

But now Koppel was giving her a chance to back out. Guinier scanned the next day's articles about her "dead nomination" and wondered why she should believe these reports when the media had gotten so much about her work so wrong. Besides, it seemed to her that Koppel had oversimplified what the articles were saying. She would later recall that she felt the articles were "more complicated" than Koppel had summarized them. She thought they were "suggesting that there were people in the White House who felt that [pulling the nomination] is what ultimately might happen." Still, Guinier thought it was up to the two aides from the Justice Department to tell her whether or not to go on. She would later laugh at the memory of them, turning to her and responding, "Well, what do *you* want to do?"

Guinier almost ached to defend herself—and to define herself. Besides, she told the aides, "Given the way the press has been reporting my views, I don't have tremendous confidence in what they're reporting on the White House views. And so I will rely on the information that I have, which is that a decision has not been made." Guinier went back to Koppel and told him she would do the show.

Guinier had never appeared on national television before, but she was so relieved to have a forum that she didn't feel nervous. "It was as if, until that time, I had been a defendant in a criminal trial in which neither I nor my attorney had been allowed to speak, while the prosecution accused me of all sorts of things. So finally, I was about to speak for myself."

KOPPEL: You've seen the headlines, because I've shown them to you. . . . You have not, I take it, heard from the White House along the lines of what was in *The Washington Post,* or what is going to be in *The Washington Post* tomorrow morning, what is going to be in *The New York Times* tomorrow. Have they at least had the courtesy to tell you that, as far as they're concerned, things are coming rapidly to a close here?

GUINIER: The nomination has proven a lot more complicated than was anticipated, but I am pleased to be given the opportunity to come on this show to talk to you about who I am and why it is that I should be the assistant attorney general for civil rights, why, if given an opportunity to testify before the Senate, that I believe the Senate will vote to confirm me.

KOPPEL: Professor Guinier, you know that I am sympathetic about the circumstances under which you have come here tonight. I think you should have been given a little more warning by the people who were your friends and your supporters here. But you didn't answer my question. My question is, have you been given any kind of advance warning from the White House that what is in tomorrow morning's major newspapers is about to happen?

GUINIER: I really can't tell you what is going to happen. I am the nominee. I am looking forward to an opportunity to present my views to the Senate . . .

Guinier had no intention of discussing what the White House might or might not do with her nomination. She had a nationwide audience, she was live, and she wasn't about to waste her chance, "my only opportunity to make my case. I did not want it to be a half-hour devoted to the White House processes for deciding and then not deciding important issues. This was an opportunity to talk about my ideas."

KOPPEL: You did indeed call for the Senate Judiciary Committee to use its power of advice and consent—I think is the way you put it—to ensure that more people from minorities get judicial appointments. Now, doesn't that amount to a quota?

GUINIER: I do not believe in quotas, I have never advocated quotas, and the one sentence in that one article was a reference to exactly what President Clinton has talked about in terms of making his cabinet look like America, and that is a more diverse federal bench. . . .

KOPPEL: But do you think it is the responsibility of the Senate, in this case, or, more specifically, the Senate Judiciary Committee, by its rejection of certain nominees or by its selection of other nominees, to get more minority judges, for example, into the judiciary?

GUINIER: I think that the Senate has an important role in its advise-and-consent capacity. . . . I believe in diversity. I believe in inclusiveness. I believe in making the federal judiciary, just like I believe in making the United States and other representative bodies, representative of all the people. And that's what I've advocated. I do not, again, believe in any particular racial quota and have never advocated a racial quota.

KOPPEL: When you talk about creating that sort of racial diversity, however, do you believe that that should take priority over the qualifications of a candidate, if the most qualified candidate happens not to be of color?

GUINIER: No, I do not believe that. And, in fact, if they had included the sentence either before or after, it would have said just that.

Guinier was enjoying this exchange. She knew that she spoke slowly and deliberately, but Koppel was giving her time.

KOPPEL: You have suggested, as I understand it, that under certain circumstances minority politicians might have a weighted vote so that, for example, just to make it very simple, a white member of a city council might have one vote, a black member of that same city council might have two votes. On the face of it, that seems patently unfair. Is that what you meant?

GUINIER: It is certainly unfair, and that's not what I meant, and that's not what I've said. People have talked about it as if I said weighted voting, but I'm talking about supermajority rules, for example, that are used right now in Mobile, Alabama, on the county commission . . .

KOPPEL: It strikes me that you may be proposing something that could lead almost to a Balkanization, in legal terms, of the United States, where Hispanics have one set of rules, and blacks have another, and Asians have another.

GUINIER: And I think that's a genuine fear if that's what I was advocating, but I'm not. What I am describing is a response to an extreme case, a proven violation, of illegal voting discrimination and a remedy that has been approved, as I suggested, by the Reagan and Bush administrations in the past.

Guinier did accept the responsibility for being so widely misunderstood.

GUINIER: Perhaps if I were being nominated to be a journalist I should not be confirmed . . . I perhaps have not been as clear as I should have, but I was writing to an academic audience . . . in some instances [the writings] are political theory that has no place in the public policy debate. They are, in other instances, not even a theory, but a framework.

KOPPEL: You still think you have a chance?

GUINIER: I have every expectation that, if given a chance, I will succeed.

KOPPEL: Okay. We close where we began, on that elegant evasion.

Guinier would remember that as the show concluded, "I just felt on some level exhilarated because this was the first moment when I was being treated with respect. Whether [Koppel] agreed with me or disagreed with me wasn't the point. He was respectful."

The next morning, Guinier was told by people at the White House and in the Justice Department that the phones were ringing "off the hook" about her appearance, "eight-to-one in my favor, twelve-to-one in my favor, and that people were really moved by the appearance and by my presentation and that they wanted to hear more." Her friends, she said, "thought it was thrilling. To them, in a sense, it was as if I had been in solitary confinement until that *Nightline* interview. And, as I'd told Ted Koppel, my mother had been seeing my name in the news, but she hadn't recognized that person as her daughter. Finally, when I came on *Nightline,* she recognized me."

But Guinier also heard that morning from top White House officials who were "very, very angry. They were very angry because I had suggested that I should have a Senate hearing." Guinier thought the criticism was absurd. Why go on *Nightline* if she wasn't going to make a case for having a hearing before the Senate? But she knew, by then, what all the anger in the White House really meant.

Early that evening, Guinier was called to a meeting with President Clinton. After they had met for the better part of an hour, Guinier disappeared in a car and Clinton emerged in the White House briefing room to say that he was withdrawing her nomination. Clinton told the press corps that he had only read Guinier's writings in detail a day earlier and that "they clearly lend themselves to interpretations that do not represent the views that I expressed on civil rights during my campaign." He described some of her proposed legal remedies as "anti-democratic," and he said the battle for Guinier would have been divisive. He said he could not fight it "if I do not believe in the ground of the battle."

Newspaper accounts would note on the following day that many nominees in trouble will ask a President to pull their names, so that the President isn't left with all the stain of the failed nomination. In this case, the papers pointed out, Guinier had apparently refused to request that her name be withdrawn. She left it to Clinton to take responsibility, publicly and privately, for the decision to deny her a Senate hearing.

Guinier held a press conference in which she didn't deny that she would have preferred to make her case to the Senate. "Although the President and I disagree about his decision to withdraw my nomination, I continue to respect the President. We disagree about this, but we agree about many things. He believes in racial healing and so do I."

Guinier told the story of her father's experience as a student at Harvard in 1929. "My father was denied any financial aid, on the grounds that one black student had already been awarded a full scholarship. He was not allowed to live in the dormitories, on the grounds that no black except the relative of a United States senator had ever resided there. He was the victim of a racial quota, a quota of one. I have never been in favor of quotas. I could not be, knowing my father's experience."

Guinier also offered a word of caution, a lesson learned during all those weeks when she had to dread waking up to the latest news accounts about her writing: "I hope that we are not witnessing the dawning of a new intellectual orthodoxy, in which thoughtful people can no longer debate provocative ideas without denying the country their talent as public servants."

That evening, Koppel ran a clip of Guinier's statement and offered a thought of his own afterward: "One has to wonder how this woman would have fared in front of the Senate Judiciary Committee. That didn't happen, though, because opponents of this nomination, working for the most part behind the scenes, set the agenda, defined the candidate, and manipulated the media. That happens all too often these days."

Guinier returned to the University of Pennsylvania Law School, where she began work on a study of the behavior of women in law school classes, and another study on new concepts for discussing race in America. She continued to hear from people who had seen her on *Nightline*. An Asian student told her his mother had watched the interview and had concluded afterward that she believed Guinier, and believed that Guinier was "a good person," because of the look in Guinier's eyes. It was the sort of comment that caused Guinier to reflect on the impact of making her case on television as opposed to making it to a newspaper reporter. No newspaper reader would have had access to the look in her eyes. "*Nightline* not only invited me into a studio, it invited me into the living rooms of the American people." For Lani Guinier, *Nightline* "wasn't so much a platform as a moment of emotional intimacy."

NINE
The Interview: Surprises

I T   W A S   S U P P O S E D   to be a simple segment about baseball and Jackie Robinson. Actually, it was supposed to be filler. The main focus of the broadcast was to be the middleweight boxing championship between Sugar Ray Leonard and Marvin Hagler. A "fun" show.

The fight was to be broadcast on closed-circuit from Caesars Palace in Las Vegas. ABC didn't have the live broadcast rights, which meant that *Nightline* couldn't go ringside until the bout was over. Hagler and Leonard weren't even scheduled to step into the ring until sometime after eight o'clock Pacific Time, eleven in the East. But most experts predicted that Hagler would win and that it would all be over in a few rounds. So the plan was for Koppel to interview ABC's Dick Schaap, who was ringside, as soon as there was a decision.

The question of what to do with the beginning of the broadcast had been resolved by a suggestion from George Will, the columnist, commentator, and baseball zealot. Will had phoned Koppel weeks earlier with a reminder that the fortieth anniversary approached of Jackie Robinson's debut as a Brooklyn Dodger. Koppel knew so little about baseball that his colleague Jeff Greenfield was fond of describing him as a "moron" about America's national pastime. But the legend of Robinson, the man who broke the color barrier in major league baseball, reached far beyond sport: Jackie Robinson's career had permanently altered the American social fabric.

So, on April 6, 1987, Koppel sat down at the anchor desk in Washington and Rick Kaplan took his seat as the show's executive producer in the control room in New York, and a few minutes before air, word came from Schaap that Leonard wasn't going down. The tribute to Robinson, he warned, might have to fill more than half the show.

Koppel introduced "two wonderful guests, who knew and loved Jackie Robinson." One of them was the sports author Roger Kahn, best known for his book *The Boys of Summer*. Kahn had been close to Robinson. He had helped him write a sports column, and had traveled with Robinson and the Dodgers in the late 1940s. Kahn had witnessed and written about what Robinson had had to endure, and it included every example of racism imaginable. Kahn had been there for a game between the Dodgers and the Cardinals when players on the Cardinals team held out their shoes and taunted Robinson with, "Shine these, boy!" He had watched Robinson play a game in Atlanta despite a death threat from the Ku Klux Klan if he did so.

Kahn had also seen Robinson's pain, after his playing career had ended, when no one offered him a job in baseball management. "Jackie and I used to talk about the issue of managing," Kahn would remember later. "He hadn't been certain that he wanted to manage, but he wanted the opportunity to make that determination. I said, 'Nobody ever called you?' He said, 'Only Vancouver. They called and asked if I'd be interested, and I said yes, and they never called back.' He was never offered a job in baseball, anywhere, and it hurt. He'd say, 'I don't like watching baseball, it's boring,' which was just one of many signs of the hurt."

Even now, fifteen years after Robinson's death, there were still virtually no blacks in the front offices; so Roger Kahn sat in a New York studio and listened to the introduction and promised himself that if Koppel didn't bring up the issue of management, he would.

The other guest, who was appearing from a box in the Houston Astrodome, planned on reminiscing about a friendship with Robinson that dated back to their days together on a Dodger farm team in the mid-1940s, before Robinson was a star. He had been known to boast that he was the one who had taught Robinson how to make a double play. His name was Al Campanis.

CAMPANIS: Mr. Koppel, it's a privilege and an honor for me to rem-
             inisce about Jackie Robinson. I played with him in 1946,
             and I can truthfully say that he's probably one of the best
             athletes that I've ever seen play the game of baseball. . . .
             He was a wonderful sight to behold.

Koppel turned to a subject raised in a videotaped interview with Robinson's widow. She had pointed out that in the forty years since her husband joined the Dodgers, baseball had not integrated "at any other level other than the players' level." Kahn immediately put a finer point on it: there were still no black general managers, no black club owners.

KAHN: I think if Jack were alive today, Jack would say, "How
             come there are no blacks running ball clubs?"

A good question to put to Campanis, thought Koppel. Campanis was now in management himself, a vice-president of the Los Angeles Dodgers and director of player personnel.

KOPPEL: Mr. Campanis, it's a legitimate question. You're an old
             friend of Jackie Robinson's, but it's a tough question for
             you. You're still in baseball. Why is it that there are no
             black managers, no black general managers, no black
             owners?

CAMPANIS: Well, Mr. Koppel, there have been some black man-
             agers, but I really can't answer that question directly. The
             only thing I can say is that you have to pay your dues
             when you become a manager. Generally, you have to go
             to minor leagues. There's not very much pay involved,
             and some of the better-known black players have been
             able to get into other fields and make a pretty good liv-
             ing in that way.

He doesn't really mean that, Koppel thought. Kaplan was signaling that it was time for a commercial, but Koppel thought he'd give Campanis a chance to clarify his statement.

KOPPEL: Yeah, but you know in your heart of hearts—and we're going to take a break for a commercial—you know that's a lot of baloney. I mean, there are a lot of black players, there are a lot of great black baseball men who would dearly love to be in managerial positions, and I guess what I'm really asking you is to, you know, peel it away a little bit. Just tell me why you think it is. Is there still that much prejudice in baseball today?

CAMPANIS: No, I don't believe it's prejudice. I truly believe that they may not have some of the necessities to be, let's say, a field manager, or perhaps a general manager.

Necessities? Did Campanis realize what he was saying? "Sometimes the most important technique for an interviewer," Koppel would say later, "is to express incredulity."

KOPPEL: Do you really believe that?

CAMPANIS: Well, I don't say that all of them, but they certainly are short. How many quarterbacks do you have? How many pitchers do you have that are black?

Roger Kahn couldn't believe what he was hearing. "I was in absolute shock. Campanis had always bragged to me that he was the one who'd taught Jackie how to make a double play. I never dreamed he'd make such blockheaded statements."

In the control room, senior producer Bob Jordan heard "this sort of collective gasp." The associate director, Gary Boyarsky, glanced over his shoulder at Jordan and whispered, "Did he just say what I think he said?"

KOPPEL: Yeah, but I mean, I gotta tell you, that sounds like the same kind of garbage we were hearing forty years ago about players, when they were saying, "Aaah, not really—not really cut out—" Remember the days, you know, "Hit a black football player in the knees, and you know—" That really sounds like garbage, if you'll forgive me for saying so.

CAMPANIS: No, it's not—it's not garbage, Mr. Koppel. Because I played on a college team, and the center fielder was black, and the backfield at NYU, with a fullback who was black, never knew the difference. Whether he was black or white, we were teammates. So it just might just be—why are black men, or black people, not good swimmers? Because they don't have the buoyancy.

KOPPEL: Oh, I don't—I don't—it may just be that they don't have access to all the country clubs and the pools.

Koppel finally broke for a commercial and sat quietly for a moment, stunned. "At first I hadn't been sure that Campanis realized what a hole he'd dug for himself. But when I gave him a chance to dig out of it, he managed to dig himself in deeper," he later recalled. "The program had by now taken a totally different direction than anyone had believed possible. This man had just said such devastatingly self-incriminating things about his attitudes, and about what was really going on in baseball."

Roger Kahn couldn't imagine why Campanis wouldn't have had some sort of prepared statement about blacks in management. At least, thought Kahn, Campanis could have resorted to one of the old clichés, something along the lines of "We're trying; it's getting better." Kahn felt sorry for Campanis, and sad. A couple of years earlier, one of Kahn's sons, a good athlete but not a great one, had been considering a baseball career instead of college. Kahn hadn't been able to persuade his son that playing in the majors was a pipe dream, so he'd asked Campanis to have a word with the boy. Campanis had obliged, advising the young Kahn that he'd never get past the minors and to "stick with the books." For that, Kahn had been a grateful father. And now he wondered, for just a moment, whether he should return the favor by bailing Campanis out.

But Kahn's greater allegiance was to the memory of the man who had been taunted by some of his opponents as "boy," to the memory of Robinson hitting a double in Atlanta just days after receiving the letter that said "We'll kill you, nigger, if you play in Atlanta," and to the memory of Robinson's sadness that baseball, in the end, didn't want him in the front office. Besides, Kahn decided, what Campanis was saying was blatantly offensive. Kahn later told a reporter, "I got to thinking that I wouldn't want to hear this kind of talk at a party, much less on a TV show in front of millions of people, so I can't bail him out of his position at all."

So when Koppel returned from the commercial break with a question for Kahn about Branch Rickey, the Dodgers' general manager who had hired Robinson, Kahn turned the focus back to Campanis.

KOPPEL: Mr. Kahn, how much courage did it take on Branch Rickey's part?

KAHN: It took enormous courage. He was threatened with ostracism by all the other owners, the people that Red Smith used to call "the fatheads who run baseball." That phrase comes to mind because I think the real reason there are no black general managers is that there are a sufficient number of fatheads running baseball who think blacks aren't intelligent enough to be general managers. Al Campanis has been a friend for forty years, and he doesn't only have my respect—the Dodger record tells us what kind of a baseball man he is. But let's say what it is—that there is a sense that the black can work in the field, he can work in the cotton field and he can work on the ball field, but ask a black to use his brain, run a team, plan a team? Oh my goodness, you're talking about real integration here.

Word was coming into the control room now from Las Vegas. The twelfth round of the Leonard-Hagler fight was about over. It had been an astonishing match, and Leonard might have actually won. The news hardly mattered anymore. Kaplan and Koppel knew they were in the middle of an entirely different broadcast than the one they had begun at eleven-thirty. "We owed it to Campanis, we owed it to the program, we owed it to the issue of race and baseball, not to just stop in mid-interview here," Koppel said later.

KOPPEL: Al Campanis, from everything I understand, you're a very decent man and a highly respected man in baseball.

I confess to you, before we began this program, baseball is not one of my areas of expertise. I'd like to give you another chance to dig yourself out, because I think you need it.

CAMPANIS: Well, let me just say this, Mr. Koppel. How many executives do you have on a higher level or a higher echelon in your business, in TV, I mean—

KOPPEL: You're absolutely right. But I—

CAMPANIS: —or anchormen? How many black anchormen do you have?

KOPPEL: Fortunately—

CAMPANIS: —let's turn about.

Sports columnist Scott Ostler would later write, "I've seen Koppel go for the jugular, grill a guest the way a hibachi grills a sirloin. This time, he seemed genuinely embarrassed for Campanis, and shocked."

KOPPEL: Yeah. Fortunately, there are a few black anchormen, but if you want me to tell you why there aren't any black executives, I'm not going to tell you it's 'cause the blacks aren't intelligent enough. I'm going to tell you it's because whites have been running the—have been running the establishment of broadcasting just as they've been running the establishment of baseball for too long and seem to be reluctant to give up power. I mean, that's what it finally boils down to, isn't it?

CAMPANIS: Well, we have scouts in our organization who are black, and they're very capable people. I have never said that blacks are not intelligent. I think that many of them are highly intelligent, but they may not have the desire to be in the front office. I know that they have wanted to manage and some of them have managed, but they're outstanding athletes, very God-gifted, and they're very wonderful people, and that's all I can tell you about them.

I am watching this man immolate himself, Kahn thought.

KOPPEL: Roger Kahn, I must say I'm flabbergasted. It seems to me we haven't made all that much progress, then, in forty years.

KAHN: Ted, we haven't.

Finally, Campanis offered what he thought was a hopeful message: Progress in the front office would happen, he said, but it wouldn't "happen overnight."

CAMPANIS: If you look back and think about the fact that it took so long for an athlete, just—you've got to realize that it's going to take a little time also for executives and managers. They have to sort of get into this just about the rate that Jackie did, which took a long time.

KOPPEL: ... I guess I don't need to remind you, Mr. Campanis, when Jackie Robinson joined, you were a kid. You were, what, in your twenties?

CAMPANIS: I was in my mid-twenties, right.

KOPPEL: Mid-twenties. All right. Well, you're a man in your mid-sixties right now. How many generations is this going to take, do you think?

CAMPANIS: Well, I don't have the crystal ball, Mr. Koppel, but I can only tell you that I think we're progressing very well in the game of baseball. We have not stopped the black man from becoming an executive. They also have to have the desire, just as Jackie Robinson had the desire to become an outstanding ballplayer.

KAHN: I can't imagine that there is no black who has the desire to be a major league general manager. There's a Don King in boxing, who seems to be a pretty good entrepreneur. There has never been a black owner of a major league baseball team.

KOPPEL: Just a matter of curiosity, Mr. Campanis. What is the percentage now of black ballplayers in your franchise?

CAMPANIS: I would say I think Roger mentioned the fact that about a third of the players are black. That might be a pretty good number, and deservedly so, because they are outstanding athletes. They are gifted with great musculature and various other things, they're fleet of foot, and this is why there are a lot of black major league ball players. Now, as far as having the background to become club presidents, or president of a bank, I don't know. But I do know when I look at a black ballplayer, I am looking at him physically and whether he has the mental approach to play in the big leagues.

By now Leonard's upset over Hagler was about as relevant to what had just occurred as a ballet. Koppel closed the show with a brief update from Dick Schaap, whose enthusiastic account of the fight now seemed completely at odds with the sad implications of the conversation that had preceded him.

Kaplan hardly paid attention to the segment out of Las Vegas. He was reeling from what had transpired in the "fun" tribute to Robinson. Thirty-five minutes earlier, he couldn't have dreamed that an homage to a sports hero of the 1940s and 1950s would make news. But it had. He would later remember feeling sick to his stomach. "I felt terrible. Campanis was one of Robinson's friends. A nice guy. But he'd just gotten in deeper and deeper and worse and worse." The show had unexpectedly laid bare the ugly racism lying behind the all-American facade of baseball.

The switchboard was lighting up from viewers across the country by the time the show went off the air. Koppel told Roger Kahn he hoped that Kahn's phone was unlisted. "The switchboard here is already going crazy," Koppel warned.

During the drive home, Kahn thought to himself, Boy, I'll bet the league gives Al Campanis a big fine. At three in the morning, Kahn's phone shook him awake. It was his son. The same son whom Campanis had advised to "stick with the books" was now a student at UCLA. *Nightline* had just gotten off the air on the West Coast. "I have never been more proud of you than I was tonight, Dad," his son told him. Kahn fell back asleep realizing the show just might make an impact.

The next morning civil rights groups, politicians, athletes, sports fans, and sports journalists issued statements condemning Campanis's remarks on *Nightline.* Both the NAACP and the Urban League demanded that Campanis be fired. Los Angeles mayor Tom Bradley called Campanis's remarks "a blight on baseball." A black player on the Dodgers condemned Campanis on television.

Later that day, Campanis and the Dodgers issued a written apology, but the furor persisted. Two days after his appearance on *Nightline,* Campanis was asked to resign by the Dodgers. Their manager, Tommy Lasorda, who had known Campanis for decades, cried as he told reporters he loved Campanis "like a brother." As for the statements on *Nightline,* Lasorda said that Campanis "was just confused."

The bigger problem for baseball was that Campanis had inadvertently revealed an ugly truth about racial attitudes in the front office, and firing him wasn't going to end what was now a national debate. "The red light of the ABC camera," wrote the *Los Angeles Times,* "became a full-scale spotlight that illuminated the sport's hiring pattern and the absence of minorities in virtually all roles." Johnny Roseboro, who'd played for the Dodgers for ten years, said in a television interview that the Dodgers were a "closed corporation." Harry Edwards, a professor of sports sociology, came on *Nightline* the night Campanis was fired and described "a plantation system in American sports, with blacks consigned to the production roles of athletes, and whites having a total monopoly on the decision-making and authority positions." Reggie Jackson of the Oakland A's told Koppel on that same program that racism was more hidden and, in a way, more pernicious than in the days of Jackie Robinson. To be black in baseball in the late 1980s, he said, "you get to fight a shadow, you get to fight an invisible thing."

Baseball commissioner Peter Ueberroth met with civil rights leaders and hired a consulting firm to help baseball clubs launch affirmative action programs. Ueberroth turned to Harry Edwards to develop a pool of former minority players and to organize management clinics around the country. Edwards had someone in mind to help him: Al Campanis. Campanis agreed. He helped Edwards develop the pool and the clinics. He even spoke to some of Edwards's college classes.

Campanis told the students, "If losing my job with the Dodgers has helped the blacks, I'm happy it happened. It was a shock at the time, but if I contributed to increased employment of minorities, I feel it was worthwhile." A year after his appearance on *Nightline,* Campanis told the *Los Angeles Times,* "It has turned to a plus for baseball and myself." By then, the pool he had worked on with Edwards had produced several black base-running and batting instructors, a black minor-league coach, and a black at the head of the league's umpire development program. A third of the nearly 550 nonplaying major league positions that had opened up over the year had gone to minorities.

Still, the top positions remained almost exclusively white. As of April 1988, of all the owners, presidents, general managers, and field managers, the only representative of a minority group was Cookie Rojas, who'd been newly appointed as the manager of the California Angels. And almost a decade after that, although the Dodgers had a black vice-president for public relations, there was only one black general manager in the major leagues, and still not one black owner.

In the spring of 1988, almost a year to the day after the Campanis broadcast, Roger Kahn arrived to cover the Dodgers in spring training and was told that for the first time, he would not be allowed to stay in the hotel complex that was the Dodgers' inner sanctum, the place where he usually met with players and managers. He tried to find out why, and asked to speak to the owner of the team, Peter O'Malley, whom he'd known since boyhood in New York. O'Malley wouldn't speak to him. Nor would the team manager, Tommy Lasorda.

Kahn remained proud, nonetheless, of his appearance on *Nightline,* and not just because of his allegiance to Robinson. That evening in 1987 would take on a more profound meaning for him as the months and years passed, for a deeply personal reason. The son who had called from UCLA, the boy who'd phoned to praise his father at three A.M., would die of an accidental drug overdose later that year. "The call from my son, when he told me he was proud of me, was the last lucid conversation we ever had."

The Campanis broadcast had a long-term impact on *Nightline.* Producer Artis Waters saw how Campanis had lifted a curtain on run-of-the-mill bigotry, and Waters concluded, "Sports is the perfect prism, a prism of American culture, attitudes, and business." Waters and reporter Armen Keteyian eventually collaborated on special broadcasts about sports and race: the dearth of black college football coaches, the relatively small number of black quarterbacks in the NFL, and the minuscule number of blacks in the front offices of baseball, years after Al

Campanis had been fired for saying on *Nightline* that blacks might not have the "necessities" to be baseball executives. They would also produce a *Nightline* documentary on the Arkansas Razorbacks basketball team, tracking the players through the final two weeks of the 1994 NCAA championship. (The Arkansas coach, Nolan Richardson, who'd been the first black coach in the Southwest Conference, would point out, bitterly, that none of the regular sportscasters ever talked about him with the kind of affection or familiarity or enthusiasm that they showed for a white coach with a lesser record like Bobby Knight.)

KOPPEL SPOKE TO CAMPANIS only once after that infamous broadcast. It happened several years later, when Koppel was in Los Angeles on business. Campanis phoned Koppel in his hotel and asked if he could see him. Koppel agreed.

A few hours later, they met for coffee in the lobby of the Century Plaza Hotel. Campanis told Koppel that he harbored no hard feelings about what had happened. He told Koppel that he had been unprepared to discuss the issue of blacks in the front office and that the question had caught him off balance. But he wanted Koppel to know that he was all right. Besides his work on behalf of minority recruitment, his life in general was going well; he was even planning to get married. Everything, he said, had worked out for the best.

"I think he wanted me to see that he wasn't a bad guy," said Koppel. "And I don't think he is a bad guy. It's very good that what happened in that interview came out. On the other hand, I'm very sorry that Al Campanis had to be the instrument for that. Because I think there are lots of people throughout American industry, and certainly in American athletics, who are genuine racists but who are smart enough to conceal it when they're on television. And Al Campanis, I don't think, is a racist at all, or was. I just think he was not a very smart old man who ended up saying some foolish things on television that reflected the reality of what was going on. He just didn't realize the impact of what he was saying."

There were two ironies about that night with Al Campanis. The first was that an homage to the fight against racism in baseball turned into an unintended exposé of the racism that still poisoned the sport. The second was that, in contrast to most guests who appear on *Nightline,* Al Campanis had no agenda, beyond his desire to pay tribute to a friend; yet he remains, as far as it is possible to know, the only *Nightline* guest who has ever lost his job as a direct consequence of remarks made on the broadcast.

MICHAEL DUKAKIS HOPED there *would* be consequences if he went on *Nightline.*

"DUKAKIS 'NIGHTLINE' SPOT VIEWED AS DESPERATE MEASURE," ran the headline in the *Los Angeles Times.* "Democratic nominee Michael S. Dukakis is appearing on ABC's 'Nightline' tonight for 90 minutes one-on-one with anchorman Ted Koppel," the story reported. " 'And that,' says William Schneider, a political scientist at the American Enterprise Institute and an independent consultant to the *Times,* 'has the smell of desperation. [Dukakis] realized he blew his last best chance [to make up ground] in the debate, and now he wants one more crack at the national audience.' "

Dukakis *was* desperate. The salad days of July 1988, when he'd led George Bush by sixteen percentage points, seemed like another campaign. With only two weeks until the election, Bush was up by thirteen and gaining.

Bush's campaign, masterminded by strategist Lee Atwater, had mercilessly forged Dukakis the New Democrat into Dukakis the Old-Fashioned Liberal. The Bush people turned every photo opportunity into an attack: Bush surveying polluted Boston Harbor, a "legacy" of Dukakis's term as governor of Massachusetts; Bush wrapping himself in a flag at a factory, silently alluding to Dukakis defending flag-burners. Then came the cynical and devastating "Willie Horton" ads.

Dukakis in the meantime had proved himself almost as adept as Bush—in hurting Dukakis. The governor even handed the opposition a new ad campaign when he posed atop a tank wearing a ridiculous-looking helmet. More damaging was his performance in one of the presidential debates. When asked how he would feel about punishing a criminal if the criminal had raped and murdered his own wife, Dukakis replied unemotionally. After that, the campaign had begun hemorrhaging and nothing seemed to stop it.

ABC News had, in September 1988, issued an invitation to Bush and Dukakis for what ABC called "an open-ended discussion," with Ted Koppel serving as a "moderator." Both men were informed that if one of them declined, then the one who accepted would sit alone with Koppel for a ninety-minute interview.

Bush conformed to the classic strategy of a candidate who is leading by a huge margin: hunker down, make no mistakes, and avoid as much as possible a situation that the candidate cannot control. Since Bush risked more than he stood to gain from appearing live with Koppel and his opponent, he declined the interview. "George Bush is a turtle with a head drawn into his shell and that is because he is ahead in the race," a political scientist told the *Los Angeles Times*. "It makes perfectly good sense to stay inside and hope the currents of the race will push him past the finish line. The last thing he needs is to let Ted Koppel stick a finger in his eye."

But Dukakis, at this point, had "nothing to lose," recalled Paul Costello, who was one of his press aides at the time. "His message certainly was not coming through. On a live program, especially a live program, there's a chance that you can get your message out. It was time to go for broke."

"They knew they were behind," Koppel would reflect later. "They knew they had to do something dramatic. They knew they had to change the public perception of Dukakis."

So, on October 25, 1988, Koppel and Dukakis met in Denver, one of the campaign stops, for a live interview, face-to-face. Koppel started out by asking Dukakis about his plunge in the polls.

DUKAKIS: We've been so polled and polled and polled that I think we're all getting a little tired of the numbers.

Tired. The word fit the candidate precisely. He looked tired. He sounded tired. He sort of slumped in his chair, his voice almost a monotone. The man was running for President and he looked as though he didn't have the energy for it. The fact was, he was exhausted. Dukakis's day had started at six A.M. in California. He hadn't arrived in Denver until early evening, at which point he'd attended a rally at the airport—attended by hundreds—instead of resting up for an interview that would be watched by millions.

Rick Kaplan, who was there with Koppel, had known as soon as Dukakis walked in the studio door, thirty-five minutes before air, that he was unprepared and overtired. Kaplan felt disgusted. He had advised the campaign to give their man some rest before the broadcast. This was make-or-break time. It occurred to Kaplan that Dukakis was "self-destructive."

Koppel urged the candidate to offer something fresh. The more Koppel pressed, the more he seemed to be badgering a worn-out man.

KOPPEL: The point that I'm trying to make, you're still coming back with the same answers that you've been giving for weeks now. And what I'm saying to you, or at least suggesting to you, is that the Bush campaign—as much as you may not like the way it's being handled—is effective as all get-out.

DUKAKIS: Well, I'm not sure. I think people are turning off in the campaign.

KOPPEL: Based on what?

DUKAKIS: Based on my own reading of what is happening out there. My own contact with people, what people are telling us. I think there's still a long way to go in this kind of campaign—thirteen days is a very long time.

KOPPEL: No, it's not. Thirteen days—thirteen days is almost nothing.

Some of Dukakis's aides, watching in a room nearby, cringed. Koppel was coming on so strong. He almost sounded contemptuous, they thought.

KOPPEL: Let me suggest as someone who's been watching from the outside, if you think you're winning right now, Governor—

DUKAKIS: I didn't say I was winning, Ted.

KOPPEL: If you think you're making ground, if you think you're picking up ground, every independent, every objective indicator—whether it's the Gallup poll, whether it's the NBC poll, whether it's the ABC poll, whether it's the CBS poll—they all show you losing ground. And you're still saying the same kinds of things—

Thomas Oliphant, who was covering Dukakis for *The Boston Globe*, would write of these exchanges: "The endless 'loser' questions were the political equivalent of the opening question in the second debate when the governor was asked about the hypothetical rape and murder of his wife." The problem, noted Oliphant, was that "not once did [Dukakis] fight back. . . . The Dukakis smile stayed tight as he was told he is failing either to understand or adjust, and the voice patiently resumed its auto-pilot journey."

KOPPEL: Let me ask you a definition. And you'll know where I'm coming from as soon as you hear the word. How do you define the word *liberal*? What is a liberal in 1988?

DUKAKIS: That's maybe a question that we ought to ask George Bush if he had been here.

KOPPEL: No, no, I'd like to hear—I'd like to hear your definition.

DUKAKIS: Well, I think all of us have combinations of liberal and conservative about us, Ted. I'm not a liberal.

KOPPEL: Governor, forgive me, that's been your answer now for three months.

DUKAKIS: Yeah, but—

KOPPEL: I'd like to hear how you define—what is a liberal?

DUKAKIS: Well, if one is a liberal in the tradition of Franklin Roosevelt and Harry Truman and John Kennedy and—

KOPPEL: Nineteen eighty-eight. Nineteen eighty-eight, Governor.

Most of Dukakis's supporters were mystified. Why was Koppel acting so hostile? In the suite of a New York hotel, where Kitty Dukakis watched with aides and supporters, there was tisking and muttering and head-shaking. There had been jubilance and jokes earlier in the evening. All that was lost now to a kind of macabre pall.

Oliphant later wrote that the problem was not Koppel but Dukakis: "He refuses to get personally angry with Bush, or even his interviewer, or to reformulate his ideas into some emotion-catching summary."

Not even Koppel could understand why Dukakis didn't fight back. "If the roles had been reversed," Koppel told a colleague later,

"I would have gone after me! I would have said, 'How dare you!' At least he could have said something like, 'This is between me and the American voter, and you may have one vote, Mr. Koppel, but that's all you've got. And there are a hundred million other voters out there, and I think they're going to make their decisions on other things.' But he seemed entirely ill-prepared—ill-prepared to do anything interesting, let alone dramatic."

DUKAKIS: Anybody who knows Mike Dukakis knows that I care very deeply about family, about community, about values, about ethics, about work and the importance of making it possible for every citizen of this country to work and earn and support themselves and their families. And—

KOPPEL: Governor, forgive me—

DUKAKIS: —again, I don't think that really carries a label with it. I've got a record, I'm proud of it. And I hope people will take a look at that record, and then make their own judgment.

KOPPEL: Let me—there's a piece of video that I'd like you to take a look at. You've seen it before. In one sense, with all due respect, let me suggest to you, I still don't think you get it.

"I still don't think you get it." For those watching with Kitty Dukakis, the statement was "like a dagger," said Paul Costello. "It was almost like a public beheading. It shocked the whole room." Mrs. Dukakis blanched. "Turn it off," she said. "I can't bear to watch." Within minutes, the suite emptied.

Even ABC News president Roone Arledge was beginning to feel uncomfortable. "I didn't feel so sorry for Dukakis," Arledge remembered, "because he should have known better. This was Dukakis's last big shot and he was just mouthing clichés. But Ted was relentless with him, and Dukakis was turning into a punching bag. Ted was becoming the heavy; I was worried he was going to end up looking like a bully."

Arledge put in a call to Denver. "It was one of the few times that I have ever called in the middle of a program to tell Ted that he was being too tough." Kaplan, who took Arledge's call, agreed that

Dukakis seemed like a punch-drunk fighter. He whispered to Koppel. "It's Koppel 9, Dukakis o." The message was that Koppel might want to back off.

"I *was* awfully close to the line at that point," Koppel said later, "and clearly, some people felt I was over the line. But I did not feel I'd crossed it. What was going through my head was the thought that so often occurs to me in a live interview: What are the people at home seeing right now? And what they were seeing was a man who didn't seem to get it. And sometimes you have to give voice to that. But even in giving voice to it, I was inviting the candidate to slap me down, to challenge my assessment, to put me in my place. He didn't. And I couldn't imagine why he didn't."

Neither could one of Dukakis's aides, who was seated just out of camera range. During a commercial break, adviser Tom Donilon raced onto the set, crouched down next to his boss, and urged, "Get mad, Governor!" But Dukakis said nothing. He looked spent.

The candidate continued to sink in a swamp of platitudes and no one could pull him out. Koppel tried to tamp down his frustration, but the effort showed. On the issue of drugs and the Medillín cartel:

DUKAKIS: So tough enforcement both at home and abroad is something that's absolutely essential in this fight, but I don't think you have to deny people constitutional rights to do it.

KOPPEL: Fine. Substance, Governor. Let's talk substance. . . .

DUKAKIS: How do you effectively break the back of that cartel when you're dealing with a guy that's been sheltering them in Panama? I mean, how do you—

KOPPEL: Governor—

DUKAKIS: How do you do that?

KOPPEL: You raise interesting questions, but I'm raising a question; I'd like to hear a substantive response from you.

In the end, an old friend of Dukakis's described the whole evening as "sad. It was just a sad end to the campaign." Dukakis's loyalists believed that Koppel had been "excessively harsh, and cruel, and personal." But the consensus was also that the candidate had blown a golden opportunity to show the passion that exemplifies leadership. He hadn't fought back.

Koppel's guess was that viewers were turning off their sets wondering, If Dukakis can't swat Koppel aside, what's he ever going to do with Gorbachev?

Oliphant summed up the political impact in the next day's *Boston Globe:* " 'Nightline' was perhaps Dukakis' last, best opportunity to break up the hardening foundation beneath the status quo of Bush's sizable lead in the polls . . . Some Dukakis advisers argue that the importance of an event like the 'Nightline' interview lies in the fact that it happened, not in what happened during it . . . Privately, though, there remains a strong conviction among others in the Dukakis family that Tuesday night was another lost opportunity to shake up the status quo."

Costello concluded that the real damage of the *Nightline* interview was what it did inside the Dukakis camp: it killed hope. "Esprit and morale are so critical to the whole movement of a campaign. And a show like this, that everybody's watching, that the campaign is watching, and supporters are watching, and it either fires you up to think you can do it or it's like taking a cold shower. This was an *ice cube* shower."

AS DISPARATE AS WERE the careers and personalities of Michael Dukakis and Al Campanis, their interviews with Koppel shared a common thread. Koppel responded to the men before him, not to the sweet old baseball veteran as described in a Dodger press release or to the man in the "Dukakis for President" television commercial. Yet both seemed unprepared for the interviewer to listen so closely to what they actually said.

Campanis and Dukakis were two of Koppel's most surprising guests. In both cases, Koppel used his own astonishment as an interviewing tool. The more he expressed his surprise at the espousals of the man who called himself Jackie Robinson's friend, the more espousals Al Campanis offered up. The more Koppel pressed for a statement of conviction from the man who wanted to be President of the United States, the more Michael Dukakis shut down and conveyed the image of a candidate with no convictions at all.

TEN
Epidemic

SERGIO GUERRERO WAS DYING. On a June night in 1991, he lay in a Palo Alto hospital, an oxygen mask clamped to his mouth. Every hour or so, he'd pick up the phone next to his pillow, dial a number, wait for a hello, peel off his oxygen mask, and launch into a tirade: "Listen to me, LeDonne! If you can't cut this thing right, I'm getting out of bed and flying to New York and cutting it myself! If I have to die in the editing room, I'll do it!" Then he'd slam down the phone.

Guerrero, after all, was a *Nightline* veteran. He *knew* how to tell a story. And damn if his own obit wasn't going to come out just the way that Guerrero wanted it.

The man at the other end of the phone, producer Bob LeDonne, took heart in each and every remonstration. This was the same arrogant perfectionist Sergio his colleagues had grown to love over the years. Sergio's deathbed panache was both admirable and comforting. Sergio was still fighting.

Nightline was losing one of its own to a disease that had not even existed—not as far as anyone knew, anyway—when *Nightline* began.

JUST BEFORE CHRISTMAS 1981, the Centers for Disease Control issued a report on mysterious incidences of rare cancers and pneumonia afflicting gay men. Six months later, the CDC issued another report on what it now called a human immunodeficiency virus. The CDC could not verify for certain the virus's means of transmission, nor could it ascertain why it had been discovered, first, in gay men and, more recently, in a few babies. Producer Bob LeDonne and correspondent Betty Rollin began to investigate who was actually contracting the disease. They found that a baby in San Francisco had acquired the virus after a blood transfusion. But other babies in other inner-city hospitals—many of whom had never received any transfusions—were also showing symptoms of the virus.

On December 17, 1982, *Nightline* presented its first broadcast on AIDS. The epidemic had yet to make page one of *The New York Times* (and another six months would pass before it would). Still, all Koppel needed to do to justify the attention that *Nightline* was devoting to the topic was recite the grim statistics.

KOPPEL: Good evening. The disease has already claimed more victims than Legionnaire's Disease and toxic shock syndrome combined: more than eight hundred cases nationwide, three hundred-plus of those fatal. And every day three more cases are identified, and yet still surprisingly few people are familiar with the Acquired Immune Deficiency Syndrome, or the acronym by which it's frequently identified, AIDS. The reason for that may lie, in part, in the character of its most common victims. When AIDS first cropped up about eighteen months ago, almost all of its victims were homosexual males who frequently changed sexual partners. Alarming enough to that particular segment of society, but, so it first appeared, not threatening to the public at large. But that seems to be changing, and the disease may be spreading.

LeDonne and Rollin had prepared a story about a hospital in Newark where eight children had contracted the virus. Four of them had already died. One, a boy named Ahmad, was the infant son of a drug addict.

ROLLIN: Ahmad Carlisle is only eighteen months old, but he has spent most of his life fighting a new, deadly disease that no one understands, not where it comes from, how to treat it, or how to stop it from spreading.

The other boy in Rollin's story was a hemophiliac. His mother expressed the terror of not knowing how to protect her child.

MOTHER: To think that you're injecting your child with blood that may kill him eventually is just frightening because you don't know what you're doing—you don't know to give him or not to give him. And you have to give him, 'cause otherwise, you know, dreadful things will happen from the hemophilia.

All of the children at the Newark hospital were the patients of Dr. James Oleske.

OLESKE: I'm frustrated that since we don't know what the agent is, we don't have any specific therapies. We have a lot of ideas, and we're trying some of the ideas. We have had now eight children. We've lost four, and we don't want to lose the other four.

The final shot in Rollin's story showed Oleske gently ministering to Ahmad, offering some reassurance to him. Rollin didn't want to end on that image, because it avoided the grim truth about Ahmad's prognosis. Instead she wanted to close with some visual reminder that AIDS appeared to be 100 percent fatal. But LeDonne had argued that Ahmad's mother deserved a hopeful ending. As it turned out, even the suggestion of hope was quickly dashed by the interview segment.

DR. JAMES CURRAN (*Centers for Disease Control, AIDS Task Force*): Well, Ted, unfortunately the cause of AIDS remains unknown [but] the overwhelming evidence now of the occurrence of this very dramatic illness in these seemingly different groups of people suggests that it probably is caused by an infectious transmissible agent . . .

KOPPEL: Is there no way to identify from a donor whether that person has—or to identify someone suffering from AIDS when you take blood from them?

DR. JOSEPH BOVE: There is no way. . . . There is no way. There's no test grades, and we don't have enough information about the cause.

KOPPEL: . . . How long after a transfusion would someone show symptoms?

DR. BOVE: One of the real difficulties we have here is this dormant or latent or incubation period is a lot longer than a few months. It may be as long as a year or longer . . . but it appears that the donor is infectious for a year, and long before the donor feels ill. So these are donors who are feeling well, who give blood and plasma for the production of Factor VIII for the hemophiliacs while they're feeling well and yet are carriers of the agent if there is an agent . . . We couldn't possibly identify those donors who gave three or two or even one year ago and are now ill.

KOPPEL: I want to phrase this next question very carefully because I don't want to be an alarmist. But it is theoretically possible, then, that as the number of people with AIDS grows, that this could move geometrically out into the general population?

DR. BOVE: It's to me not only theoretically possible but very frightening.

For the next several years, other medical stories would come and go. Producer Julie Hartenstein, who had done postgraduate work in medical journalism, would note the medical "marvels" that didn't pan out, and the medical "crises" that faded after a day or two on the front pages. Barney Clark, the first patient to receive an artificial heart, survived only a few months. Koppel interviewed him before his death. *Nightline* would also report the case of a baby named Faye, who lived for a time with a baboon's heart. Herpes, once considered so terrify-

ing a virus that *Time* magazine put it on its cover, lost power to ter-
rorize; cancer did not.

All the while, AIDS marched on. It fomented fear, it elicited questions that no one could answer, it created new quandaries and choices
that few wanted to face. It continued to kill, leaving thousands dead,
tens of thousands dying. In December 1984, almost two years exactly
since the first broadcast on AIDS, *Nightline* examined its mysteries and
myths.

KOPPEL: In the couple of years that we have known about AIDS,
               it has been a disease associated largely with gossip and a
               sort of social superstition. There are characteristics to
               AIDS that we in the public think we know: its tendency
               to strike homosexual men, drug addicts who use un-
               sterilized needles, hemophiliacs, and, for some reason,
               Haitians. But there are also things about AIDS that we do
               not know but have heard: that somehow AIDS can be
               transmitted by casual contact with a carrier, that women
               have now begun falling victim to AIDS and are passing it
               on to men who are not gay, that a sure test for AIDS has
               been or is just about to be found, that a cure is just around
               the corner. We will try this evening to separate what is
               known beyond doubt from what you've simply heard.

Americans were still struggling to understand the fundamentals of
the disease, even three years after the first CDC report.

KOPPEL: Can women get AIDS?

DR. STEPHEN CAIAZZA (*internist*):   Yes, Ted. Women can get AIDS. . . .

KOPPEL: Why Haitians?

DR. CAIAZZA: We don't know . . .

Caiazza said that the AIDS virus could be isolated from blood, and
even from saliva.

KOPPEL: Now, saliva. That would suggest that it could be passed
               on by kissing.

DR. CAIAZZA: Theoretically. But on epidemiological grounds we
                know that this is not the case . . .

KOPPEL: Is it always fatal?

DR. CAIAZZA: For the past four years, there is a mortality rate of one
                hundred percent for people who had the disease four
                years ago.

When cameras captured Rock Hudson being ferried to a hospital on a stretcher, his publicist finally announced what the tabloids had
speculated for months: Hudson had AIDS. A few days after the announcement, LeDonne put in a call to Dr. Oleske in Newark, for an
update on children with AIDS. "Where the hell have you been?"
Oleske snapped. Oleske told LeDonne that in the two and a half years
since *Nightline* had focused on his pediatric AIDS clinic, the government still ignored children with AIDS, and his clinic was desperate
for funds. No one in government *or* the media seemed to care about
the hundreds of inner-city children who were coming down with
the syndrome, Oleske complained. "You people in the media only
pay attention when it's a handsome white movie star," Oleske told
LeDonne. "No one cares about all of these little anonymous brown
and black babies who are dying before my eyes."

LeDonne began looking for more young children upon whom he
could focus, but he found that in the years since his first story, the
stigma of the illness had gotten so bad that few parents wanted their
children identified as carriers of AIDS.

The mysteries persisted. The hysteria seemed to be spreading
even faster and wider than the virus itself. *Nightline*'s producers and
correspondents began meeting with Koppel and executive producer
Rick Kaplan about new ways to approach the epidemic. Kaplan
decided it merited something unprecedented: a "national" town
meeting.

In June 1987, in a theater in Los Angeles, a panel of scientists, doctors, activists, and people with AIDS sat before an audience comprised
of a cross-section of Los Angeles. Television viewers in the Midwest
and the East were invited to phone in questions live; radio listeners,
who could tune into the "simulcast" from anywhere in the nation,
could call in too.

CALLER FROM MISSOURI: My question is, should we isolate those with
AIDS now, or wait until we have to isolate those who
are left that do not have AIDS?

CALLER FROM NORTH CAROLINA: Is it possible for a child to get AIDS
from the mother by breast-feeding?

CALLER FROM TEXAS: What's wrong with identifying the carriers of
AIDS?

AUDIENCE MEMBER: I've been married to one woman for eleven
years. And I appreciate the sex act as much as anyone.
But what my question has to do with, does anyone enjoy
it enough to die for it?

The program, which ABC scheduled on a Friday night, was
"open-ended," which meant it could wind on as long into the night
as Kaplan and Koppel deemed worthwhile. They would deem it
worthwhile for almost four and a half hours. Ratings showed that even
a three-thirty in the morning on the East Coast, millions were still
watching.

The program closed on a taped "Petacque," a natural-sound story
built around the voices of doctors and nurses treating AIDS patients.

DOCTOR: (*to elderly man with AIDS*) What are you most afraid of?

PATIENT: Pain, I guess. I'm afraid of pain.

DOCTOR: I will not let you have pain.

Koppel heard about a gay newspaper that was publishing the diary
of a man with AIDS. A camera could document the struggle against
death with unique poignancy, Koppel thought, maybe better in some
ways than a newspaper. Some of the visual changes that would take
place over time in a person with AIDS could be presented with no
words of explanation at all. He posed the concept to LeDonne: "I
wonder if you could find a person with AIDS who would allow you
to produce a video diary of his remaining days. You could do it over
the course of several months—a year, maybe. The key would be to
capture the everyday struggles, the routines, the attitudes of friends

and family—every dimension of the person's life—and the changes that take place as the disease progresses." Rick Kaplan offered more blunt instructions. "Follow someone to his grave," Kaplan told LeDonne. "That's the only way to make it true, and powerful. Find someone who will let you and a camera be there, right up until the end."

The next day, LeDonne took a cab to New York's Greenwich Village, to a rickety building housing the Gay Men's Health Crisis. He met a volunteer there, a tall, slender man with red hair, fair skin, and a wry sense of humor. He worked as one of the counselors on the AIDS hotline. His name was Ken Meeks. He told LeDonne a little about himself. He had a doctorate in economics and was a former teacher. He had been married once, years earlier, but his bride of three months had died in a car accident. For twelve years, Meeks had lived with a male companion, a pet-store owner named Jack Steinhoebel. Meeks had AIDS. He agreed to be the subject of the video diary.

LeDonne asked a veteran ABC cameraman named John Landi if he'd be interested in chronicling the life of a man with AIDS. Landi was well loved by producers for the respect and gentleness he accorded anyone who came in front of his lens. Landi and Beth Corwin, his sound engineer, told LeDonne that they would welcome the assignment.

Over the next nine months, LeDonne, Landi, and Corwin regularly dropped in on Meeks and Steinhoebel. By September, they had a video diary: Meeks and Steinhoebel having dinner with Meeks's parents, Meeks visiting his doctor, Meeks addressing an AIDS fundraiser. The final part of the diary was actually shot by Steinhoebel on a small video camera, during a cross-country train trip.

MEEKS (*home video at the Grand Canyon*):   Hi, Mom and Dad. This is
                the most glorious, colorful, beautiful, natural—what can
                I say?

The two reached the Golden Gate Bridge just before Meeks's body began to fail. A few days later, on Meeks's forty-fifth birthday, he lay in a hospital bed, surrounded by loved ones. The plan had been for Koppel to eventually interview Meeks as a coda to the video diary. But Meeks was dying. It was obvious he would never leave the hospital again. Still, he insisted that he wanted to do the interview with Koppel. It was the right way to end his diary, he told his family. So Landi's camera was brought in, and Koppel interviewed Meeks by satellite.

Meeks could not lift his head. He was skeletal. He occasionally gasped for air, and winced with pain. His red hair was just a few wisps on the pillow, now. Steinhoebel stood next to him and quietly wept.

KOPPEL: Ken, it almost sounds like what they used to call meanie jokes in the old days, to say happy birthday. But it is your birthday and you are celebrating it. Is there any happiness in it for you at all?

MEEKS: Well, of course, yes. Life is something that's exciting. Life is something that goes on. And just because there's an illness which may be terminal, that doesn't mean that you give up living.

KOPPEL: You know, in one sense this story, your story, has been a story of watching a disease take its toll. But in another sense, it has been very much a chronicle of a love story. You two love each other very much, don't you?

MEEKS: Yes indeed.

KOPPEL: That's something also that a lot of people in the straight community have a great deal of trouble understanding. I don't know whether, you know, if somebody said to me, 'Explain why you love your wife,' I'm not sure I could do that to their satisfaction, either. But let me ask you both, Why do you love each other? Jack?

STEINHOEBEL: This is the most special human being I've ever met in my life. This man has more love and compassion inside of him than a football stadium full of people. And not only does he treat me that way, he treats everyone that way.

KOPPEL: Ken, if I put the same question to you—why do you love this man?

MEEKS: Jack is the most caring, the most interested, the most wonderful person who has ever found his way into my life. I would not—I can't say I wouldn't be alive today without him, but there is some truth in that. His caring, his interest, his support. It is just tremendous.

KOPPEL: Ken, you are obviously a man who has been able to look personal tragedy in the eye . . . You know that you're near death, don't you?

MEEKS: Yes.

KOPPEL: How near?

MEEKS: Very. I'm afraid that it's going to be a matter of days, maybe not even that long.

KOPPEL: And yet you're still willing to expend what must be for you at this point an enormous amount of energy and whatever remaining strength you have for this—for this conversation. And I think I will leave it with that by asking you why it is so important to you that quite literally you are willing to expend some of your last breath on saying what you're going to say now.

MEEKS: You know, we all have things we have to do. This is one thing I feel I have to do. There are 220, 240 million people out there calling themselves Americans. There are billions of other people out there in the world calling themselves human beings. And I have an obligation to them, just as they have an obligation to me.

When Meeks died a few weeks later, Steinhoebel told LeDonne that "Ken looked on the diary for *Nightline* as his last teaching assignment." It was a chance to teach not about the process of dying, Meeks had said, but "a process of living."

A television critic for the New York *Daily News* called the broadcast about Ken Meeks "one of the most powerful half-hours in the history of television." There were hundreds of calls to ABC asking for more stories like it. Mail about the broadcast—most of it positive, a portion of it homophobic—poured into the network for weeks. The diary of Meeks marked a turning point in the way that *Nightline* would cover AIDS. There would still be programs devoted to the medical

Ted Koppel hosting *America Held Hostage,* covering the crisis in Iran that he—and almost everyone else at ABC News—thought would last "only a few weeks." *(All photos courtesy of ABC News unless otherwise indicated.)*

Above left: Roone Arledge, president of ABC News, was convinced the hostage crisis gave ABC an opportunity to create a news show that would capture the late-night 11:30 P.M. time slot. *Above right*: David Burke, vice-president of ABC News, helped Arledge win approval from ABC higher-ups to create what became *Nightline*. *Right*: Richard C. Wald, senior vice-president of ABC News, called Koppel at home on his fortieth birthday to offer him the job of becoming anchor of *Nightline*. Wald also came up with the show's name, which Koppel thought was "crappy."

Left: Ted Koppel with Bill Lord, *Nightline*'s first executive producer. *Below*: Roger Goodman, senior producer, and Rick Kaplan, executive producer, in the South African Broadcasting Company's studio; Johannesburg, March 1985.

Above left: Ted Koppel interviewed Winnie Mandela; South Africa, March 1985.
Right: Hours after Nelson Mandela's release from his twenty-seven-year-long imprisonment, Ted Koppel met the future president of South Africa; February 1990.

Right: Dorrance Smith, former *Nightline* executive producer. *Below left*: Le Duc Tho, former foreign minister of North Vietnam who helped negotiate the Paris peace agreements ending the Vietnam War, on the occasion of the tenth anniversary of the U.S. withdrawal. He was a guest on what Koppel would later remember as *Nightline*'s "worst show"; Ho Chi Minh City, April 1985.

Above: Koppel interviewing Corazon Aquino, whose triumph over Ferdinand Marcos was remarkably peaceful; Manila, February 1986.

Above: Ousted Philippines president Ferdinand Marcos interviewed by Ted Koppel; Hawaii, April 1986. *Left*: Koppel's interview of Jim and Tammy Faye Bakker in May 1987 garnered the highest ratings of any *Nightline* program in the seven years the show had been on the air. *Below*: Kermit explains the economy to Koppel; October 1987.

Koppel sitting on the "wall" specially constructed to separate the Palestinian and Israeli participants in the show broadcast from Jerusalem; April 1988.

Above: Koppel interviews Mikhail Gorbachev outside the Kremlin days before the Soviet flag was lowered and replaced by the Russian; Christmas 1991. *Right*: Koppel with "Bone," a retired gang member, and other members of the "Crips" and the "Bloods," gangs prominent in the riots that erupted in Los Angeles in the aftermath of the Rodney King verdict; Los Angeles, May 1992.

Left: Koppel and Roone Arledge backstage at the Tampa Bay Performing Arts Center before a town meeting on health care with President Clinton; Tampa, Florida, September 23, 1993. *Below*: Koppel listening to President Clinton; Tampa, Florida, September 23, 1993.

Koppel with a member of the Michigan Militia at a *Nightline* town meeting; Decker, Michigan, April 1995.

Above: Tom Bettag, executive producer; Dan Morris, chief booker; Richard Harris, senior producer; and Ted Koppel.

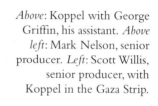

Above: Koppel with George Griffin, his assistant. *Above left*: Mark Nelson, senior producer. *Left*: Scott Willis, senior producer, with Koppel in the Gaza Strip.

"I'm Ted Koppel.
For all of us at ABC News, good night."

statistics and developments in research, but the most enlightening broadcasts on the epidemic would henceforth be the programs that focused on individuals—on faces and names.

BOB LEDONNE FOUND Priscilla Diaz, a mother of four who lived in the Bronx. Diaz's late husband had used drugs and had died of AIDS after transmitting the virus to his wife. Rather than risk the possibility that her children would be turned over to the custody of New York City and placed in foster homes, Diaz had arranged for the transfer of custody of her five-year-old twin boys, seven-year-old daughter, and fifteen-year-old son to relatives in Puerto Rico and Miami.

Diaz's children were already gone when LeDonne met her. She was nearing the end of her life. Her weight had dropped to sixty-five pounds. There was so little flesh on her face that it was all angles, topped by a bandanna because her hair had fallen out. Her voice was raspy. The only subject that seemed to bring Diaz to life was her children. She wanted to see them one last time before she died.

The local Kiwanis and hospital personnel raised the money to honor Priscilla's wish. When *Nightline* began recording the final days of Priscilla, the tiny woman with the sunken eyes was beaming with anticipation; soon she would be touching the faces of her sons and daughter.

DIAZ: I feel happy because I'm going to see them . . .

John Landi recorded the arrival of the three younger children; Priscilla clenched them against her. These three, Diaz later told the camera, were too young to understand her illness. Indeed, the children smiled and squealed and said they were just happy to be with their mother. But the oldest, fifteen-year-old Milton, looked numb. There was no emotion in his eyes at all. He understood what was happening. He understood what would happen.

MILTON: Now she's just lost everything. She's weak, but she has too much faith—that's what's keeping her alive, the faith that she has. The only thing that she don't got is us with her. That's the only thing she don't got.

When the time came for Milton to return to his grandmother in Puerto Rico, the camera recorded the final moments he would ever be held by his mother. She sobbed, caressing his head. Tears streamed down the boy's cheeks.

A few weeks after Diaz's story aired, she died. LeDonne, Landi, and Corwin attended her funeral. No more than fifteen people were there. The only flowers on the casket were from *Nightline*. But Joan Kroc, the widow of the founder of McDonald's, was so moved by Priscilla's story on *Nightline* that she donated $3 million to the hospital where Diaz had been treated, to fund an outpatient AIDS clinic.

The story did not end there. The Kroc donation created an uproar in the Bronx. The neighborhood near the hospital was comprised mostly of hardworking blue-collar families; they didn't want people with AIDS stumbling by their homes.

The hospital tried to soothe the fearful by holding a meeting in a high school auditorium. LeDonne took Landi and Corwin to record the event. "Onstage were about a dozen medical experts, religious leaders, and a couple of local politicians who swiftly faded into the background," LeDonne remembered. "The audience was packed with nearly a thousand residents who had been whipped into a fury by grass-roots community leaders. I was stunned by the fireworks. The angriest members of the audience were saying they didn't want 'dope addicts and faggots' wandering through their neighborhood for treatment at an outpatient AIDS clinic. Speaker after speaker railed against the clinic because it would bring crime and disease, the streets wouldn't be safe, property values would decline, the children would be in danger.

"The leaders on the stage tried to reason with the audience, but even a Catholic priest, who knew many of the protesters, was hooted down. It was a shouting, screaming, furious crowd.

"Ironically, one of the leaders of the protest was a chamber of commerce officer who had helped raise the money for Priscilla's re-union with her children. He came up to me after the meeting. 'I suppose you think we are all a bunch of bigots,' he said. And then he said that I needed to understand that the community was fed up with city programs that, he said, attracted alcoholics, addicts, and petty criminals to the neighborhood. The proposed AIDS clinic was 'the last straw.'

"I knew this was one hell of a story," LeDonne told a colleague years later. "This was about the irresistible forces of reason and logic versus the immovable objects of ignorance, bigotry, and fear. But it was also the kind of television story that would inflame the community even more, and cement the positions of its leaders. In addition, I sincerely believed the unwanted publicity could easily cause Joan Kroc to withdraw her $3 million gift. Or it might even force the hospital to reject it.

"So, I put the tapes of that meeting on the shelf in my office and never told anyone about them. Sometimes when you don't know what to do, it's often best to do nothing. I wasn't about to throw oil on a fire that already was raging.

"Eventually, the furor died down, reason prevailed, and the clinic was built. That was the first and only time in forty years of journalism in which I sat on a great story. I never regretted making that decision."

THE BRONX WAS NO worse than Kokomo, Indiana, where a young boy named Ryan White was driven out of town because he had AIDS. Ryan White, with his large, bright blue eyes, sweet smile, freckles, and short red hair, looked like a boy in a Norman Rockwell painting. When Ryan appeared on *Nightline* in the spring of 1988, Koppel asked him about his treatment by the people of Kokomo. Ryan sort of shrugged and recounted, matter-of-factly, what had happened.

RYAN: Well, just, you know, people have backed away, they've thrown away dishes at restaurants, they've just, you know, treated me like I wasn't even there.

KOPPEL: . . . you were telling me some of the charges that the kids were leveling against you while you were in school back in Kokomo. Just tell our audience about that, would you?

RYAN: Well, they marked my folders, they marked "fag" and other cruel sayings.

KOPPEL: I was talking about, you know, they accused you of, what, spitting on the vegetables or something?

RYAN: Yeah, spitting on the vegetables, and taking bites out of cookies and putting them back, and they said I spit on people too, which I've never done.

KOPPEL: Why do you think they were doing that? I mean, they, clearly, you had not done those—I'm assuming you didn't do those things, right?

RYAN: Right.

KOPPEL: Okay. So why would people do that, just to be spiteful or because they're scared?

RYAN: Well, I think they were scared, first and foremost, and it just led to where, you know, the fear just took control of them, and they just believed what they wanted to believe.

KOPPEL: Now, they have to be frightened of the unknown. I have to ask you to what extent you were frightened of what people think they know about AIDS, namely, you know, it is a fatal disease. To what degree, I mean, here you are, sixteen years old, at a time when most young-sters really don't have to think about death at all, that's something way down the road. How have you come to terms with it?

RYAN: Well, I believe that when you die you go to a better place. And I believe in God and everything, and I'm not really afraid of dying.

KOPPEL: Are you a very religious person now?

RYAN: I'm very religious.

KOPPEL: Have you always been?

RYAN: Not as well as I should have been.

KOPPEL: What I mean, was it really the fear of dying, or just the fact that you were subjected to so much prejudice, what is it that drove you, do you think, to religion?

RYAN: Well, I think it's a little bit of everything that's gone along with it, prejudice and the fear of dying and everything.

KOPPEL: Let's talk for a moment about the good side of things. You've been taking AZT and apparently it has been helping you. As your mother said, at one point they were

giving you three to six months, and that was three years
ago. What's the prognosis now?

RYAN: Well, it's been three years and I'm still going strong, so
            hopefully I can be around long enough for a cure.

By the time of this interview, Ryan had moved with his mother
and siblings to Cicero, Indiana. Cicero embraced them all, especially
Ryan.

KOPPEL: You have a social life?

RYAN: Yeah. I go to ball games and dances and stuff.

KOPPEL: Movies?

RYAN: Movies.

KOPPEL: What are your hobbies?

RYAN: Well, I like skateboarding, and I collect military things.

KOPPEL: Skateboarding?

RYAN: Yeah.

KOPPEL: Of all things for a hemophiliac, skateboarding?

RYAN: Yeah.

KOPPEL: I would think that would be about the last thing you'd do.

RYAN: Well, I always tried to do everything I could. (*smiles*)

Ryan died just two years after that interview.

IN THE SUMMER OF 1990, Bob LeDonne looked around for another Ryan. He hoped to find a youngster whose experiences might
suggest that the stigma of the disease was abating, a youngster whose
life could be documented the way *Nightline* had tracked the final days
of Ken Meeks and Priscilla Diaz. LeDonne found Jeremy Brooks, a
ten-year-old hemophiliac in the state of Washington whose family was
willing to take part in a video journal. LeDonne thought that blond,
blue-eyed Jeremy looked like "Tom Sawyer with glasses." But

LeDonne also found that the days of ostracizing people with AIDS weren't over.

The town in which Jeremy had grown up wouldn't let its children play with him, once word got around that he had AIDS. When LeDonne and a crew sat down to interview the family, the horror stories tumbled out one after another, as if a dam had broken. Jeremy's mother was haunted by the reaction of lifelong friends and neighbors to her son's illness. She was especially tormented by the memory of a day when Jeremy had fallen through the ice on a lake and almost drowned. None of the personnel in the local hospital wanted to touch him.

MRS. BROOKS: And when we got [to the hospital], his temperature spiked, he started vomiting, no one would come in. I'm screaming, I'm yelling, "Somebody help me," and he's throwing up. Somebody came in, handed me a towel, and walked away. And I heard them in the hall, and they were saying, "I'm not working on that AIDS kid. I'm not getting anything. You go in there."

His dentist had even said, "I'm not going to throw away my practice. I've worked hard all my life to build a thriving practice and I'm not throwing it down the toilet to work on your son." It was all I could do not to climb over his desk and choke him.

MR. BROOKS: The deciding factor was the Fourth of July. We used to get together and do the fireworks in the cul-de-sac with the neighbors. And one particular child was playing with Jeremy and his brother came up and said, "You know we're not supposed to play with that kid." And Jeremy took off, crying. We found him up on the deck in the backyard with a lawn chair folded over him, sobbing.

JEREMY: Their parents told them don't play with me, keep away.

MRS. BROOKS: [We received phone calls] telling us we better leave town or we'd be sorry. They'd stand out in front of our house with picket signs that—you know, we'd better never stop looking over our shoulder.

Jeremy's parents had moved the family to Redmond, Washington, another Cicero in terms of its kindness toward a young boy with AIDS. The move was all that was in their power to do; now they struggled with the knowledge that their protective embrace could not protect Jeremy's body from failing.

MRS. BROOKS: As a parent, we're supposed to kiss our children and make them better, and with this disease, you can't.

LeDonne had covered so many of these stories by now, yet for some reason he was dumbstruck by Jeremy's simple, plaintive reply to a question about fear.

LeDONNE: Does anything ever scare you?

JEREMY: Oh, getting sick. Just—it's—the thought of dying, that's the big scary thing.

The camera held on Jeremy's face for several silent seconds after that.

IN THE WEEKS AFTER Jeremy's story aired, LeDonne thought he might be hearing any day from the family that Jeremy had died. But Jeremy rallied. He would live for another two years.

Instead, just months after the broadcast about Jeremy, it was another person with AIDS who called to say he was failing fast. LeDonne and a camera crew had been tracking this one, too, for almost a year. But LeDonne was still shaken when Sergio said he was in the hospital with pneumonia.

Sergio Guerrero was born in Mexico, the oldest of twelve children. His father abandoned the family to poverty. At age eleven, Sergio crossed the border to live with relatives in California. He excelled in his studies, became president of his high school senior class, and won a scholarship to Yale. Sergio studied art and graduated college with honors, and was quickly hired by ABC News. In 1982, he was brought to *Nightline* to produce stories.

Sergio was outspoken, sometimes outrageous, and the office comedian. He could be exceptionally creative. Some of his most brilliant

work would never see air, because it involved hilarious mock newscasts he created on tape just to entertain the staff. Still, his stories that
did make it on the air were good enough to win a number of awards.
After five years at *Nightline,* Sergio won yet another scholarship, this
time to study for a doctorate in literature at Stanford. But he maintained close touch with a number of his ABC colleagues. Now and
then someone on the staff would pass around a stack of poems written
by Sergio that had arrived in the mail.

In 1989, a number of Sergio's friends received the same letter, in-
forming them that he had AIDS. He was then thirty-six years old. He
wrote that he intended to fight the disease, that he planned on finishing his doctorate, that he continued to paint and to write poems, and
that he was at peace.

Eventually, LeDonne and a camera crew began making periodic
forays to Palo Alto. Now the focus was on Sergio.

SERGIO: Three years ago, when I was diagnosed, I thought I was
                 going to die almost immediately. I took refuge here, this
                 place I call the land of milk and honey. I feel protected
                 here, in spite of the sour milk from time to time. . . .
                 (*shows off Emmy awards*) Coming from a little poor town
                 in Mexico to getting something like this was a quite—
                 quite a high point in my life. . . . Right now I think I'm
                 working in two years, three years, to finish the Ph.D. and
                 to get my novel published, and do a few other things out
                 there. . . . Every time I have been in the hospital, I've had
                 to face the idea that I might die. I've been in four times.
                 And each recovery period has seemed a little bit more dif-
                 ficult. When I came out last time, my hands were virtu-
                 ally incapacitated. Both of them were in braces.

Sergio's mother came from Mexico to see him. Sergio talked on
camera about the dilemma it was for a Latino woman, a devout
Catholic, to accept that her son was bisexual. What the camera saw
was a woman of grace.

MRS. GUERRERO: I do not want to have on my conscience that I aban-
                 doned him. That is why I am even closer to him, that's

why I have made the sacrifice to have come so far to be with him, to give him my support, and my love. . . . I wanted to do this interview, maybe because on one occasion I heard that a mother had rejected her son. I do not like this, because if we had them with so much love, why not accept them as they are and continue giving them love?

When Sergio called from Palo Alto to say he was in the hospital with pneumonia, LeDonne immediately locked himself in an editing room in New York to complete the final cut of Sergio's journal; it would air that evening.

Sergio's health deteriorated hour by hour; his rage did not. There was almost nothing he could control now, except the final cut of his obituary. So Sergio would periodically tear off his oxygen mask and dial LeDonne with instructions and questions: "What are you using of my mother?" "How long are you sitting on the shot of the artwork?" "Goddammit, LeDonne, this better be right!"

Sergio raged against the dying of the light by harassing LeDonne in the editing room.

Sergio knew that LeDonne knew how to handle the furor. Sergio even dialed another old colleague in between the calls to the editing room and laughed at his own outrageous deathbed perfectionism. As it turned out, even Sergio the Perfectionist was pleased with the results.

No one who knew him, however, found it easy to watch:

SERGIO: I'd like to continue living the American dream. I'd like to be able to write thirty novels, ten plays, so that they can go with this collection here. I'd like to do what I thought I was set out to do, which is to live my life not only to its fullest potential, but its full length. I'm hopeful that that will be the case, but I'm also a realist, and I just hope and pray.

Sergio was not expected to live another twenty-four hours when his story was broadcast. But a strange thing happened the morning after the show; Sergio felt better. The pneumonia abated. A week later, he returned home from the hospital. One of his best friends from his years at *Nightline,* producer Carla De Landri, would joke to colleagues that the "obit" revived Sergio. "It pumped him up," she laughed. "I think he got so angry, and then so excited, that all of the emotions—and the pride he felt when the story aired—helped him to recover . . . for a while."

In August 1991, Sergio died. Two members of his old *Nightline* family, Steve Lewis and Alison Wylegala, honored a commitment to him and scattered his ashes over a part of "the land of milk and honey" that he so loved.

ELEVEN
Tales from
the Bookers'
Vault

"**H**ELLO?"
　　　"Miss Hepburn?"
　　　"Yes."

Katharine Hepburn answers her own phone? Gil Pimentel paused for an instant to collect himself. He had expected an aide or a secretary to pick up. But there was no mistaking the voice. It almost sounded like a caricature.

"Miss Hepburn, my name is Gil Pimentel, I'm with the ABC News program *Nightline,* and we're doing a program tonight on the colorization of old black-and-white films, and—"

"Why, I think colorizing is the most *absurd* thing I've ever heard of! Imagine taking a perfectly wonderful piece of movie in black and white and adding color to it. Well, it's just *absurd.* Why would anyone want to *do* that?"

Pimentel couldn't believe it. She wanted to come on. "Miss Hepburn, this is exactly the point of view that should be represented on the program tonight. We would love to have you—"

"You mean this evening?"

"Yes."

"On television?"

"Yes."

"But I'm in a play tonight. I'll be at the theater."

"Oh, that's all right. We'll send a couple of cameras over to the theater, and you can appear from there."

"Dear boy, I'm very, very sorry. I do not want to appear on TV tonight. But were you a smart young man, you would have taken down everything I said just now. You could have recorded it and used it any way you wanted to. Goodbye."

Click.

"HELLO, TED? This is Marie. I'm in the park, and I've found the Muppets! But I don't know if they'll come on the show yet and . . . now I'm whispering because I've just screwed up their filming and . . . all the Muppets are staring at me. This is pretty weird. Have to call you back."

"Oooookay."

"HELLO?"

"Hello, *Nightline*? This is the lobby calling. Is Sally Jessy Raphael supposed to be on your program tonight?"

"No."

"Well, then, you better come tell her, 'cause she thinks she is, and she's standing right here, and she's got quite a few people with her."

THEY'RE CALLED BOOKERS: a description that fails to capture what they do to find the best guests for the broadcast.

They're investigators. They scour the world, if necessary, to find the "right" guest: someone who has a grasp of the facts on a given issue, who has an opinion on those facts, and who can articulate that opinion—live—with an earpiece in one's ear and a camera pointed at one's face and under bright lights that might make one squint.

Bookers are persuaders. Guests can be reluctant. Koppel can be reluctant about certain guests.

Bookers are travel agents and logistical masterminds. They must coordinate limousines, charters, satellites, and microwaves.

In the half-hour before a broadcast, they might be found soothing the nervous guest, plying the occasional inebriated guest with coffee—sometimes at the behest of the guest's spouse—or screaming over the phone about a lost car ferrying a guest to the studio. And in the minutes before a broadcast, the bookers are most often zombies, gazing, transfixed and edgy, at the monitors in the control room.

After all, every booker has a story about a guest who was articulate on the phone, who managed pointed arguments and original turns of phrase, only to come on the air and turn incoherent or, worse, silent.

One can never be sure.

The bookers' hours can feel like years—or minutes. The logistics can defy logic. It's a job guaranteed, if done right, to lead to burnout. Dan Morris, who ran *Nightline*'s booking department for years, didn't know who said it, but he loved the quote: "There are old bookers and there are bold bookers, but there are no old, bold bookers."

What follows are some tales from the bookers' vault.

THE YOUNG BOY HAD given an impressive phone interview. He was among a group of students recommended to *Nightline*'s booking staff by some junior high school teachers, for a program about children's fears of nuclear war.

KOPPEL: Have you at this point in your study reached any conclusions?

BOY: (*exhales loudly*) No. Not—not really.

KOPPEL: What are some of the problems that you have discussed? What are some of the problems you've tried to analyze?

BOY: Whew.

The only thing the boy seemed to fear more than nuclear war was live television.

"EVERY SHOW, my heart was in my mouth," said Susan Mercandetti, one of the show's original bookers. "You would have guests who'd said the most interesting things on the telephone, and then the little red light would go on above the camera and they'd go down the toilet. And when that happened, Bill Lord's back would go into a kind of curve, and he'd slowly turn around and say, 'Who was *that?*'

What makes a strong guest? "Intelligence. Energy. The ability to debate," said Steve Lewis, who ran the booking department in the mid-1980s. "And it's a big help if they are comfortable with the technology. They have to wear an earpiece, and they have to look into the camera."

Dan Morris believed that the riskiest bookings were the "real people—as opposed to professional talkers. Every booker has an innate fear of real people. You just never know. Will the guest freeze up? Will this be a deer-in-the-headlights situation? The worst situation is when you've booked a real person and you're in the control room before air and you see them on the monitor and they're barely breathing. And you think, Oh, no. There is nothing you can do."

THE GUEST LOOKED PALE. Tara Sonenshine took him to the greenroom and offered him some hors d'oeuvres. "Are you all right?" She asked.

"I . . . I . . . I think so. Exxxxcuse me . . . when I gggggget nnnnervous . . . I ssssssort of ssssstammmmmer."

The guest was supposed to talk about lie detectors. He had been fired from his job after having failed a lie detector test at work, but claimed the test was a setup. He had agreed to do an interview, as long as he could remain unidentified. Sonenshine had received permission to have him shot so that only his silhouette would be visible. Now, just fifteen minutes before airtime, Sonenshine was learning that the man, when anxious, had a speech impediment.

By the time they'd left the greenroom for the studio, he was having a tough time getting out a single word. Sonenshine wasn't sure he could go on the air. She began to envision a bizarre interview between Koppel and an unintelligible silhouette. But on this night, fortune smiled. As soon as Koppel asked the first question, the man paused for a few seconds and then spoke clearly, concisely, and stammer-free.

DAN MORRIS WAS LOST in a labyrinth of marble and gilt. It was six minutes before the broadcast and he couldn't find one of the key guests. He began to run through the elegant maze and wonder if this was all just a booker's bad dream. It was, in a way, a fitting climax to a day that began when Morris cornered Senator Alan Simpson in a men's room on Capitol Hill. The occasion was Anita Hill's testimony about Clarence Thomas, the Supreme Court nominee, whom she accused of making inappropriate sexual comments during her tenure as his employee.

During a break in the hearing, Morris had followed Senator Simpson into a Capitol Hill lavatory to invite him on *Nightline*. Simpson, who sat on the Judiciary Committee and was a key supporter of Thomas, said he'd be happy to appear. Then Morris explained that the other guest was Senator Howell Heflin, and that since ABC had only one camera position on Capitol Hill, Heflin would appear from there and a car would take Simpson from the Hill to ABC's studio downtown.

Morris followed Simpson back out of the men's room as Simpson wrote a number on a piece of paper. "I won't be in my office after the hearings," said the senator. "I'll be in this room. It's my quiet hideaway in the Senate building. You come and get me when it's time to take me to the studio. There's no incoming phone line, so you have to meet me."

The hearings didn't wrap up until 10:50 P.M., forty-five minutes before airtime. Morris was on his way out of the Russell Senate Office Building to find Simpson when an aide to Senator Heflin stopped him to say that Heflin was exhausted and on his way home. Morris had to have another guest to balance Simpson. He found Senator Paul Simon giving a live interview to NBC. Morris had to wait until the interview was over—to see if Simon would appear. He waited. And waited. At 11:15 the senator finished with NBC and said he'd be happy to come on *Nightline*. Morris pointed him to the ABC camera set up nearby.

Now it was 11:16 and Morris had to find Simpson. He raced from Russell across the street to the Senate. When he got inside, he found the building deserted. "No guards, not anyone. And all I had was this room number on a scrap of paper." Morris clutched the scrap of paper and began wandering through a web of elegant marble halls, past statues and paintings and gilt-limned tables. The building was absolutely silent except for the echo of his footsteps. It was eerie. "I was walking through those ornate halls, looking for room numbers. I thought I was going in the right direction, then I got to the end of a hallway, and the room I wanted wasn't there. So I tried another hallway, and hit another dead end. Now it was 11:20, and I was caught in this maze. I was panting and sweating. I was completely lost amid all those statues and paintings and the inlaid patterns on the floor, and then I started jogging up and down the hallways. It was like a strange dream—actually, it was a nightmare. At 11:25, I still couldn't find the room."

Suddenly Morris remembered he had a cell phone in his pocket and the home phone number of Simpson's press secretary, Stan Canon. Morris called him up.

"I can't find him! I can't find the senator! I'm lost in the Senate!"

Canon calmly responded, "Tell me where you're standing. What do you see."

"Thomas Jefferson!"

"Okay, I know where you are. You need to turn right."

So, like an air traffic controller who guides the pilot to safety in a melodramatic B-movie, Canon began to guide Morris toward the right door when . . . the cell phone went dead. Morris dialed Canon again. The phone went dead again. On the third try, Canon led Morris all the way to Simpson's study. Morris started pounding on the door. Simpson told him to come in. The senator was patiently reading.

It was now 11:29, six minutes before airtime.

The senator seemed amused by the flushed, sweaty young man at his door, but he quickly responded when Morris yelped, "It's time to go! Come on!" Simpson had a bad leg, but he graciously galloped alongside Morris, down halls, and out the doors of the Senate. Morris still felt he was in some strange dream, dashing across the grounds of the Capitol with the senator. Somehow, they made it to the studio in time.

THE CLARENCE THOMAS HEARINGS inspired a lot of bizarre behavior that week.

Dan Morris was escorting Nina Totenberg, a correspondent for National Public Radio, out of the ABC studios in Washington after one of *Nightline's* broadcasts about Anita Hill and Clarence Thomas. Totenberg was one of two reporters who had broken the story of Hill's allegations. During the broadcast, which featured, in addition to Totenberg, Senator Alan Simpson again and Senator Paul Simon, Simpson had challenged Totenberg to examine some affidavits and some phone records of Hill's calls to Thomas.

TOTENBERG: I do know that I do not appreciate being blamed just because I do my job and report the news.

SIMPSON: I don't care. You know, I didn't ask you to appreciate it. I'm asking you about affidavits.

Now, as Morris walked Totenberg out toward her car, they spotted Senator Simpson leaning over Senator Simon's car, chatting with Simon and Simon's wife. Totenberg marched up to Simpson and began to complain about the way he had talked to her on the air.

"Nina shouted and stamped her foot, and she used the f-word in just about every way imaginable," said Morris. "Then Senator Simpson started yelling back at her." The shouting escalated. Slowly, subtly, as if hoping not to be noticed, Simon put his car into drive and quietly pulled away, without saying another word. "Simon just sort of slinked away, leaving this screaming match behind him on the sidewalk. He just slipped right out of there," Morris laughed later.

Eventually, Totenberg walked over to her car, but Simpson followed, waving a sheaf of paper. "You've got to look at these!" he shouted at Totenberg. "These are the affidavits!"

As Totenberg got into her car, Simpson stepped between the car door and the body of the car so that Totenberg couldn't shut the door. "You must read these!" the senator shouted. "You are not an objective journalist if you don't read these!"

"Let me go!" shouted Totenberg, but the senator kept waving the papers. Finally, he stepped back, she slammed the door, and the car drove off.

Simpson stomped back to his car, and it too pulled away, leaving Morris alone on the sidewalk, mouth agape.

WHENEVER TWO GUESTS with opposing views appear from the same studio, there's always the danger that one or both might wish to continue the "conversation" after the broadcast. And if, by chance, the on-air conversation is heated, there's a decent chance that a face-to-face encounter will get ugly. Sara Just could do nothing but watch the one between Representative Robert Torricelli and Iraq's U.N. ambassador, Abdul Amir al-Anbari. Their confrontation in the lobby of ABC's New York headquarters was a sequel to an on-air blowup

moments earlier. It was May 1991 and the two guests had debated the
welfare of Iraqi children in the wake of the Gulf War. Before the
show, Just had escorted the congressman and the ambassador at separate intervals to separate studios in the New York bureau. But after the
program, whoever was supposed to take al-Anbari out by a different
exit had missed the signal.

When Torricelli saw al-Anbari in the lobby, he started right back
in where he'd left off on the air. "What's the matter with your government! Have you no morals?" Torricelli yelled.

"You Americans are so arrogant!" al-Anbari shouted back. "You
should look at your own actions!"

"Saddam is barbaric!" Torricelli countered.

"How dare you!"

It was too late to do anything but let the shouting play itself out,
which took nearly ten minutes. Finally, Just interrupted: "Gentlemen,
your cars are here."

The two men scowled and parted.

A FAMOUS ATHLETE APPEARED on *Nightline* to talk about his
recovery from drug addiction. It took two limousines and a chartered
plane, but Heather Vincent had managed to get the athlete from a remote location to a studio for the interview. Vincent went to bed feeling good about the show.

The next morning, the famous athlete's wife called Vincent: "Do
you know where my husband is?"

Vincent did not. But after calling the limousine services and the
airplane charter company, Vincent helped track him down. It turned
out that after telling Koppel he was done with drugs for good, the famous athlete had walked out of the studio, jumped back into his limo,
and gone right off on a bender.

WHERE IS YELTSIN? Gil Pimentel stood in the lobby of ABC's
New York headquarters, awaiting the arrival of the new president of
the Russian Republic. Boris Yeltsin, struggling in the shadow of Soviet leader Mikhail Gorbachev and searching for international respect,
had agreed to give his first American interview to Ted Koppel.

On the appointed evening, at the appointed hour, Pimentel stood
in the lobby at ABC feeling all puffed up. Pimentel had arranged this
coup with the charismatic Russian president. He didn't worry when

Yeltsin was five minutes late. At ten minutes, however, Pimentel started to pace. At fifteen minutes, Pimentel was muttering anxiously, "Where the hell is he?" Several minutes later, a lobby receptionist told Pimentel he had a phone call. It was an aide to Yeltsin. "I'm so sorry, Mr. Pimentel," said the aide, "but Mr. Yeltsin is exhausted."

"The blood rushed out of me," Pimentel remembered later. "We had no other guests, no other show prepared as a backup, and there wasn't any news that day. I knew that Yeltsin was staying at the Carlyle Hotel, and I went racing to the Carlyle, even though I had no idea if he'd be there. As soon as I got to the lobby, I thought, Now, where would he be? Ah, the bar. So I ran into the bar, and there he was, Boris Yeltsin, seated by himself, all alone. He had one of his huge hands in a bowl of peanuts and the other around a beer."

Pimentel walked right up to the Russian president. "Mr. Yeltsin, I'm Gil Pimentel from *Nightline,* and you were supposed to do an interview with us. I know you're really tired, but we're depending on you to do this program."

Yeltsin looked baffled. Pimentel would later remember how the Russian leader "looked at me as if to say, Why is this crazy person yelling at me?" Yeltsin, it turned out, didn't understand English. He continued to alternate between gobbling peanuts and slugging down beer while Pimentel got more worked up. "I was yelling and heaving and panting and sweating, and he still didn't have a clue who I was or what I was trying to tell him." Finally a press aide ran into the bar, apologizing to Pimentel, and suggested that perhaps Yeltsin would be feeling up to the interview by airtime. But Rick Kaplan, the executive producer of the broadcast, knew better than to count on it, and he managed to throw together another broadcast about another subject, which was a good thing, since Yeltsin never did agree to leave the bar.

"UNBOOKING" IS PROBABLY the worst part of the job. The guests for a show are arranged, and news breaks in the afternoon or evening, and the executive producer decides to go with the breaking news. Some bookers will work on finding guests for the new show. But someone has to "unbook" the guests for the show that's scrubbed.

Susan Mercandetti refused to unbook one guest. He was a Catholic bishop. She no longer remembers what superseded an interview with the bishop, but Mercandetti, the daughter of Italian Roman Catholic immigrants, recalls yelling at senior producer Stu Schwartz and at Koppel, "I am not unbooking the bishop! I'm a Roman Catholic, and I refuse to go to hell in a handbasket. Neither of *you* are Roman Catholics. One of *you* cancel the bishop!"

Then there's Sally Jessy Raphael. *Nightline* booker Dana Wolfe was sitting in her New York office at about eleven o'clock one evening when the phone rang. It was the lobby. Sally Jessy Raphael, said the receptionist, was standing there, waiting for someone to take her to the *Nightline* studio.

A few days earlier, when there had been some talk about devoting the Friday broadcast to talk shows, one of the bookers in Washington had phoned Raphael's office to see if she would be interested in appearing. Raphael's office thought the call was a firm invitation for Friday night. It wasn't, and when the subject of the show was changed to the death penalty, no one thought it necessary to notify Raphael, since no one thought she'd been booked.

But when Dana Wolfe got to the lobby, there was Sally Jessy Raphael, sheathed in gold lamé. In addition to Raphael, there stood her husband, her makeup man, her assistant, and her hairdresser. Wolfe broke the news, and then invited the group up to the *Nightline* offices to meet Tom Bettag, the show's executive producer, who apologized profusely for the mix-up. Bettag looked Raphael in the eye and said, "This has never, ever happened to me in all my days at *Nightline*." He didn't mention that he'd been at *Nightline* precisely one week.

Bettag and Wolfe found Raphael gracious and understanding, even though one of her aides had missed a family wedding to accompany her for this one appearance on *Nightline*. In fact, Raphael finally did appear for a *Nightline* town meeting about a year later, when the subject was victims who commit crimes. Even so, every now and then, the booker who insisted that she had never actually invited Raphael the first time would get a call at home from a *Nightline* colleague who would begin the conversation with "Miss Raphael is in the lobby."

IN THE EARLY DAYS, before satellites and microwave dishes were ubiquitous, guests often appeared from ABC's affiliated television stations around the country. Getting them there sometimes required not only cars and drivers but private planes. As the years have passed, most guests who don't appear out of New York or Washington do so by satellite—what is known in the business as a bird.

Once a receptionist walked into Dan Morris's office and said that someone named Peter was on the phone for him. Peter was a unit manager who arranged satellite transmissions, and earlier that day Morris had asked him to set up a transmission for a guest who would appear from a remote location that night.

Morris picked up the phone. "Peter, do we have the bird?"

"The bird?"

"The bird we talked about an hour ago."

"An hour ago?"

Morris exploded. "The fucking bird we talked about a fucking hour ago! When are you going to get off your fucking duff and get this done? What's the *matter* with you?"

"I think you have the wrong Peter. I'm Peter Rainer of the *Los Angeles Times*."

"HOW IS ZE APARTMENT hunt coming along?"

It was the same famous basso profundo tone that Henry Kissinger usually used to explain the intricacies and failings of some treaty or another. But the issue was *Nightline* booker Heather Vincent's search for a safe apartment in New York City. Kissinger knew Vincent fairly well by then. Kissinger appeared on *Nightline* relatively frequently during the mid-1980s—so frequently, in fact, that many television critics took *Nightline* to task for it.

But even now, Dan Morris is convinced that the former secretary of state was a logical and appropriate choice when the broadcast focused on international issues. "The usual suspects are the usual suspects for a reason. We've had Norm Ornstein on a number of times, too. Yet if you're doing a show about the congressional process and you need to clearly, cleanly, concisely explain what's going on, there's no one better than Norm Ornstein. There are some people who have a natural ability to communicate in this format. And when they're discovered, they're gonna be everywhere." It is therefore inevitable that "the usual suspects" will develop a rapport and, in some cases, genuine friendship with members of the *Nightline* staff.

And so it was, years ago, that when a foreign crisis dominated the news, Kissinger would pop up on *Nightline* several times over the course of a few weeks. Heather Vincent was the booker who, in those days, most often greeted Kissinger at the ABC studio in New York and sat with him before the program. "I was apartment-hunting at the time," Vincent recalled, "and I must have complained rather loudly about it to Kissinger before a show one night. So each time he appeared in the weeks that followed, as we waited for the show, he'd interrogate me about the apartment hunt."

"Does zat building have a doorman?" Kissinger would ask. "You must have a doorman." When Vincent mentioned a certain neighborhood that interested her, he weighed in, "No, zat is not a safe neighborhood. You need to be in a safer neighborhood."

A few months later, Kissinger met Vincent again at ABC's studios for another appearance on the show. He was attired in a tuxedo, having just attended a formal dinner, but he said he'd brought a jacket and tie with him for the program. Vincent walked him to the dressing room and stood outside the door. Having updated Kissinger on her adventures in New York real estate, Vincent changed the subject and started to joke about how anchors only needed to worry about their clothes above the waist. "Some anchors," she told Kissinger, "only wear shorts and sneakers. Who'd know?"

Vincent heard him say, "How's zis?" He opened the door, walked out, and there stood the former secretary of state in a shirt, tie, and a nice long jacket under which peeked just the bottom hem of his boxer shorts. Vincent howled. Kissinger smiled and said, "Maybe not," returned to the dressing room, closed the door, and put on some pants.

IF THE PRESENTATION of the Academy Awards is one of the most glamorous events of the year in Hollywood, it is one of the most dreaded, least dignified occasions for a *Nightline* booker. The Oscars usually spell trouble and torment for the bookers, particularly because *Nightline* airs just after the awards broadcast has concluded.

One year, *Nightline* booker Tracy Day had persuaded Swifty Lazar, the famous literary agent, to allow a *Nightline* camera and correspondent Judd Rose inside the restaurant Spago during Lazar's exclusive Oscar-night party. Lazar had never before allowed a television camera into the party. But Lazar told Day he was a fan of *Nightline* and that she could put a camera in an out-of-the-way corner of the room.

About fifteen minutes before the broadcast, the Spago party was well under way and Day began to wander the restaurant looking for someone famous for Rose to interview on the air. She found Michael

Caine, one of her favorite movie stars, who accepted her invitation to be interviewed. But when Day returned to the corner where the camera was supposed to be, it wasn't there. The cameraman, along with Rose, both unaware of Lazar's edict, had moved the camera smack into the middle of the entrance hall to the restaurant. It was, by now, too late to haul the camera back to its corner before airtime.

As Caine put in his earpiece, he looked up and saw, standing right behind the camera, a throng of angry celebrities, unable to enter. They included one of his best friends, Sean Connery, and the legendary comedienne Lucille Ball. Then he heard the voice of Forrest Sawyer, who was the anchor that night, announce, "We'll be talking to Michael Caine in a moment."

In the seconds before the commercial, the camera cut to Caine, who dropped his jaw and began talking to someone just off-camera. There was no audio, but just about any viewer could see that he looked angry and seemed to be saying, I'm not going to do this. That is exactly what he was saying. Caine took out his earpiece, handed Day his microphone, told her, "I don't work for ABC," and stalked off.

Rose told Day to find anyone; they had precisely two minutes. She scoured the crowd at Spago. Two minutes later, as Forrest Sawyer said, "Let's go live to Spago," there standing next to Rose was Kathleen Turner, who had responded to Day's plea to fill in. While Turner was interviewed by Rose and Sawyer, Lazar stood just out of camera range, yelling at Day to end the interview and leave, because the camera was blocking his guests.

Day stalled him long enough to conclude the interview, but not before the camera captured Rose trying to come to Day's rescue. Rose was holding his microphone out for Turner, since she had not had time to be fixed with a mike of her own, but when Sawyer took over the interview, Rose thought the camera would be on a close-up of Turner. It wasn't. While Turner chatted with Sawyer, Rose could be seen wiping sweat from his brow, whispering, nodding, and negotiating with a bald head—Lazar's—that popped up from the bottom of the frame now and then. Rose, still unaware he was on-camera, began making faces at Day that could only be interpreted as, What a disaster. Won't you be glad when this is over?

FOR ANOTHER ACADEMY AWARDS night, Heather Vincent had arranged for the actor Dennis Hopper and the director Spike Lee to be interviewed from a room inside the Dorothy Chandler Pavilion, where the awards were presented. The room was used by photographers to store their equipment.

About a half-hour after the last Oscar had been handed out, Lee and Hopper were in place, just minutes before their interview, when two security guards walked up to Vincent and said some photographers wanted to get into the room. Vincent said no, the live interview with Hopper and Lee was a minute away, and as soon as it was over, she'd let the photographers in. But the security guards ordered Vincent to let them into the room.

It was by now about thirty seconds before air. Vincent, who was in a ballgown, blocked the doorway with her five-foot-ten-inch frame and yelled at the guards, "I am too big for you to move! If you want to get through, you'll have to arrest me!"

Vincent remembered Lee giving her a sort of power salute, a "Go, man" fist in the air.

One of the guards yelled for someone to cut a hole through the wall and cut off the electrical power in the room. Vincent couldn't believe it. "It was like an episode of *Star Trek*," she said. "It was as if the enemy were saying, 'Cut off the power! Stun the main phaser banks!' "

Eventually, Hopper's pregnant wife and a female friend of Lee's stood with Vincent and helped her block the door until the interviews were over.

"SO, MRS. GORE, what are some of the specific videos you oppose?" Gil Pimentel was on the phone with the wife of then-Senator Al Gore. Mrs. Gore was campaigning at the time against violent videos being rented to children.

"Well, my husband and I rented a few and watched them, so we know what we're talking about. We rented *Faces of Death, Texas Chainsaw Massacre,* and *I Spit on Your Grave.*"

Pimentel started to giggle. He tried to stop. Then he guffawed.

"What's so funny?" asked Mrs. Gore.

"I'm sorry, Mrs. Gore," said Pimentel, still giggling, "but I just had an image of you and the senator cuddled by the fire watching *I Spit on Your Grave,* and it's kind of funny."

Mrs. Gore didn't seem to share the joke.

• • •

RICHARD HARRIS HAD BEEN running *Nightline*'s booking department for several years, but he had never had a call quite like this. A Navy lieutenant was on the phone. He identified himself as Tracy Thorne. Thorne told Harris that he wanted to come on *Nightline* and announce his homosexuality.

It was May 1992. On Capitol Hill, some members of Congress were sponsoring legislation to end discrimination against homosexuals in the military. Presidential candidate Bill Clinton was also pledging that, if elected, he would end the ban against gays in the armed services. "Thorne didn't think that those who were gay in the military should have to live a lie anymore," said Harris. "So I talked to him for a number of days. And I said to him, 'You understand what this means if you do this.' This was not one of those interviews where I wanted to have to convince him to do it. He had to convince me that he wanted to do this and that this was the right thing. I told him, 'This is going to change your life in more ways than you know.' "

The lieutenant decided he wanted to do it. But first, he told Harris, he would have to return to his hometown and tell his parents. They didn't know.

On the day of the broadcast, Lawrence Welk died. Some ABC News executives sent word to Koppel that since Welk had been a major star with ABC for many years, *Nightline* should consider devoting that evening's broadcast to Welk's death.

Harris was distraught. "I thought about this lieutenant who wanted to turn over his innermost secrets to us because he felt it was important, and who had already flown home to tell his father." Harris went into Koppel's office. "Ted, you've known me a long time," Harris began. "I've never done this before, but I've got to draw the line somewhere. I can't do this to this person."

Harris proceeded to give Koppel the entire story of the lieutenant approaching *Nightline* and of how the lieutenant had just gone home to inform his parents. Harris usually preferred not to burden Koppel with the details of booking, "but in this particular case," he said later, "given the extraordinary personal sacrifice by Thorne, I just had to make Ted understand how important this was to me as well, because I felt I would be betraying this person. Here Thorne had already told his family something that he might not have had he not been going on *Nightline*. So I just felt I had sort of a moral contract with this person." Harris finished explaining to Koppel what the lieutenant had already sacrificed and what he was prepared to sacrifice. Then Harris said, "If we can't follow through on our commitment to this person, I really have to think about leaving."

Koppel seemed surprised by Harris's passion, but he also agreed that *Nightline* should, and would, stick with interviewing the lieutenant, who turned out to be an articulate, forceful advocate of gays in the military.

Thorne paid a high price for his appearance. The following year, for having revealed his sexual orientation on *Nightline,* Thorne was discharged from the Navy, as one of the first casualties of the Clinton administration's "don't ask, don't tell" policy.

"NADINE. STOP. JUST STOP." Bill Lord was more than a tad irritated with Nadine Muchin. He had already approved the guest line-up for a program about schizophrenia, it was now after nine at night, and he wanted some peace before the show. But Muchin was standing in his office, chewing on a finger—which she always did when she wasn't satisfied. She had told Lord that they needed someone who really suffered from schizophrenia to make the show work.

Lord disagreed; he thought they had a fine broadcast ahead. They had thrown it together on deadline, just hours after John Hinckley, the young man who had shot President Reagan, was found innocent of the shooting by reason of insanity. Muchin had already arranged for medical and legal experts to be interviewed by Koppel. "Enough, Muchin. Relax," Lord ordered.

Muchin disappeared back into her office, then emerged an hour later to tell Lord she had found a woman in Chicago who ran an organization that helped schizophrenics. The woman herself suffered from the disease but had it under control.

"Fine," said Lord. "We'll add her to the mix. Order a satellite out of Chicago."

It would turn out that the woman, Marcia Lovejoy, offered the most poignant moments of the broadcast.

KOPPEL: How should we react [to schizophrenics]?

LOVEJOY: Take each person as who they are and as how they react. Understand that a lot of times we shake from the medication we're on, not necessarily because we're nervous.

We often look different, because we're often very, very poor, and live in a lot of poverty and have no hope. We live with an illness that we're told there is no recovery from, and yet we maintain our lives and try to go on and bear each day. That's very difficult to do sometimes, and I think people who have this illness and who have these kinds of problems are the most courageous people in the world because they keep on keeping on and they keep trying to make it, and often have never seen anyone who's ever recovered. There was the biggest piece of hope in my life when I went to a program and finally saw someone who is well enough to actually be staff. To talk to the person as a real person. If you have questions about what their experiences are . . . listen to what they have to say. Don't assume everything that they say negatively happened is a part of their delusion. Very many negative things happen to people in hospitals and in the community. Everything we say is not a lie or . . . a fantasy. And if you're uncomfortable or afraid, say you are, and ask the person to help you be more comfortable. If they don't want to talk about their experiences, respect their silence. Honesty is truly the best policy with any person. When you stop talking to someone about something, you put up a wall between you and them, and pretty soon they wall them in and you out, and that's what it's all about.

KOPPEL: All right. Marcia Lovejoy, your name suits you well.

Lord sat in the control room after the program, shaking his head. "Muchin doesn't let go. And it pays off."

PLAINLY PUT, bookers are pushy. They have to be. Which isn't to say they're always grateful for the trait. Dana Wolfe, who began booking for *Nightline* in 1991, was certain she had found the guest that would make her career: a foreign diplomat who had worked closely with the White House on several international crises and who was ready to reveal the details of some of those exploits for the first time. She had met with the diplomat several times. At every meeting he'd enchanted her with tales of international diplomacy and intrigue. "He was very secretive," said Wolfe, "and nobody had gotten to know him like I had. I just knew there was a broadcast here."

Koppel was reluctant. He had met the diplomat before and considered him competent but hardly vibrant. Koppel didn't share Wolfe's view that the diplomat's story was all that significant. But Wolfe insisted her instincts were right. "I pushed to the limits for this interview. I've never pushed as hard for a show." She pestered Koppel and Tom Bettag for almost a year, until they finally relented and agreed to devote an entire broadcast to the diplomat.

The show, by all accounts, was awful. The diplomat was boring. He couldn't seem to remember any of the fascinating anecdotes he had shared off-camera with Wolfe. He looked as if he didn't know why he'd been invited, and by the end of the interview, Koppel looked as if he didn't know why the man had been invited, either.

"I almost threw up in the control room," Wolfe remembered.

After the broadcast, the diplomat sat down with Wolfe and started all over again to tell his fascinating stories. Wolfe erupted. "Why didn't you say this on the air?"

The diplomat looked shocked. He didn't have an answer.

MARIE MACLEAN REACTED the way any booker would react when a guest is attempting to back out just before the broadcast. She said, "You can't."

In December 1988, Nikolai Shislin, a high official with the Soviet Central Committee who was visiting America with Mikhail Gorbachev, had agreed to appear on *Nightline* to discuss Gorbachev's address to the UN earlier that day. But about a half-hour before the show, when Maclean arrived at Shislin's hotel to pick him up for the program, he came down to the lobby without his coat.

"I'm so sorry, Ms. Maclean," said Shislin. "I must cancel my appearance on your program."

"You can't."

"Well, you see, Mr. Gorbachev has called us into an emergency meeting. I must attend."

"But you are the only Soviet representative on the program tonight. The whole show is about Gorbachev's speech." Maclean raised her voice. "You *have* to appear."

Shislin, who no doubt wanted to stop Maclean from causing a scene in the lobby of the hotel, caved and agreed to honor his commitment.

An hour later, in the middle of the broadcast, while Shislin and Henry Kissinger were discussing U.S.-Soviet relations, word came across the wires about a major earthquake in Armenia. Tens of thousands were feared dead.

Koppel announced the news and asked Shislin if he knew anything about it.

"No," answered Shislin. During the commercial break, Shislin turned to Maclean and hissed, "How can I know anything? The meeting that I'm missing for your program was obviously about the earthquake!"

Kissinger chuckled and teased Shislin, a longtime acquaintance, that he could forget about returning to the Soviet Union, since he would probably be fired for not attending the meeting.

SO HOW DID MACLEAN manage to annoy Kermit the Frog?

In October 1987, two days after the stock market plunged almost five hundred points, Rick Kaplan convened *Nightline*'s staff and announced that they were putting on a town meeting about Wall Street, to air only ten days later. The staff began brainstorming with Kaplan and Koppel about how to make the economy interesting to the lay public, when Herb O'Connor, a producer, suggested a primer on investing, "a *Sesame Street* lesson on the terminology," he said. O'Connor was speaking figuratively, but Kaplan and Koppel—both of whom had spent years with their young children watching *Sesame Street*—responded, almost in unison, "Let's use the Muppets!" Kaplan turned to Maclean: "Find Kermit!"

Maclean had heard that Kermit and his creator, Jim Henson, were filming a movie in Central Park, not far from ABC's New York offices. So she grabbed a portable phone, which in those days came packed inside a briefcase, and roamed the park until she found the movie set. A publicist asked her to wait quietly until the scene was over. Maclean nevertheless decided to open her case and hook up the phone and dial Koppel, who wanted to personally extend the invitation to Henson.

Just as Koppel said hello, the phone emitted a piercing screech.

The director yelled, "Cut! Cut!"

The entire set looked like a freeze-frame, and every face, both human and Muppet, was glaring at Maclean. "Twenty faces," recalled Maclean, "all glowering at me. All the Muppets, and all the guys holding the Muppets."

Eventually Jim Henson, who couldn't have been friendlier, took Maclean's phone and had a chat with Koppel and said that yes, Kermit, Miss Piggy, and all the gang would be happy to appear on *Nightline*.

What most of the other bookers remember about the Muppets is that their appearance at the studios generated more excitement around ABC than any human guest ever had. National and international leaders were routine visitors to the ABC studios, but not the Muppets, whose pre-taped interviews with Koppel were witnessed by scores of ABC News personnel and *Nightline* staffers, the onlookers gawking and giggling like starstruck teenagers.

By the time Kermit and Piggy and Oscar the Grouch had completed the taping, the bookers agreed that as guests go, the Muppets were about the most professional, and certainly the least demanding, in memory.

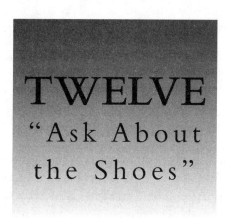

TWELVE

"Ask About the Shoes"

THE PALACE WAS EMPTY, its cavernous interior so ghostly quiet that their footsteps echoed on the marble floors. Betsy West and James Walker roamed from room to room, mesmerized. It felt as if they had entered a haunted castle, except that nothing had deteriorated. Every object left by the occupants, every bit of evidence that someone had recently lived here, was untouched. "Hurry, hurry!" their guide whispered. *Nightline* had no permission to be inside, much less to film the family quarters that Ferdinand and Imelda Marcos had vacated by stealing out a back door, onto a helicopter, and into exile less than twenty-four hours earlier. So West, who was one of *Nightline*'s senior producers, and Walker, one of the show's correspondents, tried to keep the camera crew moving without missing a detail.

Their guide was an aide to Corazon Aquino, the "housewife" who had managed to depose Marcos from his twenty-one-year reign. The aide had recognized West and Walker amid the celebrations outside and had smuggled them and their crew through a back door, to record the opulence of the family quarters before anything was altered. Not even Mrs. Aquino had seen it yet.

"There was an enormous dining room," West recalled, "and on

the table was what appeared to be a banquet that seemed to have been suddenly abandoned. There was caviar and sour cream, partially eaten, and open champagne bottles. No one had cleaned up, either because they'd left in a hurry or because there was no point in tidying up for the usurpers."

Walker tested the caviar. "It was beluga," he remembered, "and it was still fresh."

They found a family chapel. There were children's rocking chairs near the altar. And they found, on every wall of every room, photographs: shrines to Ferdinand and Imelda Marcos with world leaders, with dignitaries, with celebrities. "There were photos everywhere," said West. "My personal favorite was a huge picture of Ferdinand and Imelda posing as Adam and Eve. They were naked except for their private parts, which were covered by sugarcane leaves."

The camera crew discovered a room with a hospital bed surrounded by medical equipment. There stood a dialysis machine. Marcos had always denied reports that he was on dialysis, or even that his health was bad. But the clothes in the closets and the photos clearly indicated that this was the dictator's bedchamber.

Next came the bedroom of Imelda Marcos. West remembered that "the bed was so huge it was the size of two king-size beds put together. It was unmade—all the blankets and sheets in a tangle. A huge canopy was draped high above it."

Walker found Imelda's bathroom. "There were gold fixtures and a mirrored ceiling. And all of these glass jars of potpourri. Enormous jars, like you'd see in a florist's shop."

West's eyes focused on the bathtub. "All around the edge of this great bathtub were gallon-size bottles of French perfume."

"Then," said West, "the aide took us to the closet. He kept saying, 'Come quick, come quick,' because he wanted us to see it all before the military secured everything and stopped us. And there, in the closet, we saw these shoes. Thousands and thousands of shoes. Racks and racks. There was every style—pump, sling-back, flat heel, spiked heel. For every style, there were at least eight pairs of shoes in a row, each pair a different color."

Suddenly a soldier appeared and told West, Walker, and the camera crew to get out. He explained that the military didn't know whether the Marcoses had sabotaged the quarters. It was possible, he said, that the room they were standing in was booby-trapped. By then, the camera crew had recorded plenty.

The caviar, the gold fixtures, the perfume bottles and, most notably, the estimated three thousand pairs of shoes were broadcast on *Nightline* the next evening. The footage provided Americans with their first glimpse of what would become one of the most infamous wardrobes of modern times.

One month later, Koppel got word that Marcos, in exile in Hawaii, would grant him an interview, the former dictator's first since his fall from power. As word of it spread among Koppel's *Nightline* colleagues, one after another walked into his office with the same request: "Please, please ask about the shoes."

SIX YEARS EARLIER, in October of 1980, Ferdinand Marcos had agreed to appear on *Nightline* for the first time. But . . .

KOPPEL: Good evening. Regrettably, we have to begin tonight by telling you who will not be on this broadcast. President Ferdinand Marcos of the Philippines had agreed to appear live on this program by satellite. But when we informed his office that we would also be talking to a former Filipino senator who now teaches at Harvard, we received a long and angry cable from President Marcos's office in Manila. The text has been broadcast in the Philippines. It has appeared on the front pages of Manila's newspapers. It states, in part, that placing the president of an independent sovereign republic like the Philippines on the same forum as a convict or a fugitive from justice in his homeland would not only demean his office, it is an insult to the government and the people that it represents.

The cable was classic Marcos. It was also an omen. Not much seemed to cow Ferdinand Marcos, except the prospect of a public debate with Benigno Aquino. It was easy to squelch that possibility inside the Philippines, and Marcos had done so by declaring martial law and silencing the opposition press, by jailing Aquino on trumped-up charges of murder and treason, and finally by sending Aquino into exile in America, ostensibly for heart surgery. Marcos could do nothing, however, to prevent Aquino from talking to the American press. His appearance on *Nightline* would be Aquino's American television debut. All that Marcos could do was to refuse to share the forum.

For fifteen years, Marcos had sold himself to Washington as "our man in Manila," as America's bulwark against Communism in Asia, as the trusted guardian of two important U.S. military bases, Clark and Subic. But from the night of his angry cable canceling his appearance on *Nightline* to the night five and a half years later when he would sulk to Koppel that he was the victim of a coup d'état, Ferdinand Marcos would prove a fascinating character study. What *Nightline* would chronicle over those years was the endgame of a Cold War despot, an increasingly desperate, defensive, out-of-touch potentate slowly crumbling under the forces of democracy.

On the October night Marcos refused to appear on *Nightline,* the woman who would topple Marcos was enjoying the peace of exile with her husband in Boston, her attentions absorbed by housework and children. Her spouse—whom she called by his nickname, Ninoy—was the figure on whom U.S. officials pinned their highest hopes for political reform in the Philippines, a man whom they regarded as a key force for democracy in East Asia. That was precisely why Benigno Aquino had been invited on *Nightline.* For Aquino, the one sweet irony of exile was that it accorded him access, through this broadcast, to an important audience in Washington.

KOPPEL: Mr. Aquino, everything, of course, is relative. And we've seen some terrible dictators in your lifetime and mine throughout the world. President Marcos has really been, on balance, rather a good president, has he not?

AQUINO: Yes, on balance he has been a rather effective president. I will not use the word *good,* but he has been effective. He has been effective in controlling the military. He's been effective in controlling the opposition, in controlling the press in my country, in controlling, cowing the people. He's been very effective, but when Mr. Marcos increases his repression, he will only be increasing violence. The only way you can remove violence is to remove the original cause, which is martial rule.

Filipino television could no more carry this broadcast than Filipino newspapers could refer to it, since Marcos had his press in a stranglehold. Aquino was nonetheless certain that his countrymen would hear of the interview. Clark and Subic bases, after all, received the broadcast on the Armed Forces Network, and whatever news the bases picked up usually spread quickly around the country. More important, by 1980, a large number of Marcos's political opponents were living in the United States. They were constantly phoning home to the Philippines, mailing off clippings from the American papers and, increasingly, sending home tapes of broadcasts like *Nightline*. Aquino was counting on them. "Ninoy was very excited, pleased, and honored to be invited on *Nightline*," his wife would remember later, "because it gave him the opportunity to make known his sentiments to Filipinos in the U.S., some of whom would in turn send videotapes of that program to their relatives and friends in the Philippines."

"Filipinos knew they couldn't learn anything from the papers controlled by Marcos. The U.S. media was all they had," said Lupita Aquino Kashiwahara, Benigno Aquino's sister. "Of course, not many people had tape machines in the early eighties, but information was spread by word of mouth. That's how information was almost always disseminated. Maybe someone saw a transmission at one of the U.S. bases, or they got a phone call from a relative in the States, and then the information spread. Word of mouth was key."

There was a moment in the interview on *Nightline* when Aquino seemed not to be addressing Koppel at all, but an audience made up only of his fellow countrymen. He couched a promise to return to the Philippines with one prescient, haunting phrase.

AQUINO: I will go back because I think I'm innocent. And if Mr. Marcos would like to shoot me on that basis, so be it.

HIS RIVAL'S ARROWS, shot across American television, vexed Marcos, but they could not compare to the humiliation of a public scolding by a pope. During a February 1981 visit to the Philippines, Pope John Paul II stood before cameras and international reporters and berated Marcos for violating human rights. Marcos, in turn, asked for the pope's forgiveness, and pledged to forge a "harmonious" society. But the dressing-down by the pope was big news in America, and a heavy blow to Marcos's prestige. "At that time," recalled Raul Rabe, then a Filipino diplomat, "we had a president who was very conscious of how his image played abroad. This was very important to him. I guess he realized that his position depended a lot to the extent of U.S. support that he could get. So image was important."

In a desperate attempt at damage control, Marcos, just one day after the pope's visit, agreed once again to appear on *Nightline*, and this time he actually showed up. But with the pope gone, Marcos apparently decided that contrition was no longer necessary. He almost chuckled at the allegations that he had repressed the Muslim minority in his country.

MARCOS: I am afraid that this is principally due to the Western press making a mountain out of a molehill.

The same was true, he complained, about accusations, made by members of the Carter administration, that he imprisoned and sometimes tortured political opponents:

MARCOS: What bothered us was that the decision-makers in Washington made their decision based on the Western correspondents' reports that were distorted and sometimes false.

Even the high profile of Benigno Aquino was, according to Marcos, the fault of easily duped journalists:

MARCOS: He is not that important; it's only the Western press that is making him important. I don't know why.

Koppel thought that Marcos's attacks on the press were a classic sign of desperation. "Blaming the press," Koppel told a colleague, "is the hallmark of a rogue. Whenever a politician, anywhere, has his back to the wall, whenever he's really in trouble, he knows he can always blame journalists for getting the story wrong."

Marcos maintained a dismissive, almost weary demeanor while fobbing off the blame for his troubles on the media. When Koppel pursued the subject of Aquino, Marcos's face reddened. He seemed excited.

KOPPEL: [Aquino] claims that he cannot come back to the Philippines for fear that he will not only be jailed, but perhaps executed.

MARCOS: He was convicted for murder, for sedition, rebellion, or subversion. He appealed his case to the Supreme Court. The Supreme Court threw out his case. So now there is a warrant of arrest against him. He is also facing participation in the bombing incident that killed Americans . . . It's not something which any foreign government, like the American government, should intervene in. I think we should allow the judiciary in our country to determine whether he is guilty or not. Now if he says that he wants to come back here, sure, by all means, he can come back. But for what? He has to face up to the facts of life.

"He has to face up to the facts of life." The cliché concealed a threat. Marcos knew he had to frame his threats carefully. This was an American show, after all, with a large viewing audience in Washington. His benefactors, he could be sure, were listening. So, too, he must have hoped, was Aquino.

"He has to face up to the facts of life."
"If Mr. Marcos would like to shoot me on that basis, so be it."

Two years later, in August 1983, Benigno Aquino would feel Filipino soil underfoot once more for all of ten seconds. The only witnesses to those few seconds were the uniformed men who shot him.

Aquino's brother-in-law, ABC correspondent Ken Kashiwahara, and an ABC camera crew had accompanied Aquino on his flight home from exile. They had been there, the crew filming, when three men, apparently security guards, boarded the plane and asked Aquino to come with them, alone. Less than a minute after Aquino disappeared down some steps to the tarmac, Kashiwahara heard several shots. The next thing the camera recorded was the body of Aquino, dead on the tarmac.

Ferdinand Marcos would tell the press that he had warned Aquino not to return because of "assassination plots" against him.

Cory Aquino had not accompanied her husband on that flight into

the hands of his assassins. She had remained in Boston with their children, awaiting word from Ninoy that it would be safe to join him. She
would learn that her husband never got to see even one of the thousands of yellow ribbons that were draped all over Manila to celebrate
his homecoming. It was a detail that Cory Aquino would remember.

A few hours after learning that Ninoy was dead, Mrs. Aquino
began to pack for the funeral. A *Nightline* producer, who had been
warned that Mrs. Aquino was shy and that she preferred to remain out
of the spotlight, decided to call her anyway. Would she be interested,
the producer inquired, in speaking about her husband's assassination
on *Nightline,* before returning home?

To the producer's surprise, Mrs. Aquino said yes. Years later, she
would explain why she had agreed to appear. It was, she said, "my way
of paying final tribute to my husband. I was returning to the Philippines on August twenty-third and I was quite uncertain about my future situation in my country. More than anything else I wanted people
to know more about my husband. And they did."

The person people really got to know that night was Cory
Aquino. Her poised responses to Sam Donaldson, who was anchoring
Nightline that evening, would signal one of the first steps in the
widow's political ascent.

DONALDSON: When he left on August thirteenth and said goodbye to
you, the two of you understood that he might face grave
danger, imprisonment, and even death?

MRS. AQUINO: Well, we thought imprisonment would be it. I myself believed, you know, that would be the worst thing
we could expect. Never, never did we think this could
happen.

Mrs. Aquino would later remember that she felt "nervous" in that
interview. She did not appear to be. Her demeanor was serene, almost
august.

MRS. AQUINO: My husband felt that while he was strong and healthy,
and while he believed Marcos was, you know, still in
good health, that he could ask President Marcos to talk to

him. And he wanted to plead with Mr. Marcos to restore the democratic processes in our country. My husband believed that only Marcos, with his authority and power, could do so. So it was imperative that he go home while it was still possible for the two of them to talk.

Despite the fact that she was about to board a plane for the Philippines, Mrs. Aquino boldly, if indirectly, implicated the Marcos regime in her husband's murder.

DONALDSON: Mrs. Aquino, who do you think murdered your husband?

MRS. AQUINO: I would not like to say anything definite now. I would like to return home and talk to the people there. . . . Let me just say this. I thought that the security given my husband was really inadequate. There were only three soldiers whom I saw on television coming up the plane to take my husband. When we were still in the Philippines, and when my husband was in the detention center, whenever he could go to, you know, either the Supreme Court or the military tribunal, there would be at least twenty to thirty security men guarding him and really looking out for his security. This is really quite a strange thing to see happen, you know, only three people going up there to take him.

DONALDSON: The government says your husband was murdered by someone who had slipped in and put on the uniform of an airport worker, and had come very close with a single pistol. You saw the television pictures of that man lying there. Does that seem probable?

MRS. AQUINO: Let me say this. My relatives told me that it was very difficult to get to the airport. You had to get tickets and even where they were, you know, they were still so very far away from where the airplane was. It just doesn't seem possible. I don't know how that assassin could have possibly gotten to where he was. You know, if he were just alone.

Mrs. Aquino's final point was especially shrewd. Her husband was lying in state in the family home, she said, and over fifteen hundred people an hour were filing past the body. The message was aimed at Washington: the thousands who were paying final respects to Benigno Aquino represented a growing force for democracy.

MRS. AQUINO: Well, I am just very grateful for all these people, and I think, I hope this means that my husband did not die in vain.

DONALDSON: Mrs. Aquino, do you fear that you may be in danger, if you return to the Philippines?

MRS. AQUINO: I don't think so, and I do not worry about those things. I feel that my place should be in the Philippines now. And I am eager to be home to see my husband, to arrange for the funeral.

Benigno Aquino's quiet widow had charisma and guts. She was tough, calm, resolute. She would remember, for years, the messages of praise from viewers who "commented on how impressed they were with my unusual composure, given the tragic circumstances. In fact, Filipinos in the U.S. told me later on that my appearance on *Nightline* gave them a new impression of me. In a way, they discovered a different Cory."

Cory Aquino herself apparently "discovered a different Cory" in her *Nightline* debut. "Cory talked about that interview a lot," according to someone who later became one of her political advisers. "She was personally moved by that experience. It was a cathartic moment for her because she realized she had some inner resources of strength that surprised even her."

ONE MONTH AFTER Aquino's assassination, the pro–democracy movement caught fire. More than a hundred thousand people gathered for a "national day of sorrow," in both a tribute to Aquino and as a protest against Marcos's decision to appoint a crony to investigate Aquino's murder. At dusk, a number of demonstrators began hurling rocks at armed security men around Marcos's palace. Some of the protesters began throwing fire bombs. The police opened fire. Dozens were killed on both sides, and scores wounded.

Twelve hours later, Marcos appeared on *Nightline*. It was his first interview on American television since Aquino's assassination.

KOPPEL: Why wasn't it possible to safeguard [Aquino] when he came home?

MARCOS: We tried to protect him.

KOPPEL: You think you tried as hard as it was possible and that the security measures you took were as—

MARCOS: Oh, yes. Oh, yes.

KOPPEL: —as tight as security measures could be.

MARCOS: We tried everything [but] the opposition has succeeded in preventing the Fernando commission from conducting an investigation.

KOPPEL: Would you accept an impartial international commission?

MARCOS: International commission, what the heck. Why an international commission? This is an internal matter. We pride ourselves in believing that we can solve this. And they can come and observe if they want to, but certainly we do not dispense justice through foreigners in this country.

Marcos was doing himself more harm than good. A Filipino who was attending an American college at the time watched the interview with a number of students from his homeland: "We laughed our heads off at Marcos's excuses," he remembered later. "We called our parents back in the Philippines and said, 'You can't believe what the old man is saying now!'"

KOPPEL: Mr. President, it's a comparison that I suspect you won't like very much, but the comparison is made by some in this country between your position in the Philippines today and that of the shah of Iran in 1978.

MARCOS: Oh, come on! That's a little bit much. Come on, that's a little bit much.

KOPPEL: Why?

MARCOS: The shah didn't even know his cabinet members. He didn't know his military men. He didn't know his political base. I *have* a political base.

What Marcos had in common with the shah of Iran was the misguided belief that Washington would rescue his dictatorship. The fact was that his hold on power would never recover from the assassination of Benigno Aquino. By mid-1985, the Philippines economy was careening over a cliff despite billions in aid from Washington, the U.S. media had unleashed a torrent of reports accusing Marcos of embezzling a huge percentage of that American aid and stashing it in foreign bank accounts, the Communist insurgency was gaining strength among the ever-larger numbers of wretchedly poor Filipinos, and human rights groups across the world were charging Marcos with oppressing, imprisoning, and torturing political opponents. There had not been a free presidential election since 1969.

With the Cold War still on and Clark and Subic still serving as critical American military outposts, Washington could not afford instability. President Reagan had sent one of his closest friends, Senator Paul Laxalt, to meet privately with Marcos. It was in the wake of the much-publicized Laxalt visit that Marcos appeared once more on *Nightline,* clearly desperate to "spin" the administration and Capitol Hill.

MARCOS: The controversial reports have confused everybody. . . . We are not another South Vietnam. We have had quite a long experience with insurgency. . . . And if you want more surrenders, they're all over the papers. . . . Now with respect to the economic crisis, what is the report of the IMF and the World Bank? Both of them gave us good marks.

Koppel asked Marcos why he wouldn't call for an election sooner than the one scheduled for 1987.

KOPPEL: It doesn't have to be a snap election. Why not have an earlier election and allow there to be observers?

MARCOS: Do you know the elections are going to be held in seven
            months? Seven months.

KOPPEL: But those are not the presidential elections, sir. The
            presidential elections, as you just indicated, are more
            than a year and a half away.

MARCOS: Look, what will a presidential election give me? I already
            have the mandate of our people. At the same time, the
            International Monetary Fund and the World Bank are
            busy with us working out all these problems in the eco-
            nomic crisis. And I have my hands full . . .

Two weeks later, Marcos appeared on *This Week with David Brinkley*. Koppel had settled in at his Maryland home to watch, although he
expected nothing more from the dictator than the usual diatribes and
evasions. Suddenly Marcos announced a snap election. There would
be an election, he told the Brinkley panel, possibly in "three months
or less." Koppel was astonished. Later, Marcos would tell Koppel, "I
surprised myself" with that announcement. But he was committed to
it now. More important, he had promised that the election would be
"free," with international observers.

Raul Rabe, the man who would later become the Philippines'
ambassador to the United States, believed that Marcos had actually
trapped himself into a free election two weeks prior to the Brinkley
show, when he had appeared on *Nightline*. Rabe, then an attaché in
Hawaii, was convinced that during the *Nightline* interview, when
Koppel had mentioned "international observers," Marcos hadn't
known how to back out. "He probably would have felt more comfortable if he had conducted the elections in accordance with the way
he wanted them conducted, without the international interference
from observers. But with that placed before him, by Mr. Koppel, and
with his need to put on a good image, I guess Marcos was put into
some kind of situation where he had to consider observers."

So who would run against the dictator? "The question for the opposition was, Who was unblemished enough that Marcos wouldn't be
able to undermine their candidacy?" observed a source who played a
leading role in the movement to oust Marcos. "Cory was perfect."

"I am just a housewife," Cory Aquino told *The New York Times*.

Her modest self-appraisals would define her campaign and shape the campaign of Ferdinand Marcos.

AMONG THE MYRIAD oddities about that election in the Philippines, one of the oddest was the fact that most of the campaigning took place in the American media. Marcos was by then so dependent on the political, military, and economic largesse of the Washington government that his image as America's "stable ally," as its trusted guardian against Communism in the Pacific, was paramount.

Aquino, for her part, had no choice but to make a case for her candidacy in the American press, since Marcos had the Filipino media under his thumb. To help her reach the right journalists with the right message, she had hired an adviser from the prestigious Washington-based consulting firm of Sawyer-Miller, a savvy Englishman named Mark Malloch-Brown. "Cory was barely on Filipino TV," recalled Malloch-Brown. "We received only cursory coverage—we'd be the last item before the weather. The only exceptions were Catholic Radio Veritas and one middle-class newspaper in Manila, *The Inquirer*, which was new and only sold in Manila, and only sold a few copies at best. So the Aquino camp was in this odd situation where, other than the limited domestic outlets, we were looking to the international media, and then the international media's support reflected back into the Philippines environment."

One strategy used by the Aquino camp was to repeat an accusation about Marcos—a charge that he had embezzled U.S. aid or that he had falsified his war record—to an American journalist. "Marcos would be absolutely stunned into response," said Malloch-Brown, laughing. "And of course once he responded, it became fair game for the Philippine press to cover. So we had that whole dynamic of using the foreign media to report Cory's attacks, which in a very deliberate way drove the issues back to the Filipino people."

Marcos fought back. He ran a television ad across the Philippines that featured the face of Cory Aquino, with the voice of someone pretending to be her asking, "How can I handle the responsibility? It's too tough. This is a man's job." He ordered television stations to run the movie *The Killing Fields,* a film that depicted the terror which would befall any nation that didn't take the threat of Communism seriously. In the American press, Marcos offered not-so-subtle warnings of a Communist Philippines should he lose. "Marcos's theme was, 'No matter how much you don't like me, I'm the stable ally,' " according to Malloch-Brown. "Marcos was essentially sending the message *Après moi, le deluge*. He knew that there was the question, for Washington, of how do you have a strong government in the center after Marcos, without tipping all the way to a takeover by the Communist insurgents?"

Aquino tried to turn her status as a political neophyte to advantage, by comparing it to the corruption and cronyism of the Marcos regime. Whenever a reporter would ask her about her inexperience, she would answer that it was true that she had no experience in corruption, oppression, and in siphoning off billions intended to aid the Filipino poor.

The housewife image cut two ways. In December 1985, *The New York Times* published what the Aquino camp considered a devastating profile of her, a story that questioned whether "just a housewife" could lead the Philippines, and that gently but effectively mocked her faith that "sincerity" could compensate for lack of political experience.

But on television, Cory Aquino cut a striking figure. Even the few brief clips that ran on Filipino television projected a well-defined image. There were Aquino's trademark yellow dresses, worn to symbolize the yellow ribbons that had decorated Manila the day her husband was murdered. There were her large spectacles, which made her appear thoughtful and unaffected—the visual antithesis of the glamorous Imelda Marcos. And there was Aquino's serene demeanor, which compared favorably to Marcos's edgy defensiveness.

Koppel believed then, as he did later, that Cory Aquino was a dream candidate for television. "Television is not most or even much of the time a profound medium," he said later. "Clichés are often a convenient shorthand for us, and when a new public figure presents us with a sort of juicy cliché that Corazon Aquino bestowed on us, we seized it, relished it, and were reluctant to let go of it. She was the one who introduced herself as a woman, just a housewife, and we were unable to resist. We married it to another cliché and turned it into a battle between the housewife and the dictator."

Cory Aquino did not hesitate, therefore, to accept *Nightline*'s proposal for a televised debate between her and Ferdinand Marcos. What surprised producers was how quickly Marcos said yes to it too. The one-hour program was set for February 6, 1986, the night before the election. Koppel would moderate by satellite from Washington.

Two days before the scheduled debate, Tara Sonenshine, who was in Manila to book guests for *Nightline,* received a call from a Marcos aide. "President Marcos is terribly sorry," said the aide, "but he had forgotten that it would be illegal for him to debate Mrs. Aquino on the sixth. The constitution forbids any kind of campaigning in the twenty-four hours before the election, and a debate, you see, would constitute campaigning."

Sonenshine called Aquino's people and asked if Mrs. Aquino would be willing to move the debate up a night. They agreed. But when the proposal was put to the Marcos camp, the answer was that Marcos would only consent to the new date if he could be interviewed alone by Koppel.

Rick Kaplan decided that it was better to get something with each candidate than nothing at all. Koppel, after all, could ask the questions that an opponent might ask. Besides, Kaplan had a plan. The first step was to get the interviews with the candidates on tape. Pre-taping was necessary anyway, due to the time difference.

So, on the morning of the fifth in Washington—the evening of the fifth in Manila, Koppel talked via satellite first to Marcos, who was in his palace.

MARCOS: Everybody forgot that the sixth is not a campaign day. It is prohibited by the election code. And therefore, when you set it for the sixth we were about to violate the election code, including—the punishment includes disqualification from public office. And I certainly do not believe in violating the law. If my opponent dares to take the risk, that's her business. That's her problem. But I don't, I don't want to violate the law.

Marcos got testy when Koppel pressed him about a rash of stories in *The New York Times* and *The Washington Post* that suggested he had fabricated his war record during World War II.

KOPPEL: You have seen those newspaper articles yourself, and you have seen some of the documents, suggesting that the guerrilla group that you claim to have led in fact either did not exist at all or was just a tiny group that played no major role.

MARCOS: Then why is it recognized by the intelligence officer of General MacArthur in a paper which is certified, too, by the head of the archives of the United States? Now, look. I don't want to talk about this anymore. If you do, I'm going to walk out!

Marcos would never have walked out, however, before landing a blow for the politics of fear. Mrs. Aquino, he warned, was a risk that neither Washington nor the Philippines could afford.

MARCOS: I still believe that you need somebody who has been experienced to run our government in this time of crisis. I have nothing against her, but certainly, when, say, your son is sick and he needs an operation or he needs the expertise of a good doctor, you don't pick just anybody who has honesty and sincerity in order to cure your son . . . As president of the republic I think it's my duty to call attention to this danger.

By the time the interview with Marcos was over, Manila was closing in on midnight. Marcos turned to Tara Sonenshine with a warning: "If Mrs. Aquino speaks to Mr. Koppel after midnight, it will be the sixth of February, and she will be disqualified from the presidency." Sonenshine and a camera crew tore out of Manila to the farm where Aquino lived. They hooked her earpiece up with Koppel less than an hour before the deadline.

KOPPEL: There is a difference between running a campaign as the widow of a martyred and beloved leader and running a country, a country that is, as you yourself have pointed out, in a great deal of trouble. To those who are neutral about you, what do you say about your lack of experience?

MRS. AQUINO: Well, more than experience, I think it is credibility that counts. And the truth of the matter is that the Marcos government has lost all credibility.

This was an even steelier Cory Aquino than the widow who had appeared on *Nightline* in the wake of her husband's murder. She had this to say about the possibility that Marcos's loyalists might vitiate the vote count.

MRS. AQUINO: I just want to remind Mr. Marcos that it was he who called for snap elections, and once the people decided to participate he better watch out. If he threatens to frustrate their will again, I am afraid he will have angry people on his hands.

Mrs. Aquino was determined, unflappable. She insisted that her candidacy was no front for other opposition leaders who might hope to shunt her aside.

MRS. AQUINO: If people wanted me to defeat Marcos they would have to do it my way, and you can ask the leading politicians in the opposition. . . . There were no deals involved when I ran for president, so nobody has a hold on me. I am my own person. I intend to continue being that kind of person. As I said, I don't owe anybody any favors.

Aquino refused even to kowtow to Washington. She had made no decision, she said, about the U.S. bases in the Philippines beyond the fact that she would honor the lease agreement set to expire in 1991. She even held open the possibility that she would have Marcos and his cronies tried for corruption.

MRS. AQUINO: Mr. Marcos as well as all of his cronies will get justice, something which was denied my husband.

When the interview with Aquino was over, it was early afternoon in Washington, with hours to spare before the taped interviews with Aquino and Marcos would air on *Nightline*. Kaplan planned to use the time to create the debate that *Nightline* had originally sought. He took the tapes of the Aquino and Marcos interviews into an editing room and intercut them, issue by issue. The final result looked and felt very much like a debate, even without the cooperation of Marcos. The contrast between the two candidates in the final edited version was stark: Marcos on the defensive, Aquino serene and determined. One man who was an important Filipino official at the time said that after watching Cory Aquino that night on *Nightline,* he switched his allegiance from Marcos to her. "I believe," he said years later, "that a number of Filipino bureaucrats were impressed by Aquino's answers on that program."

ON FEBRUARY 6, 1986, Filipinos went to the polls. International observers and vote tabulators agreed that Aquino had won. But for more than two weeks, Marcos would refuse to concede. The country began to break apart. Civil war, according to a number of U.S. military men, was possibly imminent. The Filipino defense minister and the chief of staff of the armed forces defected to Aquino's side, setting up rebel headquarters on the edge of Manila at Camp Aguinaldo. And now, at the urging of the Catholic cardinal, thousands of Filipinos surrounded Camp Aguinaldo to seal it off from forces loyal to Marcos. The people greeted defecting soldiers—of whom there were more by the hour—with flowers and cheers and a gesture that meant "People Power."

Still, Marcos would not step down.

Every day since the election, Cory Aquino had been giving speeches across the country, calling on her supporters to remain nonviolent, urging them to organize their rage in the form of a boycott against products manufactured by companies owned by Marcos and his cronies. Aquino knew who she was. When Mark Malloch-Brown suggested to her that her speeches were a little rambling, she cut him off: "I know my people better than you. The speeches need to be long. They keep things calm."

And when Betsy West, now in Manila, arrived at Aquino's home to produce a *Nightline* interview, she found Aquino clad in a simple housedress, standing at the door to greet her. "Would you like some tea or something to eat?" Aquino asked as she led West to the living room. West shook her head and took a seat. Then West glanced down and saw what Aquino was wearing on her feet: fuzzy slippers. West was amazed: "Here was this woman who had just been elected president of the Philippines, padding around her house in fuzzy slippers!"

By then Cory Aquino had achieved international stature as the housewife who dared to take on a dictator. Night after night, the U.S. networks carried pictures of the widow in her yellow dresses, defiantly insisting before crowds of cheering Filipinos her right to assume the presidency. She was a made-for-television heroine, and that was becoming a problem for the White House. So far, President Reagan had supported Marcos's contention that he had won the election. Marcos would not give up as long as he thought he had Washington on his side. The White House was now the key to the transfer of power.

Aquino left it to Malloch-Brown to come up with a strategy that would turn up the heat under Reagan. One early ploy of Malloch-Brown's was to arrange a press conference for the U.S. networks with vote tabulators who were accusing Marcos of corruption. For a setting for the press conference, Malloch-Brown chose the altar of a church. He also asked Aquino to use one simple phrase in all of her speeches: "We will stand tall for freedom!" Aquino hated the phrase. When she first heard it, she wrinkled her nose: " 'We will stand tall for freedom'? It's such a silly, awkward phrase. Why should I use that?"

"Because it was the phrase that Ronald Reagan used to defend his support of the contras," Malloch-Brown responded. "When the U.S. broadcasts carry your speeches with that phrase in them, Reagan will have to notice."

But after nearly two weeks of press conferences at altars, of yellow dresses and boycotts and "People Power," Malloch-Brown returned to his Manila hotel room one night for a few rare hours of sleep, wondering what it would take to get Marcos out, short of bloodshed. His phone rang after midnight. It was Joel McCleary, a colleague from the Washington consulting firm of Sawyer-Miller. McCleary had just heard from one of President Reagan's advisers. Reagan had been on a cross-country campaign trip, McCleary said, and at every stop he'd been pelted with questions from people who had been watching Aquino on television and who wanted to know why Reagan wasn't supporting her. "The President wants to know what it will take to get Cory off his back," McCleary told Malloch-Brown. "He says that 'the little lady in yellow' is killing him in the heartland."

Malloch-Brown had a firm reply. "It will take an unconditional switch in support by Reagan to Cory. The President must make a public plea to Marcos to step down."

Malloch-Brown flopped back down on his bed and slept. Just after dawn, he walked into Aquino's campaign headquarters and an aide ran up to him. "Did you hear what Reagan just said in California? He told Marcos to step aside!"

A few hours later, a plane landed in Manila, a flight crammed with international journalists arriving for the denouement of the Philippine revolution; whether or not the military men still allied with Marcos would fight for him was unclear. Among those on the plane were Koppel and Kaplan, correspondents Judd Rose and James Walker, and a team of *Nightline* producers and camera crews. Koppel and Kaplan decided to take Tara Sonenshine and a crew and drive to Malacanang Palace.

All of the streets approaching the palace seemed to be tilting toward it, pouring thousands of protestors, like marbles, against the gates. Koppel, Kaplan, Sonenshine, and the crew finally abandoned their car to press in closer, until they were sucked into the swirling mass. Two throngs converged around them, one shouting for Marcos to leave, the other shouting for him to stay. Kaplan feared the confrontation would turn physical. He shoved his way toward some soldiers guarding the gates and asked that they allow him and Koppel inside. The soldiers insisted that Marcos was not there. So Kaplan forged a path back to the car, with Koppel, Sonenshine, and the crew jostling their way behind him, and together they raced off to rebel headquarters at Camp Aguinaldo.

The camp was an island girdled by a sea of Filipino civilians, men and women carrying yellow flowers and ribbons. When Koppel stepped out of the car, Kaplan heard several voices in the crowd shout Koppel's name, proof that somehow American television coverage of the election had been reaching the Filipino people. After reaching the camp, they entered a huge barracks in which scores of uniformed men sat at half-attention, as if waiting for something. Koppel later learned that these were recent defectors, here to vouchsafe their better-late-than-never support for Aquino. But the man they wanted to meet, Fidel Ramos, the chief of staff of the armed forces, who had defected along with Juan Ponce Enrile, the defense minister, days earlier, was behind closed doors.

A soldier who was guarding the doors looked at Koppel, opened the doors, and simply announced, "Ted Koppel from *Nightline* is here." Suddenly Ramos appeared, motioned, and said, "Ted Koppel, please come in, come in."

Koppel and Kaplan walked in and saw that Ramos was in the middle of a meeting. Seated around a table were a number of generals and colonels, examining contingency plans in case of civil war. The camera crew followed Koppel and Kaplan in the door and began recording. Ramos didn't seem to mind. In fact, he would nod at the camera and repeatedly invite Koppel to comment on the plans. Koppel declined.

AT DUSK, A HELICOPTER lifted off from Malacanang Palace, ferrying Ferdinand Marcos and his family into exile. Shots were still being fired from the palace. Betsy West, James Walker, a cameraman, and a soundman pressed behind a bulldozer at the sound of gunfire, but a minute later they fell in with a horde of civilians charging the palace.

The four ran up against a barbed-wire fence that ringed the palace grounds. Trapped, now, by the thousands of people surging behind them, they felt for a minute as though they might be crushed in a stampede. Suddenly the fence gave way. West and Walker and the crew hopped over the wire and pushed along with the mass into the public half of the palace, into what had been the offices of the Marcos regime. The sacking of the palace began immediately. "The people were throwing statues of Marcos out the window," West recalled. "They threw out pictures of Imelda, too. Men and women were just ripping open files and running through the rooms with this look of glee on their faces." A young man bounced into a chair behind an elaborately carved desk and picked up the phone, pretending to be Marcos. "Hello, Mr. President?" He sneered into the receiver, then slammed it down.

Walker and West headed for the palace's private quarters, but military forces loyal to Aquino had already sealed it off, so they grabbed the videotape of the pillaging and raced back to their hotel. They found Koppel and Kaplan in an editing room with Judd Rose, whose camera crew had captured street scenes: truckloads of young men pulling up to intersections, tossing out tires and wood, setting them on fire in jubilation. On *Nightline* that evening, Koppel would present the calm preparations at Camp Aguinaldo, the frenzied sacking of the offices at Malacanang, and the bonfires in the streets, the flames licking the air.

The next morning, thousands of Filipinos converged on the lawn outside Malacanang and laid out feasts. West, Walker, and their crew returned to record what looked like "a national holiday," West remembered. "Everyone had their kids, and they were picnicking all over the grounds. People were selling yellow scarves as souvenirs of 'People Power.' They'd even cut up the barbed-wire fence that we'd broken over the night before and they were selling pieces of it." A military parade led by the beaming face of Fidel Ramos triggered cheers from the picnickers. "Ramos was smoking a big, huge, fat cigar, and he looked incredibly pleased with himself," West recalled. West suddenly realized that Ramos was heading toward a gate that sealed off the private portion of Malacanang. "I thought, The military is not gonna open the gate, with all the public here. And, sure enough, the soldiers start climbing over the gate and then jumping down to the other side. It was all happening so fast, and I was wearing a long dress, but we got to the fence and the soldiers just sort of hoisted me up, about fifteen feet in the air, and tossed me over. A group of soldiers on the other side caught me."

Walker and the crew jumped over after her, and the four were running alongside Ramos when they bumped into one of Aquino's closest aides.

"Can you get us into the private quarters?" Walker asked.

"The military doesn't want anyone in there," the aide whispered. "But follow me, quickly. I might be able to sneak you in the back."

And so it came about, that exclusive, eerie tour of the family quarters: the half-eaten caviar and sour cream, the champagne, the gilt furniture, the Adam-and-Eve photograph of Ferdinand and Imelda, the bathtub lined with gargantuan perfume bottles. And, of course, the shoes.

West would later compare that moment in Imelda's shoe closet to her clearest memory of Cory Aquino. The media-obsessed dictator and his shoe-obsessed wife had been deposed, in the end, by a woman in fuzzy slippers.

THE IMMEDIATE AFTERMATH of a crisis was always one of Koppel's favorite moments as a reporter. There were always so many stories that couldn't be told until one side or another had consolidated power. One of the best stories came from Defense Minister Ponce Enrile, who had led the defection to Aquino. Enrile told Koppel that even as the Filipino civilians ringed Camp Aguinaldo shouting, "People Power," the rebels were badly outnumbered by troops loyal to Marcos.

ENRILE: It was a matter of life and death for us.

KOPPEL: They could have used artillery against you?

ENRILE: They could have used armored personnel carriers. They could have used the marines.

KOPPEL: Airpower.

ENRILE: They could have used helicopter gunships, or they could have used commando-type operations. They could have used artillery pieces or mortar fire.

KOPPEL: Why didn't they?

ENRILE: But they didn't.

KOPPEL: Why?

ENRILE: I don't know.

   Two days after her inauguration, Mrs. Aquino sat down with Koppel and shed further light on Marcos's final hours in power. Marcos had tried to negotiate with Aquino's people for permission to return to his home province, where he would live in a kind of internal exile.

MRS. AQUINO: I asked first, is it because that he believes that his end will come soon that he would like to die in his own home? And I was assured that it wasn't so. So I said, "Well, when Mr. Marcos has taken his rest, when he has gotten his sleep, then I have to strongly urge him to continue with his trip because it is to the greater interest of the Filipino people that he leave the Philippines right away, so that tensions will ease and that we will be able to get back to normalcy at the earliest possible time."

One month later, on the Hawaiian island of Oahu, in the shadow of Diamond Head, Marcos gave *Nightline* his first interview since his fall from power. Marcos had his own version of those final hours. He had hoped, he said, that his military would defend him:

MARCOS: The [rebel] helicopters that had attacked Malacanang—oh, I might just as well just come out with it—they were gassed and rearmed in Clark Air Force Base.

KOPPEL: So what you're really saying is that in some fashion the American government was helping the rebel forces against you.

MARCOS: In addition to which, when I arrived in Clark Air Force Base I saw our COIN planes that were supposed to be used in defense of our installations, grounded in Clark Air Force Base . . . and I also saw some . . . Philippine Air Force planes, who were supposed to be helping me and our forces. . . .

KOPPEL: You had left the Philippines giving everyone the impression that the reason there was no violence was because of your restraint, that . . . you were reluctant to cause bloodshed, Filipinos against Filipinos.

MARCOS: Yes, but we were defending, we were not on the offensive. . . . And I had difficulty immediately after that to get in touch with some of the units.

KOPPEL: Why didn't you pick up the phone and call Ronald Reagan?

MARCOS: I tried, but for some reason, I couldn't get him.

KOPPEL: Secretary Shultz?

MARCOS: Same thing. . . .

KOPPEL: Did you know where you were being taken?

MARCOS: The agreement was that I was supposed to go to Clark, then to Laoag [Marcos's home province]. They never told me that they would take me out of the country.

Marcos alternated between stubborn arrogance and self-pity:

MARCOS: I've always maintained that I am the legitimate president
            of the Philippines.

KOPPEL: Still.

MARCOS: Up to this moment. And that the only legitimate gov-
            ernment for the Philippines is the government that I
            should head.

Marcos, in the end, reminded Koppel of Richard Nixon. "The
embarrassment of their final days in power, and the humiliation of
having their power stripped away in full view of the entire world,
would drive lesser men into total seclusion. But like Richard Nixon,
Ferdinand Marcos refused to believe his own political obituary. Marcos, whatever else you thought of him, was a scrapper. He was also,
like Nixon, a very smart man, who climbed the political ladder from
lawyer to congressman to senator to president. And, like Nixon, he
was an interesting man."

KOPPEL: Where can you go? I mean, it must be a terribly humili-
            ating experience. At one point you were thinking about
            going to Spain—

MARCOS: To be treated like a pariah.

KOPPEL: Yes.

MARCOS: It's something which of course I never expected to
            happen in my whole life. But I take it in my stride. There
            is nowhere else to go. I either stay here or go back home
            and take my life into my own hands, and tell everybody,
            "Well, if you want to kill me, here I am. But you will
            start a civil war."

KOPPEL: There's an irony there, isn't there? I mean, a few years
            ago, Ninoy Aquino was in the same position.

MARCOS: No. Ninoy Aquino, there was a conspiracy against him,
            and the conspiracy was confirmed. We asked him to lay
            off the Philippines for a while because we were con-
            vinced that his life was in danger, and that we would be
            blamed for his—and we were.

KOPPEL: You are.

MARCOS: Yes, I have been. But God of course is our witness. I can swear on a dozen Bibles and people will question it. But I can tell you, if we had wanted to kill Aquino that was not the way to do it. There was a death sentence against him, and all we had to do was to let time pass by and execute him.

"Perhaps," Koppel later mused, "both Nixon and Marcos were right in placing so much faith in history. History ignores only the dull. It will relish the career of Ferdinand Marcos for many generations to come."

KOPPEL: I must tell you, when people heard I was coming out to do an interview with you, you know what most people are interested in?

MARCOS: Unh-unh.

KOPPEL: Your wife's three thousand pairs of shoes.

MARCOS: How many shoes—

KOPPEL: How many shoes—

MARCOS: —can you wear in twenty years?

KOPPEL: Exactly. How many can you?

MARCOS: Well, she gets all kinds of—buys all kinds of shoes. She has probably to change shoes twice a day, and then after a while, because she has to probably feel more comfortable, and there are parties where she can wear high heels; there are parties where she has to wear short heels.

KOPPEL: But, Mr. President, three thousand pairs of shoes, hundreds and hundreds of—

MARCOS: Twenty years. Those are collections from twenty years. . . .

KOPPEL: Four and a half million expended [by Imelda] over one month in New York.

MARCOS: Well, probably, it was not all spent for her. What is the proof that this was all spent for her? Just because she took it out of her account? . . . Right now we are hard up. We have no liquidity. We cannot even pay our security. We cannot even pay our doctors' bills. Our funding here has been below even possible healthy requirements, including food. . . .

KOPPEL: About Mrs. Marcos. Is she relatively content here?

MARCOS: She's not contented, of course. She's always crying. But she's learned to take it in stride. In fact, it is she who insists that we go home; if they want to kill us they can kill us. And she says let's do it now; why wait? And of course, I've told her that in a situation like this it is first important to think not only of ourselves, satisfy your ego and satisfy your whim, caprice, that we must first think of the country.

Almost ten years after the fall of Ferdinand Marcos, Koppel was flying to California for a story related to the O. J. Simpson trial. Seated next to him for the flight was the man who had served as Marcos's American attorney.

"As things deteriorated, Marcos preferred to make his case on *Nightline* because he trusted you," the attorney told Koppel. "He thought you were fair."

At that, Koppel and the attorney fell into a conversation over the parallels between Marcos and the shah of Iran. "Well, you know," the attorney said, "there is a parallel that has never been revealed to the media. After Marcos got to Hawaii, the Aquino government started pressing for the return of Marcos's money, and the U.S. government was exploring possible criminal charges against him, not to mention its attempts to freeze all of his assets. In fact, Washington thought that Marcos's continuing presence on American soil was a problem. The U.S. government wanted to find a new country for his exile. So members of the Reagan administration, along with those of us representing Marcos, started looking.

"Finally, it appeared that Panama—the very country where the shah had sought exile—would take Marcos. One of Marcos's sons-in-law went with one of my colleagues to Panama City to work out a deal. Two members of President Reagan's National Security Council were there too. But at some point, representatives of Manuel Noriega, Panama's military strongman, pulled the Marcos representatives away from the NSC guys and explained the deal. Marcos would have to fork over hundreds of thousands of dollars a month to the Noriega government—which meant, of course, that the money would be Noriega's extortion fee.

"The amount they were talking about was outrageous on the face of it. But that wasn't all. There was a kicker: the fee did not include linens or meals!"

Koppel thought back to every conversation he had ever had with Marcos. Every issue was magnified by Marcos into something larger than life; every position he took was extreme: the hostile threats about a Communist Philippines should he be deposed, the passionate denials that he'd embezzled American money, the angry accusation that Washington had offered military help to those who had deposed him, the pitiful representation of poor Imelda crying her eyes out in Hawaii, the fumbling attempt to pooh-pooh all the shoes. All of those extremes were embodied, really, in the closet of shoes. And now this: the dictator and his wife, with their fondness for beluga, New York skyscrapers, jewels, and shoes, had come face-to-face with another dictator whose greed was equal to their own. That the deal should collapse over sheets and towels somehow struck Koppel as just about right.

THIRTEEN
Cry, China

T HE IMAGE OF the sobbing man elicited gasps from the small group watching television in a Beijing hotel room. The man's face was contorted by grief; he was saying something to someone off-camera, but Chinese television had edited out the audio. Everyone in the room, however, knew what the man had said on the original tape. They knew because they worked for ABC and the tape belonged to them. Chinese television had stolen it.

A camera crew and an interpreter from ABC had found the man on a Beijing street, two days after the crackdown in Tiananmen Square. "It's terrible, terrible!" he had wailed. "They killed twenty thousand of our own people!"

The Chinese had apparently pirated the clip from an ABC satellite feed out of Hong Kong, or else they had received a copy of it from an official posted in the United States. This copy was grainy. The ABC producers and reporters who were gathered around the television set watched silently until Alicia Joyce, the interpreter who had originally interviewed the man, translated the Chinese characters at the bottom of the screen: *"This man is a rumor-monger. He is wanted for arrest."*

The next day the same man reappeared on Chinese television. This time the video did not belong to ABC. The man was in shackles, being pushed to jail. Someone had turned him in.

• • •

ONE WEEK AFTER thirty thousand troops of the People's Liberation Army had shot their way into Tiananmen Square in early June
1989 and mowed down hundreds if not thousands of unarmed civilians, the Chinese government was using the sobbing man as a threat,
not only to its own citizens but to foreign broadcasters. The message of
the man's arrest was that it was no longer possible to point a camera in
the direction of Chinese citizens without endangering them.

Nightline's producer on the scene phoned Ted Koppel, in Washington, with the news of the stolen clip and the arrest of the "rumor-
monger." Koppel was not surprised. He had been covering China
since his days as an ABC correspondent in Asia in the 1960s. Two days
after the bloody crackdown, he had warned the producer that more
repression would follow. Now, he said, the challenge was to come up
with new ways to cover a closed society and new ways to examine
what had happened to the foiled revolution that strange "Beijing
Spring" of 1989. "One thing you need to do," Koppel advised, "is to
find a bicycle for me like the one you've been riding around on to do
your reporting. I'm going to try to get into Beijing, if I can get a visa.
When I arrive, the first thing I'd like to do is go for a bike ride to
Tiananmen Square."

The producer asked how they would get around the government
clampdown on journalists. "Well, so far," Koppel reminded the producer, "all of you in Beijing have come up with some inspired ways
of getting around the press restrictions. Let's not stop now."

IT HAD BEEN A heady spring for the forces of democracy. Inspired
in part by "People Power" in the Philippines and, more recently, by
the death of a pro-reform official who had been ousted from the government, thousands of Beijing college students had begun, in mid-
April, a series of pro-democracy marches to Tiananmen Square. At
first, Deng Xiaoping's regime did nothing to stop the marches, but in
May, the students escalated their protest. With a sense of timing that
could be seen as either exquisite or suicidal, a score of students leading
the protest movement pitched tents in the square and launched a
hunger strike, just forty-eight hours before Mikhail Gorbachev was to
arrive in Beijing for a summit with Deng Xiaoping.

As a move to steal the international limelight, the hunger strike
was brilliant. Thousands of other college students—some from cities

thousands of miles from Beijing—journeyed to the square and set up tents in solidarity with the hunger-strikers. Foreign journalists in town to cover the summit flocked instead to the drama in Tiananmen, where the hunger-strikers were fainting, their limp bodies carried directly past the lenses of American television cameras.

Deng Xiaoping was humiliated. Almost as soon as Gorbachev was gone, Deng's regime declared martial law. Though the students ended their hunger strike, they refused to leave the square. Within an hour, all of Beijing, it seemed, poured into the streets to support them, and all of Beijing, it seemed, had boned up on "People Power." The citizens swarmed around convoys on the city's outskirts, around troops they assumed were headed for the square. The troops stopped. Military men dismounted from their tanks and engaged in friendly chat with the people. Women handed flowers to soldiers. A military crackdown, it appeared, had been stymied by ordinary people intent on democracy. Some of the hunger-strikers actually met with Premier Li Peng, and scolded him, wagging their fingers disrespectfully. Cameras from the American networks captured all of it—live.

But unlike Ferdinand Marcos, who in his final days tried to manipulate the press but did nothing to prevent broadcasting from Manila, the Chinese authorities took steps to muzzle international television coverage of the Tiananmen uprising. Just hours after the declaration of martial law, the government pulled the plug on satellite feeds out of the country. Live television broadcasts from the square, or from the streets, or from anywhere in China for that matter, were no longer possible. And yet, oddly enough, the authorities took no action against cameras *recording* in the square. Nor did they prevent the shuttling of videotapes to Hong Kong, where there was no problem with satellite feeds. Thus, producers could shoot all day long in Tiananmen, fly the material to Hong Kong in the evening, and have it fed to New York in plenty of time for airing on *World News Tonight* and *Nightline*.

So as the Tiananmen sit-in dragged on, day after day, ABC camera crews roamed the square and captured the astonishing spectacle. Tents blanketed the massive square, bound on one side by the Forbidden City and on the other by Mao's mausoleum. Young people huddled together, shared food, chatted, strummed guitars. Litter drifted between the tents. Banners draped the Monument of Heroes, where the leaders of the protest used an old mimeograph to turn out flyers on democracy. Now and then someone at the monument would take a megaphone and electrify the throng with a speech about democracy or about Gandhi, or about the Reverend Martin Luther King, Jr. There was even a marriage ceremony in the middle of it all.

Whatever else it was, Tiananmen was theater. Once in a while there would be a commotion in the crowd, arms and legs would flail, and then several students would rush in and pull someone out past the cameras and proudly announce that the man was a thief and that thieves had no place in the sit-in and that they were turning the man in to the Beijing police. The hint of vigilantism, however, was overwhelmed by a palpable sense that the protesters were engaged in a peaceful free-for-all, not law-abiding in the eyes of the regime, but abiding by their own laws just the same. The square began to look and feel like a cross between the Berkeley Free Speech Movement and Woodstock.

FROM WASHINGTON, Koppel watched anarchy blossom in Tiananmen and was mesmerized. He was certain that Deng would eventually have to end it. The regime, after all, had declared martial law. The students were flouting it before the world. Beijing would have to "save face." What concerned Koppel was that everyone who was posted in Beijing for ABC, including his own producers, were so busy covering the unfolding protests that no one had had time to step back and examine what had brought the people and government of Beijing to this flashpoint. No one was investigating the behind-the-scenes details about how decisions had been made and were being made inside the student movement, or whether the government had anticipated so much civilian support for the protesters, whether it had the backing of the military, or whether, even, it was really eighty-five-year-old Deng who had been calling the shots on the part of the regime. No one had had time to go after the background stories that would give context to the uprising. And viewers would want that context, Koppel figured, as soon as this was over. Viewers would want details and inside accounts. Looking for sources after a crackdown would be impossible; they had to be found now. It was time to start piecing together what was really happening, besides the carnival in Tiananmen, and to learn what had already happened.

So while the cameras reveled in the sights and sounds of the sit-in,

Koppel asked Tara Sonenshine to track down four scholars on China who spoke the language and who were either already in Beijing or about to travel there. Among the four that she found, one had close friends in the student leadership; the others had sources high in the regime and at the universities. Koppel informed the four that his production company, Koppel Communications, would pay them to do some behind-the-scenes reporting. "Find out as much as you can about how things have come to this. Find out what has gone on inside the leadership of the students and inside the regime," he instructed. "Find out how decisions are being made, and by whom, on both sides. Find out if there's any divisiveness. Every nugget of new information will be useful. Don't worry about cameras. Don't worry about recording anything. I assure you there's plenty of fascinating video that's not even getting on the air. We need more information."

By the end of May, *Nightline* correspondent James Walker and producer Herb O'Connor, who had covered the Deng-Gorbachev summit, were gone. With the sit-in dragging into a third week, *Nightline* was down to one producer in Beijing, Kyle Gibson.

It was dawn in Beijing when Gibson phoned Koppel. "I've been up with a camera crew all night in the square. We saw the strangest scene. Late last night this enormous procession entered Tiananmen, led by students pulling carts, and on the carts were these mammoth sections of what appeared to be a sculpture. Following behind the carts were maybe ten thousand curiosity-seekers—men, women, and children. For the next couple of hours, right in the middle of the square, the students mounted the sections atop one another. When they were done, there was this colossal statue of a goddess that looks a lot like the Statue of Liberty—she's got the crown and the torch. She must be thirty feet high. The student leaders are calling her the Goddess of Democracy. And she faces the portrait of Mao, as if she's holding her torch in defiance against him."

"No sign of the police or troops?" Koppel asked.

"No," Gibson responded. "Not in the square. In fact, once the Goddess was complete, Tiananmen was a carnival. There were small boom boxes belting out rock music. Young men were breakdancing. Parents carried their children on their shoulders to give them a better view. There was a beautiful moon, which made it all feel even more like a festival. The tapes, by the way, are en route to Hong Kong if you want to put them on the air tonight. But if the regime hates Western decadence, Ted, this was it."

"Whatever you do, don't leave Beijing," Koppel advised. "Somehow the government is going to have to get control back. Deng will not allow martial law to be flouted forever. I think there will be a crackdown, and I'll bet it's soon."

THE FOLLOWING DAY, the first of June, Gibson called Koppel again. "You need to know that we have a new base close to Tiananmen, but I don't feel comfortable calling you from there."

"Why?"

"It's my honeymoon suite."

"How nice. Would you like to tell me what you're talking about?"

"Well, as you know, ABC's headquarters are at the Sheraton—which is where I've come to phone you—but it's miles from the square. And you probably remember that the only hotel in town really close to Tiananmen, the only hotel with views of the square, is the Beijing Hotel. So Mark Nelson [the coordinating producer] tried to get a room at the Beijing Hotel for us to use as a camera location. But he found out that the hotel has stopped issuing any rooms facing the square to journalists."

"So . . . you got married?"

"Dave Green [an ABC producer] and I went in posing as honeymooners. We carried luggage, with nothing in it but blank videotapes, and Green had a phony business card. I told the clerk that we were newlyweds and that all I wanted for my honeymoon was a view of Tiananmen Square. The next thing we knew, we had this enormous corner suite on the fifteenth floor with a wraparound balcony facing the square."

"Are you filming from there yet or are you still honeymooning?"

"As soon as we got the room, we called Nelson. Nelson asked Jim Fitzgerald, who's one of the best cameramen here, to take his camera apart and to hide it in an ordinary suitcase. When Jim and his luggage showed up in the lobby, I was waiting for him, and I greeted him as if he would be my second husband and rushed him upstairs."

"Are they calling you the Slut of Beijing yet?"

"Very funny."

Gibson went on to explain that Fitzgerald had determined just the spot on the balcony where he could get a great view of both the square and Chang An Boulevard. It would be from that very spot that the world would see, in only a few days, what would turn out to be the transcendent image of the Tiananmen uprising.

ON SATURDAY NIGHT, June 3, at 9:30 P.M., the first sound of bullets snapped across the walkie-talkie of Ray Homer, a producer who had traced the low rumble of approaching tanks to the western edge of Beijing, where a massive convoy suddenly bore down on Homer and a crowd of civilians blocking the boulevard.

HOMER: There is a long, long convoy of tanks. The people are going wild. They've set a bus on fire to stop the convoy, but the tanks are plowing right through it. Now they're shooting at us.

China's ban on satellite transmissions applied only to live video, not to live audio. With walkie-talkies in the hands of producers, correspondents, camera crews, and interpreters posted all over Beijing that night, ABC had the ability to broadcast the sounds, if not the sights, of a crackdown. In London, Peter Jennings took the anchor chair and introduced the voices of the "hand-radio brigade," beginning with the voice of Ray Homer.

HOMER: Thousands of soldiers on hundreds of trucks are headed for the square. . . . Soldiers have been shooting and there has been teargas fire and automatic weapons fire . . . this is D-Day, folks.

In Tiananmen, what had been the soft thunder of the tanks in the west swelled into a roar. Frenzied civilians, men and women by the thousands, swarmed into the square carrying makeshift barricades. Kyle Gibson and Barr Seitz, a young American working as an interpreter for ABC, stood in the middle of the throng and opened their radios to transmit the shouts of the protesters, the reverberation of the approaching army, the popping of approaching gunfire.

SEITZ: I'm standing just in front of the monument facing several hundred riot police who have gathered in front of the

Great Hall of the People and who are facing the students
. . . a lot of teargas was thrown.

GIBSON: The people are yelling "Overthrow Li Peng, overthrow
Li Peng." There is gunfire just to the west of us . . . it is
starting to come this way . . . people are moving this way
very quickly . . . and we're under fire! (*sound of bullets*)

Jennings rotated between the reports from the square and the perspectives of two seasoned correspondents, Jim Laurie, who'd reached
a hospital, and Jackie Judd, who, from a balcony at the Beijing Hotel,
had an overview of the tumult.

LAURIE: This is Jim Laurie at the hospital, where dozens of very
badly wounded people are being brought into this hospital . . . there are many, many injured with very serious
wounds. The people here are extremely angry . . . they
say a government with this kind of blood on its hands
cannot last very long.

JUDD: This is Jackie Judd. I can see from here that . . . real panic
has broken out in the streets below me. People can see
and can hear the gunfire and they can see the flames and
they're running and they're trying to get off on the side
streets . . .

GIBSON: Police are fanning out and moving this way, they are
moving eastward. People are yelling, chanting for
"Strike, strike." . . . Scores of wounded have been carried
right by us on trishaws, and on carts . . . some people look
very seriously wounded . . .

SEITZ: There's another wounded . . . and another . . . and another . . . (*sound of bullets*)

For seven hours, the walkie-talkies conveyed the intermittent
thunder of civilians stampeding toward the square, the whirring of
gunfire, the screams of anguish when someone was hit, and the eerie
interludes of quiet as the civilians carried away the dead and wounded.
(The troops, it seemed, had orders to shoot at the citizens all around
the square, but not at the students at the monument, a fact that
Koppel's investigators would confirm a few weeks later.)

After one barrage, an older man pointed to the walkie-talkies and said to Seitz and Gibson, in Chinese, "Tell America, tell America what you see."

THIRTY-SIX HOURS after the troops reached the square, the first, most violent stage of the crackdown was over. Monday morning, June 5, Tiananmen was no longer blanketed by tents but by soldiers, tanks, APCs, and supply trucks. The Goddess of Democracy was a pile of white rubble. The perimeters of the square and Chang An Boulevard were quiet save for clusters of citizens who met on streetcorners to share their anguish with one another, and the occasional bursts of gunfire that would continue to punctuate the air for days. Chinese television was broadcasting clips of the "most wanted" student leaders who had escaped the round-up.

The army had yet to crack down, however, on ABC cameras recording from the balcony of the honeymoon suite, despite a couple of bullets that had whizzed over the head of cameraman Ron Dean and pockmarked the exterior wall of the balcony. At noon on Monday, Dean was pointing his camera toward a convoy moving eastward out of the square when a lone man, holding a briefcase as if he were on his way to work, suddenly walked in front of the tanks and blocked their way. The man looked tiny standing before the first tank, like an insect facing an armored beast. He scurried in one direction then the other as the tank tried to move around him, the man and tank locked in a strange dance. Then the man climbed atop the tank, knocking on it as if searching for life inside the steel. It took a group of horrified onlookers, who appeared to be civilians, to pull the man off the beast and drag him away to safety.

Dean immediately pulled the videotape out of the camera and handed it to one of the young American teachers serving ABC as an interpreter and courier. Since troops were stopping all suspicious-looking people in the streets around Tiananmen, the interpreter would have to keep it well hidden. He lifted his sweatshirt and used duct tape to bind the videocassette to his stomach. He pulled his sweatshirt back down, dashed out a back door of the hotel, and raced on his bike past patrolling soldiers to reach the ABC bureau at the Sheraton. Another courier smuggled the videotape onto a flight to Hong Kong, from where it was fed by satellite to ABC headquarters in New York. Within hours, the lone man versus the tanks became the global symbol of that Beijing Spring.

IN WASHINGTON, Koppel watched the clip of the man on the tank as it was transmitted to ABC by satellite from Hong Kong and wondered why the Chinese weren't doing more to stop the filming, much less the smuggling of videotapes out of Beijing. An hour later, he got a call from Gibson.

"Ted?"

"Where are you?"

"About five blocks from the square. One of the managers in the Beijing Hotel figured out that all of us weren't honeymooning in the honeymoon suite and he came to warn us that the army was going to take over the hotel. So we've moved to another hotel nearby. I've been bike-riding. With a very helpful Chinese friend."

"Tell me what you're seeing."

"The citizens are gathering in huddles on the street. They seem enraged. Some cry. Many are talking about the possibility of a division in the military and of the possibility of civil war. It could all be rumor; no one knows. The people we saw were hoarding food, just in case, but the troops in the city seem united. There are something like 30,000 troops in and around Tiananmen, and another 250,000 have apparently encircled the city. We can't get closer than three hundred yards from Tiananmen, but the soldiers are obviously burning the tents and God knows what else. Smoke has been rising from there all day. Chang An Boulevard is all burned-out buses and shards of glass. Barr Seitz sneaked me into a hospital, telling them we were students looking for friends. There are so many wounded they're lying in the hallways. Did you see the man on the tank yet?"

"Yes."

"Ron Dean shot that from the honeymoon suite, but Todd Carrel [ABC's Beijing correspondent] and Jim Laurie have even wandered the streets with camera crews this afternoon and the soldiers haven't stopped them yet. They've got tape of some of the burned-out buses that people used to set up barricades. Carrel says the people he's interviewing can't believe the army has done this. He saw in other parts of the city what we saw near the square: people crying on streetcorners."

"I don't think you'll be seeing people crying on streetcorners much longer," Koppel said. "You think you've seen what the regime can do, but the suppression isn't over. In many ways, it's just beginning."

"So what do we do for *Nightline* tonight?"

"What we can do on *Nightline,* tonight, and maybe all week, is to not speculate. Let's chronicle how Beijing is changing hour by hour as the regime cracks down. What we've heard this weekend suggests that every person who's there for ABC has a good eye. We'll harness everyone there and turn them into reporters, just as Jennings did Saturday night. We'll start with you. I'm going to hand the phone off to one of our producers here, and everything you just described to me, you'll describe again so that we can record your observations on tape. Then go find every producer, cameraman, editor, and interpreter, and the correspondents, if they have any spare minutes at all, and simply ask them to phone this number. We'll record whatever the caller wants to offer up in the form of personal observations, eyewitness accounts, anything that might go in a journal. Any observation about Beijing, any anecdote about what they're encountering as they try to do their jobs, is worthwhile. Then we'll weave the phone calls together with whatever video has been smuggled out."

TODD CARREL: Ten o'clock Monday morning, I went out on the streets in the northern part of the city and at first everything seemed quiet until I had run a few blocks, and then I started seeing burnt-out buses and military trucks that had been overturned. There were thousands of people on the street, but very little traffic. There were people riding bicycles, looking at the rubble, at the destruction. And in the heart of the city, a lot of people were lining up at shops to try and buy provisions, but most of the shops in the city were shut down.

KYLE GIBSON: We proceeded to a hospital, and found that, with a capacity of sixty, it was holding more than two hundred today. Down one hallway there were mattresses on the floor, and people who were wounded all lined up on the mattresses. I would not call it a scene of chaos. By Monday morning it looked more like a scene of enormous fatigue and depression on the part of the hospital workers.

JACKIE JUDD: The tanks stopped [for the man with the briefcase], and the lead tank tried moving, to one side and then to the other side, to avoid hitting him. But the protester kept running in the same pattern that the tank was moving. Finally the protester climbed on top of the tank. He stayed there for about fifteen to thirty seconds. When I saw that, I knew what it meant when the protesters had said they were willing to die for their cause. What he did was such a remarkable, brazen act of defiance.

TODD CARREL: This afternoon I went out again, farther north, and by the time I got there, there were many trucks and buses barricading what was virtually a four-lane highway. And across the buses, people had put out posters . . . they were yelling, there were speeches going on, people talking to each other, trying to rally up some support for armed resistance. One young man who was a student said, "The people want arms, the people want weapons, they want to fight the military out of their city."

KYLE GIBSON: [This afternoon] we saw an astonishing convoy headed into Tiananmen. Seventy-five troop carriers, and more trucks carrying portable kitchens, portable bathrooms, trucks carrying water tanks. Radio-communications trucks. It was clear this procession would provide the supplies to allow the military to dig in for a long time. By Monday evening, we started seeing more smoke in many directions of the city. We could hear gunfire in the south. We saw teargas. At 1:09 A.M. all the lights went out in the west of the city. It is pitch-black.

Despite the early rumors, civil war did not erupt in Beijing. But for days, no one could be certain who was calling the shots in the regime; the leadership was in hiding. Midway through the week, President Bush told the press that even *he* did not know for sure who was in power, because his calls weren't getting through.

Deborah Leff, a versatile senior producer who was pinch-hitting for a few months as *Nightline*'s executive producer, worried that the broadcast could get bogged down in unconfirmed rumors about the leadership. She felt that the show should continue through the week with what had worked on Monday: the unscripted eyewitness accounts from Beijing. The only change was that John Martin, a correspondent based in Washington, would write a narrative each evening to tie all of the perspectives together.

What those perspectives revealed, especially in the context of Martin's narratives, was an incremental consolidation of power on the part of the regime. Day by day, the crackdown intensified.

Tuesday, June 6

JIM FITZGERALD (*cameraman*):   About fifty transport trucks left the square and headed east, followed by approximately five hundred armed soldiers, who were chanting and singing, followed by two hundred troop trucks. We did hear some firing . . . They had already passed my vantage point. There are very few civilians on the streets.

JIM LAURIE: People on the street told us they heard lots of firing, lots of shooting. The longest sustained round lasted about twenty minutes, we were told, but we couldn't determine exactly who was shooting at whom.

MARK NELSON: The spokesperson at the embassy had read to me a statement urging Americans to leave the city, and leave it immediately. I told [the ABC staff] that if a staff member or a part-time member or anyone would like to leave, that is their choice, and we respect it and they should do it.

Wednesday, June 7

LYNN JONES (*producer*):   Foreigners are pouring out of the city as fast as they can. I saw cars and buses today with foreign flags, trucks with luggage, racing through the streets. The whole scene had a very unreal feeling to me, like movies we've all seen of people trying to get out of cities or countries just before a war, only this isn't a movie, it's real, and I'm here.

PHILIP DUCEAUX (*cameraman*):   [At the airport] there was a bit of pandemonium because the Chinese attendants would refuse any credit cards, and some people didn't have cash with them.

Thursday, June 8

CHRIS ANTONIACCI (*producer*):   I was [filming], trying to stay in the middle of a large crowd so I wouldn't be noticed, since the army had already said there were no pictures allowed. Suddenly somebody grabbed my shoulder and spun me around. It was a couple of Beijing police officers who shouted at me in Chinese for a couple of minutes and then led me away from the street.

Friday, June 9

JIM LAURIE: In most cases they're highlighting the arrest of workers or others who have supported the student movement. They've not actually talked about the arrest of any students. You must realize that even in this sort of environment in China today, the student still occupies a somewhat exalted, somewhat elitist place in society.

KYLE GIBSON: We found a whole new paranoia [on the streets]. We found people literally running away from us, whispering "Be careful" as they got out of the way, and saying that plainclothes police were watching us.

ALICIA JOYCE (*interpreter*):   People who managed to talk to us quietly said there's plainclothes police everywhere. They're afraid that once we leave, the policemen will come to them. And it's a very real fear.

JACKIE JUDD: In one neighborhood, we saw soldiers deliver sacks of flour. When the soldiers got back on their trucks, they waved goodbye, and the people on the streets applauded. But I want to mention that this was not a totally benign gesture or a totally benign scene, because soldiers stood patrol on the street the entire time, again with those rifles at the ready or strung across their chests.

DAVID ROSE (*ITN reporter*):   We were arrested. Three secret policemen held us for over an hour. They questioned us, asking repeatedly why we were filming when it was forbidden by martial law. Eventually they did release us, but only after confiscating our equipment, worth over thirty thousand pounds.

By the weekend, David Rose's story of being arrested was not unique. ABC's Chris Antoniacci was asked to write out a formal apology to the government for filming in defiance of the law. Troops also had opened fire on the "foreigners' compound," where a number of international diplomats and journalists, including Americans, lived. No one was hurt, but the regime had sent a fairly clear message that it might be a good time for all foreigners to leave. A few days later came the arrest of the "rumor-monger," and ABC's videotaping around Beijing ceased almost completely. The producer in charge of Beijing coverage, Mark Nelson, had ordered it, but the order was unnecessary: no one wanted to endanger the Chinese people. The authorities were putting the squeeze on journalists in general, broadcasters in particular.

Koppel, however, wasn't quite ready to succumb to the restraints. He left for Hong Kong.

Hong Kong: Chinese visa office

NAME: KOPPEL, EDWARD
OCCUPATION: SOCCER COACH

Koppel filled out the visa form carefully, and fraudulently. He couldn't take a chance by putting down that he was a journalist. In the two weeks since the move on Tiananmen, the Chinese had been denying visas to members of the international press.

NAME: SMITH, DORRANCE
OCCUPATION: BASEBALL MANAGER, SAN FRANCISCO GIANTS

Dorrance Smith was *Nightline*'s newest executive producer. He'd prepared for this. En route to Hong Kong, the plane had stopped at the San Francisco airport, where Smith had picked up a Giants cap and a baseball jacket, just to look the part. It worked. Smith got his visa. But Koppel's name was apparently on some list of journalists. His visa was denied. Smith took off for Beijing. Koppel took off for Bangkok.

Bangkok: Chinese visa office

NAME: KOPPEL, EDWARD
OCCUPATION: SOCCER COACH

This time, Koppel had a plan. The Chinese authorities didn't want journalists, but they very much wanted tourists. The trick to getting in was to not seem too determined about it—to seem a shade naive. This time Koppel would act afraid—a bit *uncertain* about going.

Koppel filled out the application with "Occupation: Soccer Coach," and took it to the visa clerk. As the official examined the paperwork, Koppel frowned and said, "I'm not entirely sure I should be going to China. I hear it's very dangerous."

"No, no, sir. Oh, no. Everything in Beijing is fine."

"Well . . . there've been some reports . . . I don't know. . . . You really think it is safe?" Koppel tried to mix the concern in his expression with a measure of fear.

"Of course, sir. Yes, yes, it's safe. You will be fine, sir." The clerk smiled reassuringly.

So it went for a few more minutes, with the clerk in the position of trying to convince Koppel that he *should* go to Beijing. Within minutes, he had his visa.

KOPPEL HADN'T BEEN off the airplane in Beijing an hour when he was riding bikes with Kyle Gibson to Tiananmen Square. It was possible, by then, to ride around the square's perimeters, where thousands of troops stood at attention, their rifles pointed outward. In an alleyway stained with blood and pockmarked by bullets, Koppel explained his plans. "We've got two projects. First, we'll try to broadcast *Nightline* from here, if we can figure out a way around the ban on satellites, and second, we've got to finish gathering the information and video that we need for our documentary. I've brought a video camera, and we'll use it as much as possible. With luck, the soldiers will think that the high-eight means we're tourists."

The next day Koppel and Gibson took a small hand-held eight-millimeter video camera and walked onto the campus of Beijing University, one of the hotbeds of the dissident movement. There was a wall on the campus where students had continued to scrawl anti-government slogans even after the authorities had seized the square. Gibson had seen a bit of graffiti here, just two days after the crackdown, that read "BLOOD FOR BLOOD." The wall was pristine now. Koppel wanted a shot of it. Chinese security men stood nearby, watched, and did nothing, apparently assuming, as Koppel had hoped, that he was a tourist. Still, he surreptitiously slipped the tapes to Gibson. "Tuck these under your sweater, in case the camera is confiscated," he urged.

Koppel had never carried a video camera on assignment before, but he began to relish the freedom it afforded. He could use the camera in some of the most restricted areas of Beijing, sometimes right under the guns of the troops. "It was wonderful to be able to work alone," he said later. "We never work alone in television. We usually move in these huge, intrusive packs, because of all the equipment. Besides, it felt good to beat the system. The little camera helped us do that."

What no one had figured out was how to actually anchor *Nightline* from Beijing. The Chinese government still had a ban on satellite transmissions out of the country. Audio wasn't a problem, since it could be transmitted on phone lines, just as the walkie-talkie reports were transmitted during the crackdown. The videotaped material wasn't a problem either, since the cassettes could be sent by plane to Hong Kong and fed to the United States via satellite from there. But if Koppel were seated at a desk in Beijing interviewing someone like the U.S. ambassador, live, how would the picture be transmitted?

Producer Bill Moore found a way. He remembered that ABC had been feeding still pictures out of Beijing with a new gadget called a pixilator. The machine turned images captured on a video camera into still photos, which could then be fed—like a fax—through a phone line to New York. Moore arranged a technological coup: to have Koppel's face "pixilated" as he anchored the show. While the audio was transmitted on a phone line, viewers saw a succession of stills of Koppel and his guests, one still dissolving to another.

When Koppel eventually screened a tape of that broadcast, he noticed that the pixilator infused an odd intensity into what might have been otherwise unremarkable interviews. "All of the excitement in that broadcast was in the technology," he told a colleague. "The effect for the viewer of hearing my interview while watching stills of the interview was almost exotic. And it sent the tacit message that we weren't the type to simply fold up our gear and walk away in the face of the tough press restrictions."

IN BEIJING, KOPPEL began meeting with the four China specialists he had retained in May to investigate the background of the uprising. They told him surprising new details about the evolution of the protest movement, about the naïveté of many of the student leaders, about the original plans for the Goddess of Democracy, and about divisions in the movement. There were revelations about the regime, too, and about Deng's role in the crackdown.

It was unclear whether any of the authorities had figured out that the soccer coach hadn't gone near a soccer field since his arrival or that the baseball manager, Dorrance Smith, hadn't even seen a ball field. But one day Koppel and Smith were in Koppel's hotel room, discussing one of the more sensitive revelations about Deng, and Koppel went over to the wet bar and turned on the faucet, leaving it running as a way of foiling eavesdroppers. Within a minute, a maid entered the suite, although it had already been cleaned, headed straight for the wet bar, turned off the faucet, and left.

The authorities would no doubt have been interested in what the soccer coach was learning about Deng Xiaoping. Deng, according to Koppel's sources, had been so humiliated by the hunger strike having upstaged his summit with Gorbachev that he vowed, right then, to use force on the students. Almost immediately after declaring martial law, Deng flew thousands of miles away from Beijing to meet with two army divisions—divisions whose soldiers didn't come from Beijing and would therefore have no knowledge of or sentimentality about the pro-democracy movement. Deng ordered the two divisions to prepare to retake Tiananmen using all means necessary. And he ordered that the troops be isolated for two weeks, during which the young soldiers were to be indoctrinated with a mission to save the people of Beijing from dangerous "counterrevolutionaries."

The inside story on the students was equally compelling. Phil Cunningham, one of the scholars with close friends in the student leadership, had discovered that the Goddess of Democracy marked the final and fatal turning point in the uprising. The unveiling of the Goddess, he had learned, was originally intended to mark the grand finale to the siege of Tiananmen. The student leaders who had commissioned the Goddess from art students "wanted to bring out the statue, have a final celebration, and go home," according to Koppel. "But what Phil Cunningham had learned was fascinating: just after the statue's debut, the student leaders took a final vote about whether they would stay or leave. The majority still voted to leave. They believed that they had made an impact, that it was time to clear the square before someone was hurt. But these same students who were protesting for democracy made an astonishingly undemocratic decision. A significant minority wanted to hold on to the square, and the students had agreed that the rule of the minority would prevail."

Cunningham had heard another story about the Goddess, one that explained why she had been carried in sections to the square. It turned out that while students were designing the statue at Beijing's Central Academy of the Arts, they had contacted some truckers to arrange transportation of the completed statue to the square. A few days later, the truckers came back to them with a warning: the secret police knew about the building of the statue and had warned the truckers that anyone who contributed a vehicle to the transport of the Goddess would have his license revoked. The art students, undaunted, kept building. They would finish the statue, then they would take a saw to it and cut it into sections that could be placed on handcarts and pulled, piece by piece, into Tiananmen, where it would be reassembled.

There was plenty of fresh meat in all that for a documentary. But in television, substance without style—i.e., compelling pictures—is the recipe for a documentary that no one watches. So while one search went on for information, a parallel investigation scoured for new, never-before-seen video. Producers didn't have to look far.

On breaking-news stories, for every interesting ten-second shot that makes it into a broadcast, there are hours of material left unused. When a story is unfolding fast, all of a network's resources are aimed at recording as much as possible in as little time as possible. Tapes pile up quickly, with no one available to screen them all. Once the daily newscasts have gleaned a few minutes' worth of material, the bulk of the original footage gets thrown—unscreened—into a library, where it is often forgotten.

Koppel suspected that all kinds of significant Beijing footage was nestled away, untouched, in ABC's Hong Kong bureau. Indeed, there were probably some scenes that wouldn't have meant much even to the camerapeople who filmed them without the knowledge later gleaned by Koppel's investigators. So while the team in Beijing finished up the editorial investigation, several producers in Hong Kong toiled away in editing rooms, combing through every single piece of video that had been shot in China by ABC since mid-April.

THE SCHEDULED AIRDATE required warp-speed production; Smith and Koppel wanted the documentary on the air before the end of June. They had good reason. The inside story of the Beijing Spring would matter most to viewers while all of the images of the protest—the marches, the hunger strike, the tents, the Goddess, and the bloody crackdown—were still fresh.

What producers needed most was a system to coordinate the findings of the Beijing investigators with the visual nuggets culled in Hong Kong. Koppel's solution was as simple as a notebook. He instructed the video team to record every shot, according to date and hour, in a large loose-leaf spiral notebook. "But keep the video logs confined strictly to the right-hand pages," he told them. The left-hand pages, he explained, would be saved for the editorial findings of the Beijing team.

Only three weeks after the crackdown, Koppel had a full notebook. On the left-hand pages was a chronology of events, as pieced together by the investigators; on the right-hand pages were the notes on what had been filmed the same day, sometimes the same hour, as events recorded on the left. The notebook became the blueprint for the documentary. Opposite the page that described Deng's humiliation and outrage over his summit losing the limelight to the hunger strike, the video notes included shots of an awkward, tense Deng standing next to Gorbachev, pictures of foreign journalists interviewing the hunger-strikers, and the student leaders in their televised, tense confrontational meeting with Li Peng. For the revelation that Deng had flown to the countryside to meet with the army about a crackdown, there was no video of the trip, naturally, but there was video from the night that Deng had made that decision, of a government official standing in the square, weeping and pleading over a megaphone for the students to leave before something terrible happened.

The biggest gold mine, visually, was material relating to the Goddess of Democracy. The team in Hong Kong had discovered scenes shot inside the Beijing Central Academy of the Arts, in late May, of students designing the statue. It was just the sort of footage that had never made it onto a broadcast because no one had originally regarded it of much significance. Only with the new information about the art students receiving the warning that the police were on to their project did the scenes inside the art school matter.

The editorial and visual components had to be pieced together like a jigsaw puzzle, but under the leadership of Terry Irving, *Nightline*'s most talented breaking-news producer, final editing had commenced by the fourth week in June. The documentary presented a day-by-day, sometimes hour-by-hour, account of the decisions taken inside Deng's regime and inside the student movement. All of the revelations were there, all of the turning points in the crisis, all of the oddities and ad hoc decisions, the coincidences and ironies that had made those few months in Beijing so searing and memorable.

Koppel and Smith wanted a title that would reflect the spirit of the uprising. They mulled over a number of possibilities, until they hit on *Cry, China: Tears of Spring*. It conveyed, they felt, exactly the right mood. In fact, they loved it.

ABC News president Roone Arledge did not, however, love it. The viewing audience, Arledge pointed out, needed to have at least some idea of what the program would offer. Arledge proposed the more straightforward *Tragedy at Tiananmen: The Untold Story*.

Smith and Koppel hated *that*. As production of the documentary drew toward completion, Smith and Koppel became even more convinced that *Cry, China: Tears of Spring* conveyed its spirit. Smith would later deny that he was inspired by the flouting of authority that was central to the documentary, but he does not deny that he found out how to write *Cry, China: Tears of Spring* in Chinese characters.

The night the documentary was broadcast, less than one month after the troops shot their way into the square, viewers saw the title graphic: *Tragedy at Tiananmen: The Untold Story*, in English. But on the left-hand side of the screen were the Chinese characters for *Cry, China: Tears of Spring*. For anyone who did not read Chinese, of course, and that included Arledge, it appeared that the Chinese characters were the translation of *Tragedy at Tiananmen*. But anyone who understood the characters knew that they read *Cry, China*. Smith laughed about it later. "At least we got to present the title we wanted to our Chinese-speaking viewers . . . It was Ted's and my little protest on behalf of artistic integrity."

In matters great and small, that spring, a rebel fever was in the air.

FOURTEEN
The Death of the
"Evil" Empire

KOPPEL HADN'T BEEN asleep an hour when the phone rang. Although it was morning in Moscow, it was the middle of the night in the United States and he had just concluded another live broadcast on the turmoil in the Soviet Union. Mikhail Gorbachev had survived a coup attempt—barely; his hold on power was tenuous. For most of the previous sixty hours, when not on the air, Koppel had prowled the offices of government officials, seeking information about a new power struggle between Gorbachev and Russian president Boris Yeltsin. "Turmoil" didn't quite describe what Koppel was witnessing; it was, he would realize later, the beginning of the end of the Soviet empire.

So it was that Koppel had just drifted off into the sort of deep sleep that punctuates a reporting vigil when the call jangled him awake. The caller was an ABC employee in the Moscow bureau. She had just heard from the office of Alexander Bessmertnykh, the Soviet foreign minister. Bessmertnykh wanted Koppel to come at once to the Foreign Ministry. Within fifteen minutes Koppel was hurtling through Moscow in a car provided by ABC. The driver, a former chauffeur for the Kremlin, commanded Koppel's awe: "At times he literally drove down the sidewalk, because there were so many traffic jams that he just couldn't get through. At times he was doing thirty, forty miles an hour on the sidewalk. And we got to the Foreign Ministry in record time. And then we just sat . . . and waited and waited and waited."

The summons from Bessmertnykh hadn't come as a total surprise: Koppel had spotted him during a Gorbachev press conference the previous day and had requested an interview. But why, Koppel wondered, had Bessmertnykh said to come immediately and then left him waiting for hours?

It wasn't until noon had come and gone that Bessmertnykh emerged from his office and asked Koppel to come in alone for a moment. "Bessmertnykh was in a very strange frame of mind," Koppel recalled. "He gave me a very warm greeting, but he seemed distracted. He started pointing to photographs on his desk."

"That's my wife," said the foreign minister. "That one is my son." And then, as though it were part of the same train of thought, he turned and looked at Koppel and said, "You know, Gorbachev just called me and fired me." Koppel was stunned. He waited for Bessmertnykh to say that in light of this shocking development, he would have to cancel the interview. Instead, Bessmertnykh said, "I want to talk to you about it." By "you," Bessmertnykh clearly meant *Nightline*.

Koppel tried to look "appropriately solemn, you know, about the fact that he'd just been fired." But what was going through Koppel's mind, as he recalled later, was *Yeeeessss! Oh, yes, absolutely!* After all, it wasn't often—say, maybe once in the entire history of the Soviet empire—that the Soviet foreign minister decided to announce his firing on American television. Then again, the empire was in chaos.

THE BIRTH OF *Nightline* coincided with the peak of Soviet expansionism. When *Nightline* began in 1980, the Soviets controlled Eastern Europe. They were arming allies in Africa, the Middle East, Asia, Central America, and Cuba. Just months before, they had invaded Afghanistan. Soon they would back the imposition of martial law in Poland. In America, Ronald Reagan, one of the candidates for President, called for massive re-armament, based on the conviction that the Soviets had achieved military superiority over the United States.

Over the next eleven and a half years, *Nightline* devoted nearly 250 broadcasts to the Union of Soviet Socialist Republics. The programs spanned the deaths of three Soviet presidents—Leonid Brezhnev, Yuri

Andropov, Konstantin Chernenko—and the rise and fall of a fourth, Mikhail Gorbachev. The coverage of Soviet-related issues ranged from psychiatry to religion, from spy scandals to spy swaps, from the White House's decision to boycott the 1980 Moscow Olympics to the Kremlin's boycott four years later of the Los Angeles Olympics, from the shooting down of KAL 007 to the melting down of Chernobyl to the tearing down of the Berlin Wall to the ultimate disintegration of the superpower itself.

But in January 1980, the notion of the death of Soviet Communism was for fantasists. President Jimmy Carter warned Congress in his State of the Union message that "the implications of the Soviet invasion of Afghanistan could pose the most serious threat to the peace since the Second World War." That night, Koppel anchored a special broadcast on the President's address. Among his guests was Vladimir Pozner, a good-looking "commentator" from Radio Moscow who spoke flawless American English with a hint of a New York accent. But wrapped inside his glossy Yankee idioms was a package of pure Soviet dogma. His country, he insisted, had not invaded Afghanistan.

POZNER: The Soviet Union, as you know, has agreements with Afghanistan, and sent in military aid on request of the Afghanistan government. We do not see that at all as an invasion, but as simply honoring our commitment.

KOPPEL: The viewpoint of the United States is that the government that invited you was found to be unfortunately dead shortly after the Soviet troops got there. Now, what is the response to that?

POZNER: Well, the response to that is that over a period of time since the April 1978 revolution in Afghanistan, the government there applied on several occasions for military aid to the Soviet Union, and it was only at the very last moment that the Soviet Union gave that aid . . . the Afghanistan government was asking for help, and we gave it. And I think that this has been blown out of all proportion.

Pozner felt the need here for an interesting addendum:

POZNER: This is my personal opinion. And I want to make it quite
            clear that I am not a government spokesman.

Pozner was accurate: he was not an *official* spokesman. What he
didn't say was that his appearance on American television required the
approval of the Soviet government. Nor did he explain that should his
performance fail to serve his government's interests, he would have
disappeared from American television without a trace. As early as
1980, the Soviets saw American television as a forum to be manipulated. A live program, in particular, afforded them the opportunity to
make propaganda without fear of being edited. Still, the forum offered
nothing without the right messenger.

Vladimir Pozner was their man. He was a gifted apologist. Pozner
had lived in New York from the age of five to the age of fifteen, when
his Russian father worked for MGM. The "Red scare" of the 1950s
had sent the Pozners to Moscow, where the younger Pozner pursued
a career in broadcasting. By the late 1970s, he had been hired by
GostelRadio, the government's broadcasting arm, as an English-
speaking commentator on Radio Moscow, the Russian counterpart
to the Voice of America. Pozner was therefore reaching for a foreign
audience.

Pozner understood why the Soviets preferred to have him broadcasting to listeners outside the borders. "I was seen in the Soviet Union
as someone who had come from elsewhere, who was, in the eyes
of some people, much too Western, and therefore I was never really
allowed to address my own audience, that is to say the Soviet audience. I was, in a way, a product made for export."

He certainly tried to look the part. In the early days, Pozner often
wore a leather jacket on-camera. The effect wasn't so much "American Cool" as it was "a Soviet-Who's-Not-Allowed-to-Leave-His-
Country's Idea of American Cool." In later appearances, especially
after he was granted permission to visit America, Pozner adopted well-
cut suits. The point, he later said, was to explode a Cold War cliché:
"American propaganda portrayed 'Russians' a certain way. They were
fat and jowly and they didn't shave very well and they were poorly
dressed, and on top of it, they had these terrible accents. And suddenly,
here I was, and I didn't fit the stereotype."

Pozner appeared more than twenty times on *Nightline* in the early
eighties. "I believed in what I was saying. I felt I had a mission. I

believed in the Soviet system—I've never said I didn't—and I believed
in the ideals of Communism. I think when you believe in something,
profoundly, then that also comes across."

There were several other devoted Soviet Communists who appeared frequently on the show: Vitaly Churkin, a Soviet diplomat in
Washington; Georgi Arbatov, a member of the Soviet Central Committee; Stanislav Menshikov, an adviser on American affairs to the
Central Committee; Artyem Borovik, the foreign editor of *Ogonyok,*
the Communist party magazine; Joe Adamov, a radio commentator;
and Gennadi Gerasimov, who first appeared as a "columnist" for a
Soviet newspaper and later as the spokesman for the Foreign Ministry.
None of them spoke with Pozner's American accent, none could
match his debonair demeanor (or the leather jacket), but all of them
irritated *Nightline*'s viewers.

In fact, the appearance by a Soviet always generated volumes of
mail. Viewers railed at Koppel for giving America's Cold War adversary a forum. Sometimes the criticism came from influential pundits.
George Will, the conservative commentator, for instance, often chided
Koppel for referring to Pozner as a "journalist."

In 1986, Koppel responded to the controversy with a special that
aired from Vanderbilt University. An audience comprised mostly of
students and faculty was invited to challenge a panel of journalists that
included Tom Brokaw, of NBC, and Roone Arledge, the president
of ABC News. The panel also included, via satellite from Moscow,
Vladimir Pozner.

AUDIENCE MEMBER: Why do we have this Russian here? That's what
            I want to know.

ARLEDGE: What's he doing here?

AUDIENCE MEMBER: Yeah, what's he doing here?

ARLEDGE: You mean on the program tonight or in general?

AUDIENCE MEMBER: Yes, sir. If we're talking about the press and the
            ideas of the press, people tell him what to say. He's not
            discussing his own topics; he's not saying anything that
            Mr. Brokaw could say. He is told what to say.

ARLEDGE: Well, I think he's here tonight because we considered
            that he would be very controversial and that people

would like to talk to him and hear what he has to say and probably question me and others about why we have him on the air, just as you're asking.

AUDIENCE MEMBER: You got me. You got me.

ARLEDGE: I mean, that's why he's here physically. The reason we have him on the air, and other Russian spokesmen from time to time, is to get their point of view.

Pozner's own response was shrewd. Whereas on *Nightline* he was always careful to insert the codicil that his opinions were his own and that he should not be interpreted as speaking for the Kremlin, tonight he turned the codicil sideways, if not upside down.

POZNER: I don't think I have been invited to go on American television to give Vladimir Pozner's point of view, which may or may not be interesting, but certainly is not a major factor in policy decisions. I've been invited to express the Soviet point of view—

KOPPEL: You are exactly right. And as someone who has invited you to come on *Nightline* many, many times, I have made precisely that point and would like to make that point to the gentleman who asks the question: (a), I don't regard Vladimir Pozner as a journalist in the American pattern. He clearly is not; he is a propagandist. But, (b), when he comes on the program, my interest is in having him on precisely because he represents the Soviet government's point of view and because we still operate under the illusion in this country that we are the stronger for it when we get not only the opinions of those who agree with us, but also the opinions of those who disagree with us.

Pozner's career, of course, didn't hinge on what American viewers thought of him. What mattered to Pozner were the reviews from his own government. It was up to Soviet officials living in the United States to watch him on *Nightline* and to relay their critiques back to Moscow. Over time he learned that one of his biggest boosters was Anatoly Dobrynin, the Soviet ambassador to the United States.

Still, Pozner would later insist he was never given instructions on what to say. "Never. Ever." But not because he was a "journalist." His bosses simply wanted cover. "No one wanted to take the responsibility. Clearly, if I did well, then everybody could, you know, slap each other on the back and say, 'Hey, great, look at the choice we made.' But if I screwed up, it was my fault."

Finally, there came a *Nightline* when Pozner "screwed up." That show, he said, put him "in danger." It was November 1982. Pozner arrived at ABC's Moscow bureau for what was becoming by now something of a routine appearance on *Nightline*. The subject of the broadcast was Brezhnev's successor, Yuri Andropov. Pozner sat down in front of the camera, put the earpiece in his ear, and waited for the program to begin. Minutes before airtime, Pozner could hear Koppel saying hello to the other guests.

"William Colby, do you hear me?"

Colby, the former CIA director, was slated to talk about Andropov's intelligence background. "Yes, Ted. Hello."

"Andre Marton?" Marton was a Hungarian-American journalist.

"Good evening, Ted."

"Arkady Shevchenko?"

Pozner blanched. Shevchenko was a defector. He had been a ranking Soviet diplomat—in fact, he had been a protégé of Andrei Gromyko—before defecting to the United States in 1978. Pozner had had no idea that Shevchenko was to be on the show. He knew that his bosses didn't know it, either. It was, after all, illegal for Soviet citizens to talk to defectors, "let alone be on a show with them. I didn't know what to do."

"I was thunderstruck," Pozner remembered. "If I just stayed there and spoke, I'd probably not have a job the next day."

By now, the show was on the air. Koppel went to Pozner first. Pozner was obviously distracted, flustered.

KOPPEL: Give us an insight into your new leader—

POZNER: I'm sorry . . . we had . . . the phone just rang on the desk here, and while I grabbed it I missed your voice—

Pozner finally offered a mundane summation of Andropov's biography, but his thoughts were still on Shevchenko, and he was frantic.

Koppel turned next to Colby, for a brief discussion of Andropov's tenure at the KGB. Now Koppel addressed Shevchenko. The defector said that Andropov had dramatically increased the foreign operations of the KGB, as well as its domestic repression.

SHEVCHENKO: The old dissident movements . . . were crushed, not by such a nice way. He [Andropov] actually institutionalized the system of the mental institution.

KOPPEL: All right. Let's hop back to Moscow for a moment and Vladimir Pozner. Have you heard anything so far with which you disagree?

"This, for me," Pozner later recalled, "was my moment of truth. I could either get up and walk away—I don't know how many million Americans watched *Nightline,* but I thought they wouldn't have understood why I did that. So I thought, well, you know, I've just got to go through with this."

POZNER: Well, Ted, I would like you to understand me quite clearly. I'm perfectly willing to speak to you and to Mr. Colby; I am not willing at all to discuss with that gentleman anything. First of all, because I see the man as a traitor to his own country. He's a man who left behind his daughter, incidentally, who went to school with my son. He left behind his wife. He's a man who's being paid to say what he's saying now. I totally don't—I can't even imagine discussing anything—even the weather—with a person like that. I do—

KOPPEL: When you say paid by—

POZNER: —not wish to discuss it.

KOPPEL: Forgive me. Paid by whom?

POZNER: Well, by someone in your country, obviously. And I simply do not want to discuss anything with him. So I'm perfectly willing to talk to you and to Mr. Colby and to any American citizen, but not to the man, to any man,

for that matter, who would betray his country, regardless
of what that country is.

KOPPEL: All right, fine. I can't force you to talk to anyone.

Pozner was able to finish the broadcast without addressing
Shevchenko, but he knew his troubles had only begun. "On the following Monday, I was called into the office of the chairman of Soviet
television, Mr. Sergei Labin. Labin was otherwise known as 'the Croc-
odile.' He was a very, very intelligent, very shrewd, and extremely
cruel man. Very anti-Semitic. And he took pleasure in scaring people."
    Labin was waiting with two deputies when Pozner walked in.
"They all sat there," said Pozner. "And I came in, and I sat down."
Pozner knew the issue was the *Nightline* appearance with Shevchenko.
"Labin looked at me with a look of disgust. He said, 'How could you
speak to this man, the dredges of the human race?'
    "I said, 'I didn't speak to him. I didn't speak to Shevchenko at all.'
And Labin said, 'Well, you didn't speak to him, but you were doing
the same show with him. How could you do this?' " At that point,
Pozner "figured I was going to be fired anyway, so I figured I had
nothing to lose. So I said, 'Well, I did it and I thought it was the right
thing to do.' " Labin "looked at me with great contempt. He said,
'Well, perhaps that's what you think, but we happen to think that it
was the wrong thing to do.' "
    Labin went on. "We also happen to think that you're simply not
capable of doing the kind of job that is necessary, and you shouldn't
be doing it anymore."
    Pozner responded, "Can I then be excused? May I leave?"
    Labin, Pozner recalled, "kind of leaned back in his chair. He
looked at me, and said, 'You don't like being criticized, do you?' "
    Pozner decided to be blunt. "I've worked here for fifteen years
and I've never heard a kind word from any of you. So, on the con-
trary, I'm used to hearing all kinds of unpleasant things."
    Labin was still angry: "You have to understand that in the kind of
job you do, you're not allowed to make mistakes. It's like someone
who dismantles a bomb: you can't make a mistake."
    "I looked at him," Pozner remembered, "and I said, 'You know,
I came to work here as a journalist, not as someone who dismantles

bombs. Second, the person who takes apart a bomb, he knows that if, heaven forbid, it should explode, his friends, the people he's working with, will try to save him. Whereas working here, if you're wounded, your own so-called friends will try to kill you.' " No one said anything.

Finally, one of Labin's deputies, a man who later would become a good friend of Pozner's, "looked up at the ceiling and in a very calm voice said, 'I wonder how they're going to punish Shevchenko for being on the same program as Pozner.' "

"And everyone started laughing, because, of course, it was absurd. Then Labin said to me, 'All right, you can go back to work.' "

Pozner would use that story to explain why he appeared so frequently on *Nightline*: no one else wanted to. "Who the hell wanted to risk it? You were walking a very, very thin line, a very narrow line."

GENNADI GERASIMOV DISCOVERED for himself how thin the line was when he, too, stumbled over it on *Nightline,* and was summoned to appear before the Central Committee of the Communist Party. Next to Pozner, no Soviet "journalist" appeared more frequently on *Nightline* than Gerasimov—although his Russian-accented English couldn't compete with Pozner's American cadence. On the other hand, Gerasimov—who had never lived in America—was far more trusted by his own government. He was, in fact, a confidant and adviser to Yuri Andropov. When he first appeared on *Nightline,* in 1982, he was a prominent columnist for a Soviet newspaper, specializing in issues involving nuclear weapons. Gerasimov was so closely tied to the top echelons of power that he required no permission from anyone before appearing on *Nightline.* Like Pozner, he now claims never to have been given instructions on what to say. The Kremlin apparently trusted him to say the right thing. "I always knew what I could say and couldn't say," he explained years later. "The censorship came from inside me." The problem arose on the one occasion when he told the truth.

In August 1983, when the Soviets shot down KAL 007, a Korean passenger jet that had strayed over Soviet airspace, the Kremlin announced that the plane was shot down because it was a spy plane in Soviet airspace. As soon as he heard of the incident, all Gerasimov could think of was *bardak,* a Russian word meaning "a house not in order." Gerasmiov knew the Soviets were not nearly the efficient, smooth-running superpower that Americans imagined them to be. He suspected—and through his impeccable connections to Andropov, he confirmed—that the shooting of KAL 007 was a screw-up.

One week later, Gerasimov was asked to discuss the incident on *Nightline.* He never referred to *bardak,* but he implied the shooting was a mistake.

GERASIMOV: Well, the plane was shot down because it was in Soviet airspace, and the pilot didn't know that it was a civilian airliner. . . .

KOPPEL: Let me ask the question very bluntly, Mr. Gerasimov. Now that you know that it was indeed a civilian aircraft, now that you know that 269 civilians died, do you think it was appropriate to shoot it down?

GERASIMOV: Of course not. I would say it in this way. That if the Soviet pilot knew for sure it was not a spy plane, it was a civilian plane, he had to try again to land it.

Gerasimov repeatedly used the words *accident* and *unfortunate* and *tragedy.* Then he implied that the blame lay with local military officials, not with Moscow.

KOPPEL: Do you think it is likely that this would have been done by a local commander at the local level, or don't you think this would have been bumped up to a somewhat higher command?

GERASIMOV: I can imagine it was done on a local basis. It was at night. I don't know really. But I think it's quite possible.

For viewers who missed Gerasimov's point, Hedrick Smith, who had covered Russia for years for *The New York Times,* deciphered the message in the next segment of the broadcast.

SMITH: I think they [the Soviets] have a pretty good sense that they've made a mistake. The repeated comments about this "unfortunate" accident and talking about a local commander having made a decision is an effort, I think, on the part of Gerasimov, and through him, the Soviet leadership, to get away from something they wish hadn't happened.

Smith was exactly right and exactly wrong. The shooting was a mistake. Gerasimov knew it. But the Soviets did not want Gerasimov saying so on American television.

The next day, Gerasimov later recalled, "I was summoned to come immediately to the Central Committee of the Communist party of the Soviet Union. And in those days, it was a serious sign that something was really wrong." When he got there, party officials sat him down and pulled out a cable from the Soviet embassy in Washington. "The embassy didn't like my message. The embassy thought I was deviating from the official party line. The official line was that we were not going to allow anybody to sneak into our airspace—it was a tough line."

Someone then produced a transcript of Gerasimov's appearance on *Nightline*. Gerasimov went over what he had said and why he had said it. After a long discussion, and after considering the fact that the complaint about Gerasimov hadn't come from the Kremlin, or even from Dobrynin, but from the number two man in the Washington embassy, the officials decided to drop the matter. "Forget about it," they told Gerasimov. "You can go home. Everything's okay."

The vigilance in Moscow over Pozner's and Gerasimov's appearances mirrored the extraordinary tensions of the Cold War. Every event, every statement had to be calculated for its possible consequences in the game of nuclear chess. On the same *Nightline* broadcast in which he suggested that shooting the Korean plane had been a mistake, Gerasimov warned that overreactions on either side could lead to something deadly:

GERASIMOV: If we are going on a collision course, it increases the danger of a big nuclear confrontation where there will be no winners.

"Nuclear confrontation." This was the sort of hyperbole at which the Soviets were adept. When Koppel had them on the defensive, it wasn't uncommon for them to pull out the nuclear theme and try to hijack the conversation. The tacit message—or threat—was that the Cold War could heat up at any time. But the real goal was to deflect attention away from the issue at hand.

THE QUINTESSENTIAL *Nightline* Cold War interview occurred in the bitter aftermath of KAL 007. American-Soviet relations had plummeted to one of the all-time lows since the 1962 Cuban Missile Crisis. What had been an unpleasant issue for the Soviets was on the verge of becoming an international crisis. Physicist Andrei Sakharov and his wife, Elena Bonner, exiled to Gorky for acts of political dissidence, had disappeared after Sakharov announced he would fast until Bonner was given permission to leave the country for medical treatment. The two had been missing for over a month when international human-rights groups raised the possibility that perhaps the Soviets were drugging the couple. French president François Mitterrand had become involved, and so had officials of the Reagan administration.

When *Nightline* decided to focus on the Sakharov case, all of the usual heavy-hitters for the Soviets were, oddly, "unavailable." The only Soviet who agreed to appear was Alexander Podakin, an attaché to the Soviet embassy in Canada. His coarse attempts to deflect the focus and put the onus on U.S. militarism are classic examples of Soviet propaganda.

PODAKIN: [The Sakharovs] would be used for another anti-Soviet outcry. And this was also concocted just to cover up some of the unseemly deeds on the part of the Western countries that are being done either in the Middle East or in Latin America or right at your door.

KOPPEL: Pretty cunning, wasn't it? I mean, here we cooked up this whole affair just so that there wouldn't be any focus on Latin America and the Middle East. You really think it's worked?

PODAKIN: I think so that it works pretty well, and your program is a good proof to that, that it works well. We'll be talking about thirty minutes about Sakharov, the case that doesn't exist, that doesn't stand between the USSR and the United States. And this would be another drift from the major problems away into some individual matters that are no concern of any foreign country at all. So instead of speaking of the danger that is looming over the United States, their people, and the USSR and our people, we are discussing some of the manmade, artificial subjects like Sakharov.

Lawrence Eagleburger, undersecretary of state, was on the show as well, and took after Podakin, denouncing the treatment of Sakharov and his wife as "a human tragedy."

PODAKIN: Speaking about the human tragedy, I would like to remind one simple fact, that this problem is brought up to cover the simple fact that there is a group of countries in the West that are doing their best to start another huge confrontation between East and West and getting ready for the war. And in this context we may speak of the human tragedy for the whole mankind that the West is preparing for us and trying to cover up with a simple, single individual case like Mr. Sakharov.

KOPPEL: Mr. Podakin, you seem to be a man of subtle intelligence. If that was in fact the Western intention, surely it would be terribly easy for the Soviet Union to undermine that simply by answering the question that so many people in the free world are asking, namely, Where is Andrei Sakharov? What kind of condition is he in?

PODAKIN: The West knows perfectly well where is Mr. Sakharov. And again, if we are going to discuss something, there are major problems. Let us discuss some of the problems that exist right in the United States. There could be discussions of the people who are on mass scale deprived of their rights to work.

KOPPEL: We'll do that—

PODAKIN: There could be discussions of the people who are deprived of their right to have a shelter over their heads and so on and so forth.

KOPPEL: You're quite right, we could do that. And I'll be happy
to appear on Soviet television to do that anytime you invite me to do so. For the moment, however, we're going
to take a break. . . .

PODAKIN: Under [his wife's] guidance and protection, Sakharov
asked the United States to deliver a nuclear blow at the
Soviet Union and pinpointed some of the most vital targets of the Soviet Union, mainly the most populated
cities. . . .

EAGLEBURGER: My blood pressure is rising. I've never heard so much
nonsense in my life. Mr. Sakharov at no point told
the United States what targets should be hit in the Soviet Union, much less encouraged us to attack the Soviet
Union. What we are seeing here again tonight with regard to the way the Soviet spokesman is dealing with this
issue is he's dragging one red herring after another across
the issue, talking about propagandists, talking about
being somebody who's targeting—wants us to target the
Soviet Union. All of this to avoid talking about the most
serious question, which is, here is a man and here is his
wife, two human beings who are being massively mis-
treated by the Soviet Union, and the Soviets are unprepared to say he's healthy and alive—

PODAKIN: But what about those millions in the Soviet Union that
the United States was prepared nineteen times to bomb
nuclear—

EAGLEBURGER: Oh, for heaven's sake.

PODAKIN: —in the postwar history, Mr. Eagleburger?

EAGLEBURGER: This is just such nonsense. I don't know how to deal
with it. You make up these—

PODAKIN: And you know the facts.

EAGLEBURGER: Yeah, I know the facts all right.

PODAKIN: And this is not the way to—

EAGLEBURGER: This is nonsense.

PODAKIN: Okay, sir.

KOPPEL: Where are we then?

EAGLEBURGER: Where we are is nonsense.

What every Soviet spokesman knew and tried to exploit was the fact that Americans in the early 1980s were fairly obsessed with the arms race. Ronald Reagan had followed through on his campaign promise and had initiated one of the largest military buildups since the start of the Cold War. *Nightline* focused on the related stories that flowed out of that buildup: Salt II, "Star Wars," the MX missile, nuclear winter, and the disastrous summit at Reykjavik between Reagan and Gorbachev. Running through all those broadcasts was the unspoken but tangible threat of nuclear annihilation, an undercurrent of gloom and apocalyptic portent.

In early 1982, just as Reagan was about to deploy Pershing and Cruise missiles in West Germany, a book by Jonathan Schell called *The Fate of the Earth* captured the attention of newspaper editorial pages, opinion magazines, and Washington think tanks. It laid out a nightmare, in grim detail, of the consequences of a nuclear exchange. At the same time, a movement to freeze all nuclear weapons production was sweeping America and Europe. That April, *Nightline* held what would become the prototype of a town-meeting broadcast, at Harvard. The focus was the nuclear freeze movement, with a debate featuring former secretary of state Henry Kissinger, former national security adviser McGeorge Bundy, nuclear theorist and futurist Herman Kahn, Monsignor Bruce Kent, leader of Britain's Committee for Nuclear Disarmament, Richard Burt of the State Department, and for the Soviets, Gennadi Gerasimov.

The allusions to catastrophe reflected the increasingly fierce debate—in the United States, in Europe, and in the Soviet Union—over how and when to check the nuclear buildup.

KISSINGER: The dilemma is that if we announce that we will not use nuclear weapons, we are tempting nuclear blackmail.

BUNDY: The crucial point in the current exchange over how you use them is that nobody has a good answer to that. And that question becomes even harder if you ask who's going to use them first, because the more people look at what happens after they get going, the harder it is to give a confident answer to the question, How do you stop?

KAHN: First and foremost, there is no respectable study that indicates that all human life would be destroyed by nuclear war . . . the Russians are terrified of nuclear war; we're terrified of nuclear war; it's not going to be an exuberant experience one bit.

GERASIMOV: We are very much worried about this talk of potential for the first strike, and we see new weapons systems which are being developed on the other side of the ocean, a system which has this potential of first strike against us. We know that we are vulnerable, and we said many times that there can be no winner in a nuclear exchange.

Long after the Harvard symposium, Gerasimov said he had never really believed that the Cold War would result in a nuclear exchange. In 1982, however, he seemed bent on emphasizing that very possibility. Twice during the broadcast, he referred to the Schell book. He called it his "bedtime reading." But his expression of alarm at the ubiquity of civil-defense shelters in America was an absurdity Koppel couldn't resist noting.

GERASIMOV: I remember that when I was in your country I saw here, there, and everywhere black-and-yellow signs of fallout shelters. And I even found in the basement of the house where I lived several defense all-purpose survival crackers. It's very big.

KOPPEL: It's one of our big strategic secrets, Mr. Gerasimov.

GERASIMOV: Actually I keep it as a souvenir. This big can—it's a six-and-three-quarters-pound can. I keep it in my house.

KOPPEL: Don't open them, though. Most of them are spoiled. Mr. Burt?

BURT: Yeah, I would tell him not to eat any of those crackers.

The subject Gerasimov was determined to avoid was Afghanistan. The reason, he recalled years later, was that he was fiercely opposed to the invasion. Among trusted friends, he would quote from Rudyard Kipling, and ask, "If the British failed in Afghanistan, why should we succeed?" Of course, to reveal those sentiments publicly at the time was unthinkable for a career Soviet official. He knew, however, that in a two-hour broadcast Koppel was bound to refer to the matter. When Koppel did, Gerasimov danced away from the subject and back to the issue of arms control: "I just went with the topics I wanted to discuss, but didn't touch the topics on which I couldn't say what I thought."

GERASIMOV: We were the winner in the last war, but there was no boom. It was a period of very hard times. It was a period of recovery. And military aggression was very far from our minds. But the American atomic bomb was very close to our fears.

KOPPEL: I'm sure that Afghanistan is delighted that things are so much better now.

GERASIMOV: You see, you have your own opinion on Afghanistan, but in the context of our discussion the thing that I want to emphasize is that Salt II was torpedoed, and almost buried, before Afghanistan.

The most prescient question of the evening was raised by a member of the audience. The issue was nuclear proliferation. In 1982, the potential threat was Libya.

QUESTIONER: Most of the debate on nuclear weapons recently has centered around the U.S.-Soviet standoff. How much danger do you see in the spread of nuclear weapons to governments with unstable regimes, to governments with unpredictable leaders, for example, Libya's Qaddafi, and to political terrorist organizations?

KISSINGER: I agree with the thrust of the question. I think the proliferation of nuclear weapons into the hands of more and more irresponsible countries is one of the great dangers of our period. It is an issue on which all the existing nuclear powers seem to me to have a common interest to prevent the further proliferation of nuclear weapons.

MSGR. KENT: There's no way you can contain this Pandora's box. If nuclear weapons are good for Britain and good for America and good for Russia, then they're good for anybody who can get a hold of them. And that's the way the world is going, until some voices of sanity are heard—and we haven't heard very many this evening, I'm sorry to say.

No "sane" voice in that broadcast could have predicted that only nine years later, the catalyst for unchecked nuclear proliferation would be the political collapse of the Soviet Union.

ON MONDAY MORNING, August 19, 1991, while Mikhail Gorbachev was vacationing at the Crimean Sea, eight officials, many handpicked for their posts by Gorbachev, announced that he was sick and that they had formed an "emergency committee" to run the country. The committee included the head of the KGB, the minister of defense, and the vice-president of the Soviet Union.

Gorbachev wasn't sick at all. This was an old-fashioned Stalinist coup. The committee of eight wanted to end reform. The next day, Gorbachev was supposed to attend a signing ceremony that would cede enormous amounts of independence to the Soviet republics. So the coup plotters surrounded his house in the Crimea, cut his phone lines, and had Gorbachev and his family placed under house arrest.

Koppel was in Washington when he heard of the coup. His first thought was that it would succeed. "In fact, that first day, when I heard President Bush express his continuing support of Gorbachev and his conviction that Gorbachev would be returned to power, I thought, 'What an incredibly decent and probably stupid thing to do.' I mean, I thought it was a very brave thing to do, but I thought President Bush was whistling in the dark. I thought it was over."

Vladimir Pozner thought so too. He'd been out jogging that Monday morning, near his dacha outside Moscow. Pozner had recently quit his job at Soviet television after getting into trouble for criticizing the government on the air. He'd accepted a job in the United

States hosting a new television show with Phil Donahue. (*Nightline*, he admitted, had made him famous in America.) On this morning in August, he and his wife were in the last stages of preparing their move. So, after an early run, he turned on the television just as a friend of his who anchored the morning news began reading a statement by the "emergency committee" announcing its authority and Gorbachev's "illness." Pozner noticed that his anchor friend looked "green around the gills."

"My wife and I were totally petrified," Pozner later recalled. They jumped into a car and headed for their apartment in Moscow. "We drove along with tanks that were rumbling in," tanks ordered by the coup plotters. As soon as he and his wife arrived home, "the phone just started jumping off the hook. And one of the first calls was from ABC: would I go on *Nightline*?

"Here was my situation," Pozner explained. "I was going to America, I had left Soviet television, I had resigned from Soviet television. I had my visa. I had my passport; so did my wife. My daughter was in Berlin. My son was, at that time, on a trip in the United States. I said to myself, If I go on *Nightline*, first of all I'm going to be arrested—because I had no doubt that they would stay in power, because to me it was clear that with the army, the KGB, the party all behind these people, there was no way they were going to lose. It's going to be the end of everything for us. What are we supposed to do here? Maybe the wise thing to do is just grab our hats and go to the airport—I do have tickets—and try to get on any plane and get the hell out of here.

"I told ABC, 'Look, I don't know what's going on. Let me get my bearings; I will definitely make a statement. But I've got to, you know, get a clear view of this.' And I went out, and I walked around the city, and I walked and I looked, and then I went to see some friends. And I spent about five or six hours doing that. And when I got back, I had made a decision that, yes, I would go on *Nightline*." But Pozner's decision came too late for him to appear that night.

There was a young Soviet who did agree to appear on that show. His name was Andrei Kortunov. He was a Soviet analyst for the Institute for the Study of the USA and Canada.

KORTUNOV: You know, I think that the fact that we still have communication shows that the people who are taking the power in Moscow do not have political will. They

cannot detain Yeltsin, they cannot cut off international
communications, and I think that they are losing momentum, that time is playing against them, and probably
they do not have a political leader who can take responsibility for some radical actions that could antagonize the
population and terrify the people in Moscow.

Koppel thought Kortunov was brave, heroic even, for criticizing
the coup makers when it was still possible that they might succeed.

Later that week, Koppel spotted Pozner in Moscow. By then
Pozner had appeared on the Tuesday edition of *Nightline*. "Had you
appeared on the first show," Koppel chided him, "you would have
been a hero. Instead, you waited until the second night, which means
you are simply a very decent man, which you are." The comment
stung Pozner. He would never forget it.

What Kortunov had counted on when he criticized the coup so
early was the moral and charismatic force of Boris Yeltsin. Yeltsin had
begun a massive counterrevolution from inside the Russian Federation
Building. By Tuesday morning, tens of thousands of Muscovites loyal
to Yeltsin had surrounded the building. Some of the troops sent in by
the coup plotters had switched sides and were now protecting Yeltsin
and his supporters. Later that day Yeltsin mounted one of the tanks,
took a megaphone, and urged the crowd to defy the coup, to demand
the return of Gorbachev, and to call for an end to the dictatorship of
the Communist party. The citizens of Moscow, and television viewers around the world, were enthralled.

Elsewhere in Moscow, "coup flu" seemed to be sweeping through
the high echelons of Soviet power: it was an epidemic of cowardice.
Many Soviet officials who were afraid to either endorse the coup or
to denounce it—uncertain as to whether or not the coup would succeed—simply didn't show up for work, claiming illness. Among those
who called in sick on Tuesday was Foreign Minister Bessmertnykh. By
then, even a couple of the coup plotters seemed to have disappeared,
claiming an attack of the "flu."

On Tuesday Koppel left Washington and flew to Moscow along
with Tom Bettag, *Nightline*'s new executive producer, and several
Nightline colleagues. Koppel wasn't at all certain their plane would be
permitted to land. The fact that it did land on Wednesday afternoon

indicated to Koppel that the "emergency committee" declared by the coup leaders might not have such a firm grip on power. "You know, when things went wrong there, the Soviet Union was the kind of place where everything would just shut down and the radio station would start playing martial music. You wouldn't be allowed in; you wouldn't be allowed out. And so it struck me as more than passing strange, when I got to Moscow, that things seemed as sort of relaxed as they did. There was no great sense of urgency."

It turned out, of course, that at almost the very moment Koppel and crew were landing, the coup plotters, having garnered almost no support from the military and realizing their power grab was a debacle, had flown to the Crimea to try to cut a deal with Gorbachev. He declined, ordered all of the plotters arrested, and returned early Thursday morning to Moscow.

"I was surprised at the ineptitude of the plotters," Koppel later recalled. "And I still don't get it. I still don't understand what happened. I still don't know to what degree Gorbachev may have been either a witting or unwitting dupe of what was going on. It was the most incompetent power grab, I think, that the Soviet Union has ever seen. These guys really had it in their capacity to take over the Kremlin, and certainly to take over the government. And they blinked."

When Gorbachev arrived at the Moscow airport, a number of "loyalists" greeted him on the tarmac. Among them was Foreign Minister Bessmertnykh, fully recovered from his "illness."

IT WAS NOW LESS than thirty-six hours later, and Bessmertnykh was telling Koppel that he had just been fired and wanted to talk about it on American television. He was using *Nightline* no differently than scores of U.S. officials and celebrities in trouble: to put his own spin on his troubles.

For Koppel, Bessmertnykh's motives didn't matter. What mattered was that the foreign minister would possibly shed fascinating light on what in the past the Soviets had shrouded: the mysterious and often sinister struggle for power inside the Kremlin. Koppel knew as well as anyone how unusual was the opportunity. As a former diplomatic correspondent in the mid-1970s, he had endured the drudgery of trying to extract something fresh and compelling out of U.S.-Soviet bilateral negotiations. He would roll his eyes at the memory of Soviet foreign minister Andrei Gromyko's predictable silence. "In those days, we were lucky if Gromyko offered a 'Good morning, boys!' Soviet foreign ministers just didn't give interviews. They sure as hell didn't give interviews thirty minutes after they'd been fired. And here Bessmertnykh was saying, 'Let's do the interview.' " So Koppel hustled his camera crew and producer into Bessmertnykh's office, and the cameras rolled.

KOPPEL: Mr. Foreign Minister, is it still appropriate, in fact, to call you Mr. Foreign Minister?

BESSMERTNYKH: Well, maybe not so. I have just had a telephone conversation with my president and he informed me that he believes I was quite passive during the three last days of the emergency situation. So we discussed my position, and I have resigned. And because this is not true at all, and I was not given any information on which the conclusion is based, unfortunately, it is not the best way to do it, but I would like to tell the story as it was, because you are the first person whom I meet after the telephone conversations besides my deputies and my chiefs of the departments, whom I immediately informed about the telephone conversation with the president.

Koppel asked Bessmertnykh about the difficulty of his predicament.

BESSMERTNYKH: It is a difficult moment, but, you know, you have to consider I am seasoned in difficult situations. A diplomat's life is not an easy one. I am a professional diplomat. I have spent dozens of years in this profession, and I have always served the country and the people, and I always believed that the *perestroika* policy, the policy of new thinking, is my policy, because I was always the part of the team that worked it out.

Just the situation of today, which brings so much confusion, a lot of emotions, misjudgments, probably is the reason for the decision which has been taken by the president. But I understand him. He is in shock. He is now advised by someone around him and he is suspicious. His best friends, Yazov and Kryuchkov, have betrayed him. So I understand the man. I just want to—the world to know and my colleagues in the world to know, I am the man I always was.

And as for the particulars of this tragic three days, I'll be prepared to discuss them with you, so that you should know what terrible life you went through when you were here.

Then Bessmertnykh revealed something far more serious than his own fate. Had the coup succeeded, he told Koppel, the United States would have been facing a much more hostile Soviet superpower. Just after the putsch was under way, the "emergency committee" sent Bessmertnykh a kind of working paper on the United States:

BESSMERTNYKH: It was called something like "Emergency Committee's Statement on President Bush's Declarations." It was terrible, a terrible document. It was the start—if it was sent or published, it would be the start of a new cold war.

KOPPEL: Why? What did it say?

BESSMERTNYKH: Oh, it was an angry paper saying that President Bush is interfering and he is dictating to us and he is not—he does not—he never understood us and he will never understand us, and we don't need this kind of relationship. And that previous relations were not so good because the Soviet part too much submitted itself to American pressures, but no more, just stop it today, that kind of stuff. . . . And I was doing a dangerous thing, but I have written on the paper, "Completely unacceptable."

Twenty minutes into his interview with Bessmertnykh, Koppel's crew told him they needed to pause to change tapes. During the break, Koppel was trying to fill time and asked Bessmertnykh whom he had informed, so far, of his dismissal. Bessmertnykh said the call from Gorbachev had only just happened.

Koppel: "Does Jim Baker know?"

Bessmertnykh: "No. Do you think I should tell him?"

Koppel: "Well, he is, you know, the secretary of state. And I'm sure he'd like to know that you're out of office."

Bessmertnykh: "Maybe I should do that right away."

Koppel decided to lob one, although he was certain the answer would be no: "Do you mind if we film the phone call?"

Bessmertnykh: "No, that's fine."

Again Koppel stifled the urge to shout *"Yessss!"*

So it was that after Bessmertnykh had explained how he had been dumped, and how he had tried to fight off the hardliners and their plans for a new Cold War, *Nightline* viewers were allowed to eavesdrop on a bizarre call to Jim Baker. The secretary of state was on vacation at his ranch in Wyoming, where it was almost five o'clock in the morning.

BESSMERTNYKH: Hello, Jim? Good morning. Is it early morning there? I'm sorry. I hope I haven't wakened you. Jim, it's a very important piece of information for me, but I think it will be also for you. I have just resigned, and I wanted you to be the first among the foreign ministers to know about it. (*pause while listening*) Yeah. I just want you to know, since we don't have probably much time to discuss it, but I would like you to know that I have been, I am, and I will be always the man of *perestroika* and new-thinking policy, and I have been protecting and pursuing it all the time. And it is just because of this commotion and confusion in our capital, in the afterwards of the coup d'état, that things happened that, in my view, should not have happened. But anyway, I was blamed for being passive during the last few days, although out of the three days, two days I was sick.

But anyway, that was the case against me, and it is impossible in this situation to continue the duty, and the president—I had a talk with the president and the president shall probably be declaring that somewhat later.

Baker was about to learn that while he may have been the first foreign minister to hear the news about Bessmertnykh, he was not the
first foreigner. In fact, he was not even the first American.

BESSMERTNYKH: Actually you are the first one to know—brought—
                 brought up to it—and Ted Koppel is somewhere
                 around, and he was the first man to whom I talked about
                 the situation since it happened. I promised him yesterday
                 to meet today.

At this point Koppel knew it would be a brief conversation: "I'm
sure much of the brevity was a consequence of Jim Baker saying,
'Hell, I'm not going to go through a long conversation with him if
Koppel's in the office with him right now.' "

BESSMERTNYKH: (*listens*) Yeah, please do that. Thank you very much.
                 Thank you, Jim, and my best regards to Susan. Thank
                 you. Yes. Thank you. Bye-bye.

Koppel finished the interview with Bessmertnykh and raced the
material to the ABC Moscow bureau—this was news, after all, and
some of it would have to air prior to *Nightline*. Marshall Goldman, an
American expert on Soviet affairs, was at the bureau, where he was
serving as a consultant for the week. He told Koppel he had just heard
that Gorbachev and Yeltsin were on their way to the Parliament.
    Koppel and Goldman ran for the car again, the same car with the
same crazy driver. This time the chauffeur didn't bother with side-
walks; he jumped into the lane reserved strictly for Kremlin brass. Suddenly Koppel realized they were in Gorbachev's motorcade. "We
pulled up in front of the Russian Parliament three or four cars behind
Gorbachev's car. The camera crew and I jumped out of our car, and I
just rushed over to Gorbachev, and he said, 'I can't talk to you right
now.' But he shook hands with me, and the guards at the Parliament
saw that I seemed to be with Gorbachev, so I just kept walking with
him and told the camera crew, 'Just keep on walking.'
    "And Gorbachev walked right into the entrance of the Par-
liament, and there was an elevator waiting with a couple of his
security guards. And we all just squeezed into the same elevator.

Gorbachev didn't say no, and his guards didn't say no, and the guards at the Parliament thought we were with him, so we just went up in the elevator with him." Gorbachev walked into the Parliament, leaving Koppel and his crew in an anteroom. "We were the only reporters there."

Koppel couldn't watch what happened next: as Gorbachev addressed Parliament, Yeltsin approached him on the stage, wagged his finger, and scolded the Soviet president for not realizing that his own cronies had betrayed him. Yeltsin demanded that Gorbachev read a list of names, out loud, of those who had supported the coup. Gorbachev looked stunned, humiliated.

Koppel saw none of it from the anteroom. When Gorbachev and Yeltsin walked out, Koppel remembered, "I went to Gorbachev first. I was still naive enough to believe that Gorbachev was, after all, president of the Soviet Union, and I thought he was still the big guy. So I went to him first." Yeltsin was livid. His fury was captured on videotape, where he can be seen standing in the background, stewing, all but shouting out: *he* was number one now; *he* should be interviewed first. "Certainly, if I had known about his speech," Koppel said, "I probably would have gone to Yeltsin first and gotten him to explain why he was being so disrespectful and harsh to Gorbachev in public. But I didn't. And I don't think Yeltsin has ever forgotten it. I have tried to interview Yeltsin on a number of occasions since then, and it has been made clear in a number of different ways that he really doesn't want to talk to me."

LESS THAN SIX MONTHS after this faux pas, Koppel returned to Moscow to witness the death of the Soviet Union. Yeltsin's counter-revolution was complete. The Soviet empire would formally dissolve during the week of Christmas. The Russian Republic, presided over by Yeltsin, would assume the occupancy of the Kremlin, the Soviet seat at the UN, and most important, Yeltsin would take control of the Soviet nuclear arsenal.

Koppel and Rick Kaplan, former executive producer of *Nightline* and by then in charge of ABC's *PrimeTime Live,* had negotiated an agreement to produce a documentary with Russian television. It would capture the last breath of the Union of Soviet Socialist Republics and Mikhail Gorbachev's final days in the Kremlin. For almost a week in December 1991, Koppel enjoyed unprecedented access to

Gorbachev. On the first day, the cameras captured him reading a Moscow newspaper article that claimed he'd already resigned. He laughed.

GORBACHEV: (*quoting newspaper*) "Gorbachev's resignation decree has been signed . . . and the decree has been signed by Gorbachev himself!"

Clearly visible on Gorbachev's desk was the briefcase holding the launch codes for the Soviet nuclear arsenal.

Several days later, Koppel asked if he could film Gorbachev wandering around outside the Kremlin. Koppel was instructed to meet Gorbachev at a certain spot on the Kremlin grounds on the morning of December 24, Christmas Eve, Gorbachev's final day in power. Koppel and Kaplan arrived at the appointed time and place. All of a sudden, they saw Gorbachev's limousine pull up almost a quarter-mile away. Koppel could see that a cameraman from Russian television was positioned right next to the car, beginning to film. That was fine, since the arrangements were to share material. Then Koppel saw Gorbachev emerge from the car. Koppel still didn't move. He thought he was following instructions. "And as Gorbachev got closer and closer, I saw him looking around and looking a little bit annoyed, and it suddenly occurred to me: Hell, he's looking for me. You know, he's wondering, Where the hell is Koppel? You know, I'm doing this stupid walk-through of the Kremlin, and I'm not doing it for me; I'm doing it for him!"

Koppel grabbed his camera crew and tore across the Kremlin courtyard to catch up with Gorbachev.

KOPPEL: Your thoughts this morning when you left home . . . when you said goodbye to your wife?

GORBACHEV: (*through interpreter*) Well, you know, today is a culmination of sorts. I've said many times I've been feeling over the recent days absolutely calm and free. So today I wouldn't say anything has changed, because everything's been decided already. Everything is clear. . . . And, you know, the psychological stress is hardest until you make the decision. The most important thing is to make the decision.

KOPPEL: You look more relaxed today than you did yesterday.
             Yesterday you looked a little tired. Today you look as
             though you're at peace with yourself.

GORBACHEV: Thank you very much!

Later that afternoon, Koppel and his cameras eavesdropped on another extraordinary phone call. What they captured was the final contact between the leader of the Soviet Union and the President of the
United States.

GORBACHEV: (*through interpreter, on the telephone*) George, my dear
             friend, I greet you. Let me begin by saying something
             pleasant. I would like to say Merry Christmas to you and
             to Barbara and to your entire family. . . . I have here on
             my table the decree of the president of the USSR. In
             connection with my resignation, I also resign the duties
             of the commander-in-chief. And I transfer the authority
             to use nuclear weapons to the president of the Russian
             Federation. Everything remains and will remain under
             very strict control. You can have a very quiet Christmas
             evening.

The interpreter's microphone picked up the voice of President
Bush through the phone line:

PRESIDENT BUSH: I appreciate your comments on the nuclear ques-
                  tion. This is of vital significance, of course. And I com-
                  mend you for the way you've handled that.

A few hours later, Koppel met again with Gorbachev. Now the
nuclear briefcase was gone.

GORBACHEV: The nuclear button is now already with Yeltsin.

Koppel closed the broadcast with a final observation for viewers at
home. This documentary, he noted, had come about as a joint venture with government-run television.

KOPPEL: Soviet television now also passes under Russian control.
             So it is probably quite accurate to say that this program
             may have been one of the final acts of U.S.-Soviet co-
             operation.

The closing shot from Moscow, Christmas night: The Soviet flag
drifting down the Kremlin flagstaff. In its place, moments later, the flag
of the Russian Republic fluttering in the night breeze.

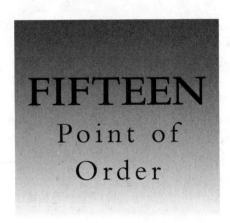

FIFTEEN
Point of
Order

KOPPEL HAD KNOWN this moment was coming. Before
the broadcast, Koos van der Merwe had warned him. Van der
Merwe, one of South Africa's leading arch-conservatives, had
agreed to share the stage of the Johannesburg theater with several of
his political opponents as long as no one onstage was affiliated with the
African National Congress. But should a member of the ANC join in
the debate, even if only by satellite, van der Merwe had warned that
he would walk off.

Koppel, of course, would not have convened the *Town Meeting in
South Africa* without a representative of the ANC. In fact, he had invited two. Seated in the front of the theater was Walter Sisulu, a
founding member of the ANC, recently released from prison after
twenty-six years, and appearing via satellite from Zambia was Thabo
Mbeki, the current ANC foreign minister. After a few minutes of debate between the politicians onstage, Koppel had just put a question to
Mbeki when van der Merwe interrupted.

VAN DER MERWE: Mr. Koppel, a point of order!

KOPPEL: A point of order. Well, it's not a parliamentary debate that
we're engaged in here, Mr. van der Merwe, but go ahead.

VAN DER MERWE: I have indicated to you before the debate started that at a particular moment I will arrive at an insurmountable difficulty.

KOPPEL: Which is?

VAN DER MERWE: Which is that my party is not prepared at this time in history to debate with the African National Congress and the Communist party. As long as they are bent on intensifying the armed struggle to kill and maim people to accomplish their ends, there is no way that we will talk to them.

"This time in history," referred to by van der Merwe, was, in a sense, only three days old. The previous Sunday morning, February 11, 1990, hundreds of thousands of jubilant supporters had gathered at the gates of Nelson Mandela's prison. When Mandela emerged, free for the first time in twenty-seven years, the passionate swarm engulfed him. It was a moment of supreme exultation for many South Africans, for the oppressed black majority in particular. For others, especially whites allied with van der Merwe's Conservative party, Mandela's freedom ignited confusion and prompted fear for their future.

The whole point of scheduling a *Nightline* town meeting immediately after Mandela's release was to showcase the reaction to it; but the concept was inherently risky. The Johannesburg auditorium was the vessel for a combustible stew of emotions. Hundreds of South Africans of every race and political allegiance were crammed inside for the dawn broadcast, which was airing live in the United States. And though a few had arrived rubbing sleep out of their eyes, no one was looking tired now.

KOPPEL: (*to van der Merwe*) I understand that you're leaving, and you have already indicated to me that if we brought Mr. Mbeki on the program that you would, and I told you we would, and so you are of course free to do what you have to do, and I'm free to do what I have to do. But let me just ask you, why is it that you're so worried about talk? What is it—I mean, you seem to be not only a forceful but a very intelligent gentleman who is able to express his opinion forcefully—

VAN DER MERWE: Flattery will bring you nowhere.

KOPPEL: Well, it may bring this part of the conversation to a somewhat more abrupt halt. What I'm asking you is, why are you afraid of discussion? What is it that makes you nervous about it?

VAN DER MERWE: You are implying that I am nervous or afraid. I am not. I am a soldier of the South African Defense Force, amongst others. I've been trained. I fought in the operational area; if it's necessary I'll do it again. I fear nobody, including you. So it's not a matter of fear or that—

(van der Merwe is interrupted by someone shouting in the audience)

Van der Merwe's "I fear nobody, including you"—directed at Koppel—kicked the tension level inside the auditorium up a notch, and might have kicked it up two notches had van der Merwe himself not lost the floor seconds later to the shouts of a young white man in the audience. At Koppel's insistence, the man moved to a microphone in the aisle:

MAN: I'm not particularly interested if the rest of the world hears, sir. I'm only interested—Mr. van der Merwe, I'm chairman of a group called Veterans for Victory, and I also served in the operational area—*(loud booing in audience)* They all know me, sir. This audience is definitely loaded against you, sir. And I commend you, because you're the only person with enough strength of character and enough guts and enough balls to stand up and say what you really think—*(more loud booing)*

Helen Suzman, an anti-apartheid activist on the stage, asked the man where he lived.

MAN: I live just around the corner from you, ma'am.

SUZMAN: Oh, my word. I must move. *(members of audience clap and cheer)*

MAN: Please, please do! Let me tell you something, ma'am—

SUZMAN: You come from Australia?

MAN: I was brought up in Australia, yes.

SUZMAN: That's what I thought. *(members of audience shout at man, "Go home!")*

KOPPEL: Hold on, folks, just a second—if I may—

MAN: Everybody says "Go home," huh? Let me tell you something—*(more of audience yells, "Go back to Australia!")*

The man looked more agitated now. He began to complain that conservatives weren't fairly represented onstage. He had a plea for van der Merwe:

MAN: Mr. van der—don't leave, Mr. van der Merwe, don't leave. Just don't talk to the sons of bitches, but don't leave! Sit there!

KOPPEL: All right. It's all right. You'll be relieved—*(clamoring in audience)*—you'll be relieved to hear that at whatever time it is, 12:20 A.M., in the United States, most of the children are in bed, and even we have heard words like that before.

While van der Merwe took up a debate with Suzman, the man in the audience picked up a briefcase and strode down an aisle toward the stage. Koppel thought the briefcase contained a gun. So did the show's executive producer, Dorrance Smith, who was squeezed in a truck that served as a control room outside the auditorium. So too did Lionel Chapman, the producer seated next to Smith. Chapman's eyes darted from monitor to monitor. On one screen was a close-up of Koppel's face. Koppel looked as if nothing extraordinary were happening. But another screen showed the man nearing the stage, and no one was stopping him. Chapman lunged for the door of the truck, but he knew he'd never get to the stage in time to do any good.

Inside the auditorium, the guards didn't make a move. Correspondent James Walker was standing in the back, wondering what to do. The man with the briefcase brushed past Richard Harris, *Nightline*'s head booker, who was standing in the aisle to coordinate questions from the audience. Harris froze. "I know this sounds illogical," Harris would explain later, "but I didn't want to get in the camera shot. The first rule of a producer, after all, is never get in the shot. So I hesitated, and held my breath. It all seemed to be in slow motion."

It was up to Koppel. The man came right up to the edge of the stage, set his briefcase upon it, and began to open it.

Koppel's expression remained placid, but "I really did think he had a gun in there," he later recalled. "All kinds of things went flashing through my mind: 'Should I dive off the stage and try to knock the briefcase out of his hand? I'm really going to feel stupid if there's nothing but papers in there!' Anyway, I figured that at that point, there wasn't a damn thing I could do about it."

Abruptly, the man yanked a sheaf of papers out of the case and began waving them in the air. Koppel told him to return to a microphone. After thirty seconds of paper-waving, the man walked back up the aisle to his seat.

THE MAN WITH the briefcase has become, in *Nightline* lore, the symbol of the tension and unpredictability that are intrinsic to every *Nightline* town meeting. The format tends to produce moments that risk chaos. Each broadcast has its own tempo and tone, but they all come down, in the end, to a tug-of-war among Koppel, the panelists onstage, and the live audience, for control of the debate.

"I have always felt that whatever control I have over a town meeting is largely smoke and mirrors," Koppel once told a colleague. "It truly is a little bit of the lion tamer with a chair. What is the chair going to do? What are you going to do, beat that lion to death with the chair?"

"Technological problems aren't what you worry about in a town meeting," according to Tom Bettag, *Nightline*'s executive producer since 1991. "Ted can smooth over trouble with a dead microphone or something like that. It's the human component that you never have complete control over. We're always worrying. Do we have the people to make this thing come alive? Or, do we have too many people to make it come too alive, and is this thing going to explode on us?"

One or two such shows have come close.

• • •

NIGHTLINE'S TOWN MEETINGS are not regularly scheduled; instead, they are produced in response to an event or issue that seems to have captivated the nation, if only for the moment. Hence the title that sounds like an oxymoron: *A National Town Meeting*. Among the scores of town meetings was one on the stock market crash of 1987, one on drugs in America in 1988, one on Anita Hill versus Clarence Thomas in 1991, and another on the O.J. Simpson verdict in 1995.

Nightline's first town meeting, like most good ideas, was a hybrid of other ideas that came before it. There was nothing new, for example, about an anchor working with a live audience; Phil Donahue had been doing that long before *Nightline* was born. Even at ABC News, there were a couple of prototypes, dating to the early 1980s. In 1981, George Watson, an ABC News vice-president, launched a program in which Koppel and a panel of media critics and journalists took questions from a live audience. The show, called *Viewpoint,* still appears on occasion in the *Nightline* time slot, but focuses only on media issues. The closest thing to a real town meeting, before the format had a label, was the symposium on a nuclear freeze, staged in a theater at Harvard University in 1982.

Not until 1987 did another issue inspire as much fear and confusion across the nation as the potential for nuclear war. The issue was AIDS. The disease was creating a state of near national panic. It occurred to Rick Kaplan, who was running *Nightline* then, that the country was anxious to talk about AIDS, that people wanted to express their fear, to ask questions, perhaps to voice their rage.

On a Friday night in June 1987 *Nightline's* first town meeting was broadcast from a theater in Los Angeles. To describe it as multidimensional wouldn't convey its reach. It had everything. Among the more than twenty panelists—most of whom sat around an enormous horseshoe-shaped desk—were prominent AIDS doctors, researchers, academics, civil rights activists, a California congressman, the mayor of San Francisco, a Catholic priest, and a prostitute. The panel also featured the playwright Harvey Fierstein to address cultural controversies, the actress Morgan Fairchild to address Hollywood's approach to sex, and even a Bank of America representative to discuss corporate health-care plans. Another panelist was Leonard Matlovich, a gay man who had been kicked out of the Air Force and had since learned that he had AIDS. In the auditorium sat a cross-section of Los Angeles:

students, parents, young professionals, residents from impoverished areas, and people with AIDS. Viewers across the country were given an 800 number on which to call in their questions. The ABC radio network even carried a live "simulcast" of the broadcast, so residents of the West Coast, where the televised program would be delayed, could nonetheless listen and phone in questions.

That wasn't all. Kaplan had commissioned taped stories from local ABC stations across the country, more than twenty altogether, each focusing on a specific aspect of AIDS in those communities. The stories would be interspersed throughout the broadcast. "Our plan," Kaplan recalled later, "was that every time Ted wanted to shift the focus, we would have a taped piece on the subject to get things started, to turn the discussion. But we had had to work carefully with the local stations when they were producing these stories, to make sure that the narration would make sense to radio listeners, who, of course, couldn't see anything. This was a real town meeting, in the sense that stations across the country had contributed stories and we had the capability for viewers to phone in and we had the simulcast on radio in all fifty states. No one had ever before combined so many elements into one broadcast.

"And all the pressure was on Ted, because he was the one who had to conduct a conversation with a panel, an audience, satellite guests, phone-in callers, and radio listeners. It was a tremendous juggling act."

It was a long juggling act: the show lasted more than four hours. The discussion percolated. Koppel introduced a taped story every time an exchange succumbed to predictable polemics, like this one between Congressman William Dannemeyer of California and Harvey Fierstein. Dannemeyer was advocating legislation that would make it a crime for someone with the HIV virus to engage in sexual activity with another person.

DANNEMEYER: We're not going to tolerate them transferring this fatal virus to another human.

FIERSTEIN: That's insanity. That is complete insanity.

DANNEMEYER: Well, let me advise you, sir, that we have had a law in California since 1957 which makes it a misdemeanor for a person with a venereal disease to have sexual relations with another human.

FIERSTEIN: Has it ever been used?

DANNEMEYER: That's not the point, it's the law.

FIERSTEIN: That's what you people do—

DANNEMEYER: We make laws to establish standards—

FIERSTEIN: That's how you make your living—

DANNEMEYER: —that citizens are asked to observe.

FIERSTEIN: That's how you make your living. You pass laws that nobody uses.

The real town meeting began when Koppel turned to phone calls from viewers and radio listeners. Their questions revealed a thirst for basic and potentially life-saving information.

CALLER FROM CALIFORNIA: If you are an IV-drug user and you don't share your needles, are you still a high-risk factor?

CALLER FROM NEW HAMPSHIRE: I'm calling to find out if you can get AIDS from a mosquito bite.

CALLER WHO IDENTIFIED HERSELF AS DENTAL ASSISTANT: I'm really concerned about how concerned we should be [about] wearing gloves and masks.

YOUNG WOMAN: My boyfriend refuses to wear a condom. And I wondered if there's anything that I can do to protect myself.

Graphic moments were inevitable. One caller who asked about cunnilingus and condoms may have hung up even more confused after an exchange among Koppel, Dr. Paul Volberding of San Francisco General Hospital, and Carol Leigh, a prostitute:

VOLBERDING: A condom for oral sex, for cunnilingus, doesn't help.

KOPPEL: No, no, no. I guess I didn't make myself clear. What I'm saying is, if you're going to engage in oral sex and then thereafter have regular sex, it still makes sense to use a condom. Right?

VOLBERDING: Definitely, definitely.

LEIGH: I think it's urgent to recommend a condom for oral sex, especially on the first date with a partner that one doesn't know.

VOLBERDING: I meant cunnilingus, not date.

LEIGH: Oh.

KOPPEL: I must say, first dates have changed a lot.

The ratings would show that even as the program ended, despite the fact that it was almost 4 A.M. in the East, millions were still watching. Kaplan felt triumphant. Koppel felt satisfied: "I thought we'd tried to stuff ten pounds into a nine-pound bag. But it was a glorious piece of live television theater. And it was groundbreaking to spend, in early 1987, nearly four and a half hours of network television time on AIDS. There certainly was no question that the format would work well for us, given the right subject."

NO *NIGHTLINE* TOWN MEETING has ever matched the length of the one on AIDS, but each has had its own defining moment, or, sometimes, a defining feature.

The issue of race, in particular, elicited passions so fierce that they could be difficult to harness inside the framework of a live broadcast. The first town meeting that touched on race issues, broadcast in April 1989, catalyzed so much anger and frustration in the audience that Koppel feared he might lose control of the program. The topic was the link among drugs, crime, and racism in the cities, especially in the District of Columbia. The setting was a church in the heart of one of Washington's African-American neighborhoods. In the nave sat community leaders, residents, ex-cons, and recovering drug addicts from the neighborhood; in front of them, two officials of the Bush administration: Jack Kemp, secretary of housing and urban development, and William Bennett, the director of drug policy. Among the other panelists was Washington mayor Marion Barry.

The hostility between the audience members and the panel mounted with the heat—which itself was mounting considerably, given all the television lights and the overflow audience. Early in the program a local resident ratcheted up the rhetoric by admonishing Bennett that "you're not going to create a fascist America!"

Another member of the audience challenged Bennett to address the economic obstacles faced by African-Americans:

AUDIENCE MEMBER: What are you going to do about racism? . . . What do you and your office plan to do about the racism and how it affects our communities in terms of gentrification, in terms of black African-Americans who can't afford to live in their own communities? Where is the responsibility going to lie?

BENNETT: It is wrong to sell somebody drugs, whether you are white or black. Let's be perfectly clear about—

AUDIENCE MEMBER: That's not the question. I'm talking about racism.

BENNETT: That is part of the issue.

AUDIENCE MEMBER: The question is racism. (*audience cheers, claps*)

BENNETT: Racism is terrible and awful and repugnant wherever we see it and we must do everything we can to get rid of it, [but] the drug problem is an emergency and we've got to get after it.

Bennett was having trouble making himself heard over the clamor in the church. Koppel and his producers could feel that the rage was spreading and worried that the church might not be able to contain it. Richard Berendzen, the president of American University, was sitting in the audience. "I thought *Nightline* had been irresponsible in fomenting all of this emotion under these conditions," he told a producer after the program. "There was so much frustration in the audience. I was certain there was going to be violence before the night was over."

Not even Mayor Barry was able to calm the group. Less than a year later, Barry himself would be arrested for drug possession. But on this night, his drug use was no more than a rumor and Barry was advocating education and treatment for users.

BARRY: Most of the emphasis has been on locking people up. I'm for that too, if you have to—

AUDIENCE MEMBER: No! Hell, no!

BARRY: Wait a minute. Wait a minute.

AUDIENCE MEMBER: Hell, no!

BARRY: I say if you have to. The emphasis ought to be on prevention—(*audience member tries to interrupt*)

KOPPEL: Hold it just a minute, sir. We'll—(*shouting in audience*)

Koppel's favorite tactic, when he senses he is losing control of a town meeting, is to "appeal to the good manners of the audience. To do so is to suggest that everyone there has good manners. It's almost quaint. And it usually works." But on this night, by this point in the program, the people in the church were in no mood for etiquette. Koppel had two more tactics available: shutting down all microphones but his own and cutting to a commercial break. He wielded both by announcing: "Folks, if it's just going to be the people with the loudest lungs, then, you know, I mean, I got the microphone, okay? And you don't. We're going to take a break and we're going to get a little order here."

"I'm the only person who has his own microphone in the hall," Koppel would explain later. "I'm the only person who has the director and the producers and the sound technicians and the cameramen. They are all working with me. They're on my side, by which I mean, if I start to get into trouble I can cut the microphones in the audience, and I can also say, 'We are going to go to a commercial.' Of course, things can still get out of hand during the break. If an audience wants a town meeting to go out of control, it can. I don't have any guards around me. I don't have any people who are going to make someone sit down. We are live. If someone wants to make a fool of himself or herself or if someone wants to make a fool of me, they can do that too."

Sometimes, though, passion serves. It can culminate in one profound moment. That's what eventually happened in the stifling church in Washington. After a man in the audience had suggested that the U.S. government was using drugs to commit genocide against African-Americans, a woman who identified herself as Mrs. Patricia Godley stood and spoke, her voice rising.

GODLEY: I'm a mother, you understand. I heard a lot of things in here said. My son passed two weeks ago when he got killed, but that's okay. That's not even—that's not even the issue, that he's dead. The issue is that I have another one. And if other people have sons, you understand what I'm saying? I heard the man say on the television, this is addressed to you, sir, that parents need to get more involved. Okay. I'm a recovering addict. I'm a recovering convict. I've never been a parent, you understand? Society says that I have to be responsible. I'm trying to be responsible. I'm trying to be a productive member of society. I came from nothing because I thought nothing of myself. Today I see myself as someone, something!

Now Godley glared at the panel. She leaned forward. Her voice jumped higher. Most of the hecklers fell silent and still.

GODLEY: I lost my child but I have not had a drink or a drug behind his death, because that's not going to bring him back to me. What I do know is that I have another child that I know that needs me desperately. You all take us to jail, you all think I'm going steer straight. Bullshit! Pardon my expression. We learn how to survive in the penal system. That's no problem. All we have to do is overlook somebody telling us when to get up, and go to bed.

           You sent my son to Oak Hill, to teach him a lesson. Judge, that city was a menace to society. No one took the time once to work with him to evaluate him, to see what the penal system could do to help him to be more productive. My son was handicapped. He could not read or write. And it was not his fault. I'm the addict, not him. I brought him into this world, suffering. I did not know any better at the time, but that does not fix the wrong that I did. I can't give it back, I can't take it back. But I'm trying today. What can you do to help me to be something I've never been, a parent? I'm trying to assist my child. Can you do that? . . .

I'm working hard. I pay my bills, goddammit, I ain't on welfare. You understand what I'm saying? I'm a working taxpayer today. I'm off parole. I walked it down, because I wanted to. You can open up all the jails in the world that you choose to, but if you don't get to the core of the human being that you are incarcerating, nothing is ever going to change. Nothing. Make me know that I'm worth fighting for, instead of closing the door in my damn face. It took a judge, one judge, A. Franklin Burgess, Jr., to see something in me that I didn't see in myself. When you shooting drugs you can't see nothing. You don't care about nothing. How could I care about me?

You got a lot of addicts out there that are suffering. I am recovering today, but you have a lot of them out there, man, that are suffering still, that don't see no hope, that don't see no way out. Do you know that jail is a relief? They glad when you lock them up! They get three meals, hot, and a cot, and clothes to wear, get to take a shower. They get more than they get on the street. They need some help. We're learning that their life is worth something more than a piece of rock in a pipe, a piece of junk in a pipe, you understand? I got a fourteen-year-old baby that I want to see live to see— (*man tries to interrupt*)

KOPPEL: Oh, sit down, sir, will you?

GODLEY: But I'm powerless over that part. . . . I can't put enough locks on my goddamn door to keep him in. If I'm going to work, if I'm going to take care, where do you go when you got people—you got young boys twenty-one years old out here with apartments of their own, seventeen, pay their own rent. Ain't no mother in there. They tell them, "Well, look, if you see my son, please send him home." Ain't nobody in there but kids. Kids dictating to kids. . . . Some of you all need to come down off them high horses you're up on and deal with it.

Because you're watched on TV, you got a lot of clout, Mr. Koppel, you got a lot of clout. You understand? You had an education and everything. Granted, I ain't mad 'cause you had it. I have no animosity in my heart, because you had the potential to excel. I don't have that. I want the chance to excel. Make me feel like I can do it. That's what our children are asking for. The punk rock, the rapping, all that, that's not what I'm talking about. I'm talking about trying to give a child, the child, while they're young, man. You can take them off them porch out there and teach them that they have the potential to excel because somebody cares. Not just mouth service. The mouth will say anything but actions don't lie. Thank you.

KOPPEL: There's one thing I've learned in twenty-six years in this business and that is, every once in a while, someone comes up and says it like it is. And there's not much point in trying to say any more. That lady wrapped it up for us.

"When somebody like that woman gets up and unleashes her experience, her anger, her fears, and her hopes, and does it with such conviction, unrehearsed, it's electrifying," recalled Koppel. "A moment like that, something truly unplanned, is rare. The spontaneity itself is so unusual for television that the viewers at home can feel it, and so do the members of the live audience. Many town meetings will fall into lulls, or the discussion won't be moving forward, then, all of a sudden, one person can change everything."

Since the night Mrs. Godley silenced the church and closed the show, it has become an axiom of *Nightline* town meetings that spontaneous, resonating exchanges take time to develop. They rarely occur in the first half-hour. They surface after the people in the audience have had time to adjust to the lights and cameras, to the opinions and expertise presented by the panelists, and to Koppel as ringmaster. After that, inhibitions fall away. The later the hour, the more likely that what has seethed will erupt.

Once, though, an audience seethed and erupted before cameras were even pointed its way. What resulted was the only spontaneous town meeting in *Nightline* history. It was also the purest town meeting, in a sense, because the audience members were the ones who called for it. They demanded it.

It happened on the first day of May 1992. Less than forty-eight hours earlier, the aquittal of four policemen for the beating of a black motorist named Rodney King had ignited riots across South Central Los Angeles. Tom Bettag had arranged for Koppel to anchor *Nightline* from the basement of South Central's AME Methodist Church, where he would interview a panel of people involved with the local community.

An hour before the program, more than a hundred local residents walked into the church and asked where they were supposed to sit for the *Nightline* show. According to Koppel, "We had told the minister of the church that if he wanted to invite a few people to come and watch, he was certainly free to do that. Instead, he'd invited about one hundred fifty people and had told them it was going to be a town meeting. We had no idea."

Bettag decided to set up a section of seats so that the 150 could remain and observe the panel discussion. The panelists took their seats. They included the Reverend Cecil Murray, the pastor of the church; Maxine Waters, the congresswoman for the district; John Mack, the president of the Los Angeles Urban League; and Jim Galipeau, a probation officer. Two gang members had been invited on the panel as well, but a representative of the church forbade them to come in. He told a *Nightline* producer that he was acting on the orders of the Reverend Murray. So, shortly before the program, Koppel walked across the street with a camera and taped an interview with the two young men. The tape ran at the beginning of the program.

The Reverend Murray was furious. When Koppel turned to the panel, Murray protested that the facts were being distorted and that he had never restricted the gang members from the church. Many of the residents seated in the audience nodded as the Reverend Murray complained, for the better part of ten minutes, about misrepresentation. He was implying that Koppel and his staff weren't to be trusted.

MURRAY: It's a calumny against the black church for that [tape] to
            be shown to America—

KOPPEL: Reverend—Reverend—

MURRAY: —and to say we discriminate against our brother.

KOPPEL: Figuratively speaking, Reverend, and only figuratively
            speaking, I have broad shoulders. If you need to use me
            that way, you go ahead and use me that way.

Those in the audience who believed Murray lost faith in Koppel long before the program was over. The rest lost faith when Koppel concluded the discussion with the panel, looked into the camera, and said, "Good night." For an instant, the men and women in the seats looked shocked. Then they began to shout and jeer. "What about *us?*" "What happened to the town meeting?" "What's going on?"

"They were outraged," Koppel later remembered, "because they had been invited to participate in a town meeting, and they felt they were being cheated out of the experience." Several of them stood up and moved toward Koppel and the panelists. Murray, Waters, Mack, and Galipeau asked them to calm down.

Bettag, who'd been outside the church in a truck serving as a control room, walked into the room and saw a crowd circling around Koppel. "Everybody was yelling at everybody," Bettag remembered. "A lot of them were screaming at Ted. So I tried to yell at the crowd that I was the one responsible for this and that if they had a problem, it shouldn't be Ted taking the heat. It should be me. And, boy, they took me up on that one."

A group surrounded Bettag and continued to demand a town meeting. Bettag looked at Koppel.

"All right," Koppel announced. "All right. Fine. You want a town meeting, let's do a town meeting. Right now."

Roger Goodman, the show's director, had also ventured from the control truck into the chaos. Goodman had been the one who, in 1985, had managed to turn archaic television facilities in South Africa into a production base for *Nightline*'s historic broadcasts there. In

Jerusalem in 1988, it was Goodman who had supervised the building of the "wall" down the middle of the stage—less than twenty-four hours before airtime. Goodman knew what to do now. While the crowd backed away from Koppel and Bettag and took their seats, he quickly instructed his crew to put up a few more lights in the room. He told the cameramen to put the cameras on their shoulders, to move freely around the room and record what they could.

By now, *Nightline* was off the air on the East Coast. It didn't matter. "The crowd was so angry and upset, that we were doing this, as much as anything else, just to sort of calm them down," said Koppel. "At that moment, it did not even occur to me that this would ever end up on the air."

The camera crews started recording nonetheless, and John Mack launched the meeting with a plea.

MACK: We have a city that's burning to hell, we have a city that's going to hell because a whole lot of things have not been done, ought to be done. Let's please, please, for once in our lives, act with some intelligence and let's ask some questions and have a discussion that's going to get us somewhere, and not just—other than just a feel-good session, so we can come in and talk about how we jammed Ted Koppel, or some other kind of B.S. like that.

AUDIENCE MEMBER: *(to Koppel)* If there's some way you can get some communication over to Mr. Bush, as long as he is in office, that these militia dollars that he's spending to send out the militia and create violence and more tension that he calls it's going to be peace and to do whatever he can at all cost for peace.

WATERS: Everybody gets concerned when we don't, you know, take the opportunity to talk about how we can use power. Ted Koppel has a TV show, and of course, emerges as one of the most significant journalists with power in the country, but he really don't have any more power than we got, and let me tell you that. Until you understand it, you'll be constantly asking Ted Koppel to get a message to Bush that *you* should be sending him.

(*shouting from members of audience*) Just a minute, wait just a minute. Just a minute— It is wonderful if Ted Koppel can come and cover and get and do that, but Ted Koppel is not going to change George Bush's mind . . . I'm a very powerful person. I believe that each of you are very powerful people, I believe collectively we can be magnificently powerful. But don't ever let me hear you believe that any one white man in America is more powerful than you are, okay?

MACK: We've got to do some stuff for ourselves, and also bring our collective power to bear and deal, not with Ted Koppel, but deal with our elected officials here, our mayor, our city council, our police department and all the other folk, our governor, all the other folk who can do something about changing the stuff that's got to be changed in Los Angeles.

AUDIENCE MEMBER: Well, I know that Ted Koppel is—who he is, and I know that Ted Koppel is only—represents the mentality of white racism in America. I heard him refer to all of the giants in our community as "you people" several times. What does "you people" mean and "you folks" mean? When are we going to have the opportunity to be mad because we deserve to be?

KOPPEL: All right—

Koppel understood why he was the prime target. "There was only one other Caucasian on the panel. So, by the process of elimination, all of the audience's anger against the white establishment was directed against me. I never felt it was a personal assault on me, and I didn't feel in any way threatened by it, but it was sort of left to me to deal with all the accusations against white society and the white establishment."

WOMAN: What do we have to wait for? We are upset, we are mad, because we have seen our black men killed, we have seen our black men castrated, our children murdered and shot in the head. When do we have the right to be mad? When do "you people" have a right—

KOPPEL: You have the right—

WOMAN: —to be mad and vent anger?

KOPPEL: Ma'am, you have the right to be mad, you have the right to be angry, but let me—

WOMAN: Well, why do you come and ask us "Why is this going on?"

KOPPEL: Let me, with all respect—

WOMAN: . . . "What is this all about?" (*shouts and cheers from audience*)

KOPPEL: Do you want an answer? Would you like an answer? May I give you an answer?

WOMAN: If you could.

KOPPEL: I can understand if you think that every single white man, woman, and child in this country has a tinge of racism in them, but you've also got to believe that there are other gradations. Some of us are worse than others, some of us are better than others, and if we're ever going to have a dialogue with one another, if we're ever going to reach our hands out to one another, you can't lump us all together any more than we can lump you all together.

"It could have just as easily turned to physical violence," recalled Koppel. "We could have just as easily had people throwing things at me or at the panel. There was that feeling throughout that it could turn that way. Ironically, precisely because none of it was planned, it had the feeling of being the most genuine town meeting that we've ever done, and one of the most interesting."

MAN: Let's don't turn Ted Koppel into the man in the truck and beat him down. Let's be one of those four men that took up that man and saw indecency, and let's show America we are the moral fiber of this country.

YOUNG MAN: You ask why this is happening? 'Cause

My Country 'Tis of Thee
is a racist land of liberty,
land where my father died
'cause he was chained and he was tied
from every mountainside
and justice rings.
No justice, no peace.
First there was quiet,
then there was a riot.

These were the residents of South Central who didn't want to riot but who desperately needed to be heard. Koppel and the panel listened, and responded, for more than ninety minutes. The camera crews roamed the room without the advantages of tripods and preset positions. What they captured was gritty, occasionally shaky, and exceptionally intimate. Koppel and Bettag screened the footage the next day, and they found it compelling—as if the viewer were spying on this convocation born of anger. The best of it aired on the following Monday night's broadcast.

IF SOUTH CENTRAL had a polar opposite, it may have been, once upon a time, the tiny, quiet, all-white farming community of Decker, Michigan. Then, in late April 1995, the deadliest act of domestic terrorism in American history raised the question of whether a soporific backwater like Decker could be a breeding ground for murderous rage.

Just days after the bombing of the Alfred P. Murrah Federal Building in Oklahoma City, James and Terry Nichols, two brothers with a farm a few miles outside Decker, were arrested as material witnesses to the bombing. Their friend Tim McVeigh, at that point the only person formally charged with the bombing, had also listed the Nichols farm as his place of residence.

The night of the Nicholses' arrest, *Nightline* reported that the two brothers had sought membership in the right-wing Michigan Militia but had been rejected for their "extremist" anti-government views. A man from Decker who appeared on the program told Koppel that the brothers, along with McVeigh, had practiced making small bombs on their farm.

In that same broadcast, Koppel interviewed another Decker native, Phil Marawski, who said, "I've probably met a hundred people who felt—who had the same ideas, who would do the same thing, but you know, it's still—they can talk about it and talk about it and talk about it, but you don't really believe it's going to happen, until something like this happens." Marawski pointed to the 1993 federal assault on David Koresh and his sect, the Branch Davidians, at Waco, Texas. "If you go across the country, you'll find there's numerous groups that the common beef is Waco. . . . There's a feeling out there that when the government came down so very hard on David Koresh, that that was a battle cry, that was the war cry. And these people actually justify themselves that this is an act of war. Now, that's how they think. I'm not saying it's right, but that's how they think."

Koppel walked off the *Nightline* set that evening wondering how prevalent were these groups—and this attitude—as conveyed by Marawski. He cautioned a colleague who guessed that this sort of fierce mistrust of Washington was probably rare: "I think it's dangerous to dismiss out of hand everyone who has any sympathy whatsoever with an event like this as kooks. I'm not talking about the people who would blow up a building. I'm talking about people who will look at the bombing and say, 'I abhor the act, but I understand the anger and frustration that may have prompted it.' Those people should not be dismissed as easily. If there is this much anger, if there is this much resentment against the federal government in the country, then it behooves us to find out why, and what it is that people are so upset about."

On the Sunday after the bombing, Koppel was watching *This Week with David Brinkley*. One of the guests was a member of the Michigan Militia. The Brinkley panelists pressed the Militia leader for answers as to when and for what reason his group might take up arms and against whom. But the harder they pressed, it seemed, the more defensive the man became, and the less forthcoming. Koppel wondered if the people of Decker and the neighboring communities might not be more candid. After all, in the course of a single weekend, the arrest of the Nicholses had turned Decker into one of the most notorious towns in America. How did that feel to the residents? What if *Nightline* could summon them all together and ask? "I thought it probably made sense to go to Decker and to simply listen to them. A town meeting—a *real* town meeting—no panels, no experts, no phone-in questions, where the only participants would be people who lived in the region, expressing their points of view. I'd just try to listen, as much as possible."

That Sunday afternoon Koppel called Bettag at home. "What would you think of a town meeting in Decker?"

"Great. Let's do it." Bettag answered. The two of them immediately agreed that from what they'd read about the town, it was relatively isolated. They would need time—several days at least—to move in all the equipment necessary to produce a live town meeting. They thought that the soonest they could possibly air from Decker would be the following Friday.

The next day, however, Bettag phoned Koppel. "I've got good news and bad news," he said. "The good news is that management in New York loves the idea of a town meeting in Decker. The bad news is they want us to do it tomorrow night."

Within twenty-four hours, a convoy of trucks and vans, along with a horde of crews, producers, bookers, and reporters, invaded tiny Decker. Technicians streamed in and out of the little white clapboard United Methodist Church, trailing snakes of black cable behind them. The pastors of the church, the Reverends James and Jean Rencontre, had offered the building to *Nightline*. The Reverend James Rencontre knew how traumatized local residents had been by the national attention, and by the association of their town with the bombing in Oklahoma. He thought it important to give the people a forum from which to address the nation, and to address one another. "I'd been a counselor for many years," he said later, "and I knew this could serve like group therapy for the people of the area. It would be a chance to express their feelings." The Rencontres had also, at *Nightline*'s behest, spread word of the town meeting across the county. Bettag had told the Rencontres that once all the people of Decker who wanted to attend were seated, the residents from other towns would be invited to fill up whatever space was left.

But Tuesday afternoon, as the armada of vehicles, equipment, and personnel engulfed the church, a woman who lived across the street gazed out her window and panicked. It wasn't the commotion but what stood in the middle of it all: a Ryder truck. It had been rented by one of the ABC technicians to transport equipment, but it looked no different than the Ryder vehicle that had blown up the Federal Building in Oklahoma City.

The woman found Bettag. The truck had so unnerved her, she said, that she had sent her children out of town for the day. Bettag understood; he too had cringed at the sight of the truck. Now, though, there wasn't much he could do but assure the woman that *Nightline*'s monstrous convoy would be gone within twenty-four hours.

Director Roger Goodman, meanwhile, had discovered that the church was so small there wouldn't be room for most of the cameras. He realized he'd have to station a number of the cameras outside the building and point them through the windows.

The town wasn't much bigger. Decker's power supply was so ill-equipped for this technological avalanche that late in the afternoon, the town suffered a blackout. Bettag would later wince at the recollection. "We didn't just blow the power for the church. We blew Decker's only transformer, and therefore the power for all of Decker."

Leon Gittens, *Nightline*'s business manager, got on a phone and learned that the power company didn't have a truck within forty miles of Decker. So ABC personnel rigged up power for the church off a generator located in one of the trucks. Eventually, just before dark, the power company arrived and bestowed a brand-new transformer on the town.

By then, news of the town meeting had spread by radio, by television, and by word of mouth across the region. At a quarter past ten, more than a hundred people who had lined up outside were brought into the nave. Only a handful were from the actual town of Decker, whose population numbered less than forty. The bookers had found that of the small pool of townspeople, a number were elderly; others had early-morning farm work and didn't want to be out of their homes at such a late hour. Several simply didn't want to be associated with the events in Oklahoma in any way. Some were afraid of trouble.

So were many of those who filed into the church. The cause of their alarm was a small group of men sitting in two pews toward the back. The men were dressed in fatigues—the uniforms of the Michigan Militia. Koppel and Bettag had invited Norman Olson, the commander of the Militia, even though he lived in another part of the state. "We wanted Olson in the meeting," Bettag explained later, "because the Militia was already being characterized in so many different ways that it seemed to us the commander would be able to say what was true and what wasn't true. And the reports were that a few members of the Militia lived not all that far from town. More important, the Militia had been, by now, linked to Decker in the national media. Many of the townspeople weren't happy about it, so we told the people who were angry about Olson and his men being invited that they could say so. This was their chance to express their opinions of the Militia on national television. One of the main reasons we were here, after all, was to get the average citizens of this area to react to how people like Olson were portraying their part of America."

A number of audience members were more than angry about the Militia's presence—they were afraid. Several approached Bettag and warned of rumors that violence might erupt. Trouble of that sort was perhaps the only possibility that Bettag was not worried about. "The truth was that the Michigan Militia was going to be on its best behavior, and we knew it. They were not going to do anything that could be vaguely construed as violent because, in the wake of the terrorism in Oklahoma City, everybody was scared to death of violence. The atmosphere was tense, of course, because everyone was so afraid. But in my gut, I didn't think it was an explosive situation."

The stress showed on the faces of the grandmothers, grandfathers, men, women, and a few teenagers who packed the church. The Militia members looked grim, too, especially Olson. He scowled. He had been reluctant to appear. He had told producer Richard Harris that he feared being made a scapegoat.

Koppel pulled Olson and his men to a downstairs room. "Look, I don't want you to misunderstand," Koppel told them. "This is a town meeting with the people of Decker and their neighbors. I think what you folks have to say is important and needs to be heard, but if any one of you starts giving a speech I'm going cut you off, and I'm not going to let you speak to the detriment of the townspeople who want to be heard. You will be heard, but understand, you're going to get your fair share of time and no more than that."

Koppel also met with James Rencontre and told the pastor that if he was uncomfortable with where the conversation was headed, if he felt, for example, that the people of the community weren't getting a fair representation, then he should stand up, interrupt Koppel, and say so.

A few minutes before airtime, Koppel stood before the people gathered in the church and thanked them for coming. "We are not here to put your views up to ridicule," he told them, "but to let you speak for yourselves. But I must warn you, these programs go by very quickly. If you have something to say, let me know. If you hold back and wait, the time will be gone. You will be surprised, even with ninety minutes, at how few of you actually get a chance to speak." Then he tried to break the tension. He looked at his watch and said, "So who's gonna milk the cows tomorrow morning?" There was soft laughter, then silence again.

The program began with a story about the area by Dave Marash, a correspondent for *Nightline*. Marash had interviewed several people who posed the possibility that it was the federal government that had blown up its own building in Oklahoma City. Others didn't agree, but were still enraged by the government's actions at Waco. An expert on extremists told Marash that a "populist revolt from the right" was under way in the country and that it involved many more Americans than the Michigan Militia or its local sympathizers.

After the Marash piece, Koppel began the conversation by asking who among those gathered in the church believed that the federal government might have been involved in the Oklahoma bombing. About fifteen out of the one hundred seated in the nave raised their hands, including an older woman who spoke in soft, measured tones.

KOPPEL: It's a dreadful, dreadful thing to think about our government, isn't it?

WOMAN: True.

KOPPEL: Why do you believe it?

WOMAN: Look at Waco. Look at what they did to that man [supremacist Randall Weaver] up in the hills. How can you shoot a woman and child? [referring to the FBI's killing of Weaver's wife and son] . . . What's going on in our country? Why? . . . They're trying to cover things up, it looks like to me.

Another woman, Nancy Adams, said she was "upset" with media coverage of the Nichols brothers.

KOPPEL: These are your neighbors.

ADAMS: Yes.

KOPPEL: You cannot believe that they would have had anything
              to do with that.

ADAMS: No, I can't.

Koppel was just starting to wonder if anyone among the eighty-five who had not raised their hands at his first question would openly disavow the anti-government movement, when Kim Reed, the local assemblyman, asked to speak.

REED: The one thing I don't understand is why some of these
              faction groups feel so threatened by their govern-
              ment. . . . The last election, if it didn't teach us anything
              else, it should have taught us that people in this country
              still have the ability, through the ballot box, to com-
              pletely change the direction that their government
              goes. . . . I just hope we're not headed into a time where
              instead of making change with ballots, that we make it
              with bombs.

Koppel thought Reed showed guts. "He surprised me. Here was the guy, after all, who could be elected out of office by these people. So what he was saying struck me as quite brave."

The owner of the local radio station echoed the sentiments of Reed, and so did the retired publisher of a local newspaper. But Olson's chief of staff stood to complain about the media coverage of the Militia, and a friend of James Nichols stood and suggested that the FBI had unlawfully taken over the work of the sheriff. Koppel called on the sheriff for a response.

SHERIFF: I don't believe I was personally mishandled with the au-
              thorities. What we have to understand here, that this case
              has been assigned by the President of the United States
              to be investigated by the FBI. It's their case.

Koppel then turned to Olson, since Olson advocated the aboli-tion of all enforcement officers except sheriffs. More than half an hour had passed with Olson sitting glum and silent. But now he stood and unfolded a piece of paper. His hands seemed unsteady. His voice trembled slightly.

OLSON: This is a letter I received—a letter I received today. It has only two lines to it. It comes from Tulsa, Oklahoma: "We are coming for you. Pray for your soul." Thank you, media.

KOPPEL: Mr. Olson, let me just interrupt you for one brief moment, and we will—we are going to have to go to a commercial in a second, we'll come back and you can speak again—I can show you a dozen letters like that that I receive every week of my life. You know, there are a lot of fruitcakes out there. I'm sorry that you receive letters like that, but believe me, I routinely package them and send them off to the FBI.

Several members of the audience chuckled. Olson looked furious. The next day, Koppel was wishing he hadn't said what he'd said—not because he had embarrassed Olson, but because he'd missed a crucial point. Koppel explained his mistake to a colleague. "The morning after the show, as I thought back on how upset Olson was, his voice trembling and all, I remembered that he'd given me a long lecture on *Nightline* the previous Friday about how the only legitimate law enforcement official was the sheriff, because the sheriff was elected by the people. So what I should have said when he pulled out that letter was, 'Not much point in showing that letter to your local sheriff, is there? Go to the sheriff in Oklahoma City and *he's* not gonna do much for you.' One of the reasons that you need a *Federal* Bureau of Investigation, after all, is that sometimes a crime is committed or threatened across state lines—and local law enforcement just can't handle it. It struck me as this ultimate irony that here is a man who, first of all, is creating this group around him that's supposed to be ready to stand in armed resistance against the government of the Unites States, should the government stand against him, who is afraid because he gets a message from some kook in Oklahoma. Second, I was struck by the irony of a guy who would abolish any federal law enforcement agency but who ultimately could only be protected in this instance by the federal agency."

As the town meeting moved toward a conclusion, Koppel asked Olson what he was afraid of.

OLSON: I am afraid of our constitutional republic . . . of slipping into a totalitarianism where the government controls the people. We've enjoyed two hundred twenty years of a people controlling the government, and things are changing, and I think we sense it. I sense it. I sense it very deeply.

Now all the members of the audience who had objected to the very presence of the Militia realized that time was running out. Emotions that had simmered for almost ninety minutes found a voice—two voices, actually.

MARTY HEMKE: I've been here for over twenty years, and I appreciate what the media is doing, but . . . I'm afraid, more afraid of them guys (*points to Militia members*) than I am the media or the government. I mean—I feel like I'm at war every time hunting season comes around. But it just seems that I don't want—I'm shocked at how many of my neighbors are really feeling so anti-government and so just—they seem so cold about everything that took place in Oklahoma City, and it just affected me so deeply, and to think that this evil is like permeating my atmosphere scares me, and I am glad the media is letting me know about those guys, 'cause I'm keeping my eye on them.

For the better part of an hour, Ruth Shaw had been raising her hand for a chance to speak. Shaw, the wife of a farmer, was worried that viewers would think the Michigan Militia was a part of life in Decker and that those who didn't belong to it were afraid of it. "I was worried that the real Decker had gotten lost," she explained later, "and I knew that I had to speak up quickly, because the show was about to end."

RUTH SHAW: I'm Ruth Shaw, and my husband and his family farm
in the area. And first of all I'd like to say to the Oklahoma
City people that we're very sorry for what has happened.
And I'd also like to say that we're not a bunch of Militia
people up here. In fact, I didn't even know the Militia
existed until I heard it on the newscasts. And I just
wanted to say to the country that we're just normal
people up here, and we're just like everybody else, just
normal people . . . I just feel like I'm almost ashamed to
say that I'm from Decker.

Koppel announced that less than a minute remained, which
may have emboldened Marty Hemke. She lit into a man named
Doug Hall, who had identified himself as a chaplain in the Militia.
Hall had said the fact that the Militia frightened people "troubles
my heart."

HEMKE: When people are living in my backyard and making
bombs and are paramilitary, that's frightening.

HALL: Wait a minute.

HEMKE: I don't want a war in my backyard. I don't want you
guys training in my backyard, making bombs—

HALL: The problem is, I don't want—

HEMKE: There's ways to change things without guns. I've seen
what guns do. I've seen firsthand.

That exchange closed the broadcast. Ruth Shaw walked out of the
church and wondered if Americans would think that half the citizens
of Decker toted guns and that the other half cowered in fear of the
gun-toters. The Reverend James Rencontre was sorry that not more
of the citizens of Decker proper had chosen to attend, and sorry that
of those who did, not many spoke, but he felt relieved, and surprised,
that the meeting had stayed calm. "I have watched the Michigan Militia on a lot of other shows, and they can get out of hand, very quickly.
That's as mellow as I've ever seen something involving members of
the Militia."

"I wanted to keep it calmer than most town meetings," Koppel would say later. "It would have been awfully easy to stir everyone up, but I'd promised the people in the church that this wasn't going to be a circus. There'd been enough hyperbole about Decker, Michigan, in the press."

A few days later, Norman Olson was removed from his command of the Michigan Militia. The direct cause of Olson's demotion was a comment he had made to the press about the Japanese being involved in the Oklahoma City bombing. But his appearance in the town meeting—the fierce scowl, the trembling voice as he read the threatening letter—probably contributed to an erosion of confidence in the ranks.

Meanwhile, the Rencontres began receiving a number of letters from viewers across the country. A woman from Texas said she could empathize with the people of Decker because of the problems Texans still had in disassociating themselves from the Kennedy assassination. A Michigan woman wrote, "You did our [state] a great favor. We must mourn deeply, but we must also heal."

Koppel thought that the concerns of the Michigan residents and of the people of Decker in particular were understandable, "but it wasn't our job to go in there and say what a nice place Decker is. We are not in the public relations business. No matter where we hold a town meeting, no matter what the subject is, it is not our job to portray the residents, or the audience, or the issue in any particular light. It is not our job to flatter. It is our job to go in and listen. Period."

SIXTEEN
The Candidate

THE CANDIDATE WAS TICKED. The polls said he would win, the plane was on schedule, the staff was managing not to screw up, but the man was steamed. Yes, the hour was late and the cabin air nothing if not stultifying, but that was usually the way it was on the road. The problem was that on the night before Election Day 1992, Bill Clinton was losing—at hearts.

He began to swear.

And *Nightline* had him miked.

Each time Clinton tossed down a card, he'd hiss and grumble, seethe for a second or two, then spew an indelicate curse. All the while on a monitor overhead, a tape of Dana Carvey as George Bush provided a background whine: "Please, please vote for me."

The few staffers on the plane who were still awake and not a part of the card game were chuckling softly at the Carvey tape. They tried to stifle their laughter in front of the *Nightline* crew, until Carvey-as-Bush pleaded, "Don't wanna be a one-termer." At that point a sudden collective guffaw rolled through the cabin.

At the hearts table, Paul Begala laughed nervously for about five seconds. Then he spotted the mike and his face fell. Clinton had just been dealt a new hand, and Begala saw the candidate flush red and he knew what was coming. The strategist started to glower at the man across the table, the man who would be President, the man who was about to fulminate again next to an open microphone. Begala stared at the candidate as if by staring he could stop him from another eruption. Clinton threw down a card and let forth with another "Fuck!" Begala's eyes shifted nervously to the *Nightline* camera crew. A look of panic crossed his face. He jumped up and darted out of the picture.

Begala raced down the aisle toward the back of the plane, where Koppel was writing a script.

"Your crew is getting a bit of rough language from the governor," Begala said.

"I know," Koppel responded evenly.

"Well, you can't use it."

"Of course we can."

"But the network wouldn't permit it, would it?"

"Oh sure." Koppel smiled. "We can use anything. We're on late-night."

"Well, you wouldn't want to use *these* words."

"Listen," said Koppel. "One time we did a show on the Mafia, and an informer used the word *motherfucker*. We put *that* on the air."

Oh man, thought Begala. This was bad. Begala had never liked the idea of allowing *Nightline* behind the scenes for the last hours of the campaign. Life "behind the scenes" was behind the scenes because it was *supposed* to be behind the scenes. It wasn't that the show would cost Clinton any votes—it couldn't, since Koppel was holding all of the material for a documentary to air the night after the election. But what about the President-elect? Would the expletives sound any more genteel on Wednesday than on Monday? Begala thought not.

"What's it gonna take," Begala asked Koppel, "to get you to go easy with the language?"

Koppel paused. Begala held his breath.

Koppel: "Maybe we can cut a deal."

Begala sweated some more.

Koppel smiled. "I'll give you . . . two *shits* for one *fuck*."

Begala looked sick to his stomach.

Koppel kept smiling. "Or, maybe we could lose the bad words in exchange for, oh, say, your giving *Nightline* the first exclusive interview with the President-elect."

By now Begala's complexion resembled the pallor of a heart-attack victim. He squinted silently at Koppel for a moment, then stalked back up the aisle, brushing past *Newsweek* reporter Jonathan Alter. Alter had heard the bulk of the conversation. He walked over to Koppel and asked if *Nightline* would dump the cuss words.

Koppel's reply: "I'll cut 'em some slack on the *fuck,* but I can't guarantee anything on the *shit.*"

THE CUSS-WORD POKER fairly well reflected what had been, for the better part of a year, a weird relationship between *Nightline* and the Clinton campaign. Few successful campaigns for the presidency have overcome as many near-death experiences as the 1992 campaign of Bill Clinton. Time and again, from January to November, Clinton's consultants would examine what James Carville, the campaign's chief strategist, called their "toolbox" of media options, from which they'd have to select just the right forum for the crisis of the moment. Sometimes they wanted *Nightline,* sometimes they didn't.

Koppel understood the mentality. It made sense. *"Nightline,"* Koppel would remind his staff, "is used all the time." Politicians, public officials, and candidates would cooperate with the broadcast when and if they stood to gain by it. No one came on *Nightline* because of altruism; certainly, no politician ever did. That fact never bothered Koppel, because it was also true that he never tackled a broadcast without an agenda of his own. Sometimes his task, as he saw it, was to weed a conversation of platitudes and to steer a debate into a specific and useful set of arguments; sometimes it was to give context to an event, or to flesh out the details of a story. Even if all that a broadcast achieved was a clear or meaningful presentation of an issue, then it might or might not have been a mistake from the point of view of the guests, but it would have been useful to the audience.

But from Carville's perspective, *Nightline* was a "tool in the toolbox." A campaign problem, he said, was like a "board that is sort of falling down. So you look up, and is it a screw or a nail that is loose that is causing the board to fall down? All right, if it's a nail, you pick up a hammer. If it's a screw, you pick up a screwdriver."

WHAT THE CLINTON campaign needed on January 23, 1992, was a sledgehammer. A supermarket tabloid called the *Star* had published a story by a woman named Gennifer Flowers, claiming she'd been Bill Clinton's lover for twelve years. She said she had tapes of his calls.

Tabloids don't normally funnel much to the story coffers of *Nightline*, but this story was different. "This wasn't," in Koppel's words, " 'Martians Invade Secaucus, New Jersey.' " What the *Star* had published, Koppel thought, was a story that "appeared to have some truth in it. They had a real person, making real accusations; there were real quotes, and there was a real tape." The tape was a recording of telephone conversations between Flowers and a man she claimed was Bill Clinton. Early on the morning of January 23, *Nightline* sent senior producer Scott Willis to the offices of the tabloid to listen to it.

"I'm no expert," Willis later told Koppel. "But the voice sure sounds like Bill Clinton. And yet there's no way to verify if anything's been done to this tape."

Koppel decided to call George Stephanopoulos, Clinton's close adviser, to see if the governor wanted to respond. Stephanopoulos said he'd call back. Koppel hung up, wondering whether *Nightline* should go anywhere near this thing. It made him uncomfortable. A debate ensued among Koppel, executive producer Tom Bettag, Scott Willis and the other senior producer, Mark Nelson, chief booker Richard Harris, and Jeff Greenfield, one of *Nightline*'s correspondents. The question was, Without independent confirmation, did the Flowers allegations merit a broadcast?

"We went through it," according to Koppel. "We went up the hill and down the hill and ultimately felt we just didn't have enough independent information to do that program." Koppel and Bettag decided to kill the broadcast.

The Clinton camp, however, never knew of *Nightline*'s decision. Carville later recalled feeling only that "this story was breaking and we wanted to get in front of it as fast as we could before it got in front of us." The next decision, said Carville, was to choose the right forum: "You could hold a press conference that afternoon. You could do Larry King. You could send out a statement. There's all kinds of tools that you have in your box. It's just a question of which one you use." What drew the campaign to *Nightline* was that the candidate could be interviewed live. "What you get is what you see. There's no editing. If your candidate is good live, that is always going to be an advantage to him. Now, you don't have any control over what you're asked, but you do have control over your answers." In addition, compared to live broadcasts on cable, *Nightline* had "the numbers: more people actually see it." But the key reason to pick *Nightline,* according to Carville, was that "if you go on there, it is a definitive answer that you're not running away and you're not hiding."

The campaign insisted upon two non-negotiable conditions for an interview with the candidate: the first was that Clinton must be face-to-face with his interlocutor. That way Clinton could use body language and eye contact to gain more control over the interview. The second was that Hillary Clinton had to be by her husband's side.

"You don't have to be a great political strategist," said Carville, to know that "if somebody is telling you you don't have a very good marriage, you want people to see that you're together."

So it was that, unaware of Koppel's decision to abandon a broadcast on the Flowers allegations, George Stephanopoulos called Koppel back. "If the governor does come on your show tonight," said Stephanopoulos. "Will you agree to interview him face-to-face?"

"Of course," Koppel replied. He knew immediately where Stephanopoulos was headed; the call, in Koppel's eyes, automatically rendered moot his reasons for abandoning a broadcast on the subject.

"And will you allow Mrs. Clinton to be there in the interview? The governor will not do this without her next to him."

"Consider it done," said Koppel.

"All right," said Stephanopoulos. "We haven't made a final decision yet, but we'll get back to you."

Koppel convened the *Nightline* staff and announced, "I think it's a whole new ball game. Clinton has clearly decided he's going to address this thing head-on, and I think we have to prepare to do this topic tonight."

Next Koppel got a call from ABC reporter Mark Halperin, who was in New Hampshire covering the Clinton campaign and had spent an extensive amount of time with the candidate. Halperin had learned that the Clintons might appear on two ABC shows that night: first, *Prime Time Live*, then *Nightline*. Going on both shows would triple Clinton's viewing audience: *PrimeTime Live* reached an estimated 15 million viewers; *Nightline,* around 7 million. The advantage of *Prime-Time Live*—besides numbers—was its earlier time slot: what the Clintons said in their own defense could make the morning papers. Where *Nightline* would help would be in reaching the "opinion-makers—the elites," according to Carville.

Within the hour, Halperin called Koppel again. Now he was in a motorcade with Clinton, headed for the airport. The candidate had apparently decided to go ahead with *PrimeTime Live* and *Nightline*—if, that is, he could make it to Washington in time and if Hillary, who was campaigning in Atlanta, could link up with him. "As far as I was concerned," Koppel recalled later, "that was it: Clinton was going to appear; we were definitely doing the show."

But while Koppel and his staff began gearing up for the broadcast, sleet in New Hampshire was reducing the Clinton motorcade to a crawl. The candidate would never make it to Washington in time for *PrimeTime Live,* which meant that he had lost the larger audience, as well as a shot at the morning papers. Clinton and his strategists used the slow drive to reconsider their options.

The sleet settled it. By the time Clinton reached the airport, the weather had gotten so bad the plane couldn't fly. And in Atlanta, where Hillary Clinton was supposed to board a plane, thunderstorms were delaying air traffic. In the elegant vernacular of Carville, "There wasn't shit moving on the East Coast."

"We get the call," said Koppel, "that it's not gonna happen. They just can't make it." Almost immediately, Koppel learned that the Clintons were shopping for another venue. A source close to the campaign told Koppel that an appearance on Friday's *Nightline* or on *20/20,* which also aired on Friday, would be impossible. The governor had to be in Little Rock that night, for any last-minute pleas in the case of a controversial execution. For the governor to talk about Gennifer Flowers on the very night of the execution wouldn't look good. And the story couldn't be allowed to persist—without a response from the Clintons—until Monday. Koppel's source told him that the Clintons would definitely go public on some show over the weekend, perhaps CNN's *Newsmakers* or *This Week with David Brinkley.*

The point that mattered to Koppel and Bettag was that Clinton was still planning to address the issue directly and publicly. That, in their view, meant it was perfectly appropriate for *Nightline* to go ahead with the story that night, even without the Clintons. "I was convinced then," Koppel would say later, "and I remain totally convinced now, that it was absolutely a legitimate story once Clinton had made the decision to confront this thing head-on."

The story was, as Koppel saw it, "Bill Clinton is going to address the issue of his philandering, and he's gonna do it on television. And

he realizes if he doesn't head this thing off, his campaign is dogmeat."
Before the night was over, however, it would be Koppel who would
be dogmeat.

THE BROADCAST BEGAN with Koppel explaining that only the
weather had prevented the appearance of the Clintons and that "this
is clearly a story that the Clintons want to meet head-on and together,
and they still plan to do that, although not tonight." Then Koppel
blew it.

His first question to his first guest, Larry Sabato, a nationally
renowned political scientist at the University of Virginia, was not
about the details of Flowers's accusations; it was about the media
"feeding frenzy," as if *Nightline* weren't at the trough. Sabato landed
the first blow of the night.

SABATO: I think this is a classic case of lowest-common-
denominator journalism. This is being driven by a
sleazy supermarket tabloid. And since when did *The
New York Times,* or for that matter *Nightline,* allow the
subjects it covers to be driven by that kind of news
organization?

Koppel got a reprieve from Jonathan Alter, who was covering
Clinton for *Newsweek* and who felt ambivalent.

ALTER: The *Star* story today was something you held with as-
bestos mittens. You know, it was one of those radio-
active stories that I don't think anybody really wanted to
deal with. But, to mix a metaphor, it's like a big elephant
sitting in the living room and when the entire campaign
comes to a screeching halt over an issue like this, it's hard
to avoid it completely.

The next guest seized the show, refocused the debate, set the
agenda, and, for good measure, addled Koppel. Mandy Grunwald was
a Harvard-educated media consultant to Democratic candidates. Her
business partner, Frank Greer, had been hired to advise Clinton, but
so far, Grunwald had not. Earlier in the evening, a *Nightline* producer
had discovered that Grunwald was in Washington, which meant that

the weather would be no obstacle if Grunwald would agree to pinch-hit for the Clintons. After trying to talk the producer out of doing the show altogether, Grunwald said she would call back. Then she called Greer and the other operatives in New Hampshire. The consensus was that Clinton could do worse than to have a woman—a smart woman, no less—defend him on charges of adultery and that Grunwald should go ahead.

She later claimed she was terrified. She did not sound it. In fact, she executed a classic defense of a candidate under siege: change the subject, turn your agenda into a weapon, then slash and burn and scorch, but whatever you do, stay on the offensive.

MANDY GRUNWALD: This is the first program that *Nightline* has done on any topic relating to the Democratic presidential candidates. You haven't been talking about the middle class. You haven't talked about why Bill Clinton has captured people's imagination. Here you are—

KOPPEL: Oh, now, wait a second. Wait a second. You're making a charge that's not accurate. We've done a number of programs on the middle class. We've done a number of programs on—

GRUNWALD: You have not—

KOPPEL: —the issues, unemployment. You're quite right, we haven't done a program on Bill Clinton.

GRUNWALD: But here we are just a couple weeks before the New Hampshire primary. People are about to go out there and vote. Jon's absolutely right. They have real concerns. And you're choosing with your editorial comment by making this program about some unsubstantiated charges that started with a trashy supermarket tabloid. You're telling people something that you think is important. That's not context. You're setting the agenda and you're letting the *Star* set it for you.

KOPPEL: All right, let me—

GRUNWALD: And I find that troubling.

Koppel didn't take more than a minute to realize that Grunwald had taken control of the show, and that she was on the better side of the argument to boot. "What was going through my mind was, *Mandy, you got me. You're absolutely right. This is a trashy way to go about doing this story.*" He still felt that the philandering allegations were worth a broadcast. "But the way we handled it was wrong. I realized that I'd made a mistake in terms of the editorial direction of the program."

So Koppel tried to change editorial direction. He tried to steer Grunwald into a debate about the accuracy of Flowers's story.

KOPPEL: Would the public, for example, Mandy Grunwald, have a right to know—I understand this is hypothetical. If it turns out later on that these charges were true, would the public have a right to know and would it make a difference if Governor Clinton has been covering up something he knows to be true?

GRUNWALD: I think you're getting on the wrong subject here. The question is your judgment here about who these sources are. There's a lot of cash involved in these stories.

"Wow!" Bettag exclaimed in the control room. "She's really throwing some punches!"

And every punch punched up the Clinton camp. Grunwald was deflecting attention away from the adultery charges altogether by turning the spotlight on the responsibilities of the press.

GRUNWALD: We know that the *Star* has a record, let's put it that way, of paying money for stories, cash for trash. We know that's an element of this story. I would think you'd be rather concerned before you write these allegations about a man who just might be a good President for this country at a time when we need somebody to make some changes. I think you would want to check out the story a little bit more before you devote a half-hour to it.

KOPPEL: You're an—well, we're not devoting a half-hour to the story itself. We're devoting a half-hour to precisely the kind of discussion—

GRUNWALD: But that's just a neat little way to get at the story.

"When somebody's got me," Koppel said later, "they got me.
And Mandy nailed me."

Jonathan Alter was fascinated. "Once Mandy started taking Ted
apart, I knew that I was watching something highly unusual."

KOPPEL: (*to Grunwald*) So far you've done a very effective job of
               putting me on the defensive and asking me questions,
               which is perfectly appropriate.

That was James Carville's favorite moment. "If Ted Koppel tells
you that you've put him on the defensive," said Carville, "then that
makes you."

In the final round, Grunwald threw two more punches: one on
behalf of the candidate, one against the press.

GRUNWALD: He said something rather rare already in this campaign.
            He and Hillary said that they haven't had a perfect mar-
            riage. I mean, there aren't a lot of candidates you've talked
            to who have admitted to not being perfect. I think that's
            a pretty good start. But they've also said that they've put
            that marriage back together and that their commitment is
            to each other and to this campaign and to the country, and
            I think that ought to be enough. I don't have enough faith
            in the press to believe that it's going to be.

Grunwald would later remember walking out of the studio and a
producer coming up to her and saying, "Nobody does that to Ted."
Is that a good thing? Grunwald wondered. She wasn't certain whether
she had done Bill Clinton a favor or humiliated him.

But Koppel knew. He told a colleague, "Mandy ate me for lunch."

Clinton's strategists knew too. James Carville said that when
Grunwald took on Koppel, "Mandy made her name." One thing was
certain: by Sunday, after the Clintons had decided to appear on a special edition of *60 Minutes* airing just after the Super Bowl, Mandy
Grunwald was among the top aides by their side, preparing the candidate and his wife for the interview. Within two weeks, she was on the
campaign, full-time. When pressed about the show years later, Grunwald laughed. "Okay, you want me to say it? I owe my career to Ted
Koppel!"

What still sticks with Jonathan Alter is how many times he's been asked about that show, even years later. The thing is, what people usually ask Alter is whether he *saw* the *Nightline* on which Mandy Grunwald beat up on Ted Koppel. Sometimes Alter never even bothers to explain that he was one of the other guests. Who would remember?

WHAT MANDY GRUNWALD had done that night in January was to lay out a battle plan for the year: if the candidate is accused of something, find a secondary issue that can be wielded as a weapon and then use it; attack, attack, attack. Less than three weeks later, the Clinton camp would pull out the plan and use it to ward off another monster of a crisis. And once again, the camp would use *Nightline* as a tool.

Eight days before the New Hampshire primary, Carville had to break the news to Clinton that his candidacy was disintegrating. This time the issue wasn't women but the Vietnam draft. A few days earlier, *The Wall Street Journal* had published a story that questioned how Clinton had avoided military service. The piece charged that in 1969, at a time when Clinton was likely to be drafted, he had received a deferment by enrolling in the Reserve Officer Training Corps at the University of Arkansas, and by stating his intention to attend law school there. But the *Journal* said he had never participated in the ROTC program and had never even applied to the law school. Instead, he'd returned to England that September for a second year of study at Oxford. Later that autumn the United States enacted a new lottery for the draft. Clinton submitted to the lottery and drew a high number. At that point, according to the *Journal*, Clinton informed the ROTC that he would not be joining its program in Arkansas, and remained in England all year.

The thrust of the piece was that Clinton's declaration to enroll in the ROTC had shielded him from the draft at a time—just before the lottery was introduced—when he would have been conscripted. The *Journal* also pointed out that when Clinton did apply to law school that winter, he did not apply to Arkansas but to Yale. The article quoted an ROTC recruiter who said that Clinton "was able to manipulate things so he didn't have to go" into the service. The recruiter's name was Colonel Eugene Holmes.

The *Journal* article had come out on a Thursday. By late Sunday night, Carville had to tell Clinton that a new poll showed that over the previous four days he had plummeted by fifteen to twenty points. Clinton moaned, "We're dropping like a turd in a well."

Two days later, Ted Koppel was sitting in his office when Tara Sonenshine walked in with a letter. She had received it from a long-time source, a retired Air Force general. Koppel knew him well. But the letter had nothing to do with the general. And although the general was not willing to say exactly where he had obtained it, he did tell Sonenshine that he had never met either the author or the addressee. The letter was written in December 1969. It was addressed to a Colonel Eugene Holmes, the commander of the Reserve Officer Training Corps at the University of Arkansas. The author of the letter was a twenty-three-year-old Rhodes scholar named Bill Clinton. It said, in part, "I want to thank you, not just for saving me from the draft." The letter went on to explain Clinton's tortuous decision not to join the ROTC.

Koppel looked at the letter. He knew that his source, the retired general, was not only a Republican but also a major actor in the Iran-contra scandal. It didn't take a genius to deduce that whoever had leaked the letter to the general, the leaker surely wasn't interested in helping Clinton. And yet, "you develop an instinct over years in this business," said Koppel years later, "where you can look at something like that and you say: 'This looks like the real thing.' It could very easily have been a phony, a dirty campaign trick. But this looked like the real thing."

Koppel put in a call to David Wilhelm, Clinton's campaign manager. Koppel read the letter and said it looked legit. *Nightline* would like Clinton to come on the show and respond to it. Koppel then added one note of reservation to Wilhelm. It was about Koppel's source. Obviously, Koppel could not reveal where the letter came from. But he was concerned about the fact that his source had once worked for the Pentagon. There was a possibility, he told Wilhelm, "that somebody was playing a dirty trick" on the Clinton campaign. Koppel felt he owed the campaign "the courtesy of knowing" that it was possible that the Pentagon was coming to the political assistance of George Bush. But Koppel also told Wilhelm that it was impossible to confirm these suspicions.

That morning, Carville, Begala, and Stephanopoulos were riding in a van in western New Hampshire when their beepers went off. The message was to call Wilhelm—urgent. Carville had the van pull off at a motel and paid ninety dollars for a room just for a private phone line. They called Wilhelm. He told them about his telephone conversation with Koppel.

Next, the consultants reached Clinton. Clinton called Koppel. Clinton did not deny the legitimacy of the letter. But he wanted to know more about what Koppel had said to Wilhelm . . . something about the Pentagon. Koppel repeated to Clinton what he'd said to Wilhelm—that the letter may have come out of the Pentagon, but that he couldn't be sure.

"The Pentagon" were the only words the Clinton camp needed to hear. In his memoirs of the campaign, Carville would write, "Now we had some evidence that they were monkeying with the election here. Now I had an enemy." Now he had a *strategy.* Carville was going to do exactly what any good strategist should do: take the offensive. He called Koppel and said, "We've got to blow this damn thing up about the Republicans using the Pentagon."

Koppel again warned Carville that *Nightline* had no proof of who had leaked the letter to his source. Carville didn't care. Neither did Clinton. They had a plan now. "What we wanted to do, of course, was change the subject," Begala explained later, "to pivot and blast the Pentagon or the Bush people for this alleged leak." The issue, Carville would write, "kind of turned a corner for us in New Hampshire. It lit a fire, raised the bloodlust, gave us something to fight."

The next morning Clinton called Koppel at home and said he would go on *Nightline* that night. But first, Clinton said, he would break the news of the letter himself, in a press conference that very morning. The campaign desperately wanted to shape the public perception of the letter or, in Carville's vernacular, to "get out ahead of it."

Within an hour or two, Clinton was standing in an airport hangar in New Hampshire, surrounded by press, announcing that he was releasing a letter he had written to his ROTC commander in 1969, that the Pentagon was trying to bring down his candidacy, and that he would appear on *Nightline* that evening to talk about it. Jonathan Alter was there for *Newsweek.* He had been covering Clinton for months. He thought Clinton looked "stunned." Alter remembered that the reaction of most of the press was, "Whoa, is this the end of the whole thing? We'd just been through Gennifer Flowers. Is this thing just going to explode on us right now?"

As soon as Clinton had finished, Carville stepped into the fray and "pivoted and blasted" and pursued the hard offense, turning the focus away from the issue of Clinton and the draft and toward the issue of campaign dirty tricks. He was frothing. Of course Carville's counter-attack didn't make any sense if the Pentagon was *not* involved in getting the letter to Koppel, so he stuck with that assumption and harped on it: "What in the world business does the Pentagon have in the middle of a political campaign?"

Within minutes, when Koppel got word of what Clinton and Carville were saying, *he* was frothing too. The Clinton camp, he felt, "was dishonest, in a fashion, given what I'd told them. I truly did not know where the letter came from." Within a few more minutes, Koppel had a call from his source, the retired general, who had also heard about the press conference. Now, *he* was frothing. No, the source told Koppel, the letter had not come from the Pentagon.

Meanwhile, there were at least three journalists in that hangar in New Hampshire who did not for one minute think that Ted Koppel had gotten the letter through the Pentagon. They thought he'd done something more dastardly. And by now, *they* were frothing. These were colleagues of Koppel's, fellow employees of ABC. And they wanted to know one thing: Was Ted Koppel a thief?

The three angry men were correspondent James Wooten, reporter Mark Halperin, and ABC producer Michael Bicks. It turned out that they themselves had been in possession of the letter for several days and were planning to reveal it as an exclusive scoop for *World News Tonight* with Peter Jennings. They were certain that their source for the letter had not leaked it to anyone else. In fact, Wooten had presented the letter to Bill Clinton on Monday—two days prior. Wooten had already taped an interview with Clinton about it. For the past day and a half, Wooten and Bicks had been nailing down a few more details, and trying to reach Colonel Holmes, before going on the air with the letter.

Wooten, Halperin, and Bicks were dumbfounded. The only way Koppel could have gotten that letter was by chicanery. They wondered if one of *Nightline*'s producers or minions had committed outright theft. Perhaps *Nightline* had a hacker, someone who had broken into Wooten's or Halperin's computer files. The most serious possibility was that a *Nightline* staffer had actually stolen their copy of the letter and had duplicated it.

Several concerned ABC executives heard of the mysterious *Nightline* scoop and called Koppel, demanding to know how his people had stolen Wooten's letter. Now it was Koppel's turn to feel dumbfounded. Until that moment, no one at *Nightline* had any idea that *World News Tonight* had the letter too. "Strange as it may seem," said Koppel, "I don't know what Peter Jennings and his staff do on *World News Tonight,* and he doesn't know what we're doing on this program."

So now Koppel had two catastrophes. First, he had to issue a statement contradicting Clinton and explaining that *Nightline*'s source had now insisted that the Pentagon had nothing to do with the letter. Second, colleagues from his own network thought Koppel and Company were a bunch of thieves.

Koppel's first priority, however, was that night's broadcast. He decided that the entire letter should be read on the air, before the bulk of the interview with Clinton. Koppel felt that, taken as a whole, "the letter gave a fair picture of a very conflicted young man, who wasn't altogether sure what the hell he ought to be doing," and yet "a fairly sophisticated young man, who was laying the groundwork here for being able to move and wanted any number of different directions, should the occasion call for it." Koppel believed the letter, read in its entirety, shed "a lot of insights into Clinton." So he placed yet another call to the Clinton people, to offer the candidate the opportunity to read the letter. Should they decline the offer, Koppel said that he would read it. "It did not occur to me for one moment," Koppel said later, "that Clinton would be dumb enough to read it."

Right about that. Simple havoc lay in store if Bill Clinton read the letter: any opponent could tape it, edit it, and just like that, he's got Clinton saying "thank you for saving me from the draft."

On the other hand, Carville felt strongly that having Koppel read the letter, with all the references to anguish, conscience, and self-regard, would serve Clinton enormously. In fact, from the moment Halperin handed him the letter on Monday, which was the first time he'd ever read it, Carville believed it would lift Clinton out of the crisis. Begala remembered Carville reading the letter that first day and shouting, "Governor, this letter is going to be your best friend!"

So that night, after a few exchanges with Clinton and after reaffirming that the letter had not come from the Pentagon, Koppel read it. Some passages:

> The draft was justified in World War II because the life of the people collectively was at stake. Individuals had to fight if the nation was to survive, for the lives of their countrymen and their way of life. Vietnam is no such case. . . . The decision not to be a resister and the related subsequent decisions were the most diffi-cult of my life. I decided to accept the draft in spite of my beliefs for one reason: to maintain my political vi-ability within the system. . . . After we had made our agreement and you had sent my 1-D deferment to my draft board, the anguish and loss of self-regard and self-confidence really set in. I hardly slept for weeks and kept going by eating compulsively and reading until exhaustion brought sleep. Finally on September 12, I stayed up all night writing a letter to the chairman of my draft board, saying basically what is in the preceding paragraph, thanking him for trying to help me in a case where he really couldn't, and stating that I couldn't do the ROTC after all and would he please draft me as soon as possible. I never mailed the letter, but I did carry it on me every day until I got on the plane to return to England. I didn't mail the letter because I didn't see, in the end, how my going in the Army and maybe going to Vietnam would achieve anything except a feeling that I had punished myself and gotten what I deserved. So I came back to En-gland to try to make something of this second year of my Rhodes scholarship.

While Koppel read, one side of the screen showed the words, and the other side showed Clinton listening and occasionally nodding. The effect was compelling: Old Bill Clinton listening to Young Bill Clinton.

Back in New Hampshire, a pack of journalists had gathered in a motel room to watch. Paul Begala walked in and found, he said, "the

entire mood of the press corps changed. It took them out of feeding
frenzy mode and into a reflective stepping back, thinking about it in
the context of 1968 or 1969 and not 1992. You could just feel it. They
sat for two or three or four minutes, or however long it took Koppel,
and they listened in as the words crawled up the screen. They listened
to what this guy was really going through."

But after completing the reading, Koppel began to challenge Clinton on the details.

KOPPEL: (*quoting from letter*) "I didn't see, in the end, how my
             going in the Army and maybe going to Vietnam would
             achieve anything except a feeling that I had punished
             myself and gotten what I deserved. So I came back to
             England to try to make something of this second year of
             my Rhodes scholarship, and that is where I am now."
             That doesn't sound like the voice of a young man who
             expects that he is likely to be drafted.

CLINTON: No, but you've got to look back at what happened in the
             intervening time. . . . If you look at the records and look
             at what the draft board says, they point out that my de-
             ferment was withdrawn in October, I was put back in
             the draft pool, then the lottery came in, then I got a high
             draft number. . . . In the end, I didn't think it right to
             have a four-year deferment and I ought to go back in the
             draft. . . . I was trying to make that case . . . and if you
             read the whole letter in context, I think it makes that
             plain.

Koppel thought Clinton "was very cool and collected and in command of himself."

KOPPEL: December first, you get your high lottery number; De-
             cember second, the letter goes off to Yale Law School;
             December third, you write your letter to Colonel
             Holmes. That's just a coincidence of timing, I mean,
             there's nothing to read into it.

CLINTON: I say, I just don't remember, and there's nothing to read
             into it. . . . Before I knew my lottery number, I was in

the draft. If I had drawn number one or number ten, none of this would have happened and we wouldn't be having this conversation today.

Jonathan Alter wrote in his journal that Clinton's appearance was "impressive," and that "I began to think maybe he might even be able to survive the wave that seemed to be crushing him that day."

As time was running out, Clinton squeezed in one final line, provided to him by Mandy Grunwald:

CLINTON: All I've been asked about by the press are a woman I didn't sleep with and a draft I didn't dodge.

One of the advantages of live television—for Clinton—was that he had saved that line until the end, so that Koppel had no time to challenge him, and viewers would remember it. In his journal, Alter said that "was the only time [Clinton] squarely and bald-facedly lied during the campaign."

It didn't matter to Clinton's consultants. Perceptions ruled. Carville thought the line was one of the best of the whole campaign. When Begala heard it, he thought, *Now we've made the turn. He's out of battling back and he's now back fighting for what got him in the race.*

The next day, Clinton's polls showed he was on the rise again. Over the course of the week, he fought back to a second-place finish in New Hampshire, just behind Paul Tsongas, a political restoration good enough for his own campaign to proclaim him "the Comeback Kid."

As for Koppel, he spent the next few days defending his staff from the suspicion that they had stolen the Clinton letter. So where, exactly, had *Nightline*'s copy of the Clinton letter originated? Koppel and members of the *Nightline* staff compared what information the general would provide about the path of the *Nightline* copy with information gleaned from *World News Tonight* staffers about their copy.

They discovered a freakish chain of circumstances.

Wooten and one of his producers had received the letter first. They had received it while in South Carolina over the weekend from an impeccable source, a former aide to the head of the ROTC at the University of Arkansas, and they had guarantees that no one else in the press had the letter. The ABC producer wanted an extra copy of the letter for safekeeping, and took it to the desk clerk of his hotel, asking that the clerk run off a duplicate. Unfortunately for the producer, the clerk knew how to read, and what he had been given to copy looked interesting. So the clerk ran off one extra copy, ABC got its original back, along with the copy it had ordered, unaware that the clerk now had his own personal copy of the letter.

Then, said Koppel, the clerk "faxes his copy of the letter to a friend in Virginia, who by absolute coincidence has the office across the hall from my friend the retired general. The guy goes running across the hall to the general and says, 'Take a look at this. It's incredible. Do you know anyone who might be able to use this?' And the general says, 'Yeah, I might know someone.' And he calls us."

So, had *Nightline* stolen the letter? "Well," said Koppel, "it turned out that we had. Only we didn't know it."

THE LONG ELECTION YEAR was in its final hours when Ted Koppel and a camera crew boarded Clinton's plane. Down on the ground in Little Rock, a second *Nightline* crew recorded the delirium of the "War Room," as the campaign headquarters was called. James Carville was wearing black gloves.

CARVILLE: These are my lucky charm, these gloves. I've got to keep my hands clean and pure for when I touch the victory.

At almost the same hour, at a rally with Clinton in Cleveland, Paul Begala was explaining for Koppel the meaning of his own good-luck charm: a tie with skulls and crossbones on it.

BEGALA: This is my *de cuello* tie, the Mexican death sign.

KOPPEL: And why are you wearing that tie?

BEGALA: No prisoners, no mercy, no quarter. We don't want to coast into this, man. We just want to drive a stake through their heart.

It was George Stephanopoulos, who, a few days before the election, had signed off on giving *Nightline* almost unlimited access to the final hours. The logic behind his decision was simple and shrewd: barring an electoral catastrophe, Clinton was going to win. If *Nightline* could capture the exaltation of his winning the presidency and could convey the experience to the viewer, the documentary might help preserve the momentum of victory for an extra day.

What Koppel hoped to convey was not so much the rapture but the subtle psychological shifts as victory closes a campaign and launches a presidency. "The theme for the documentary," said Koppel, "was what happens at that moment a person becomes President of the United States? There is a change that takes place. People see him differently. They will talk to him differently."

In the final forty-eight hours, Clinton refused to declare victory in front of the cameras, but his relaxed, delighted expression revealed him. A *Nightline* camera captured him backstage after a rally, where a quartet of young African-American men softly sang to him. The candidate basked in the harmony. But even as late as election eve, en route to another city, when Koppel asked the Clintons if they could feel the victory yet, they shook their heads, in unison. Mrs. Clinton pursed her lips, as if it were bad luck to acknowledge the polls.

Only later that Monday night, when the chances of losing grew increasingly remote, did caution give way to giddiness. A thunderous welcome in Paducah, Kentucky, pumped Clinton so high that he phoned headquarters to gloat. *Nightline*'s crews captured the call from both ends: on the plane, Clinton teased the War Room that Paducah was his idea; Hillary, seated next to him, laughed and nodded; in Little Rock, Carville and his troops circled around the speaker phone, listened, and applauded. The scene that followed that call, as weary, happy young volunteers gathered around Stephanopoulos and Carville, would seem especially poignant, and innocent, with a few years' hindsight:

STEPHANOPOULOS: Tomorrow we're going to win and that means that more people are going to have better jobs, people are going to pay a little less for health care, get better care, and more kids are going to go to better schools. So thanks. . . .

CARVILLE: Outside of a person's love, the most sacred thing that they can give is their labor . . . And I think we're going to win tomorrow and I think that the governor is going to fulfill his promise and change America and I think many of you are going to go on and help him.

No one in the room moved. A few wept. Carville's voice trembled badly as he struggled to finish.

CARVILLE: I was thirty-three years old before I ever went to Washington or New York. I was forty-two before I won my first campaign. And I'm happy for all of you all. You've been part of something special in my life and I'll never forget what you all have done. Thank you.

At dawn the campaign plane lumbered into Little Rock. Clinton took the microphone and shouted over the intercom, "Elvis lives!"

Hours later, exit polls indicated that "Elvis" was about to become "Mr. President-elect." The psychological shifts that Koppel had sought to document began to emerge.

GEORGE STEPHANOPOULOS: It's hard—it's different. I never called him Bill. I always called him Governor. But I was sitting on the couch an hour ago and I don't know what to call him when he calls. And I was really—like—do you say, "Mr. President"?

MICKEY KANTOR (*campaign chairman*):   It'll be a new thing for a lot of us who are close to him, but I think it will be different.

KOPPEL: Can you still call him by his first name?

KANTOR: I won't, no. Not anymore. He's President-elect Clinton, as far as I'm concerned.

JAMES CARVILLE: I'm scared. I think it's a little bit like—I'm kind of scared to see him the first time. I mean, my only other experience has been with governors and senators. I mean, I know that once someone gets elected, the relationship changes. It's inevitable. I have no idea what it's going to be like when you see somebody as the President-elect. I mean, I've never talked to a President.

Election night, in a Little Rock hotel, the Clintons and the Gores reveled with their supporters. A few blocks away, in a makeshift editing suite in the basement of a hotel, Koppel and his producers met and compared notes on what they'd recorded of the final hours on the plane and in the War Room. They had less than twenty-four hours to carve out the best material and forge it into a one-hour prime-time documentary. The only way to get it done in time was to have Koppel, who had already been awake for almost forty-eight hours with Clinton, stay up one more night and write and record the narration, segment by segment. Each segment would have its own producer, tape editor, and cutting room. Koppel thought the whole process, including the simultaneous shoots on the plane and in Little Rock, was "like making a statue and saying, 'Here, you work on this part; you work on that part; you work on the following part; you do the hand; you do the head; you do this.' And there is no way to know if the pieces fit until you put it on the air." The "pieces" would include Carville with his gloves, Begala with his tie, the quartet serenading Clinton, and the conference call from Paducah.

As for the hearts scene? It went in too. The shot that Koppel and his producers selected was a pan from the TV, where Dana Carvey's George Bush was prattling on, over to the card game. The camera captured the back of Clinton's head just as he tossed a card and muttered something, but whether it was or was not an expletive was made moot by the fact that it was drowned out, lost to the sound of Carvey whining and staffers guffawing.

And the good audio of the dirty words? "It never occurred to me—ever—to use that," Koppel said later. "When people are giving you that kind of flexibility to come and go, move in and out, there are just certain things you don't do." Poor Paul Begala had sweated blood for nothing. "I was just yanking his chain," recalled Koppel, "but I thought he'd get it right away."

CALL IT BEGALA'S REVENGE, even though he had nothing to do with it: two hours before airtime, the final segment of the documentary did not exist. It was supposed to be Clinton's first post-election interview. Stephanopoulos had promised it to Koppel and had guaranteed that it would happen in time to use it at the end of the documentary. But now it was six o'clock, and after hours of waiting in the backyard of the Governor's Mansion in Little Rock, Koppel played with Socks, the First Cat-elect, and wondered whether the President-elect might be a no-show.

Tom Bettag, who was supervising the final editing back at the hotel, realized that he was looking at a six-minute hole in his prime-time special. He would later insist to his colleagues that he would have thought of *something* to do with the time . . . though he always remained vague about what that something could have been: "I know we would have been okay. Somehow, something would have happened and we would have been okay." Bettag would say it with both a smile and a jitter in his voice, as if he was quite glad he didn't have to *prove* that they would have been "okay." For, just after six, Clinton emerged from the mansion and roamed the back lawn with Koppel, the cameras rolling.

KOPPEL: Has someone told you yet, because I honestly don't know the answer. Is it at this point appropriate to call you Governor or Mr. President-elect? What's—

CLINTON: I think Governor.

KOPPEL: Is there such a title as Mr. President-elect?

CLINTON: Well, no. I don't think much about titles. I don't know. It never occurred to me. . . .

KOPPEL: You still feel like the same person, but you know you're not, don't you?

CLINTON: Well, I have more responsibilities now. I have a higher— even a higher sense of obligation. I'm happy about it.

The interview lasted almost half an hour. Before closing, Clinton asserted his first priority. By delivering it for prime time, he knew it would make the next day's papers: "I'm going to focus like a laser beam on the economy."

Minutes later, Koppel thanked Clinton and prepared to take the tape from the crew and race it over to the editing suite, where Bettag would tack the best of it onto the end of the documentary. Koppel paused for a moment. He handed Clinton the reporter's notebook that he'd clutched and scribbled on over the previous two days. "Would you mind," Koppel asked Clinton, "jotting a note?"

Clinton wrote, *"To Ted Koppel, who has been present for some of the best and worst moments of my campaign."*

SEVENTEEN
Adventures
in Hi8, and
Other Tales

"TOUGH? YOU WANT to know if prison is *tough*? I wasn't here seven minutes, Ted, and this huge woman with whiskers came up and kissed me on the lips."

"Is she homosexual?"

"Her name is Juice, Ted. What do *you* think?"

Deanna Lee knew that she sounded like a shrew, but incarceration tends to do that to a person. She glanced over her shoulder at the line of women waiting to use the phone and wished that she'd never had wine the night Koppel started talking about the penal system over dinner. Somehow, by dessert, Lee had volunteered to take a video camera inside a women's penitentiary. For two weeks the *Nightline* producer would live like a prisoner, with no special privileges, except for the privilege of recording the experience.

It was now day three for Lee inside Alabama's Tutwiler Prison. Until this phone call she hadn't talked to anyone outside. Not that she hadn't tried. Two previous attempts to reach Koppel had been stymied by a couple of eager new *Nightline* interns who'd thought they were doing the right thing in refusing to accept collect calls from an Alabama prison.

So, after more than forty-eight hours inside Tutwiler, and after a fifth half-hour wait for the only phone (twice she'd waited but hadn't even made it to the head of the line before lockdown), all that Lee had needed to hear was the voice of a colleague finally accepting her call and she'd started shouting, "Get Ted *now,* and if not taking my calls is some kind of trick by all of you to freak me out, then I'm not going through with this!"

Koppel had picked up in time to hear the last part, but hadn't responded, because Lee was still shouting something about "rotary dial," "one chance," and "lockup." Finally, Koppel assumed a low, soothing tone, to ask Lee why, after only two days, she sounded so broken. "I'm interested in this high pitch you're at already. Exactly what's so terrible? Is it *that* tough in there?"

That's when Lee described the "welcome kiss" from Juice.

"It might be interesting," Koppel replied, his voice still calm, "in fact, it might help you, if you could become friends with Juice. She might be able to bring some of the homosexual population together for you to talk to."

Lee rolled her eyes and didn't answer.

Koppel asked her to tell him more about what made prison so intolerable. "What's the worst part of the day?" he asked.

It dawned on Lee that Koppel was easing into the kind of interrogation he conducted so often with his guests. She thought that this must be what it's like to be on the show, and to have "the feeling that Koppel is trying to pull something out of your brain." She decided to oblige his curiosity, though she wasn't sure where he was headed.

"The food is unbelievably bad."

"Like school food?"

"No, much worse. You want to know how bad it is? I'm totally constipated. My stomach is killing me and I've only been in here a few days."

"I'll bet that's a common problem. And I bet it has more to do with than just the food, right? I mean, it must be kind of awkward going to the bathroom."

"Of course it is. It's these open stalls. Twenty-five toilets in a row, no walls. Male guards walk right through. It's embarrassing. So everybody tries to go to the bathroom late at night, when they can be alone. It's the whole question of dignity."

"Well then, I bet this combination of the food problem and the dignity factor means there must be a lot of constipation, and therefore a lot of home remedies. It would be interesting to hear what some of the prisoners come up with—how they deal with all that."

Lee finally asked Koppel why he was asking her all of these personal details.

"You've got your camera, right?"

"Of course I've got my camera."

"Well, when we get off the phone, find a ledge or someplace to set it, stand in front of the lens, and talk about your day the way you just have with me. From now on, keep a daily video journal not only of life in general for the women there, but of your own personal experiences and feelings. And see if you can interview the other prisoners about the issues we've discussed."

"Okay."

"And call me every day from now on, Deanna, so that we can see how it's going."

"I assume you'll tell the interns to accept my calls from now on."

"Will do."

THE FIRST TIME Koppel ever held in his hand one of the small video cameras that came out in the mid-1980s, he felt a rush of envy for anyone clever enough to take the technology and run with it. The eight-millimeter cameras could set a television reporter free. Inside oppressive regimes, a reporter with a hand-held camera would look like any tourist, which meant that he or she could document scenes off-limits to journalists. And the portability of a Hi8 could extend television's reach to some of the more geographically remote, even exotic parts of the world, areas inaccessible to the larger cameras and technical equipment—microphones and lights—normally used in network news, not to mention the ungainly standard network entourage of reporter, cameraperson, sound engineer and, often, a lighting technician.

"One of the great frustrations for those of us who work in television news," Koppel once complained, "is that we don't travel light. We come with a lot of people. We bring a lot of gear. There are all kinds of stories we can't even cover with that kind of equipment, and the ones we do cover are usually affected by our very presence. It's hard for this unwieldy entourage to remain unobtrusive."

It was in Beijing, two weeks after the massacre in Tiananmen
Square, that Koppel first experienced the freedom of working in Hi8.
The soldiers under whose guns Koppel pointed his camera thought
he was a tourist. He returned from the trip with advice to his colleagues that they cart along video cameras whenever their assignments
involved geographically remote or politically oppressive countries.

Ten days after Iraq invaded Kuwait, *Nightline* correspondent Forrest Sawyer carried a Hi8 into Baghdad. Even as the Iraqis kept the airport closed to regularly scheduled flights and continued to withhold
visas from the U.S. network personnel, they'd arranged a charter to
ferry Koppel from Jordan into Iraq, for the purposes of an exclusive
interview with Iraqi foreign minister Tariq Aziz; Sawyer was on the
plane. Sawyer's plan, while Koppel had the large network cameras tied
up in the interview, was to take the hand-held camera and find some
of the U.S. and British citizens being detained by the Iraqi government. Anything he could document of the hostages, Sawyer figured,
would be "gold."

Sawyer met two Americans who led him to the al-Rashid, the
hotel where most of the hostages were being detained. As soon as he
pulled out the camera and aimed it around the hotel's cavernous, ornate lobby, Sawyer was engulfed by security guards.

"What are you doing?" one of them asked.

Sawyer had encountered plenty of hostile military personnel over
the years, but what worried him was Koppel. In forty-five minutes, at
a television studio nearby, Koppel's interview with Aziz was set to
begin. If the guards discovered that Sawyer was from ABC, they might
well get word to the Foreign Ministry in time to quash the Aziz
interview.

"Why are you here?" the guards asked.

Sawyer decided he needed to stall. "Oh, you know, just here, just
hangin' out at the ol' Rashid."

"Tell us where you are from."

"America. Uh, New York."

The security men went off and huddled for a while. Sawyer kept
checking his watch. The two Americans who'd accompanied him
stood by quietly, looking slightly afraid. The guards came back and
asked him a few more questions, to which he shrugged as if he
couldn't understand. They huddled again. Finally, once enough time

had passed that Koppel and Aziz would be sitting down to start the interview, Sawyer told the guards who he was. They released him and the two Americans, but they kept the video camera.

The next day, Sawyer returned to the al-Rashid, to see what more he could learn about the hostages. When he arrived, he found Koppel deep in conversation with the guards. One of the guards was holding the video camera, shaking his head.

Koppel was explaining something about how the camera wasn't "intended" to be used for the purposes of news coverage. The guards finally handed him the camera.

At that moment, Sawyer spied his videotape still inside the machine. For some reason, the Iraqis hadn't confiscated it. He pointed it out to Koppel, who furtively removed the tape and carried it on to Jordan a few hours later. That night, when Koppel anchored the broadcast from Amman, he used the tape to underscore the fact that U.S. citizens were being held against their will in Baghdad.

KOPPEL: What is offbounds these days is the al-Rashid, the Rashid Hotel. It is, by world class standards, an elegant hotel, a beautiful hotel. It is also the place where some thirty-six Americans are being held against their will . . . These pictures of the Rashid Hotel, where the detainees are being held, were shot surreptitiously and without the permission of the Iraqi government by my colleague Forrest Sawyer.

Sawyer, who was still back in Iraq, waited for word of the unauthorized tape to get back to officials. He fully expected they'd throw him out. They did not. Sawyer continued to report from inside the capital for several weeks.

IT WAS A FEW months after the Baghdad trip that Tom Bettag took over as *Nightline*'s new executive producer. Bettag, a veteran of CBS and a former executive producer of the *CBS Evening News,* deemed experimentation the oxygen of any long-running broadcast. He hoped to diversify the *Nightline* format and to infuse the broadcast with some of the pioneering spirit—what Bill Lord had once called the "astronaut mentality"—that had defined its earliest days. *Nightline,*

Bettag thought, should take the viewer on adventures. The Hi8 was the ideal vehicle.

The first Hi8 project under Bettag featured the work of a photographer from *Life* magazine, Ed Barnes. Near a small village in Haiti, Barnes boarded a twenty-seven-foot boat with 121 refugees who were hoping to reach Miami. Before the Coast Guard intercepted the tiny craft and took the group to Guantánamo, Barnes recorded his nights and days with the refugees, all of them jammed in so tightly that there was no way to lie down. The video conveyed something entirely different about the Haitian refugee crisis than the usual reports out of Washington. It wedged the viewer inside the crisis; it wedged the viewer right between the frightened faces of men, women, and children trying to float to safer land.

Barnes's work whetted Bettag's appetite, and Koppel's, for more stories that could only be portrayed by the portability and gritty realism of Hi8. So when Deanna Lee proposed taking a hand-held camera into prison, they told her to go for it.

LEE PUT IN REQUESTS with penitentiaries across the country. Nineteen said no. Tutwiler Prison, in Alabama, agreed. There were all sorts of negotiations about how and in what situations Lee could use the camera, and there were all kinds of papers for her to sign, absolving the prison of any liability should she run into trouble. Lee was told she wouldn't be treated any differently than any of the prisoners except for this: she had to wear colored clothing. The rest of the prisoners wore white smocks during the day, and officials wanted to be able to spot Lee easily. Other than that, she'd sleep in a dorm with 104 other women, some of them thieves, some of them drug dealers, some of them murderers. In June 1992, surrendering everything that belonged to her but her camera, Lee entered Tutwiler Prison.

Koppel's idea for Lee to befriend Juice may have been his most important advice. The day after that conversation, Lee ended up working with Juice on a road crew, and when Lee managed to chop down a tree, Juice started to show her respect. Juice agreed to gather some of her friends for a group interview.

The women were seated around a table in the prison yard when Lee pointed her camera at them and started to ask them about the homosexual relationships.

INMATE 1:   That is the way of living in here.

INMATE 2:   It passes time.

INMATE 3:   I'm not a homosexual, but I am a flirt . . . I'll flirt with anybody.

The women told Lee that they even built family structures.

INMATE 4:   We call each other wife, husband, mother, daughter, son. . . .

LEE: You want to get out, you go back to your real daughter. But then what happens to your family in here?

INMATE 5:   Well you have to let 'em go, 'cause my family's more important to me out there than they are in here. . . .

INMATE 6:   You see somebody else's kids, it's heartache.

On another day, Lee got through to Koppel again. She began to fill him in on some of the drudgery of her routine when he interrupted her. "You sound kind of down."

"Well, we just had mail call, and of course, I didn't get anything. Why would I get any mail? But I just get sort of upset for all the women who don't get mail. The ones who get something are just so damn excited . . . showing pictures around and things like that. I filmed it, but I put the camera down 'cause I got kind of watery eyes, and I knew why."

"Talk about it a little," Koppel said.

Lee thought he sounded like a shrink. "I guess," she replied, "it must be that contact with the outside world and with your friends. And, you know, it's bugging the hell out of me that the phone here isn't a push-button phone, so I can't even check my answering machine. Even if you can't return the call, you love to hear who has called. I can't do that. I miss that, and I'm doubly upset by this stupid mail thing."

"If you could have anything sent to you right now," Koppel asked her, "what would it be?"

"The first thing that comes to mind is too stupid to tell you."

"What is it?"

"Well, I don't even wear this sort of thing at home, but a colored, flowery satiny nightgown."

"Why? To be feminine?"

"Not really. It's just that you should see the things the women put on at night here in the dorm. It's their only chance for individuality, because they have to wear this awful white smock all day long. If someone gets a scarf in the mail, she can't wear it in the day, but she'll use it for chiffon sleeves for her nightgown. You should see the colors and the brightness. Anything that's not linen or cotton comes out at night. It's their only chance to show individuality and some self-esteem. So it's really important, and if you're stuck wearing the prison-issue nightgown, you feel awful."

Lee got off the phone and, as it was the established routine now, she immediately talked about the nightgowns into the camera. Then she conducted interviews about mail call.

INMATE 7:   You need that connection with that world out there, be-
              cause without that world, it's like you're totally thrown
              into another world and you're disconnected from every-
              thing and everybody. And if you don't get that mail,
              from family or somebody that, you know, you was close
              to out there in the free world, it's like you just been to-
              tally rejected from that world altogether. Nobody cares
              about you anymore.

On the eleventh day, Lee got out of prison. She had more than enough material, and Koppel was about to leave on a story and wanted to record an interview with her in the studio before her memories faded. The interview, and Lee's edited version of the tapes, aired in the course of two nights. The women of Tutwiler looked straight into the lens, a technique that gave the viewer the odd sensation of feeling like one of the prisoners.

There were Juice and the other women at the picnic table, look-ing into the camera and explaining their need to feel like members of a family. And there were the women who longed to wear something, anything, colorful. And there were the women at mail call—the ones who gleefully waved their letters and postcards, and the ones who got nothing.

. . .

SKELETAL FIGURES LAY prostrate at his feet, the sun beat down on the bloated tummies of glassy-eyed children, and wandering among them, pointing a video camera at the dying, was the director of *Field of Dreams*. Phil Alden Robinson was here in Somalia because the United Nations had invited him here as an observer. It hadn't been the UN's idea for Robinson to bring along a video camera; that was his idea. Earlier that autumn of 1992, Robinson had notified *Nightline*'s producers of his plans and had asked if they might be interested in the material, and the word back was, "Perhaps. We'd love to see what you get." At any rate, it was only natural for Robinson to "observe" through a lens.

What his lens captured were the sunken eyes and flat expressions of the famished Somali people. What his microphone captured was the ghastly dissonance of death. "We went into a meeting center on the second day," he later recounted, "and there was this young boy on the floor making a terrible death-rattle sound in his throat. When I walked in, I heard him, but couldn't see him. My eyes hadn't adjusted yet. I saw this person obviously dying and I just wanted to flee. I couldn't bear being there. I didn't want to look at him. I made myself shoot. I kept saying to myself over—and I kept wanting to pan away. I kept saying to myself, 'No, just keep shooting. Don't turn the camera away. Just keep shooting.'

"I learned that it gave me distance; that having the camera gave me just enough distance so that I could stand to be there. That was the only way I could look at this, by having the lens between the boy and myself."

Robinson's second stop with the UN was Sarajevo. The bullets of Serb snipers cracked and popped around the building, or what was left of it, that housed the local newspaper. Editors and reporters kept working. "The newspaper editor takes me in the hallway and he kneels down. I didn't even know where we were going and all of a sudden he's kneeling and I thought I should kneel. He's pointing to where the snipers are out the window." Robinson aimed his camera out the broken window and held it there for a long time.

Robinson returned to Los Angeles and sent word to Tom Bettag of what he had on tape. Bettag seized on it. His idea was to have a producer "debrief" Robinson on camera and then to overlay the interview with the video. But when senior producers Scott Willis and Mark Nelson phoned up Robinson to talk about *Nightline*'s proposal, he responded, "I could be more articulate if you would let me write something as opposed to responding to questions. Why don't you let me make a little movie? This is what I do . . . I'll make a little film." After a quick chat with Bettag, Willis told Robinson, "All right, give it a shot." Robinson hadn't expected to convince the producers so easily. The *Nightline* people, he'd say later, "were very open to the idea, which I was happily surprised by."

Within a few weeks, Koppel turned his entire program over to Robinson's journal of Somalia. The lens of the small camera held the viewer uncomfortably close to the dying. There wasn't the psychological distance that most news reports, narrated by professional reporters, allow. The viewer was made to stand there over the dying little boy. The camera held still on his eyes. There was no reprieve from the scene, until the boy's eyes rolled back.

A few weeks later, *Nightline* devoted a half-hour to Robinson's Bosnia tapes. Robinson edited the material so that the pace of the final package was much slower, conveying more tension, than most evening-news pieces. The scene with the editor and the sniper, as Robinson described it, "is one long take of walking in the hall and kneeling and then discovering that broken-up, shot-up part of a building, and then he points out the window. 'That's where the snipers are.' I just sit on it, because if you make a cut, somehow, subliminally the audience knows we're editing the experience for them. I would like them to feel like they are there."

Robinson ended the Bosnia documentary on a poignant note: a Sarajevo theater group performing the musical *Hair*. The final shot faded out as the audience clapped and sang along: *"Let the sun shine, let the sun shine in."*

Robinson would offer his amalgam of artistry and journalism to *Nightline* again when he recorded a day in the life of Los Angeles's new police chief, Willie Williams. And he would take a Hi8 back to Sarajevo once more, where he found a woman, a poet, who had spent her life there. She gazed wearily into the lens as if the audience were a long lost friend who hadn't seen what had happened to her beloved city. Her name was Farida Deracovic. She led the viewer, by way of Robinson's lens, on a grim tour. She'd written a fairy tale once; now she and Robinson stood in the shell of a theater where her fairy tale had been performed.

DERACOVIC: This was a sport and cultural complex . . . I was the main organizer for cultural programs. This was a grand dancing hall. It was beautiful, once upon a time, you know. We had concerts, mostly rock and roll, and sometimes classical.

ROBINSON: Why would they pick this target?

DERACOVIC: Because it was one of the main places where the youth of Sarajevo came, you know. It was kind of a symbol for Sarajevo youth. . . . I remember the grand premiere of my fairy tale in this theater.

The Hi8 would become a tool for peering into any number of civilization's grim pockets. It was mobile enough and unobtrusive enough to personalize Curry's Woods, a New Jersey housing project, where Koppel roamed with the author Richard Price. The project had inspired some of the settings and characters in Price's novel *Clockers,* about inner-city teenagers. The badly lit hallways, with their peeling paint and broken glass, seemed to close in around the lens. Outdoors, the camera was still trapped in concrete; there was no horizon to give perspective or to suggest the promise of escape.

The central character upon whom Koppel and Price focused their attention was a fourteen-year-old boy named Hassan, who hid in his room, tinkering with appliances, to stay out of trouble. Hassan was still considered a good boy by his teacher. His mother, single and raising four children, told Koppel that she would kill anyone who tried to turn her children on to drugs. But Koppel and Price spent most of their time interviewing the male role models available to a boy like Hassan. The camera pulled in close to these men, from a concerned housing cop to a charismatic part-time drug dealer, as they interacted with the young boys of the project. No one who passed by the lens seemed to care about a video camera aimed at them; they all seemed jaded, too worn down for affectation. A young boy approached a part-time drug dealer, Frankie McCord.

BOY: Frankie, you saw my father?

FRANKIE: Not today. Yesterday.

Virtually all of the boys of the project seemed to be searching for a father, or a father figure. The housing cop, who had started an activity center to keep the boys out of trouble, told Koppel that he would be lucky to sway 25 percent of the boys to stay on the right side of the law. People like Frankie, a charismatic "hustler's hustler" in Price's words, offered a more complicated alternative.

KOPPEL: Most of those kids playing ball behind us over there. What do you think is going to happen to them?

FRANKIE: If you come out here in another five years from now, those same little kids playing ball will be on the other side, selling drugs.

KOPPEL: Because of guys like you?

FRANKIE: Yeah, yeah.

KOPPEL: Do you have the decency to be ashamed of that?

FRANKIE: Sure. Sure.

KOPPEL: So why do you do it?

FRANKIE: (*shrugs*) For money.

The closer the camera got to the men of Curry's Woods, the more it revealed them. Hassan's cousin, a twenty-seven-year-old named China, who had served time for dealing drugs, looked like a scrawny teenager in his rag-tag clothes, a baseball cap worn in the requisite backward style. But when the camera sat tightly, for minutes, on his face, his expression was resigned, old; the corners of his mouth were pulled down. He knew that his fate should be a cautionary tale for Hassan.

PRICE: Do you have any advice for him other than stay in school, having been—growing up in the same place he has?

CHINA: Don't be a follower. (*fights off tears*) Be a leader. Just do something that's positive. Stay—stay away from the knuckleheads. (*starts to weep*)

China didn't sob. But the lens was so close that his effort to quickly flick away a tear and his attempts to stop his chin from trembling were magnified.

Producers Peter Demchuk and Rick Wilkinson were screening these scenes in an editing room when it occurred to them to flip a switch that took the color away. It looked right. Black-and-white was truer to the colorless world of Curry's Woods, so that was how the documentary, *Hassan's Choices,* was broadcast. It also had black bands at the top and bottom of the screen, to give it a "letterbox" effect, as if the viewer were spying through a keyhole.

The intimacy and immediacy of Hi8 would inspire its use, more and more, on *Nightline.* The point, Tom Bettag told his staff, was that if a perspective was compelling, *Nightline* would use it. The possibilities, he said, were "limitless."

THE WAY HI8 coverage evolved on *Nightline* was typical of how the show in general was evolving under Tom Bettag. He could recognize the potential in the experiments that had predated him, and was more than happy to incorporate those innovations into the show's repertoire. A good idea, as far as Bettag was concerned, could come from anywhere. The point was to keep breathing life into *Nightline* by diversifying the format in as many ways as possible.

Bettag's style was unusual for an executive producer. He was diffident and unassuming. He liked to listen to ideas. He'd listen to anyone—a senior producer or an intern. One intern, a college student from Stanford, pitched a story idea about a friend trying to make it in professional tennis, and within a week Bettag had her set up with a production team to put together an entire documentary-style broadcast about the tennis player.

Producer Bryan Myers liked to describe Bettag's approach as "mellow. It allowed us to do our jobs." Peter Demchuk noticed that Bettag "had a way of quietly listening, of wanting to hear what you were thinking, that was so exciting. And he sent the message that the show didn't have to cling to the old format anymore. It didn't have to depend on Ted sitting in the studio conducting live interviews. There was this feeling that the show could do anything, that it could be about anything. And that feeling, for a producer, was like looking at blue sky."

The anchor saw "blue sky" too. He'd been looking to shake up the show, to get away from the traditional format, when Bettag came on board. Koppel had been anxious, for example, to find a way to revive all of the techniques that he and Dorrance Smith had developed to produce the 1989 documentary on Tiananmen Square. He knew that the video-on-the-right, information-on-the-left system of collating story and picture could be applied to any event. So when Bettag first assumed the helm and mentioned that he'd been a big fan, in particular, of the Tiananmen documentary, Koppel renewed his commitment to finding another event, or crisis, that would serve the format.

ON THE SECOND DAY of May 1992, Koppel and a camera crew stood in a lot strewn with charred cars near the intersection of Florence and Normandy, in South Central Los Angeles. Koppel's guides to the area were two retired gang members, or "OGs" as they called themselves, which meant "Original Gangsters." Bone had belonged to the Athens Park Bloods, and Li'l Monster to the 8-Trey Gangster Crips. They pointed out the corner where so much of the rioting had erupted two days earlier, after four policemen were acquitted in the beating of black motorist Rodney King. News reports showed that men and women of all races had joined in the looting, if not the arson and the beatings that had left fifty-one dead. Now, Li'l Monster told Koppel that none of the gangs had had an organized plan to riot, but . . .

LI'L MONSTER: . . . a hundred police converged upon us on this corner right here and tried to manhandle our homeboys, you know. They had sisters in headlocks; and . . . we weren't going for it. We weren't going out like Rodney King. So when we pushed them up out of here . . . what they left was a bunch of brothers and sisters out here in the street highly upset.

KOPPEL: And what did that have to do with that trucker?

LI'L MONSTER: The trucker was not black. That's what he had to do with it.

KOPPEL: That's all he had to do, was not be black?

LI'L MONSTER: That was—that was his claim to fame, he was not black.

Koppel moved with the OGs to a park controlled by Bone's old gang. Their conversation stopped when several cars approached the lot and slowed down. The camera panned to the street.

LI'L MONSTER: It's a funeral procession.

BONE: And those are Crips right there.

KOPPEL: Those two cars?

BONE: Now, Ted, you're in jeopardy right now. You don't even know it. One of them cars can easily pull up and say, "Oh, there go the park boys right there," and they could come right here with an AK-47 and you are in jeopardy right now, you are in jeopardy.

The camera zoomed in on the young men in the cars. They dropped their hands out of the windows and made signals.

LI'L MONSTER: And you can see a person right there throwing up signs.

BONE: You see him throwing up signs? You see them throwing up signs at us?

KOPPEL: Yeah, I see it.

LI'L MONSTER: That's why we don't want our kids playing out here.

The cars finally picked up speed and moved on.

The next day, on a flight back to Washington, Koppel thought about the silent interplay between the gang members, and about Li'l Monster's version of what had happened in the first few minutes of the riots. He wondered how the residents of South Central had communicated with police during the first hours of bloodshed, and how city officials had communicated with one another. Who gave orders? Who didn't? It had required the National Guard, after all, to quell the violence. When did officials realize that a catastrophe was unfolding in South Central? And why hadn't they been able to stop it?

Koppel realized he had his next Tiananmen. *Nightline* would reconstruct what had happened in Los Angeles on April 29, hour by hour, perhaps minute by minute. A day later, producers Jay Weiss and Gordon Platt were on their way to Los Angeles with Tara Sonenshine. Koppel's instructions were simple: "Find out what happened, from the perspectives of residents, store owners, police, the mayor's office. Get every detail. And cull through every tape that was shot on the day and night of the riots. There's probably stuff there just like there was in

China, material that no one has ever bothered to screen carefully." Koppel also advised Weiss and Platt to look for still photos that might shed a different light on events.

Platt checked out the bylines of newspaper pictures. He tracked down a freelance photographer named Bart Bartholomew, who had been standing not far from Florence and Normandy after the acquittals were announced on television and radio. Bartholomew showed Platt a fascinating series of still photographs as residents of South Central gathered in the street, in shock over the news. The stills, when scanned in sequence, showed the expressions dissolve from shock to anger. Bartholomew told Platt that the crowd had turned on him and grabbed his camera, and that there'd been a frightening moment when he scrambled to get in his car and get away.

Back at ABC's Los Angeles bureau, one of *Nightline*'s production associates, Kathy Kennedy, spent the better part of four days and nights screening everything that had been shot between April 29 and May 1. She came upon a home video that ABC had obtained from a South Central resident. It showed a photographer surrounded by some angry men and women, and the photographer pulling back from a swarm as an arm threw a punch at him. Another arm reached for his camera, until he dashed to a car and disappeared. When Kennedy showed it to Weiss and Platt, they recognized the photographer. It was Bartholomew. The video showed that as he pulled away, part of the crowd engulfed some police officers who'd arrived on the scene. The camera had recorded the moment as the police, overwhelmed and outnumbered, began running to their cars and completely retreated from the scene.

Producers intercut the stills and the video to create a portrait of the early minutes of the unfolding riot. There were the photos of the shocked expressions after the announcement of the acquittals, and the video of the cops in retreat. The montage dramatized the facts unearthed by *Nightline*'s investigative unit: L.A. officials were entirely unprepared for this contingency. In the minutes and hours of escalating violence, there was virtually no communication between the mayor's office and the police department. The investigative producers had in fact learned that in the hours just after the verdict, police chief Daryl Gates had attended a fund-raiser in a suburb and no one had been able to reach him.

The completed documentary, *Anatomy of a Riot,* aired less than a month after the riots. It presented a chronology of the minutes and hours after the acquittals of the police officers. Taken as a whole, the chronology portrayed total paralysis at the levels where quick decisions might have quelled the violence. Gates would later tell Koppel on the air that the show was a hit piece, but he did not refute the breakdown in communication. In fact, six months after the broadcast, a commission chaired by Warren Christopher would issue a report that confirmed the conclusions drawn by the documentary.

Anatomy of a Riot worked so well it became a prototype. It would become standard procedure, at the end of a crisis, for a team of producers to start culling details and pictures. When it wasn't Koppel narrating the story, it was often Chris Bury, who had a natural talent for reconstructing all the critical events of a crisis, sometimes within a few days of its conclusion.

Every "anatomy" would have a few key revelations, some editorial, some visual. And sometimes, as in the case of a rebellion against Boris Yeltsin, the biggest surprise would be one of perspective.

IN OCTOBER OF 1993, the Russian White House was a charred shell. When four *Nightline* producers flew into Moscow, they were given three weeks to review every tape of the failed revolution against Boris Yeltsin and to cull the critical scenes into *Anatomy of a Revolution*. The violent storming of the government television stations by allies of the rebel parliamentary leaders, and the shelling of the parliament building by troops loyal to Yeltsin, were scenes that had already made it onto American newscasts. But producer Lisa Koenig unearthed a gold mine of material not seen by most U.S. viewers. It was shot by a French camera crew from inside the Russian White House while Yeltsin's troops bombarded the building with shells. Rebel leader Alexander Rutskoi could be seen crouched under a window, shouting desperately into a phone at the chief justice of the constitutional court. Rutskoi had hoped the judge would save the lives and the cause of the rebels.

RUTSKOI: *(translation)* I'm begging you! You're a believer! Fuck you! The sin be on you!

Across the room, sitting on the floor motionless, his back against a wall, was Rutskoi's comrade, the parliamentary leader Ruslan Khasbulatov. His face was ashen, gaunt. His eyes looked glazed. He appeared catatonic.

The *Nightline* producers had a wealth of footage to build *Anatomy of a Revolution*. What they didn't have was much time or editing space. ABC's Moscow bureau was so small its closets were converted into editing rooms for the project. Producer Leroy Sievers would later remember how he and his editor, Eric Wray, didn't see a hotel room for days leading up to airtime. They found a cot and set it up next to their editing equipment. "We took turns taking naps on the cot," Sievers recalled. "We were racing against such a tight deadline that in the last several days before air, we didn't have time for more than fifteen-minute naps—just enough to keep us going. You know, when you lie down for fifteen minutes, you're afraid you're going to wake up and it'll be eight hours later. So you don't really sleep. You sort of lie down, but you're really tense."

The tensions attendant to production could never compare, of course, to the horror and occasional danger of field assignments, but Sievers and his colleagues knew all about war zones and disasters, and knowing the difference *still* didn't make marathons in closets-cum-editing rooms any fun. The only process more punishing, Sievers would tell a colleague, was another form of storytelling introduced by Bettag, an innovation requiring that all production, from first shoot to final edit to broadcast, be compressed into a single day.

The format was called *Day in the Life*. Koppel and Bettag had actually borrowed the idea from the CBS program *48 Hours*. Koppel always liked the concept, which was to use that specific amount of time as the limits that defined a story. A team of producers and camera crews would descend on some location and cover it from every angle for forty-eight hours. All of the different perspectives would eventually be threaded into a single unfolding diary. The actual *48 Hours* program eventually loosened up its time constraints, but Koppel and Bettag decided to try to adopt the original idea, or, to put it in Koppel's words, "We shamelessly stole it. We'll take a good idea where we can find it." Bettag actually tightened the time frame to one day, from first shoot to airtime.

Producer Kathryn Kross and correspondent Jackie Judd tried out the format first, to cover a day in the life of an anti-abortion protest.

The twelve-hour constraint pushed the story along. The pace demanded the viewer's attention.

Then Bettag applied the format to the 1992 New York presidential primary. Koppel and a team of camera crews followed a day on the campaign trail with candidates Bill Clinton and former California governor Jerry Brown. Brown's morning began with a heckler at a Jewish social services center. Clinton's afternoon wound down with a member of a newspaper editorial board referring to him as "Slick Willie." Neither event, in isolation, would have generated much national attention, but when the scenes were laid end-to-end in a chronicle of the day, they contributed to a larger portrait of humiliation, frustration, and exhaustion. Koppel opened the broadcast by asking, "Why would any rational human being subject himself to this level of punishment?" Koppel could have been asking the same question about his staff. To present the chronology of that one campaign day in New York required a grueling military-style dawn-to-midnight operation. Editors and producers worked in relays as videotapes came into a central editing location from cameras assigned to each candidate. Peter Demchuk would later marvel at what the format required in particular from the editors, but Bettag never doubted that they were up to it. He thought *Nightline* had the best videotape editors in the business. In fact, as soon as *One Day in New York* was off the air, Bettag was already thinking of other sorts of stories that would come alive in a tight dawn-to-dusk chronicle.

The key, Bettag decided, was to get unusual access. One factor in the success of the New York primary show was that Bryan Meyers had placed a wireless microphone on Clinton. When a rally fell flat, Clinton, forgetting he was miked, exploded and chewed out an aide. The greater the behind-the-scenes access, the more even a seemingly mundane moment might convey something profound. So *A Day in the Life of Wall Street* caught the cafeteria worker at Salomon Brothers gauging how the economy was doing by what the customers were eating; *A Day at Camden Yards* showed the hot-dog vendor trying to make a few more dollars before the advent of a baseball strike.

Sometimes the struggle for access was part of the story. *A Day in the Life* of Oliver North's campaign for the U.S. Senate opened with North trying to avoid Koppel and the *Nightline* cameras altogether by ducking out of an early-morning rally through the back door. The evasion did not work. Senator Edward Kennedy, on the other hand, brought Koppel right into his van one dawn as he set out for a Boston suburb, hustling for votes. When Hillary Clinton joined Kennedy and his wife at a day-care center, the three led the children in a round of "Itsy Bitsy Spider." It may have been the position of the microphone, but Kennedy seemed to be singing louder than anyone, as if knowing nursery school songs were a prerequisite of political leadership. The scene begged a question that Koppel would find himself asking a lot after spending a day with one politician or another: "Is high office worth this to you?" Kennedy's answer was long, but it came down to "Yes."

Kathryn Kross produced several of these one-day marathons; she considered them to be the most grueling of all her assignments. But the one she would remember best was *A Day in the Life of Tampa General*. Bettag had timed it to coincide with the debate over the Clinton health-care plan, as a window into the problems of tackling the costs of medical care. Kross knew that the premise was terrific. What she wasn't sure about, on the morning of this particular project, was her anchor. At dawn Koppel trudged into the hospital looking very much as though he should be admitted as a patient.

"What's wrong with you, Ted? You look awful."

"Thank you. I think I have the flu."

"Will you make it to airtime?"

"If I don't, I'm in the right place."

Koppel actually did make it to airtime, with one of the best broadcasts of the one-day genre. It began with the sun barely breaking the Florida horizon and a sixty-eight-year-old man arriving for surgery on a blocked artery. A hospital administrator explained that the man's surgery was covered by Medicare. Another patient, a sixteen-year-old boy, sat in bed, waiting for an operation to remove a cyst from his brain. His mother told Koppel that she was uncertain whether either of the family's two insurance companies would pay. It was barely eight in the morning when the cameras caught a helicopter landing next to the emergency room. It ferried the victim of a car accident. Just hours later, one of the doctors tallied up the cost of the victim's care so far:

DOCTOR: She's had a CAT scan of her head and abdomen and several plain X rays and lab tests. She probably already has a—somewhere in the neighborhood of a $25,000 hos-

pital bill. She doesn't even appear to be injured severely. . . . But this is what is the standard of care—

KOPPEL: Who's going to pay for that $25,000? I mean, you don't
              know if she's insured, right?

DOCTOR: That's right. In other words, it doesn't really matter if
              they're insured or not.

The broadcast was not a good omen for anyone with dreams of
tackling the American health-care system. But it was great television.

KOPPEL AND BETTAG had always known that one day there
would be a tragedy whose scale would overwhelm the capability of a
camera to convey it. And they knew that when it came, a polished,
dispassionate format wouldn't work. The personnel behind the scenes
would have to step in front of the camera and serve as eyewitnesses. In
fact, years before Bettag came to *Nightline,* Koppel had established a
policy of using behind-the-scenes personnel as reporters whenever the
need arose. In 1988, after a massive earthquake in Armenia left tens of
thousands dead, rescue workers were still struggling to free survivors
when a *Nightline* producer reached the epicenter with a satellite dish.
Koppel was told he'd have to wait a day for an ABC correspondent to
make it to the site for a live interview, but Koppel didn't want to wait.
He put the producer on-camera and told her to report. It was six
months later, during the crisis in Beijing, that Koppel expanded on the
innovation, commissioning first-person stories not only from his producer, but from all of the off-camera personnel stationed there. The
lesson of the Beijing reports, for Koppel, was that all of those eyewitness accounts brought texture to a story and that the very entourages
whose size he so often lamented presented a big advantage over print,
and television seldom capitalized upon it.

Koppel found a kindred spirit on this issue in Bettag, who loved
almost any innovation that humanized a place. Using behind-the-scenes
personnel as reporters created an intimacy, immediacy, and informality
that suited *Nightline.* Bettag had agreed with Koppel that one day their
colleagues in the field, working behind the scenes of a tragedy, would
convey the scope of it in dimensions that pictures could not.

The day came with the Rwandan civil war.

• • •

THE DYING REFUGEES of Rwanda were in some circle of hell that no one had ever seen before. *Nightline* made it the burden of its own personnel—cameraman, sound engineer, producer, and correspondent—to abandon professional detachment; to speak for the dying, and for the dead. The witnesses stood one after another before a camera. Each voice was distinct. The same horror was conveyed in their haunted eyes.

FLETCHER JOHNSON (*camera*):   You are of two minds. You've got to be able to make the picture, and in effect, you are in a position to use these people to make a point. But they are also in need, they are in desperate need, and I found myself unable to take a picture without—without doing something for them, and Trevor and I had a lot of water and crackers for a lot of those folks. . . .

We shot a couple of kids who were wandering aimlessly . . . the thought that goes through my head is my son, and the idea of him possibly being out here in the same situation is—is just staggering.

TREVOR BARKER (*sound*):   . . . the babies crying, it's just—it's so ear-piercing . . . you feel so hopeless.

LEROY SIEVERS (*producer*):   . . . I think the worst part of it, when we feel that we're intruding, is literally, you can take pictures of people and you realize that they're dying. I mean, that's the last thing they're going to see is us and our cameras, and that's the ultimate intrusion.

JIM WOOTEN (*correspondent*):   . . . What happens here is that this story is so overwhelming that it breaks through almost immediately whatever defense mechanisms you have learned to apply over the years, whether it's a mode of detachment, of a cynicism, or some sort of artificial steely hardness. It breaks through almost immediately.

I'll tell you a small story. We got off the plane last Friday, here at the Goma airport. We unloaded supplies, which took about ten minutes. We walked around and found places to put our tents, which took about another ten minutes. And I turned around and saw a woman putting the body of her little girl down on the side of the road, fifteen feet away from me. I had been here twenty minutes, and the story had already broken through whatever defense mechanisms I had built up. . . .

KOPPEL: You don't need to answer this, Jim, if you don't want to, but what do you dream?

WOOTEN: Well, frankly, I—I see my children and grandchildren here, and as I said to someone the other night who was getting out of here, I said, "You better be careful and not squeeze your kids or your grandkids too hard when you get home."

EIGHTEEN
Page Two

O NE APRIL NIGHT in 1995, a few hours after the House
of Representatives, led by Speaker Newt Gingrich, passed a
tax cut bill, Koppel introduced *Nightline* on a distinctly personal note:

> I think I like this bill a lot. You understand, of course, that
> I speak as a wealthy network anchorman whose wife has
> been handling the family taxes since we got married thirty-
> two years ago. But, if I understand this thing correctly, the
> cut in the capital-gains tax is going to put a nice chunk of
> extra change in my pocket. Actually, it looks as though it's
> going to put a nice chunk of change in almost everyone's
> pocket, except the poor. I don't see them making a whole
> lot of money out of this, but then, why should someone
> be getting a tax credit anyway if he's not paying any taxes
> to begin with? . . . I know it sounds as though the rich and
> the middle class are benefiting at the expense of the poor,
> but I must have it wrong, so let's see if we can straighten
> it all out.

Viewers who phoned in to ask why in the world he was bragging
about his income apparently didn't appreciate the sarcasm. But they
couldn't deny that Koppel had gotten their attention.

That, above all, was the mark of a good introduction. Koppel's introduction had evolved over the years into a distinctive segment of the broadcast. It provided context, it set a tone, and it conveyed an attitude—Koppel's. Fact, for a moment, was superseded by impression. The words were his own. The aim, above all, was to entice.

At *Nightline,* the introduction is called Page Two. The term comes from the way the broadcast is organized. Every element—whether a live segment or a taped story—is given a number corresponding to where it will occur in the show. The assigned number becomes the page number for that element in the script package that goes to the control room. Invariably, Page One is the minute-long opening, with the familiar stars and space animation. Page Two is always Koppel's introduction.

In the early days of the show, Koppel's introductions were laconic, dispassionate, and conventional. For example, the show that aired on June 2, 1980, began with Koppel saying:

> Our subject tonight is taxes, actually, the income tax levied
> by the state of California, because tomorrow, as part of
> their state primary, the voters of California will decide
> whether they want to cut their taxes by fifty percent.

"When *Nightline* began," Koppel recalled, "my training as a journalist did not naturally lead to what we would later think of as Page Two. As a journalist you're taught to start with the most important aspect of the story, and get the who, what, where, when, why, and how into the first couple of paragraphs. You're taught to save the extraneous material for later."

Then somewhere in *Nightline*'s second or third year, about the time when, according to Koppel, "I sensed the show was really *mine,* that I wasn't simply interchangeable with other anchors," he began writing longer, more interpretive introductions. On June 28, 1983, for instance, Koppel introduced a show on the furor over allegations that a briefing book intended for use by Jimmy Carter during a debate with Ronald Reagan, his Republican challenger, had been stolen.

> The wolves are howling again. Just the tiniest trickle of
> blood on the ground and the pack is in full throat, and
> once again their quarry is the President of the United

States. Or so it must seem. After all, what's at stake here? Preparations for a debate in a campaign that ended more than two and a half years ago. And if someone in candidate Reagan's camp was guilty of some slightly unethical behavior, did that make any difference in the outcome of the election? Probably not.

When Rick Kaplan came to the program in 1984 as executive producer, he encouraged Koppel to write even more personal, lively, even surprising Page Twos. Kaplan's research had shown that most viewers decided whether or not to stay with the program within the first two minutes. So he hired special producers to create well-edited, dramatic video packages for the show's opening announcement, and he pushed Koppel to think of innovative introductions. The idea was to convey to the viewer as quickly as possible that "this is *not* the evening news," said Kaplan.

August 30, 1984
Subject: Science and the Beginning of the Universe

Prepare to limber up your mind, to bend it in directions it has possibly never known before. We're going on a journey through time and space that reduces the entire span of human history to a heartbeat.

October 31, 1986
Subject: Homosexuality: The Vatican Condemnation

We have probably dealt with more controversial subjects than the one that we're approaching tonight, but I don't remember when. We're going to be talking about values and morality, and whether something abnormal is necessarily immoral. Of course, we're not just talking about abnormality in general, we're discussing homosexuality in particular.

Gradually, Koppel began using Page Two as inveiglement—an intellectual appetizer. He started to craft more and more unconventional preambles.

June 10, 1987
Subject: The Teamsters Union

There is the case of the man struggling to identify the cause of three crippling hangovers. On the first night, he had drunk himself into a stupor with brandy and soda; on the second night, the drink was scotch and soda; and finally, he succumbed to bourbon and soda. Finding soda to be the only constant element in his drinking, he identified that as the source of his misery and became, thereby, the perfect example of imperfect logic.

We can, and over the next few minutes will, be pointing out the unfortunate regularity with which presidents of the International Teamsters Union end up in jail. Whether that, however, justifies the logical conclusion that the entire 1.7 million-member union is under the influence of organized crime is something that has yet to be proved in court. The Justice Department, the FBI, and the Labor Department have apparently decided, however, that it's worth trying, and they are preparing a massive lawsuit aimed at forcing the Teamsters' twenty-one-member executive board out of office.

"Page Twos have evolved to the point that now," said Koppel, "when news breaks, they almost always begin with extraneous information, something that may have the viewer asking, 'Whoa, where's he going?' "

April 1, 1994
Subject: Life with a Top NCAA Basketball Team, the Arkansas Razorbacks

Doris Day was a very popular singer, of course, but she also specialized in the Hollywood role of a beautiful young woman who wouldn't fool around before marriage. The late piano virtuoso and humorist Oscar Levant reduced all of that to a savage one-liner: "I knew Doris Day," he said, "before she was a virgin."

The line comes to mind because the NCAA, which lost its virginity a long time ago, keeps pretending that it isn't so. It maintains a rigid 1950s Hollywood-style appearance of virtue, and God help any player who accepts as much as a hamburger from a fan.

Everyone else, meanwhile, is chasing the almighty buck, and if yours is not one of the sixty-four teams which makes it into the NCAA tournament, you're out of the money and out of luck. Schools lose alumni contributions, coaches get fired, and the behind-the-scenes frenzy of wheeling and dealing for players becomes more unseemly than ever.

Page Two is where Koppel puts his signature on the program. It can be very personal, an offering up of some autobiographical detail:

May 30, 1986
Subject: Baldness

Somehow I don't think that we're going to make it through an entire program on this subject without my addressing a question that seems to have preoccupied quite a few of you since *Nightline* began more than six years ago.

No, I'm not. And yes, it is. That is, I'm not bald, and yes, for what it's worth, that is my own hair up there.

June 18, 1992
Subject: Poetry in America

When I was a child growing up in England, parents—not just mine, but almost all parents—placed enormous stock in the health-giving power of cod-liver oil. Despite the fact that I was repeatedly told how good it was for me, I learned to loathe cod-liver oil.

Unfortunately, some parents and many teachers dispense poetry the same way. We would like, if humanly possible, to undo some of that damage tonight. Indeed, perhaps a warning is in order. Poetry has the power to arouse and inflame, to evoke the most private of emotions. It can be polemical or funny, it can rhyme, but it doesn't have to, and there is some danger that you may enjoy it.

Most nights, Koppel's personal imprint is an attitude. A contrarian streak, for example, runs through hundreds of introductions. This was how he led into a taped story about his visit with gang members in Los Angeles the weekend after the 1992 riots there:

May 4, 1992
Subject: Gangs in Los Angeles

On Saturday, I spent most of the afternoon with a bunch of murderers, drug dealers, robbers, and probably the architects of quite a few crimes I've never even thought of. And I'm only slightly embarrassed to say that I liked them very much and was extremely impressed with a great deal of what they had to say, and the passion with which they said it.

The editorial comment surprised many, and offended a few. It unquestionably piqued interest. Some of his colleagues, and more than a few viewers, thought Koppel had gone over the line.

No one's interest—or ire—was more piqued by Koppel's introduction to Oliver North than Oliver North. He happened to be sitting not five feet from Koppel at the time. Producers who were there say the color drained from North's face as he listened.

January 28, 1994
Subject: Oliver North

Perhaps the most beloved figure in American popular culture, from Huck Finn to Rhett Butler, is the charming rogue. Fifty years ago, Clark Gable and Errol Flynn built entire careers on their portrayals of the charming rogue. These days we have Mel Gibson and Harrison Ford, and David Letterman and Ollie North. Oh, yes, the appeal of the gap-toothed grin is not limited to the world of entertainment. But there has to be something of the rebel present, the ability to flip an authority figure the bird with such a disarming air of innocence that no offense is taken. "Sincerity," George Burns once noted, "is the secret of success. If you can fake that, you've got it made."

Ollie North, who just yesterday announced his candidacy for the U.S. Senate from his home state of Virginia, is such a charming rogue that he may well be elected before constituents even stop to consider what are the qualifications he has for the job. That is not as dismissive a statement as it may seem. Mr. North is smart, tough, and extremely hardworking. He is also—and he'll have an opportunity to respond to all of this later in the program—he is also an accomplished liar, and a shameless self-promoter.

When Koppel said the words *accomplished liar,* North blanched. "He almost did a double-take," according to a producer in the control room. North never complained about the epithet on the air or afterward to Koppel, but a few weeks later, he stood before fifteen thousand Virginia Republican delegates and pledged, "Clinton, Congress, Koppel, and above all, Chuck [Robb]—we'll beat 'em all like a dozen eggs!"

There is something about media-savvy rogues that inspires notably pithy Page Twos.

February 22, 1988
Subject: Televangelist Jimmy Swaggart Confesses

You have to have seen Jimmy Swaggart work his congregation, this linebacker of a preacher sacking Satan to the ecstatic approval of all those decent, open-looking churchgoing people. Sometimes the voice no more than a husky whisper, going all the way up the scale to roaring denunciation. He makes them laugh; he makes them cry; he makes them fear for their very souls. Striding back and forth across the altar, the Bible opened and closed so many thousands of times that it just lies there, form-fitted on the palm of his hand, drooping over either side. A Jimmy Swaggart sermon grabs and holds with an hypnotic fascination, and that's just on an average Sunday. Yesterday, Swaggart was fighting for his very survival. And whether you count yourself among his friends or most cynical critics, take a look at someone who is a master of communication.

November 15, 1991
Subject: Who Is the Real David Duke?

Take it from someone who has spent most of his adult life working in this medium, television and David Duke were made for one another. He has the looks, as the current edition of *Newsweek* puts it, "of an affable game-show host." Countless newspaper and magazine profiles have pointed out that there was a little cosmetic surgery along the way. Quite a few people in public life had similar assistance; the rest of us might well benefit from it.

The only professionals who fall prey to Page Two more often than the media-savvy are the media elite. Koppel lambastes his profession a lot, but not without confessing membership.

September 16, 1992
Subject: The Media

Good evening. It's long been a suspicion of mine that many of us who choose journalism as a career do so because it allows us to remain adolescents past the age of forty. Our work is endlessly interesting, because we move constantly from story to story, we are rarely held to account for the consequences of our reporting, we are free to hold others to much higher standards than we are inclined or able to meet ourselves and, in exchange for all of this, especially those of us in television journalism, our egos are regularly massaged while we are paid more than we're worth.

December 10, 1993
Subject: The Media

It is probably a good thing that you will rarely, if ever, find large mirrors hanging from the walls of a newsroom. I'm not altogether sure that I would like to catch a glimpse of myself when word of some disaster reaches us. The sudden pumping of adrenaline that goes with the arrival of a big story may be a useful part of journalism, but it's not terribly attractive.

You've heard the expression "one man's meat is another man's poison." Unfortunately, in our line of work, everybody else's poison tends to be our meat. Because the consequences of violence and crime are so often graphic and more or less self-explanatory, they provide easy, and therefore frequent, targets for television news. I fear that if several of you showed up in my driveway to gauge my reaction to the slaughter of my wife on a commuter train or the rape of my daughter in some alley, I might lose some of my enthusiasm for the First Amendment, but those are the kinds of issues that we are here to talk about tonight.

Does Koppel find it gratifying to write Page Two? Sometimes. Any night, for example, when he has the chance to skewer both politicians *and* journalists, and for good measure the Washington establishment, the weapon of choice is gleeful sarcasm.

December 15, 1987
Subject: Gary Hart Reenters the Race for President

So there we were last night, a bunch of Washington media people and a number of prominent politicians, attending a special screening of a new movie, *Broadcast News*. Before the movie began, someone in our row turned around and asked Colorado congresswoman Pat Schroeder, who herself had toyed with the idea of running for President, what her friend Gary Hart was doing. That quickly evolved into speculation about whether Hart might yet return to the presidential sweepstakes. And there was general agreement, among this small group of plugged-in, worldly wise politicians, lawyers, and newspeople, that if there was one thing Gary Hart was not dumb enough to do, it was to get back into the presidential race. That was last night. Today, Gary Hart announced that he was back in.

May 11, 1994
Subject: The Paula Jones Lawsuit

It is spring here in Washington, and hypocrisy is in full bloom. President Clinton's political enemies, who can barely contain their glee over the Paula Jones allegations, have discovered how deeply committed they are to the cause of rooting out sexual harassment. Many of the President's supporters, on the other hand, who had no trouble at all bridging the gap between allegations and conclusions when it came to Anita Hill's charges against Clarence Thomas, have now become supersensitive to the distinction. Allegations, they now appear to be saying, are inappropriate topics for discussion.

It is, as always, simply a question of whose ox is gored.

We in the media, of course, are guarding our sacred turf between the brothel-keepers and the parking lot owners. We got it, we sell it, we've still got it. Scandals make good copy, no matter who's involved. In the meanwhile, whatever the merits of Ms. Jones's allegations, the President and his defenders have to take appropriate measures and, oh yes, he has to run the executive branch of government.

For all the Page Twos that poke fun at journalists, there are those that betray a deep affection for the practice of journalism. Koppel's memories of life as a foreign correspondent have inspired a slew of introductions. He'll throw in a personal reminiscence if it can, in any way, lure the audience to a different perspective. The storytelling is a way to give historical context without putting viewers to sleep.

October 18, 1985
Subject: The Philippines

A personal observation. Back in 1969, I was covering events in Southeast Asia for ABC News. The main story in those days, of course, was Vietnam, but there was another bubbling crisis in the region that our producers felt needed coverage, and I was dispatched to do a lengthy report on *The Philippines: A Presidency in Crisis.* Sixteen years ago, as now, the presidency was that of Ferdinand Marcos. It's worth recalling, if only to make the point that President Marcos is no stranger to controversy, and that he is one of the world's truly great survivors.

June 14, 1989
Subject: China after Tiananmen Square

I've been covering China for more than twenty years. Back in 1969, when I was based in Hong Kong, my cameraman and I would drive up to the new territories, to a hilltop as close to the Chinese border as we could get. He would erect a large antenna, and then we would put a television set on a board inside the trunk of his car, where it was relatively dark. At the other end of the board, extending out the back of the trunk, he would place his camera, facing the television set. And then he would film the output of Can-

ton TV, grainy, black-and-white, but the only window
into China that we had in those days.

Connecting a far-off place to Koppel's personal experience can
help the viewer to relate. When Koppel wrote a powerful introduction about his colleagues in Rwanda, about how overwhelmed they
were by the catastrophic disease and death that enveloped them, he
was, in part, expressing appreciation for their work. But he was also
attempting to transport the viewer to the scene and, by elaborating on
the expertise of the witnesses, to convey the monstrous scale of the
tragedy.

July 29, 1994
Subject: Rwanda

Let me tell you something about my colleagues here at
Nightline and ABC News, the reporters and the producers
and the technicians. Most of them have either worked here
for quite a while, or they were veterans by the time they
got here. They have witnessed—most of them, that is—a
lot of bad things over the years. That, after all, constitutes
much of what we do, drawing up this daily catalog of the
worst things that happen to people. Still, I have rarely seen,
in fact I have never seen, my colleagues quite as shaken
as on their current assignment covering the Rwandan
refugees in Zaire, and that is what most of this program will
be about, a debriefing of our cameraman and soundman,
producers and correspondent. How do you live and work,
eat and drink and sleep, when people are starving and dying
of thirst and disease all around you?

The references to his colleagues are almost always appreciated by
them. Almost always. One exception was an introduction to a program about working mothers. On that night Koppel managed, without even mentioning a single name, to incite pretty much the entire
female staff of *Nightline*.

March 16, 1989
Subject: The "Mommy Track"

Let's start here at home. Of the five senior-most jobs here at *Nightline*, three are held by men, two by women. Among the men, each of us is married, with children. The women are unmarried. And that pattern holds true for most of *Nightline*'s production staff. While both men and women work extraordinarily long hours—sixty- to eighty-hour weeks are not unusual—many of the men have children; only one of the women does.

The introduction launched a chorus of gasps and groans of horror and embarrassment from the women in the New York and Washington control rooms. Senior producer Besty West shouted, "Here we are, the *Nightline* women! Single! Lonely! Desperate!" Deborah Leff, the other senior producer referred to by Koppel, wanted to crawl under a console and hide. Leff, like West, had covered stories from the floods in Bangladesh to an anti-nuclear protest in New Zealand, but having viewers learn about her marital status, she remembered, "was absolutely mortifying." (The female staffer with a child was producer Diane Mendez. She would laugh, many years later, that almost a decade separated the ages of her two children. The first was born just as *Nightline* began. The second wasn't conceived until Mendez had left the show in 1990 for the saner schedule of *World News Tonight*.)

On the other hand, the day that Koppel was to anchor a program on phobias, it seemed that every producer and reporter on the staff had a phobia, or knew someone who had one, and wanted Koppel to hear about it. Koppel was "shrink for a day," lending an ear as one colleague after another unloaded some fear—or the rumor of someone else's fear. That night, Koppel threw it all into an "everything but the kitchen sink" introduction.

January 14, 1988
Subject: Phobias

One producer on our staff revealed that she has a phobia of ship propellers. Another is adamant that we address his phobia tonight, namely, the fear of flying. And yet another revealed that his mother used to suffer terribly from the most common phobia of all, agoraphobia, which refers loosely to the fear of crowded places and of leaving one's home.

The ship-propeller phobic hadn't told Koppel about her fear until after eleven P.M. Her timing almost ensured that she would be mentioned, anonymously, in the introduction. At that late hour, Koppel was only just beginning to write. Koppel almost always writes the introduction as late as possible, no earlier than a half-hour before airtime. "I usually wait until then because I have to feel that slight panic: Oh man, I haven't done Page Two yet, and it's thirty minutes to airtime!" Herb O'Connor, a producer who worked on *Nightline* for several years, used to know, when Koppel would stroll into his office around 10:50 at night for a game of Nerf basketball, that he was probably trying to think of an introduction. Koppel would quietly shoot some hoops for ten or fifteen minutes, then straggle away again. Whether he'd thought of a good lead or had simply procrastinated, O'Connor could never tell.

"When I've thought of a good introduction," Koppel has said, "I've almost always written it as fast as my fingers could hammer it out." Some nights, he has observed, Page Two writes itself. If there is a possibility that viewers will be puzzled by the selection of a certain topic, "then I always think it's a good idea to tell, in as straightforward a way as possible, how we came up with this particular idea for a show."

October 28, 1987
Subject: Cremation

A few weeks ago I was stuck at LaGuardia Airport because of a flight that was delayed by several hours. Desperate for something to read, I picked up a magazine I'd never seen before, *The National Law Journal,* and found myself reading an article on cremation litigation. That piece is what prompted this program.

LaGuardia has popped up twice in those "how-we-arrived-at-this-topic" introductions. Koppel thinks it's a coincidence.

February 24, 1994
Subject: Is Environmental Science for Sale?

A number of years ago, I ran into then-Senator Al Gore at LaGuardia Airport. We were both waiting to catch the shuttle down to Washington, had some time to kill, and so we sat down to grab a cup of coffee. Senator Gore used the occasion to sketch out on a napkin one of his chief ecological concerns, depletion of the ozone layer. Ever the environmental activist, Senator Gore was proposing a *Nightline* program on the subject.

He's the Vice-President now, of course, but he is still proposing. A few weeks ago, Mr. Gore called to draw our attention to some of the forces, political and economic, behind what he would regard as the anti-environmental movement. The Vice-President suggested that we might want to look into connections between scientists who scoff at the so-called greenhouse effect, for example, and the coal industry. There was also a connection, he said, to the Reverend Sung Myung Moon's group, and with Lyndon LaRouche's organization. I told the Vice-President that we'd do two things. We'd look into whatever his staff gave us, and that if we did anything on the story, I would explain to you how it was that we came to be doing it in the first place.

The choice of an esoteric subject merits one kind of explanation; the choice of a scandal or fad impels more of a defense. Koppel has written several variations on the theme "Some of you may think this is beneath us, but most of you are talking about this story—admit it."

July 20, 1984
Subject: Miss America Dethroned over Sex Scandal

You should know that we were not going to do this story. We know that some of you will feel that we should have trusted our initial instincts. But we have spent the better part of the day now observing a simple reality: everywhere we went, people were talking about the Vanessa Williams story, and everyone has an opinion. So we are bringing together tonight one of this country's leading feminists, a former Miss America who until today was regarded as perhaps the most outspoken and atypical of that very small sorority, a woman who is vice-chairman of Penthouse International. We have frequently on this broadcast focused on subjects that we thought were important but which we feared might bore you. We finally concluded that there is no point in avoiding a subject simply because almost every-body is interested in it.

December 1, 1983
Subject: Cabbage Patch Doll Mania

Let's be blunt about this thing. Are there more important stories today than the Cabbage Patch doll madness? You bet. Anything that more people are talking about? Possibly, but the answer to that one is not quite as clear. Those squishy dolls have become such a popular item over the last few weeks that consumers are brawling over them and store managers from Allentown, Pennsylvania, to Lawrence, Kansas, have decided to either sell the dolls by lottery or give them away to charity rather than put up with the customer violence.

Page Twos can be fun. They can be pedagogic. Some Page Twos are both.

December 7, 1988
Subject: Gorbachev and the UN

It was, coming from the leader of the Soviet Union, a truly extraordinary proposal. There he stood before the UN General Assembly, calling for complete disarmament, the destruction of all atomic and hydrogen bombs, the aboli-tion of all military bases on foreign territory, the elimina-tion—over a period of four years—of all land armies, navies, and air forces, the return of dozens of millions of men to peaceful, creative labor. It was absolutely breath-taking in its vision and daring, and it led absolutely no-where. Because that was not Mikhail Gorbachev's speech today, it was Nikita Khrushchev's address to the UN twenty-nine years ago, on September 18, 1959.

But which lesson do we infer from that historical foot-note? George Santayana's warning that those who ignore the lessons of history are condemned to relive them, or

Mark Twain's cautionary tale of the cat which sat on a hot stove and never sat on a hot stove again? Of course, it never sat on a cold stove, either.

November 21, 1986
Subject: Inside Insider Trading

I was reminded this afternoon of a famous story about one of the fabled Rothschilds, the European family of financiers. This story is famous, though it may be apocryphal. Some years back, you may recall, the British and the French collided in a decisive battle at a place called Waterloo. Knowing who won that battle before anyone else knew would give a London banker certain obvious advantages. A French victory would create one set of circumstances; a British victory, clearly, another set. Mr. Rothschild, so the story says, was the first to know the outcome because he had arranged for someone to observe the battle and then release some London-bound homing pigeons carrying news of the outcome. Insider trading? No, some very thoughtful preparation, but others could have done the same. Knowing where to draw the line in such matters is, in a sense, what this program is all about tonight.

April 24, 1992
Subject: The Big Bang Theory

Well, it does tend to put things in perspective. I mean, initially, we felt a little awkward about doing this big-bang broadcast tonight. After all, the story broke yesterday. And then, we thought, here's an event that cosmologists are still trying to pinpoint to within, give or take, five billion years, that somehow being a day late on the story doesn't seem all that critical.

Now, the most popular version of this story was authored, it's generally believed, about 3,200 years ago by Moses while he and the children of Israel were wandering around in the Sinai Desert. You've all heard it before, the first two verses of the first chapter of Genesis. "In the beginning, God created the heaven and the earth, and the earth was without form, and void, and darkness was upon the face of the deep, and the spirit of God moved upon the face of the waters."

It's a breathtaking beginning to what is, arguably, the

greatest book ever written, but it's a little short on specifics. Like a great deal of what is written in the Bible, it calls for us to accept a lot on faith. A great many devout people of all religions are offended by the very spirit of inquiry that tries to fill in with facts what so many, for so long, have accepted on faith.

Here's the latest. Cosmologists think they have found new evidence to support the big bang theory.

March 18, 1994
Subject: The Tyranny of Fashion

It is not the sort of thing you ever worry about when you're hungry or poor and homeless. Fashion is not the sort of thing that occurs to most of us until we have a little disposable time and money. Indeed, one can speculate on that first Neanderthal man who decided to wear his animal skin at a slightly more rakish angle, but we will probably never know who it was that made the first prehistoric fashion statement, or why.

Certainly, though, for as long as we've been recording the social evolution of man, fashion has been a part, if sometimes an inexplicable part, of that history. Why, for example, do so many millions of men, to this day, still wrap a piece of silk or other cloth around their necks, in a variety of slipknots, and then pull it tight? I can't think of a single logical reason why any one of us would do that, but we do. I have deliberately stressed what men do in the name of fashion, because we often act as though the obsession with fashion was strictly the province of women. It's not, of course.

The broadcast on fashion featured a closing essay as well.

There is something obscene, of course, about an industry that creates artificial needs and appetites in a world which still has so many genuinely needy people. But, in a curious way, a vibrant fashion industry tends to flourish only where freedom of expression is permitted. Sometimes, as in China, for example, you can track the growth of freedom in what people are wearing long before it's reflected in what they're saying. During the height of the repressive Cultural Revolution, for example, everyone in China wore the

Mao suit, and then only in grays and navy blue. China is still a repressive society, but less so now than during the sixties and seventies. China today is a far more colorful place than it used to be twenty or thirty years ago. Perhaps there is a relationship between the return of colors and cosmetics and a certain level of political relaxation. Now, wouldn't *that* be a nice fashion statement?

Closing thoughts are occasional, although they have become more common since Tom Bettag began running the show. Bettag's logic was simple: "Some topics simply merit a final message from the anchor." But it was Koppel alone who decided that a show about medical incompetence was going to play nicely into a personal closing message.

June 23, 1986
Subject: Medical Incompetence

And now a brief personal note. I am about to follow in the distinguished footsteps of President and Mrs. Reagan, Vice-President Bush, and tens of thousands of lesser-known citizens in that, over the years, I have apparently spent more time in the sun than was good for me. I have a small basal cell carcinoma on the lower lid of my right eye. This form of skin cancer is easily treatable, but it does require minor surgery. That means that for the next few days I'll have some stitches and a black eye. Never being one to turn down a few days off when I can get them, I'm going to do just that for the rest of this week. At least until the swelling goes down.

I tell you this for several reasons. One, to serve as an object lesson to those of you who spend too much time in the sun. Two, to urge those of you who love outdoor activities too much to give them up altogether—and I still count myself among your number—to use a sunscreen. The higher the number the better. Three, to ask those of you inclined to write get-well cards not to do so. You'll only make me feel guilty if I don't write back. And finally, to assure the very skilled surgeon who's going to be operating on me tomorrow that tonight's program on medical incompetence had nothing, absolutely nothing, to do with you.

NINETEEN
Exchanges

April 12, 1983
Subject: Election Day in Chicago
Guest: Harold Washington, mayor of Chicago

KOPPEL: One last question. You seem almost placid. I've seen you more excited almost every other day prior to now. One would think you would be almost euphoric at this point. You don't seem to be at all.

WASHINGTON: I'm extremely elated. It's very uncomfortable in this studio. I'm sitting in a chair which must have been designed by a person who loved the guillotine. It's the most awkward position I've ever been in. As a matter of fact, for subsequent interviews, I think I'll stand up. This is miserable.

June 17, 1982
Subject: Watergate Revisited
Guests: Bob Woodward, Carl Bernstein
(Pulitzer Prize winners for Watergate coverage)

KOPPEL: Was either of you—this may seem like a totally off the wall question—but was either one of you married at the time?

WOODWARD: No.

BERNSTEIN: No. Neither of us was married at the time.

KOPPEL: It sometimes occurred to me—and I was married during that period—and I kept thinking, "Boy, if I had to say to my wife, 'I'm sorry, honey, it's two o'clock in the morning, I know, but I've got to go off and see this source and I can't tell you . . .' " Do you think if you'd both been married, history would have turned out differently?

BERNSTEIN: I think we're so reluctant to talk about history turning out differently, let's try it a little differently. Had we both been married, I think perhaps we would not have had the time to cover the story that we gave to it. Clearly, we were there in the middle of the night all the time. I mean, it was—I'm not sure I could ever do that again.

WOODWARD: *(to Koppel)* Are *you* still married? You spend all this time up late at night.

BERNSTEIN: That's right. *You're* the one that does a show at eleven-thirty at night.

KOPPEL: My wife knows where I am late at night, and she knows how long it takes me to get back, too. Let's get back now—

WOODWARD: But this is being taped in the afternoon.

KOPPEL: You're absolutely right.

March 9, 1984

Subject: The Super Rich
Guests: Dina Merrill, actress and heiress, and Fran Lebowitz, author

KOPPEL: Did you know you were rich?

MERRILL: Not really, no. I just knew that I had a wonderful family. And one of the places that we lived was out on Long Island; we had a farm. When I came home from school I used to go in the cow barn and milk myself a glass of milk with foam on top, and it was great. You know, I didn't really think about it that much.

KOPPEL: Ms. Lebowitz, what did you do when you were growing up?

LEBOWITZ: I never milked myself a glass of milk. And, in fact, I would consider that a disadvantage. If I was rich I wouldn't bother—don't bother doing it now.

KOPPEL: What is so grand, do you think, about being rich?

LEBOWITZ: I think it's probably the money.

November 18, 1986
Subject: Iran
Guest: Former President Jimmy Carter

KOPPEL: Is it ever possible, given the political realities in this country, for a President of the United States to ignore the fate of fifty hostages, five hostages, one hostage?

CARTER: Ted, I think you're one of the few Americans who might say that he benefited from the Iranian hostage crisis, because a substantial portion of your career—

KOPPEL: I've heard that observation made.

CARTER: —has been derived from it . . .

February 4, 1987
Subject: Liberace's Death
Guests: Jamie James, Liberace's publicist; Milton Berle, comedian

BERLE: I walked on the stage and ad-libbed with [Liberace] and he had on a red sequins sport jacket with glittering, glamorous things, and he was funny, too, I'll tell you that. He had some great sense of humor. I said, "What is that supposed to be?" And he said this line to me, which I didn't expect, he said,—I said, "That looks great." He said, "Yes, it's 20,000 fireflies in heat."

KOPPEL: Let me get back to Jamie James for a moment—

BERLE: Why, do you want to leave me?

KOPPEL: No, because if I ask you one question, you'll take an-
            other nine minutes, so I got—I want to get—

BERLE: Oh, shut up.

April 1, 1987
Subject: Jokes and Pranks
Guests: Alan Dundes, anthropologist and folklorist

DUNDES: You have pranks at boarding schools, you have them in
            the military. I mean, in boarding school, what do you
            do—you put the salt in the sugar shaker or you short-
            sheet the beds. You put bouillon cubes in the shower
            heads—I mean, there are fantastic—I mean, there are
            stories about wonderful pranks, too. They're usually set
            in engineering schools—

KOPPEL: Wait—wait a second. Bouillon cubes in the shower heads?

DUNDES: It's kind of sticky.

June 9, 1988
Subject: George Bush's Candidacy for the Presidency
Guest: George Bush

BUSH: And, Dan, I'll take all the credit, all the blame—

KOPPEL: No . . . Dan, Dan's the other fellow. . . the trial of Oliver
            North, which means it's going to be all over the front
            pages and all over the television news every day. It's going
            to be dogging you, you know that.

BUSH: No I don't, because, Dan, you've made a fatal error
            there, a fatal flaw in your analysis.

KOPPEL: I'll tell you what. If you stop calling me Dan, try calling
            me Peter or Tom or—

BUSH: Did I do it again?

KOPPEL: Well, that's all right. You can call me anything you like,
             but, you know, it's—

BUSH: It's Freudian. Hey, listen, it's Freudian.

KOPPEL: It's getting a little bit repetitious.

BUSH: I am not trying to be clever. I'm, I'm—

KOPPEL: No, no. I know you're not.

BUSH: I promise you, it's Freudian.

July 19, 1988
Subject: Jesse Jackson's Speech to the Democratic Convention
Guest: Jesse Jackson

JACKSON: The most difficult thing was, with my state of nerves and
             concentrations, was getting down to a thrust . . .

KOPPEL: You strike people sometimes as arrogant, if anything, but
             not a man who is nervous. Why were you nervous?

JACKSON: Well, in part my athletic background. You learn to play
             in the big game and you learn to keep your concentra-
             tion, so it's a kind of discipline I learned while playing
             ball in school . . . And so I felt more than an ordinary
             weight on my shoulders, and that gave rise to some real
             tension.

KOPPEL: I was just about to make the point, and forgive me, I got
             a little distracted there for a second. You—

JACKSON: I didn't know you could get distracted, Ted.

KOPPEL: Yeah, I didn't either.

JACKSON: Your getting distracted, and my getting nervous. It's
             really about—

KOPPEL: You—you—it's quite an evening, isn't it?

JACKSON: It's our evening, Ted, you know?

February 17, 1989
Subject: Tap Dancing
Guests: Sammy Davis, Jr.; Gregory Hines;
Steve Condos, veteran tap dancer

KOPPEL: (to Hines, Condos, and Davis) Would you dance us off,
           guys?

HINES: Ted, you going to join us?

KOPPEL: I'll be dancing with my buns right here on the seat.

November 9, 1989
Subject: The Berlin Wall: Is It Coming Down?
Guest: Vitali Kobesh, Soviet commentator

KOBESH: The German Democratic Republic is a sovereign state,
           and they are doing their job, and it is their job. And if
           they want to live with a multiparty system, it's their busi-
           ness, and we welcome it.

KOPPEL: But is it their business if they want to reunify with West
           Germany? Can they do that?

KOBESH: To unite?

KOPPEL: Yes.

KOBESH: Ted, tell me, would you like Germany to be united, but
           friendly?

KOPPEL: I'll tell you what. When I come on your program I'll an-
           swer your questions; now you're on my program.

KOBESH: Okay.

KOPPEL: You answer mine, all right?

October 28, 1987
Subject: Cremation
Guest: Jessica Mitford, author, The American Way of Death

MITFORD: (after Koppel interviews lawyers about cremation) Well, I was fascinated listening to the discussion of the lawyers about these bits of tissue, et cetera. I felt that I was in the middle of a lunatic asylum while you were all talking there. . . .

KOPPEL: To what degree are you concerned at all, though, that there is this commingling of ashes, that the relatives do not know, necessarily, what is happening to the body?

MITFORD: Who cares if you're commingled? I mean, would you, Ted Koppel, care, really, if you were commingled, say, with Johnny Carson?

KOPPEL: Well, you know, Johnny Carson is all right, but there are some that I would prefer not to be commingled with. . . .

MITFORD: The fact that more and more people are now choosing cremation, I thought, showed a great strain of developing sanity on this subject until I began listening to the people on this program.

July 6, 1983
Subject: The Guru's Cult Takes Over Antelope, Oregon
Guests: Ma Anand Sheela, president, Rajneesh Foundation; Margaret Hill, former Antelope mayor

HILL: We simply do not have enough water to service the type of facility which they wish to put in there. Rather than address that issue, they charged us with religious discrimination.

SHEELA: I think you need to shut up for a while.

KOPPEL: I'm sorry, I didn't hear what you said, Sheela.

SHEELA: I said she needs to shut up for a while because what she—

HILL: You have told me to shut up one too many times.

SHEELA: She's absolutely off the wall in running the city. She has been off the wall in judging people. She doesn't know what she's doing.

KOPPEL: All right, let me just raise a question with you, Sheela, because I must say that, in terms of demonstrating this great love for humanity that you profess, I don't see a lot of it reflected here this evening.

June 24, 1983
Subject: Romance Novels
Guest: Vivian Stephens, Harlequin Books

KOPPEL: The industry as a whole earns about half a billion dollars a year. Is that right? Is that worldwide or here in the United States?

STEPHENS: I can't hear you right now, but I think I can answer your question.

KOPPEL: That's the way it usually is.

STEPHENS: They do a lot of books. Last year Harlequin did 200 million books. That's a lot. I think that women are looking for a certain kind of entertainment, so they are the repeaters. They go back every month to buy books. I'm sorry, I can't hear you at all right now.

KOPPEL: Well, that's all right. I wasn't saying anything.

January 4, 1984
Subject: Why Are We in Lebanon?
Guests: James Zogby, American Arab Anti-Discrimination Committee;
Howard Squadron, American Jewish Congress

KOPPEL: James Zogby is executive director of the Arab American Anti-Discrimination Committee. I got that backwards, Jim, I apologize—it's the American Arab Anti-Discrimination Committee . . . And now to Howard Squadron, who's president of the American Jewish Committee.

SQUADRON: It's the American Jewish Congress, Ted.

KOPPEL: I beg your pardon. I'm screwing 'em all up tonight. But evenhandedly, you will agree.

SQUADRON: Yes, certainly evenhandedly.

October 11, 1991
Subject: Supreme Court Nominee Clarence Thomas vs. *Anita Hill*
Guest: Senator Alan Simpson

KOPPEL: When something is leaked, it is not the press's job to suppress it, it is the press's job to look into it, check into its accuracy and, if indeed the charge is factual—that is, that the woman made it—then the press reports it, right?

SIMPSON: Well, Ted, I've heard that old saw before. You leave off two words when you talk about the public's right to know.

KOPPEL: I didn't use the public's right to know.

SIMPSON: I know, I know. I am. It is the public's right to know the truth.

KOPPEL: No. It is the public's right to know the facts, sir, and there is a difference.

October 13, 1981
Subject: Televangelism
Guest: Mother Superior Angelica, founder,
Eternal Word Television

MOTHER SUPERIOR ANGELICA: I don't know much about commercial networks. All I know is that God wants this network to be a spiritual growth network, a teaching, sharing, loving network. And I'm hoping, with His grace, that we can continue on that vein. I think we will.

KOPPEL: Well, you've got a good sponsor.

February 20, 1985
Subject: IRA Guns: A Cash Controversy
Guests: James Prior, former secretary of state for Northern Ireland; Martin
Galvin, NORAID (Irish Northern Aid committee)

GALVIN: But the real monies that finance violence and terrorism in Ireland and the enemies of democracy are those openly collected by British taxpayers and openly used to arm 30,000 occupation forces of the British Army Royal Ulster Constabulary and Ulster Defense Regiment.

KOPPEL: Mr. Galvin, at the risk of—at the risk of cutting you off in midstream, I'm going to do it nevertheless, because I'm going to suggest that we go through my questions first and then we'll get to the answers you want to give to questions I haven't asked.

March 2, 1984
Subject: Video Violence
Guest: Gene Simmons, of the rock group Kiss

(after excerpt from rock video by Kiss, called "All Hell's Breakin' Loose")

KOPPEL: Well, I've got to confess, I'm not sure what's wrong with it. It looks like an old Douglas Fairbanks movie done in drag. What's the point of it?

SIMMONS: Those are girls, incidentally.

KOPPEL: Well, I know they are, yes. I gathered that much. I'm not *that* button-down.

May 17, 1984
Subject: Lawmen in Disguise
Guest: Anthony Bouza, Minneapolis police chief
who defends police going undercover

KOPPEL: You would not masquerade as a doctor. For one thing—

BOUZA: I didn't say that, Ted. I said that I would not practice medicine. There is nothing to prevent the police from masquerading as a doctor.

KOPPEL: Well, I think you're wrong, but we're going to find out in a moment. I mean, you know, the thing that will prevent you from masquerading is the same thing that would prevent me from masquerading as a doctor—I don't have a license.

BOUZA: Oh, no. I think you would be prevented from practicing medicine. I don't know that if you went to a dinner party and identified yourself as Dr. Ted Koppel, world-renowned psychologist, that you would necessarily be subject to arrest. You'd have to be practicing.

KOPPEL: Well, let's say M.D., and someone chokes at the dinner and all of a sudden they turn to me and they say, "Hey, we didn't call for a doctor because we've got you there, doc." Right?

BOUZA: Good luck. I would suggest that that's the time to adopt your clerical collar and give him the last rites.

KOPPEL: All right, well, I'm glad you've got such a sense of humor about it.

May 14, 1985
Subject: Medical Malpractice
Guests: Stanley Rosenblatt, attorney; Dr. James Sammons,
executive VP, American Medical Association

SAMMONS: There is a crisis in professional liability in this country. The thing that Mr. Rosenberg was not saying is—

ROSENBLATT: Rosenblatt, sir. Rosenblatt, sir.

SAMMONS: I beg your pardon.

ROSENBLATT: Try to get the name right.

SAMMONS: Yeah, well, if I can remember it, I will.

ROSENBLATT: Try to get some of your facts right, beginning with my name.

SAMMONS: I am going to if you'll shut up long enough. I'm going to tell the answer to the question. . . .

ROSENBLATT: If you're a doctor and have had four years of medical school and internship, served a residency, and you don't have enough confidence in your own ability to know that you're dealing with a headache instead of a brain tumor and when you're pretty sure you're dealing with a headache you order a CAT scan at several hundred dollars, you are an incompetent, gutless doctor and should be out of the profession.

SAMMONS: Ted? Ted, that is just absolute garbage.

ROSENBLATT: Defensive medicine is a disgrace.

SAMMONS: And he knows it. And the fact of the matter is—

ROSENBLATT: I know no such thing, sir, except that you—

SAMMONS: You don't have—you don't have—

ROSENBLATT: —you don't practice medicine. You run around the country as a politician—

SAMMONS: For your information, Mr. Whatever-your-name-is—

KOPPEL: Well, gentlemen, I'm afraid we're going to have to take on good faith that there are solutions because I don't think we've heard any of them tonight.

August 17, 1982
Subject: Stock Market Rally
Guests: George Will, ABC commentator; Joseph Granville,
stock market forecaster

KOPPEL: Joe Granville, your final conclusions. Are the interest rates going to go on coming down? Just the interest rates.

GRANVILLE: All right. Here's my answer, Ted, and I want every American tonight to go to sleep and think about what

I'm about to say. In 1980 the Dow went up 245 points following my buy signal and we went up 24 points in the Dow for every rise of one point in the prime rate. In 1981–82, the Dow Jones industrial average went down 35 points per every drop of one point in the prime rate. And now you ask me what do interest rates have to do with the market and I answered it for you. Nothing. Follow the market, not interest rates.

KOPPEL: No, I didn't ask you that, Joe. Forgive me. I always ask you what tomorrow's weather is going to be and you start off by telling me about the Ice Age. I'm asking you, are interest rates coming down? Do you accept that interest rates are going to go on coming down?

GRANVILLE: And I say, Ted, in 1929 to 1932, interest rates crashed and so did the market. Enough said.

KOPPEL: So you think interest rates are not going to go on coming down. Please just give me a straightforward answer, would you?

GRANVILLE: I simply say follow the market and not interest rates. Most people follow the interest rates, and if you had done that between 1929–1932, you would have been wiped out.

KOPPEL: George, what is he saying?

WILL: I think he's saying read his newsletter.

April 26, 1993
Subject: Book Promotion
Guest: George Shultz, former secretary of state

KOPPEL: I'd like to move away from your book now. We're going to take a break.

SHULTZ: I don't know why you want to move away from my book. What was the . . . what was the title of—

KOPPEL: Only because Bosnia hadn't happened—

SHULTZ: What was the title of my book, by the way?

KOPPEL: Beats the hell out of me. If you—

SHULTZ: *Turmoil and Triumph.*

KOPPEL: If you haven't found a way of weaving it into this conversation yet, you'll learn it by the time you finish your book tour.

September 29, 1983
Subject: The Shooting of KAL 007 by the Soviets
Guest: William F. Buckley, Jr., columnist

BUCKLEY: Mr. Koppel, if you asked me the question "Does the Soviet Union wish it hadn't happened?" I think I would reply, "Yes, they wish it hadn't happened."

KOPPEL: No, but I'm asking—

BUCKLEY: If you asked me a second question, "Given the fact that it did happen, is the Soviet Union going to be worse off?" I say not necessarily, because they have taken precisely this step of attempting to create the vision of America as a hysterical war-mongering country, which might serve to arouse a resentment against the deployment of missiles, which was pretty well thought to have been put to bed with the elections in Great Britain and Germany earlier this year.

KOPPEL: Well, Mr. Buckley, while your questions are excellent, as they always are, nevertheless let me go back to mine, humble as it may be.

February 21, 1992
Subject: After Nine Months in Orbit,
the Cosmonauts Who Can't Go Home
Guests: (from orbit) Alexander Volkov and Sergei Krikalev,
cosmonauts (who were launched into orbit
before the end of the Soviet Union)

(Floating behind cosmonauts is a life-size doll, resembling a woman)

KOPPEL: Let me begin by asking you, Colonel Volkov, who is the young lady strapped in behind you?

VOLKOV: It's our space friend ... unfortunately, she doesn't understand either English or Russian. So we'll have to translate whatever you say to her.

KOPPEL: Very good.

February 24, 1995
Subject: The Age of Jazz
Guests: Lionel Hampton, vibraphone, age 86;
Milt Hinton, bass, age 85; Doc Cheatham, trumpet, age 89

KOPPEL: Doc, you said you don't like to talk about or discuss politics too much, so let me ask you to talk about the future of a ninety-year-old musician in this country.

CHEATHAM: The future?

KOPPEL: Yeah.

CHEATHAM: (*chuckles*) Looks pretty bad!

May 29, 1984
Subject: Iran, Iraq, and Persian Gulf Oil
Guests: Riyadh al-Qaysi, Iraqi ambassador to the UN;
Said Rajai Khorassani, Iranian ambassador to the UN

KOPPEL: Do you gentlemen communicate with one another at the United Nations? Do you talk to each other?

AL-QAYSI: Well, Mr. Koppel, let me answer this question quite candidly. I am quite glad that you raised it. You see, despite the fact that there is an armed conflict between our two countries, there are full-fledged diplomatic missions in our capitals. Yet the Iranian ambassador, for some strange reason, even refused to interact with me on television.

KOPPEL: Well, I mean, you've certainly been interacting for the past few minutes and I'm delighted to see it. I hesitate—

AL-QAYSI: I'm delighted that he's interacting with me. He refused, since our last appearance on *Nightline*.

KOPPEL: Well, I hesitate to describe what we've just seen as a dialogue, but at least it is an exchange of ideas. And let me address to you, Ambassador Rajai, then, the question of whether you think such an exchange of ideas can be useful.

RAJAI: Not at all.

KOPPEL: Not at all?

RAJAI: No.

TWENTY
Final
Thoughts

JOURNALISM, AS ANY of my colleagues who love the profession can testify, is an addictive pastime. Like all addictions, it engenders illusions. Like the proverbial dog howling at the moon, we come to believe, at times, that we are responsible for its rising. Thus inflated by the perceived importance of our mission, we race through our lives becoming more or less fleetingly acquainted with the major issues and players of our time, while our wives, husbands, or significant others deal with the more trivial aspects of existence, like creating homes, sustaining relationships, and raising children. As long as it is voluntary, there is nothing inherently wrong with this division of labor; but it is rarely voluntary and surely is always galling to be left with the impression that the imperatives which call a journalist away from home are so much more important than the ones which might oblige him to stay home. That case will be increasingly difficult to make as the issues that occupy the attention of American television journalists become even more banal.

Even at the time of its inception, *Nightline* was something of an anomaly. In order to come into existence it required an extraordinary convergence of factors:

The creativity, drive, and ambition of Roone Arledge, who was then ascending to the height of his power and influence within ABC, happened along at precisely the time that the network was prepared and able to invest substantial resources into the development of a truly competitive news division. The story of U.S. diplomats, intelligence officers, and Marines held hostage by forces both mysterious and largely unsympathetic to the American public triggered a ravenous appetite for more information than could ever be satisfied by a few minutes each evening on the dinnertime news programs. Most of the television magazine programs now on the air did not then exist. ABC had, in previous years, experienced modest success with *The Dick Cavett Show* at 11:30 P.M., but in 1979, it had nothing to compete with *The Tonight Show*. In short, the network was primed to gamble and had little to lose by letting its news division, now led by a legendary producer, experiment.

Had a similar convergence of events occurred five years earlier, during Watergate, Sam Donaldson would likely have gotten the nod to anchor the program, since he was the principal ABC correspondent covering that story. This, though, was a foreign policy story and I was ABC's senior diplomatic correspondent. Most significant of all, my better-known colleagues at the time had no reason to leave CBS or NBC News to take a flier at ABC, then a distant third in the news sweepstakes.

The chances, in other words, of all these factors converging at the right time, sufficient to convince a major network to invest millions in developing and promoting a news program, anchored by a less-than-charismatic diplomatic correspondent, in order to challenge Johnny Carson and *The Tonight Show,* still causes me on occasion to shake my head in amazement. It nearly didn't happen at all; it almost certainly would not happen now. Even in sixteen years, the American public's attention span appears to have diminished. We in television have certainly contributed to the phenomenon. Little did we know twenty-five years ago, when critics began focusing on our treatment of important events through "sound bites," that our willingness, back then, to let the "bites" run thirty, forty seconds or more would one day be regarded as something approaching a high water mark of journalistic responsibility.

Nightline has been imitated in Spain and Great Britain, in Australia and South Africa, but not really here in the United States. By all that is perceived to be conventional wisdom in television, the program is an unlikely model for success. Having survived, even flourished, for sixteen years now, *Nightline* is something of a flying pig in that, having seen it, you are well advised not to question the aerodynamics; you simply marvel at the fact that it gets off the ground at all. That it has, that it does, is due to the remarkable synergy that occasionally permits great producers, reporters, camerapeople, videotape editors, researchers, guest bookers, and others to work together in the relatively sheltered corner of a network schedule. Seven o'clock on Sunday evenings has provided a similarly protected environment over many more years to our colleagues at *60 Minutes*. It doesn't happen often. I am all the more grateful, then, to have shared the journey with so many wonderful colleagues and friends.

A few years back, my friend Rick Kaplan and I were spending December twenty-fourth at the Kremlin, putting the finishing touches to a program about the end of the Soviet Union. We were in an antechamber, waiting for an interview with Mikhail Gorbachev. One of Gorbachev's security men came up to Rick and wished him a Merry Christmas. "I don't celebrate Christmas," said Rick, "I celebrate Hanukah."

The Russian looked puzzled. "Why," he asked, "do you celebrate Erich Hoeneker?" Even at the time, the confusion between the Jewish holiday and the disgraced East German president was something less than a thigh-slapper. It was somewhat less amusing to all of our families back home, waiting to celebrate, variously, Hanukah and Christmas with us. It has been that way all too often over the years: holidays, birthdays, anniversaries missed. I shudder to think how many school plays, doctors' appointments, leaking roofs, and flooded basements the various *Nightline* staffers and I have missed over the years because we were "on assignment." I wonder how many marriages have been brought to the brink and how many others never came to be because of the enormous demands that the four thousand-plus *Nightline* programs have exacted. It will not change anything; but it should be said. To all the husbands and wives, children and other family members; to all the lovers and friends who did what we should have done, because we were not there to do it, thank you. For good or ill, what you have just read would never have happened without you.

Index

ABOUT THE AUTHORS

TED KOPPEL has been the anchor of *Nightline* since its inception in 1980. As an ABC News correspondent for seventeen years before that, he covered the civil rights movement, the Vietnam War, Latin America, Asia, and the Middle East. He and his wife, Grace Anne, live in Potomac, Maryland, and have four children.

KYLE GIBSON is a native of Iowa and a graduate of Yale University. She joined *Nightline* on the day of its premiere and became an Emmy Award–winning producer for the broadcast, covering national and international stories, notably the protest and subsequent massacre at Tiananmen Square in China. In 1989 she became a producer for *PrimeTime Live,* and in 1990 and 1991 she covered the White House as an ABC News correspondent. After living overseas for several years, Gibson now resides in Washington, D.C.